ANNUAL EDITIONS

Personal Growth and Behavior

Twenty-Second Edition

02/03

EDITOR

Karen G. Duffy

SUNY College, Geneseo

Karen G. Duffy holds a doctorate in psychology from Michigan State University and is currently a professor of psychology at SUNY at Geneseo. She sits on the executive board of the New York State Employees Assistance Program and is a certified community and family mediator. She is a member of the American Psychological Society and the Eastern Psychological Association.

McGraw-Hill/Dushkin
530 Old Whitfield Street, Guilford, Connecticut 06437

Visit us on the Internet
http://www.dushkin.com

D1510892

GCLS/GLASSBORO BRANCH
2 CENTER STREET
GLASSBORO, NJ 08028

Credits

1. **Becoming a Person: Foundations**
   Unit photo—© 2002 by Cleo Freelance Photography.
2. **Determinants of Behavior: Motivation, Environment, and Physiology**
   Unit photo—WHO photo.
3. **Problems Influencing Personal Growth**
   Unit photo—© 2002 by Cleo Freelance Photography.
4. **Relating to Others**
   Unit photo—© 2002 by Cleo Freelance Photography.
5. **Dynamics of Personal Adjustment: The Individual and Society**
   Unit photo—© 2002 by Cleo Freelance Photography.
6. **Enhancing Human Adjustment: Learning to Cope Effectively**
   Unit photo—Courtesy of Louis Raucci.

Copyright

Cataloging in Publication Data
Main entry under title: Annual Editions: Personal Growth and Behavior. 2002/2003.
1. Personality—Periodicals. 2. Adjustment (Psychology)—Periodicals. I. Duffy, Karen G., *comp.* II. Title: Personal growth and behavior.
ISBN 0–07–250628–8   658'.05   ISSN 0732–0779

© 2002 by McGraw-Hill/Dushkin, Guilford, CT 06437, A Division of The McGraw-Hill Companies.

Copyright law prohibits the reproduction, storage, or transmission in any form by any means of any portion of this publication without the express written permission of McGraw-Hill/Dushkin, and of the copyright holder (if different) of the part of the publication to be reproduced. The Guidelines for Classroom Copying endorsed by Congress explicitly state that unauthorized copying may not be used to create, to replace, or to substitute for anthologies, compilations, or collective works.

Annual Editions® is a Registered Trademark of McGraw-Hill/Dushkin, A Division of The McGraw-Hill Companies.

Twenty-Second Edition

Cover image © 2002 by PhotoDisc, Inc.
Printed in the United States of America   1234567890BAHBAH5432   Printed on Recycled Paper

Editors/Advisory Board

Members of the Advisory Board are instrumental in the final selection of articles for each edition of ANNUAL EDITIONS. Their review of articles for content, level, currentness, and appropriateness provides critical direction to the editor and staff. We think that you will find their careful consideration well reflected in this volume.

EDITOR

Karen G. Duffy
SUNY College, Geneseo

Advisory Board

Sonia L. Blackman
California State Polytechnic University

Linda Corrente
Community College of Rhode Island

Robert DaPrato
Solano Community College

Mark J. Friedman
Montclair State University

Roger Gaddis
Gardner-Webb University

Richard A. Kolotkin
Moorhead State University

Angela J.C. LaSala
Community College of Southern Nevada

David M. Malone
Duke University

Karla K. Miley
Black Hawk College

Terry F. Pettijohn
Ohio State University

Victor L. Ryan
University of Colorado–Boulder

Pamela E. Stewart
Northern Virginia Community College

Robert S. Tomlinson
University of Wisconsin, Eau Claire

Charmaine Wesley-Hartman
Modesto Junior College

Lois J. Willoughby
Miami Dade Community College–Kendall

Staff

EDITORIAL STAFF

Ian A. Nielsen, Publisher
Roberta Monaco, Senior Developmental Editor
Dorothy Fink, Associate Developmental Editor
William Belcher, Associate Developmental Editor
Addie Raucci, Senior Administrative Editor
Robin Zarnetske, Permissions Editor
Marie Lazauskas, Permissions Assistant
Diane Barker, Proofreader
Lisa Holmes-Doebrick, Senior Program Coordinator

TECHNOLOGY STAFF

Richard Tietjen, Senior Publishing Technologist
Jonathan Stowe, Executive Director of eContent
Angela Mule, eContent Developer
Joe Offredi, Technology Developmental Editor
Janice Ward, Software Support Analyst
Ciro Parente, Editorial Assistant

PRODUCTION STAFF

Brenda S. Filley, Director of Production
Charles Vitelli, Designer
Mike Campbell, Production Coordinator
Laura Levine, Graphics
Tom Goddard, Graphics
Eldis Lima, Graphics
Nancy Norton, Graphics
Juliana Arbo, Typesetting Supervisor
Karen Roberts, Typesetter
Jocelyn Proto, Typesetter
Cynthia Vets, Typesetter
Cathy Kuziel, Typesetter
Larry Killian, Copier Coordinator

To the Reader

In publishing ANNUAL EDITIONS we recognize the enormous role played by the magazines, newspapers, and journals of the public press in providing current, first-rate educational information in a broad spectrum of interest areas. Many of these articles are appropriate for students, researchers, and professionals seeking accurate, current material to help bridge the gap between principles and theories and the real world. These articles, however, become more useful for study when those of lasting value are carefully collected, organized, indexed, and reproduced in a low-cost format, which provides easy and permanent access when the material is needed. That is the role played by ANNUAL EDITIONS.

Have you ever watched children on a playground? Some children are reticent; watching the other children play, they sit demurely and shun becoming involved in the fun. Some children happily and readily interact with their playmates. They take turns, share their toys, and follow the rules of the playground. Other children are bullies who brazenly taunt the playing children and aggressively take others' possessions. What makes each child so different? Do childhood behaviors forecast adult behaviors? Can children's (or adults') antisocial behaviors be changed?

These questions are not new. Lay persons and social scientists alike have always been curious about human nature. The answers to our questions, though, are incomplete, because attempts to address these issues are relatively new or just developing. Psychology, the science that can and should answer questions about individual differences, is the primary focus of this book, and has existed for just over 100 years. That may seem old to you, but it is young when other disciplines are considered. Mathematics, medicine, and philosophy are thousands of years old.

By means of psychology and related sciences, this anthology will help you explore the issues of individual differences and their origins, methods of coping, personality change, and other matters of human adjustment. The purpose of this anthology is to compile the newest, most complete, and readable articles that examine individual behavior and adjustment as well as the dynamics of personal growth and interpersonal relationships. The readings in this book offer interesting insights into both the everyday and scientific worlds, a blend welcomed by most of today's specialists in human adjustment.

This anthology is revised each year to reflect both traditional viewpoints and emerging perspectives about people's behavior. Thanks to the editorial board's valuable advice, the present edition has been completely revised and includes a large number of new articles representing the latest thinking in the field.

Annual Editions: Personal Growth and Behavior 02/ 03 comprises six units, each of which serves a distinct purpose. The first unit is concerned with theories and philosophies related to self-identity. For example, one theory, humanism, hypothesizes that self-concept and self-esteem, our feelings about who we are and how worthy we are, are the most valuable components of personality. This unit includes articles that supplement the theoretical articles by providing applications of, or alternate perspectives on, popular theories about personal growth and human adjustment. These include all of the classic and major theories of personality: humanistic, psychoanalytic, behavioral, and trait theories.

The second unit provides information on how and why a person develops in a particular way—in other words, what factors determine or direct individual growth: physiology, heredity, experience, or some combination. The third unit pertains to problems commonly encountered in the different stages of development: infancy, childhood, adolescence, middle age, and adulthood.

The fourth and fifth units are similar in that they address social problems of adjustment—problems that occur in interpersonal relationships and problems that are created for individuals by society or culture. Unit 4 concerns interpersonal topics such as friendship and shyness, while unit 5 discusses broader societal issues such as racism, gender roles, and cults. The final unit focuses on adjustment or on how most people cope with problems of daily existence.

Annual Editions: Personal Growth and Behavior 02/ 03 will challenge you and interest you in a variety of topics. It will provide you with many answers, but it will also stimulate many questions. Perhaps it will inspire you to continue your study of the burgeoning field of psychology, which is responsible for exploring personal growth and behavior. As has been true in the past, your feedback on this edition would be valuable for future revisions. Please take a moment to fill out and return the postage-paid article rating form on the last page. Thank you.

Karen G. Duffy
Editor

Contents

To the Reader   **iv**

Topic Guide   **xi**

Selected World Wide Web Sites   **xiv**

UNIT 1
Becoming a Person: Foundations

Six selections discuss the psychosocial development of an individual's personality. Attention is given to values, emotions, lifestyles, and self-concept.

Unit Overview   **xvi**

1. **Positive Psychology: An Introduction,** Martin E. P. Seligman and Mihaly Csikszentmihalyi, *American Psychologist,* January 2000
   Two prominent psychologists trace the ***history of psychology*** with an emphasis on how psychology changed its focus from ***human deficits*** and problems to positive human characteristics such as ***well-being, contentment, and optimism.***   **2**

2. **Making Sense of Self-Esteem,** Mark R. Leary, *Current Directions in Psychological Science,* February 1999
   Self-esteem may not solely be a measure of self-evaluation but rather a result of social acceptance. A redefinition of self-esteem that includes ***evaluations from others*** helps explain the antecedents of self-esteem as well as the relationship between ***low esteem*** and ***psychological problems.***   **6**

3. **Repression Tries for Experimental Comeback,** Bruce Bower, *Science News,* March 17, 2001
   Sigmund Freud proposed an ***unconscious*** part of the psyche where we ***repress memories*** that we are trying to forget. Modern ***scientists*** are finding ways to measure these elusive memories, but the debate continues as to whether the unconscious exists.   **9**

4. **Private Lives: Discipline and Knowing Where to Draw the Line,** Jan Parker and Jan Stimpson, *The Independent,* May 3, 1999
   Managing a child's ***misbehavior*** can be trying for parents and caregivers. Based on ***behavioral theory,*** the authors provide guidelines for when and how to use ***punishment.***   **10**

5. **The Stability of Personality: Observations and Evaluations,** Robert R. McCrae and Paul T. Costa Jr., *Current Directions in Psychological Science,* December 1994
   There is substantial evidence for the ***stability of personality*** as well as for ***individual differences*** in personality traits. The authors review research on personality that supports their views and critique research methodology that does not.   **12**

6. **How Culture Molds Habits of Thought,** Erica Goode, *New York Times,* August 8, 2000
   Culture is a powerful force in determining how we process and interpret various pieces of information—social or otherwise. Erica Goode reports that through a series of ***controlled studies,*** psychologists are able to demonstrate that culture greatly influences mental life.   **15**

The concepts in bold italics are developed in the article. For further expansion, please refer to the Topic Guide and the Index.

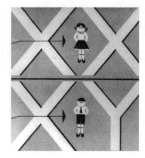

UNIT 2
Determinants of Behavior: Motivation, Environment, and Physiology

Ten articles examine the effects of culture, genes, and emotions on an individual's behavior.

Unit Overview   **18**

7. **The Tangled Skeins of Nature and Nurture in Human Evolution,** Paul R. Ehrlich, *The Chronicle of Higher Education,* September 22, 2000

   Are we slaves to our **genes** or does **culture** modify our psyche and behaviors? According to Paul Ehrlich, attributes of an organism are the product of the ***interaction between biology and culture*** or learning.   **20**

8. **The Gender Blur,** Deborah Blum, *Utne Reader,* September/October 1998

   With the blurring of **gender boundaries,** author Deborah Blum asks just how much **biology** rather than our **training in society** contributes to maleness and femaleness. She provides everyday examples of the blurred boundaries and examines research on the topic of **gender roles** and their origins.   **27**

9. **The Personality Genes,** J. Madeleine Nash, *Time,* April 27, 1998

   Does **DNA** shape behavior and **personality**? For example, is there a gene that causes some individuals to seek novelty? Molecular biologists who believe the answer is yes are busy pursuing the study of **genetic influences** on our personalities.   **31**

10. **Where We Come From,** Nancy Shute, *U.S. News & World Report,* January 29, 2001

    By studying **DNA,** some humans are now capable of tracing their various inherited or **ancestral roots.** Some African American individuals, for example, are learning that they have Jewish and Native American origins. The usefulness of such knowledge—good or bad—is not yet fully understood.   **33**

11. **Autism Is Likely to Be Linked to Several Genes,** Hugh McIntosh, *APA Monitor,* November 1998

    Autism, a **brain disorder** that usually manifests itself early in life, may be linked to **genes** on several different **chromosomes.** Viruses, drugs, and other factors may cause **damage** to these chromosomes in the **embryo,** thus increasing the chances for autism.   **39**

12. **The Future of the Brain,** Norbert R. Myslinski, *The World & I,* August 2000

    New **brain imaging techniques** are reviewed by Norbert Myslinski. New possibilities such as more precise, less invasive **brain surgery** are discussed as outcomes for utilizing this technology.   **42**

13. **The Biology of Joy,** Jeremiah Creedon, *Utne Reader,* November/December 1997

    Biologically speaking, scientists are close to knowing what **pleasure** is. In the 1970s, **endorphins** were heralded as the key to human pleasure and joy. Today scientists are closing in on refined information about the causes of and controls for pleasure.   **47**

14. **The Tick-Tock of the Biological Clock,** Michael W. Young, *Scientific American,* March 2000

    The **human brain** seems to have a built-in, 24-hour **biological clock** that persists even in the absence of day and night. Heart attacks, body temperature, pain threshold, stress hormones, and other bodily changes are linked to this clock, according to Michael Young.   **52**

The concepts in bold italics are developed in the article. For further expansion, please refer to the Topic Guide and the Index.

15. **Into the Zone,** Jay Tolson, *U.S. News & World Report,* July 3, 2000

The ability to **visualize, tolerate stress,** and be **mentally tough** contribute to "flow." **Flow** makes for great athletes, dancers, and executives. How to develop, experience, and enhance flow as suggested by cutting edge **research** is at the heart of this article.   **56**

16. **Mind Over Medicine,** Howard Brody, *Psychology Today,* July/August 2000

Can we really heal ourselves? Does believing something alter our **health** trajectory? Howard Brody examines research on the **placebo effect** and answers "yes" to these and other questions about the **mind's power over the body.**   **60**

UNIT 3
Problems Influencing Personal Growth

Ten articles consider aging, development, self-image, and social interaction, and their influences on personal growth.

Unit Overview   **66**

17. **The Seven Stages of Man,** Constanza Villalba, *New York Times,* February 17, 1999

This brief article reviews a variety of **genetic, biological, and social changes** that men experience at each **stage of life.** Many informative statistics related to psychology, health, socialization, and so forth are presented.   **69**

18. **Fetal Psychology,** Janet L. Hopson, *Psychology Today,* September/October 1998

Birth may be a significant occasion, but it is only one milestone in a series of important **developmental events,** many of which precede birth. Janet Hopson reviews the latest findings on just how fascinating and significant **fetal life** is.   **71**

19. **Four Things You Need to Know About Raising Baby,** Joanna Lipari, *Psychology Today,* July/August 2000

Modern research with **infants** is demonstrating that babies are not the passive receptacles we once thought they were. Joanna Lipari reveals four **myths** about infants and how science has altered our thinking.   **75**

20. **What Ever Happened to Play?,** Walter Kirm with Wendy Cole, *Time,* April 30, 2001

Children's **free time to play** has decreased more and more as **children and parents** fill free time with other activities, all designed to create **"superkids."** Play is normal, natural, and necessary, according to the authors.   **78**

21. **Parenting: The Lost Art,** Kay S. Hymowitz, *American Educator,* Spring 2001

Parents blame **schools** and schools blame parents for **children's misconduct and failure.** Kay Hymowitz explores this complicated web of blame and helps the reader to understand better today's parents and their relationship to their children.   **81**

22. **Disarming the Rage,** Richard Jerome, *People Weekly,* June 4, 2001

Over a third of sixth- to tenth-graders—5.7 million American children—report being the victims of **bullying.** Some **victims** turn their **rage** outward and start shooting; others turn it inward and commit **suicide.** Why bullying occurs and how schools and parents can stop or prevent it is highlighted in this article.   **86**

23. **A World of Their Own,** Sharon Begley, *Newsweek,* May 8, 2000

Modern **teens** are still very **peer-driven,** but their lives in other ways are quite different from teens of **previous generations** due to the **Internet** and other **social changes.** What they say they want and who they think they are provide the focus for this article.   **90**

The concepts in bold italics are developed in the article. For further expansion, please refer to the Topic Guide and the Index.

24. **The Road Ahead: A Boomer's Guide to Happiness,** Barbara Kantrowitz, *Newsweek,* April 3, 2000
Baby boomers are reaching age 50, the age between *adulthood* and *old age.* Boomers again have the chance to redefine *cultural norms* just as this large generation did in the past—from health to spiritualism to finances as well as to other aspects of life.   **93**

25. **Live to 100? No Thanks,** Susan L. Crowley, *AARP Bulletin,* July/August 1999
The American Association of Retired People (AARP) surveyed over 2,000 individuals and found that most people opt for *quality of life* rather than *quantity of life* in old age. AARP also discovered that the *older people* are, the older they want to be when they die. *Declining health* and lack of money are the main concerns about old age.   **96**

26. **Start the Conversation,** *Modern Maturity,* September/October 2000
Death is a stigmatized topic in *American society.* This article is designed to *motivate* people to assess their own feelings about death, to plan for the future, and to feel more comfortable with the issue.   **98**

UNIT 4
Relating to Others

Ten articles examine some of the dynamics involved in relating to others. Topics discussed include friendship, love, the importance of family ties, and self-esteem.

Unit Overview   **105**

27. **Friendships and Adaptation Across the Life Span,** Willard W. Hartup and Nan Stevens, *Current Directions in Psychological Science,* June 1999
Friends foster a *sense of well-being* across a *life span,* although adults and children may conceptualize and interact with friends differently. The friends who provide the most "social capital" are those who are *well-adjusted* and *socially competent.*   **107**

28. **Emotional Intelligence,** Casey D. Cobb and John D. Mayer, *Educational Leadership,* November 2000
Emotional intelligence or *EQ* involves correctly *perceiving emotions,* especially those of other people. Two *models of EQ* as well as *methods for measuring* it are explored. This article also includes a discussion of what schools can do to foster EQ.   **111**

29. **Nurturing Empathy,** Julia Glass, *Parenting,* June/July 2001
Empathy (or experiencing another's feelings) is an important human attribute. How and why empathy unfolds in young *children* is explained. *Tips for parents* who want to encourage empathetic behavior in their children are also included.   **116**

30. **What's in a Face?,** Beth Azar, *Monitor on Psychology,* January 2000
A controversy in psychology exists about the importance of the *face* as a mirror of a person's *emotions.* Some argue that the face influences *social interactions;* others argue that the face tells others something about another person's overall *moods.*   **120**

31. **How to Spot a Liar,** James Geary, *Time Europe,* March 13, 2000
Humans and animals regularly deceive others. *Nature,* however, provides *clues* to help others decipher *deceit.* In humans, the face is a particularly revealing feature, so much so that computers are being programmed to detect *liars.*   **122**

32. **Shyness: The New Solution,** Bernardo Carducci, *Psychology Today,* January/February 2000
Bernardo Carducci discloses new research on *shyness*—where it orginates and how it can be overcome. The author pays special attention to the *Internet* as a means for overcoming shyness.   **125**

The concepts in bold italics are developed in the article. For further expansion, please refer to the Topic Guide and the Index.

33. **Revealing Personal Secrets,** Anita E. Kelly, *Current Directions in Psychological Science,* August 1999
When do people reveal their **secrets**? Why do some secrets remain undisclosed? Anita Kelly reviews **research** and reveals the answers to these and other questions. **131**

34. **Welcome to the Love Lab,** John Gottman and Sybil Carrere, *Psychology Today,* October 2000
Using three dialogues from **couples,** the authors demonstrate how to detect **troubled relationships.** Results of actual research are also shared in order to enable the reader to detect problems as well. **136**

35. **Finding Real Love,** Carey Barbor, *Psychology Today,* January/February 2001
Do we tend to sabotage **intimate relationships**? The answer is "yes," especially when we **attach to a partner** who reminds us of **a parent who had negative characteristics.** The **defenses** we use in such a relationship and how to overcome them are the focus of this article. **141**

36. **Prescription for Passion,** David M. Buss, *Psychology Today,* May/June 2000
Is **jealousy** necessary? David Buss answers the question, saying that not only is jealousy a normal part of **personality,** but it can help ignite passion and therefore hold **couples** together. **145**

UNIT 5
Dynamics of Personal Adjustment: The Individual and Society

Seven selections discuss some of the problems experienced by individuals as they attempt to adjust to society.

Unit Overview **149**

37. **The Teening of Childhood,** Kay S. Hymowitz, *American Educator,* Spring 2000
Today's **children** are born into a "kid kulture," where they are introduced early to such concepts as **teen in-crowds.** Barbie, modern **television,** and **advertisements** targeted solely to children are modern inventions that encourage our children to grow up too fast. **151**

38. **The Betrayal of the American Man,** Susan Faludi, *Newsweek,* September 13, 1999
After the **feminist revolution, American men** were left wondering what is the ideal man. Susan Faludi traces the evolving masculine **gender role.** **159**

39. **Coping With Crowding,** Frans B. M. de Waal, Filippo Aureli, and Peter G. Judge, *Scientific American,* May 2000
Early research with rodents on **crowding** strongly suggested that crowding leads to high levels of **aggression.** New research with **primates** and **humans** suggests that primates are capable of flexible **adjustment** to all kinds of **environmental conditions,** including crowding. **168**

40. **Nobody Left to Hate,** Elliot Aronson, *The Humanist,* May/June 2000
Negative school climate can alienate students and foster **racial and ethnic prejudice.** Elliot Aronson discusses his method, known as the **jigsaw classroom,** as a means to reduce such alienation and to promote **racial harmony.** **173**

41. **Speak No Evil,** Dennie Hughes, *USA Weekend,* May 4–6, 2001
One of the most difficult conflicts is **family conflict.** The battle of the sexes is a close second. This article emphasizes how and why **miscommunication** occurs and how to improve communication, or at least to "fight fair." **178**

The concepts in bold italics are developed in the article. For further expansion, please refer to the Topic Guide and the Index.

42. **Work, Work, Work, Work!,** Mark Hunter, *Modern Maturity,* May/ June 1999

The biggest part of adult time is spent at **work** because the lines between our **private lives** and our working lives are blurring. Survival tips for **coping** with the increased pressure to work, work, work are part of this informative article. **180**

43. **Don't Face Stress Alone,** Benedict Carey, *Health,* April 1997

Many Americans are **Type A** and competitive, and they prefer to face **stress** alone. Research, however, is demonstrating how beneficial **social support** or talking to others can be in times of distress. **184**

UNIT 6
Enhancing Human Adjustment: Learning to Cope Effectively

Six selections examine some of the ways an individual learns to cope successfully within today's society. Topics discussed include therapy, depression, and interpersonal relations.

Unit Overview **187**

44. **Self-Help: Shattering the Myths,** Annie Murphy Paul, *Psychology Today,* March/April 2001

Self-help books are full of advice, but is it sound advice? Not exactly, according to the author of this article. Annie Murphy Paul holds self-help advice under the microscope of **scientific scrutiny** in order to shatter some of the **myths and misinformation** contained in these books. **189**

45. **Think Like a Shrink,** Emanuel H. Rosen, *Psychology Today,* September/October 1998

Most clients go to **psychotherapists** because they recognize that they have **distorted perceptions.** Therapists strip away **defensiveness.** Emanuel Rosen supplies some heuristics or rules of thumb used by psychologists that we, too, can apply to assess our own or another's **mental health.** **194**

46. **Bad Choices: Why We Make Them, How to Stop,** Mary Ann Chapman, *Psychology Today,* September/October 1999

We tend to take the path of least resistance so often that we continue our own **destructive behaviors,** such as smoking. We can learn to minimize the **immediate rewards** or to make the **long-term negative consequences** seem more immediate. **197**

47. **Chronic Anxiety: How to Stop Living on the Edge,** *Harvard Health Letter,* July 1998

Chronic anxiety differs from healthy feelings of nervousness. **Anxiety disorders** are the most common disorders affecting Americans and often coexist with **depression.** How to recognize and treat these disorders is the focus of this article. **200**

48. **Up From Depression,** Jeff Kelsey, *Healthline,* January 1999

Depression is perhaps the most treatable of all **mood disorders. Psychotherapy** and **pharmacotherapy** are both useful. Jeff Kelsey also provides guidelines for determining if you are depressed. **203**

49. **Secrets of Happiness,** Stephen Reiss, *Psychology Today,* January/ February 2001

What is **happiness**? Steven Reiss examines the answer to this important question. Satisfying **physical needs** or obtaining large sums of **money** is not the answer. Reiss concludes that there are **basic human values** such as curiosity, acceptance, and tranquility. Satisfying our most important values leads to happiness. **206**

Glossary **209**

Index **219**

Test Your Knowledge Form **222**

Article Rating Form **223**

The concepts in bold italics are developed in the article. For further expansion, please refer to the Topic Guide and the Index.

Topic Guide

This topic guide suggests how the selections in this book relate to the subjects covered in your course. You may want to use the topics listed on these pages to search the Web more easily.

On the following pages a number of Web sites have been gathered specifically for this book. They are arranged to reflect the units of this *Annual Edition.* You can link to these sites by going to the DUSHKIN ONLINE support site at *http://www.dushkin.com/online/.*

ALL THE ARTICLES THAT RELATE TO EACH TOPIC ARE LISTED BELOW THE BOLD-FACED TERM.

Adolescents
22. Disarming the Rage
23. A World of Their Own
37. The Teening of Childhood

Aging
24. The Road Ahead: A Boomer's Guide to Happiness
25. Live to 100? No Thanks
26. Start the Conversation
27. Friendships and Adaptation Across the Life Span

Anxiety disorder
47. Chronic Anxiety: How to Stop Living on the Edge

Autism
11. Autism Is Likely to Be Linked to Several Genes

Behavior
4. Private Lives: Discipline and Knowing Where to Draw the Line

Behaviorism
4. Private Lives: Discipline and Knowing Where to Draw the Line

Biochemistry
13. The Biology of Joy

Biological cycles
14. The Tick-Tock of the Biological Clock

Brain
12. The Future of the Brain
13. The Biology of Joy
14. The Tick-Tock of the Biological Clock

Bullying
22. Disarming the Rage

Children
2. Making Sense of Self-Esteem
4. Private Lives: Discipline and Knowing Where to Draw the Line
11. Autism Is Likely to Be Linked to Several Genes
17. The Seven Stages of Man
18. Fetal Psychology
19. Four Things You Need to Know About Raising Baby
20. What Ever Happened to Play?
21. Parenting: The Lost Art
22. Disarming the Rage
23. A World of Their Own
29. Nurturing Empathy
37. The Teening of Childhood
40. Nobody Left to Hate

Circadian rhythms
14. The Tick-Tock of the Biological Clock

Cognition
18. Fetal Psychology
19. Four Things You Need to Know About Raising Baby

Computers
32. Shyness: The New Solution

Conflict
41. Speak No Evil

Crowding
39. Coping With Crowding

Culture
6. How Culture Molds Habits of Thought
7. The Tangled Skeins of Nature and Nurture in Human Evolution
37. The Teening of Childhood
38. The Betrayal of the American Man
42. Work, Work, Work, Work!

Death
26. Start the Conversation

Decision making
46. Bad Choices: Why We Make Them, How to Stop

Development
20. What Ever Happened to Play?
21. Parenting: The Lost Art
24. The Road Ahead: A Boomer's Guide to Happiness
27. Friendships and Adaptation Across the Life Span

Development, human
17. The Seven Stages of Man
19. Four Things You Need to Know About Raising Baby
20. What Ever Happened to Play?
23. A World of Their Own
25. Live to 100? No Thanks

Development, social
2. Making Sense of Self-Esteem
17. The Seven Stages of Man
27. Friendships and Adaptation Across the Life Span

Emotions
13. The Biology of Joy
18. Fetal Psychology
19. Four Things You Need to Know About Raising Baby
28. Emotional Intelligence
30. What's in a Face?
32. Shyness: The New Solution
36. Prescription for Passion
47. Chronic Anxiety: How to Stop Living on the Edge
49. Secrets of Happiness

Empathy

    29. Nurturing Empathy

Facial expression

    30. What's in a Face?

Family

    19. Four Things You Need to Know About Raising Baby
    41. Speak No Evil
    42. Work, Work, Work, Work!

Fetal development

    18. Fetal Psychology

Freud, Sigmund

    3. Repression Tries for Experimental Comeback

Gender

    8. The Gender Blur
    38. The Betrayal of the American Man

Genes

    7. The Tangled Skeins of Nature and Nurture in Human Evolution
    8. The Gender Blur
    9. The Personality Genes
    10. Where We Come From
    11. Autism Is Likely to Be Linked to Several Genes

Genetics

    7. The Tangled Skeins of Nature and Nurture in Human Evolution
    9. The Personality Genes
    17. The Seven Stages of Man
    19. Four Things You Need to Know About Raising Baby

Groups

    39. Coping With Crowding

Health

    16. Mind Over Medicine

Interpersonal relationships

    27. Friendships and Adaptation Across the Life Span
    28. Emotional Intelligence
    29. Nurturing Empathy
    30. What's in a Face?
    31. How to Spot a Liar
    32. Shyness: The New Solution
    33. Revealing Personal Secrets
    34. Welcome to the Love Lab
    35. Finding Real Love
    36. Prescription for Passion
    39. Coping With Crowding
    43. Don't Face Stress Alone

Jealousy

    36. Prescription for Passion

Joy

    13. The Biology of Joy
    49. Secrets of Happiness

Love

    34. Welcome to the Love Lab
    35. Finding Real Love

Lying

    31. How to Spot a Liar

Marriage

    34. Welcome to the Love Lab
    35. Finding Real Love
    36. Prescription for Passion
    38. The Betrayal of the American Man
    42. Work, Work, Work, Work!

Medicine

    16. Mind Over Medicine

Men

    8. The Gender Blur
    17. The Seven Stages of Man
    38. The Betrayal of the American Man

Mental illness

    47. Chronic Anxiety: How to Stop Living on the Edge
    48. Up From Depression

Middle age

    24. The Road Ahead: A Boomer's Guide to Happiness

Mind-body

    16. Mind Over Medicine

Motivation

    15. Into the Zone

Nature vs. nurture

    7. The Tangled Skeins of Nature and Nurture in Human Evolution
    8. The Gender Blur
    9. The Personality Genes
    10. Where We Come From
    11. Autism Is Likely to Be Linked to Several Genes
    12. The Future of the Brain
    13. The Biology of Joy

Nonverbal communication

    30. What's in a Face?
    31. How to Spot a Liar

Parenting

    4. Private Lives: Discipline and Knowing Where to Draw the Line
    19. Four Things You Need to Know About Raising Baby
    21. Parenting: The Lost Art

Perception

    45. Think Like a Shrink

Personality

    2. Making Sense of Self-Esteem
    5. The Stability of Personality: Observations and Evaluations
    18. Fetal Psychology
    19. Four Things You Need to Know About Raising Baby
    32. Shyness: The New Solution
    49. Secrets of Happiness

Play

    20. What Ever Happened to Play?

Prejudice

    40. Nobody Left to Hate

Prenatal development

    18. Fetal Psychology

Psychoanalysis
3. Repression Tries for Experimental Comeback

Psychology, history of
1. Positive Psychology: An Introduction

Psychology, positive
1. Positive Psychology: An Introduction
13. The Biology of Joy

Psychotherapy
45. Think Like a Shrink
48. Up From Depression

Punishment
4. Private Lives: Discipline and Knowing Where to Draw the Line

Reinforcement
4. Private Lives: Discipline and Knowing Where to Draw the Line

Repression
3. Repression Tries for Experimental Comeback

Research, psychological
18. Fetal Psychology

Reward
4. Private Lives: Discipline and Knowing Where to Draw the Line

Schools
22. Disarming the Rage
40. Nobody Left to Hate

Secrets
33. Revealing Personal Secrets

Self-esteem
2. Making Sense of Self-Esteem
32. Shyness: The New Solution

Self-help
44. Self-Help: Shattering the Myths

Shyness
32. Shyness: The New Solution

Social behavior
21. Parenting: The Lost Art
22. Disarming the Rage
28. Emotional Intelligence
29. Nurturing Empathy
30. What's in a Face?
39. Coping With Crowding
40. Nobody Left to Hate

Social support
32. Shyness: The New Solution
43. Don't Face Stress Alone

Sports
15. Into the Zone

Stability of traits
5. The Stability of Personality: Observations and Evaluations

Stress
18. Fetal Psychology
38. The Betrayal of the American Man
43. Don't Face Stress Alone

Theories
5. The Stability of Personality: Observations and Evaluations

Type A personality
43. Don't Face Stress Alone

Violence
22. Disarming the Rage

Women
8. The Gender Blur

Work
15. Into the Zone
42. Work, Work, Work, Work!

World Wide Web Sites

The following World Wide Web sites have been carefully researched and selected to support the articles found in this reader. The easiest way to access these selected sites is to go to our DUSHKIN ONLINE support site at *http://www.dushkin.com/online/*.

AE: Personal Growth and Behavior 02/03

The following sites were available at the time of publication. Visit our Web site—we update DUSHKIN ONLINE regularly to reflect any changes.

General Sources

National Institute of Child Health and Human Development (NICHD)
http://www.nichd.nih.gov

The NICHD conducts and supports research on the reproductive, neurobiologic, developmental, and behavioral processes that determine and maintain the health of children and adults.

Psychnet
http://www.apa.org/psychnet/

Get information on psychology from this Web site through the site map or by using the search engine. Access *APA Monitor,* the American Psychological Association newspaper; APA Books on a wide range of topics; PsychINFO, an electronic database of abstracts on over 1,350 scholarly journals; and HelpCenter for information on dealing with modern life problems.

UNIT 1: Becoming a Person: Foundations

Abraham A. Brill Library
http://plaza.interport.net/nypsan/service.html

The Abraham A. Brill Library, perhaps the largest psychoanalytic library in the world, contains data on over 40,000 books, periodicals, and reprints in psychoanalysis and related fields. Its holdings span the literature of psychoanalysis from its beginning to the present day.

JungWeb
http://www.cgjungboston.com/

Dedicated to the work of Carl Jung, this site is a comprehensive resource for Jungian psychology. Links to Jungian psychology, reference materials, graduate programs, dreams, multilingual sites, and related Jungian themes are available.

Sigmund Freud and the Freud Archives
http://plaza.interport.net/nypsan/freudarc.html

Internet resources related to Sigmund Freud can be accessed through this site. A collection of libraries, museums, and biographical materials, as well as the Brill Library archives, can be found here.

UNIT 2: Determinants of Behavior: Motivation, Environment, and Physiology

American Psychological Society (APS)
http://www.psychologicalscience.org

APS membership includes a diverse group of the world's foremost scientists and academics working to expand basic and applied psychological science knowledge. Links to teaching, research, and graduate studies resources are available.

Federation of Behavioral, Psychological, and Cognitive Science
http://www.am.org/federation/

At this site you can hotlink to the National Institutes of Health's medical database, government links to public information on mental health, a social psychology network, and the Project on the Decade of the Brain.

Max Planck Institute for Psychological Research
http://www.mpipf-muenchen.mpg.de/BCD/bcd_e.htm

Several behavioral and cognitive development research projects are available on this site.

The Opportunity of Adolescence
http://www.winternet.com/~webpage/adolescencepaper.html

This paper calls adolescence the turning point, after which the future is redirected and confirmed, and goes on to discuss the opportunities and problems of this period to the individual and society, using quotations from Erik Erikson, Jean Piaget, and others.

Psychology Research on the Net
http://psych.hanover.edu/APS/exponnet.html

Psychologically related experiments on the Internet can be found at this site. Biological psychology/neuropsychology, clinical psychology, cognition, developmental psychology, emotions, general issues, health psychology, personality, sensation/perception, and social psychology are addressed.

Serendip
http://serendip.brynmawr.edu/serendip/

Organized into five subject areas (brain and behavior, complex systems, genes and behavior, science and culture, and science education), Serendip contains interactive exhibits, articles, links to other resources, and a forum area for comments and discussion.

UNIT 3: Problems Influencing Personal Growth

Adolescence: Changes and Continuity
http://www.personal.psu.edu/faculty/n/x/nxd10/adolesce.htm

This site offers a discussion of puberty, sexuality, biological changes, cross-cultural differences, and nutrition for adolescents, including obesity and its effects on adolescent development.

Ask NOAH About: Mental Health
http://www.noah-health.org/english/illness/mentalhealth/mental.html

This enormous resource contains information about child and adolescent family problems, mental conditions and disorders, suicide prevention, and much more.

Facts for Families
http://www.aacap.org/info_families/index.htm

The American Academy of Child and Adolescent Psychiatry provides concise, up-to-date information on issues that affect teenagers and their families. Fifty-six fact sheets include many teenager's issues.

www.dushkin.com/online/

Mental Health Infosource: Disorders
http://www.mhsource.com/disorders/

This no-nonsense page lists hotlinks to psychological disorders pages, including anxiety, panic, phobic disorders, schizophrenia, and violent/self-destructive behaviors.

Mental Health Risk Factors for Adolescents
http://education.indiana.edu/cas/adol/mental.html

This collection of Web resources is useful for parents, educators, researchers, health practitioners, and teens. It covers a great deal, including abuse, conduct disorders, and stress.

Suicide Awareness: Voices of Education
http://www.save.org

This is the most popular suicide site on the Internet. It is very thorough, with information on dealing with suicide (both before and after), along with material from the organization's many education sessions.

UNIT 4: Relating to Others

CYFERNET-Youth Development
http://www.cyfernet.mes.umn.edu/youthdev.html

An excellent source of many articles on youth development, this site includes a statement on the concept of normal adolescence and impediments to healthy development.

Hypermedia, Literature, and Cognitive Dissonance
http://www.uncg.edu/~rsginghe/metastat.htm

This article, subtitled *The Heuristic Challenges of Connectivity,* discusses EQ (emotional intelligence) in adults and offers an interactive study, the Metatale Paradigm, that is linked to story sources. Click on *http://www.uncg.edu/~rsginghe/metatext.htm* for access.

Emotional Intelligence Discovery
http://www.cwrl.utexas.edu/~bump/Hu305/3/3/3/

This site has been set up by students to talk about and expand on Daniel Goleman's book, *Emotional Intelligence.* There are links to many other EI sites.

The Personality Project
http://personality-project.org

The Personality Project of William Revelle, director of the Graduate Program in Personality at Northwestern University, is meant to guide those interested in personality theory and research to the current personality research literature.

UNIT 5: Dynamics of Personal Adjustment: The Individual and Society

AFF Cult Group Information
http://www.csj.org/index.html

Information about cults, cult groups, and psychological manipulation is available at this page sponsored by the secular, not-for-profit, tax-exempt research center and educational organization, American Family Foundation.

Explanations of Criminal Behavior
http://www.uaa.alaska.edu/just/just110/crime2.html

An excellent outline of the causes of crime, including major theories, which was prepared by Darryl Wood at the University of Alaska, Anchorage, can be found at this site.

National Clearinghouse for Alcohol and Drug Information
http://www.health.org

This is an excellent general site for information on drug and alcohol facts that might relate to adolescence and the issues of peer pressure and youth culture. Resources, referrals, research and statistics, databases, and related Internet links are among the options available at this site.

Schools Health Education Unit (SHEU)
http://www.sheu.org.uk/sheu.htm

SHEU is a research unit that offers survey, research, and evaluation services on health and social development for young people.

UNIT 6: Enhancing Human Adjustment: Learning to Cope Effectively

John Suler's Teaching Clinical Psychology Site
http://www.rider.edu/users/suler/tcp.html

This page contains Internet resources for clinical and abnormal psychology, behavioral medicine, and mental health.

Health Information Resources
http://www.health.gov/nhic/Pubs/tollfree.htm

Here is a long list of toll-free numbers that provide health-related information. None offer diagnosis and treatment, but some do offer recorded information; others provide personalized counseling, referrals, and/or written materials.

Knowledge Exchange Network (KEN)
http://www.mentalhealth.org

The CMHS National Mental Health Services Exchange Network (KEN) provides information about mental health via toll-free telephone services, an electronic bulletin board, and publications. It is a one-stop source for information and resources on prevention, treatment, and rehabilitation services for mental illness, with many links to related sources.

Mental Health Net
http://www.mentalhealth.net

This comprehensive guide to mental health online features more than 6,300 individual resources. It covers information on mental disorders, professional resources in psychology, psychiatry, and social work, journals, and self-help magazines.

Mind Tools
http://www.psychwww.com/mtsite/

Useful information on stress management can be found at this Web site.

NetPsychology
http://netpsych.com/index.htm

This site explores the uses of the Internet to deliver mental health services. This is a basic cybertherapy resource site.

We highly recommend that you review our Web site for expanded information and our other product lines. We are continually updating and adding links to our Web site in order to offer you the most usable and useful information that will support and expand the value of your Annual Editions. You can reach us at: *http://www.dushkin.com/annualeditions/.*

UNIT 1

Becoming a Person: Foundations

Unit Selections

1. **Positive Psychology: An Introduction**, Martin E. P. Seligman and Mihaly Csikszentmihalyi
2. **Making Sense of Self-Esteem**, Mark R. Leary
3. **Repression Tries for Experimental Comeback**, Bruce Bower
4. **Private Lives: Discipline and Knowing Where to Draw the Line**, Jan Parker and Jan Stimpson
5. **The Stability of Personality: Observations and Evaluations**, Robert R. McCrae and Paul T. Costa Jr.
6. **How Culture Molds Habits of Thought**, Erica Goode

Key Points to Consider

- Can you trace the history of psychological thought? Where do you think psychological and psychiatric thinking will head in the future? Do you think events at any given point in world history have influenced the theories of psychologists and psychiatrists?

- Do you think self-concept is the most important human construct? Do you think that the development of self is driven by biology? Why or why not? What else do you think prompts the development of self-concept? How do you think evaluations from others affect our self-concept, especially self-esteem?

- Do you believe in the unconscious and repression? Why or why not? If yes, can you provide examples from your own life of their influence? What other concepts are important to Sigmund Freud's conceptualization of humans?

- What contributions, if any, has Freud made to our understanding of human nature?

- What is behaviorism? To what general principles do behavioral theorists subscribe? Should we utilize punishment to alter or manage children's behaviors? Which is most preferred—reinforcement or punishment? Why?

- What is a personality trait? Do you think personality traits remain stable over a lifetime? Do traits remain stable across situations; that is, are they carried from church to school, for example? From where do personality traits originate? Are they biological or learned? Do traits collectively comprise self-concept or is self comprised of more than traits?

- Which theory of human personality (humanistic, behavioral, psychoanalytic, or trait) do you think is best and why? How do these theories differ from one another; for example, how does each deal with the "nature" (goodness or badness) of humans?

- What role does culture play in shaping our mental life? Are there differences among cultures? How so? Do any of the above theories take culture into account? If not, should they?

 **Links: www.dushkin.com/online/**
These sites are annotated in the World Wide Web pages.

Abraham A. Brill Library
http://plaza.interport.net/nypsan/service.html
JungWeb
http://www.cgjungboston.com/
Sigmund Freud and the Freud Archives
http://plaza.interport.net/nypsan/freudarc.html

A baby sits in front of a mirror and looks at himself. A chimpanzee sorts through photographs while its trainer carefully watches its reactions. A college student answers a survey on how she feels about herself. What does each of these events share with the others? All are examples of techniques used to investigate self-concept.

That baby in front of the mirror has a red dot on his nose. Researchers watch to see if the baby reaches for the dot in the mirror or touches his own nose. Recognizing the fact that the image he sees in the mirror is his own, the baby touches his real nose, not the nose in the mirror.

The chimpanzee has been trained to sort photographs into two piles—human pictures or animal pictures. If the chimp has been raised with humans, the researcher wants to know into which pile (animal or human) the chimp will place its own picture. Is the chimp's concept of itself animal or human? Or does the chimp have no concept of self at all?

The college student taking the self-survey answers questions about her body image, whether or not she thinks she is fun to be with, whether or not she spends large amounts of time in fantasy, and what her feelings are about her personality and intelligence.

These research projects are designed to investigate how self-concept develops and steers our behaviors and thoughts. Most psychologists believe that people develop a personal identity or a sense of self, which is a sense of who we are, our likes and dislikes, our characteristic feelings and thoughts, and an understanding of why we behave as we do. Self-concept is our knowledge of our gender, race, and age, as well as our sense of self-worth and more. Strong positive or negative feelings are usually attached to this identity. Psychologists are studying how and when this sense of self develops. Most psychologists do not believe that infants are born with a sense of self but rather that children slowly develop self-concept as a consequence of their experiences.

This unit delineates some of the popular viewpoints regarding how sense of self, personality, and behavior develop and how, or whether, they guide behavior. This knowledge of how self develops provides an important foundation for the rest of the units in this book. This unit explores major theories or forces in psychology: self or humanistic, behavioral, psychoanalytic, and trait theories. The last article is included because it references an important element that many of these theories ignore—culture.

The first article reviews the interesting and circuitous history of theories in the area of personal growth and development. In "Positive Psychology," renowned psychologists Martin Seligman and Mihaly Csikszentmihaly discuss the history of psychology and its recent evolution from focusing on human foibles and problems to an emphasis on the more positive aspects of human existence. They also include commentary on how psychology will evolve in the future.

The next series of articles introduces to the reader some of the various theories about human nature. In the first article related to humanistic psychology, the reader is provided with a critique of the concept of self-esteem. As noted earlier, some theorists, namely the humanists, believe that self-concept is the crux or glue of personality. Self-esteem is a related concept and refers to our perceived self-worth. In "Making Sense of Self-Esteem," Mark Leary suggests a redefinition of the construct as well as a closer examination of the effects of low esteem.

The next article in this unit relates to a different theory, the psychoanalytic theory of Sigmund Freud. Psychoanalysis, a theory as well as a form of therapy, proposes that individuals possess a dark, lurking unconscious that often motivates negative behaviors such as guilt and defensiveness. This notion is quite a contrast to the more positive thinking of the humanists. This article reviews an important construct in this theory—repression. Modern psychologists, using sophisticated research techniques, are attempting to establish that repression does indeed occur.

The next article pertains to a third theory—behaviorism. Behaviorism expunges thought, emotion, and abstract concepts such as self from psychological philosophy. In "Private Lives: Discipline and Knowing Where to Draw the Line," using principles from operant conditioning or learning, the authors discuss how parents and teachers can better manage a child's behavior. The authors provide guidelines on how and when to use reinforcement and punishment, with punishment being the most controversial and least desirable of the two. The next essay in this unit offers a contrasting viewpoint on human nature, known as the trait or dispositional approach. Trait theories in general hold that personality is comprised of various traits that perhaps are bound together by our self-concept. This review of relevant research claims that most personality traits remain constant over time, a view that is in sharp contrast to other theories—humanistic theories that propose continued growth, the psychoanalytic stage theory of Freud, and the behavior change model of learning theories and behaviorism.

Finally, this unit would not be complete without an article on culture. Most of the above theories (humanism, psychoanalysis, behaviorism, and trait theory) are laced with Western thought. However, cross-cultural psychologists are teaching us that there are other ways of construing the world and the self, suggesting that these theories might not be universally applicable. In "How Culture Molds Habits of Thought" several studies are highlighted that demonstrate that culture, rather than any single over-arching theoretical principle, influences mental life.

Positive Psychology

An Introduction

A science of positive subjective experience, positive individual traits, and positive institutions promises to improve quality of life and prevent the pathologies that arise when life is barren and meaningless. The exclusive focus on pathology that has dominated so much of our discipline results in a model of the human being lacking the positive features that make life worth living. Hope, wisdom, creativity, future mindedness, courage, spirituality, responsibility, and perseverance are ignored or explained as transformations of more authentic negative impulses....

Martin E.P. Seligman
University of Pensylvania

Mihaly Csikszentmihalyi
Claremont Graduate University

Entering a new millennium, we face an historical choice. Left alone on the pinnacle of economic and political leadership, the United States can continue to increase its material wealth while ignoring the human needs of its people and that of the rest of the planet. Such a course is likely to lead to increasing selfishness, alienation between the more and the less fortunate, and eventually to chaos and despair.

At this juncture the social and behavioral sciences can play an enormously important role. They can articulate a vision of the good life that is empirically sound while being understandable and attractive. They can show what actions lead to well being, to positive individuals, and to thriving communities. Psychology should be able to help document what kind of families result in children who flourish, what work settings support the greatest satisfaction among workers, what policies result in the strongest civic engagement, and how our lives can be most worth living.

Yet psychologists have scant knowledge of what makes life worth living. They have come to understand quite a bit about how people survive and endure under conditions of adversity. (For recent surveys of the history of psychology see, e.g. Koch & Leary, 1985; Benjamin, 1985; and Smith, 1997). But we know very little about how

normal people flourish under more benign conditions. Psychology has, since World War II, become a science largely about healing. It concentrates on repairing damage within a disease model of human functioning. This almost exclusive attention to pathology neglects the fulfilled individual and the thriving community. The aim of Positive psychology is to begin to catalyze a change in the focus of psychology from preoccupation only with repairing the worst things in life to also building positive qualities.

The field of positive psychology at the subjective level is about valued subjective experience: well-being, contentment, and satisfaction (in the past), hope and optimism (for the future), and flow and happiness (in the present). At the individual level it is about positive individual traits—the capacity for love and vocation, courage, interpersonal skill, aesthetic sensibility, perseverance, forgiveness, originality, future-mindedness, spirituality, high talent, and wisdom. At the group level it is about the civic virtues and the institutions that move individuals toward better citizenship: responsibility, nurturance, altruism, civility, moderation, tolerance, and work ethic.

Two personal stories, one told by each author, explain how we arrived at the conviction that a movement toward positive psychology was needed and how [a] special issue* of the *American Psychologist* came about. For Martin E.P. Seligman, it began at a moment in time a few months after he had been elected president of the American Psychological Association:

The moment took place in my garden while I was weeding with my five-year old daughter, Nikki. I have to confess that even though I write books about children, I'm really not all that good with children. I am goal-oriented and time-urgent and when I'm weeding in the garden, I'm actually trying to get the weeding done. Nikki, however, was throwing weeds into the air, singing, and dancing around. I yelled at her. She walked away came back and said,

"Daddy, I want to talk to you."

"Yes, Nikki?"

"Daddy, do you remember before my fifth birthday? From the time I was three to the time I was five, I was a whiner. I whined every day. When I turned five, I decided not to whine anymore. That was the hardest thing I've ever done. And if I can stop whining, you can stop being such a grouch."

This was for me an epiphany, nothing less. I learned something about Nikki, about raising kids, about myself, and a great deal about my profession. First, I realized that raising Nikki was not about correcting whining. Nikki did that herself. Rather, I realized that raising Nikki is about taking this marvelous strength she has—I call it "seeing into the soul,"—amplifying it, nurturing it, helping her to lead her life around it to buffer against her weaknesses and the storms of life. Raising children, I realized, is vastly more than fixing what is wrong with them. It is about identifying and nurturing their strongest qualities, what they own and are best at, and helping them find niches in which they can best live out these strengths.

As for my own life, Nikki hit the nail right on the head. I was a grouch. I had spent 50 years mostly enduring wet weather in my soul, and the past 10 years being a nimbus cloud in a household full of sunshine. Any good fortune I had was probably not due to my grumpiness, but in spite of it. In that moment, I resolved to change.

However, the broadest implication of Nikki's teaching was about the science and profession of psychology: Before World War II, psychology had three distinct missions: curing mental illness, making the lives of all people more productive and fulfilling, and identifying and nurturing high talent. The early focus on positive psychology is exemplified by such work as Terman's studies of giftedness (Terman, 1939) and marital happiness (Terman, Buttenwieser, Ferguson, Johnson & Wilson, 1938), Watson's writings on effective parenting (Watson, 1928), and Jung's work concerning the search and discovery of meaning in life (Jung, 1933). Right after the war, two events—both economic—changed the face of psychology: In 1946 the Veteran's Administration (now Veterans Affairs) was founded, and thousands of psychologists found out that they could make a living treating mental illness. In 1947, the National Institute of Mental Health (which, in spite of its charter, has always been based on the disease model, and should now more appropriately be renamed the National Institute of Mental Illness) was founded, and academics found out that they could get grants if their research was about pathology.

This arrangement brought many benefits. There have been huge strides in the understanding and therapy for mental illness: At least 14 disorders, previously intractable, have yielded their secrets to science and can now be either cured or considerably relieved (Seligman, 1994). But the downside, however, was that the other two fundamental missions of psychology—making the lives of all people better and nurturing genius—were all but forgotten. It wasn't only the subject matter that was altered by funding, but the currency of the theories underpinning how psychologists viewed themselves. They came to see themselves as a mere sub-field of the health professions, and we became a victimology. Psychologists saw human beings as passive foci: Stimuli came on and elicited responses (what an extraordinarily passive word!). External reinforcements weakened or strengthened responses. Drives, tissue needs, instincts, and conflicts from childhood pushed each of us around.

Psychology's empirical focus shifted to assessing and curing individual suffering. There has been an explosion in research on psychological disorders and the negative effects of environmental stressors such as parental divorce, the deaths of loved ones, and physical and sexual abuse. Practitioners went about treating the mental illness of patients within a disease framework by repairing damage: damaged habits, damaged drives, damaged childhoods, and damaged brains.

Mihaly Csikszentmilhalyi realized the need for a positive psychology in Europe during World War II: As a child, I witnessed the dissolution of the smug world in which I had been comfortably ensconced. I noticed with surprise how many of the adults I had known as successful and self-confident became helpless and dispirited once the war removed their social supports. Without jobs, money or status they were reduced to empty shells. Yet there were a few who kept their integrity and purpose despite the surrounding chaos. Their serenity was a beacon that kept others from losing hope. And these were not the men and women one would have expected to emerge unscathed: they were not necessarily the most respected, better educated, or more skilled individuals. This experience set me thinking: What sources of strength were these people drawing on?

Reading philosophy, dabbling in history and religion did not provide satisfying answers to that question. I found the ideas in these texts to be too subjective, dependent on faith, or dubious assumptions; they lacked the clear-eyed skepticism, the slow cumulative growth that I associated with science. Then, for the first time, I came across psychology: first the writings of Carl Jung, then

Freud, then a few of the psychologists who were writing in Europe in the 1950s. Here, I thought, was a possible solution to my quest—a discipline that dealt with the fundamental issues of life, and attempted to do so with the patient simplicity of the natural sciences.

However, at that time psychology was not yet a recognized discipline. In Italy, where I lived, one could take courses in it only as a minor while pursuing a degree in medicine or in philosophy. So I decided to come to the United States, where psychology had gained wider acceptance. The first courses I took were somewhat of a shock. It turned out that in the United States psychology had indeed became a science, if by science one meant only a skeptical attitude and a concern for measurement. What seemed to be lacking, however, was a vision that justified the attitude and the methodology. I was looking for a scientific approach to human behavior, but I never dreamed that this could yield a value-free understanding. In human behavior, what is most intriguing is not the average, but the improbable. Very few people kept their decency during the onslaught of World War II; yet it was these few who held the key to what humans could be like at their best. However, at the height of its behaviorist phase, psychology was being taught as if it were a branch of statistical mechanics. Ever since, I have struggled to reconcile the twin imperatives that a science of human beings should include: to understand what *is*, and what *could be*.

A decade later, the "third way" heralded by Abraham Maslow, Carl Rogers, and other "humanistic" psychologists promised to open a new perspective in addition to the entrenched clinical and behaviorist approaches. Their generous vision had a strong effect on the culture at large and held enormous promise. Unfortunately humanistic psychology did not attract much of a cumulative empirical base and it spawned myriad therapeutic self-help movements. In some of its incarnations it emphasized the self and encouraged a self-centeredness that played down concerns for collective well-being. We leave it to future debate to determine whether this came about because Maslow and Rogers were ahead of their times, or because these flaws were inherent in their original vision, or because of overly enthusiastic "followers." But one legacy of the 1960s is prominently displayed in any large bookstore: The "psychology" section will contain at least 10 shelves on crystal healing, aromatherapy, and reaching the inner child for every shelf of books that tries to uphold some scholarly standard.

Whatever the personal origins of our conviction that the time has arrived for a positive psychology, our message is to remind our field that psychology is not just the study of pathology, weakness, and damage; it is also the study of strength and virtue. Treatment is not just fixing what is broken; it is nurturing what is best. Psychology is not just a branch of medicine concerned with illness or health; it is much larger. It is about work, education, insight, love, growth, and play. And in this quest for what is best, positive psychology does not rely on wishful thinking, faith, self-deception, fads, or hand-waving; it tries to adapt what is best in the scientific method to the unique problems that human behavior presents to those who wish to understand it in all its complexity.

What foregrounds this approach is the issue of prevention. In the last decade psychologists have become concerned with prevention, and this was the presidential theme of the 1998 American Psychological Association meeting in San Francisco. How can we prevent problems like depression or substance abuse or schizophrenia in young people who are genetically vulnerable or who live in worlds that nurture these problems? How can we prevent murderous schoolyard violence in children who have access to weapons, poor parental supervision, and a mean streak? What we have learned over fifty years is that the disease model does not move us closer to the prevention of these serious problems. Indeed the major strides in prevention have largely come from a perspective focused on systematically building competency, not correcting weakness.

Prevention researchers have discovered that there are human strengths that act as buffers against mental illness: courage, future mindedness, optimism, interpersonal skill, faith, work ethic, hope, honesty, perseverance, the capacity for flow and insight, to name several. Much of the task of prevention in this new century will be to create a science of human strength whose mission will be to understand and learn how to foster these virtues in young people.

Working exclusively on personal weakness and on damaged brains, however, has rendered science poorly equipped to effectively prevent illness. Psychologists need now to call for massive research on human strength and virtue. Practitioners need to recognize that much of the best work they already do in the consulting room is to amplify strengths rather than repair the weaknesses of their clients. Psychologists working with families, schools, religious communities, and corporations, need to develop climates that foster these strengths. The major psychological theories have changed to undergird a new science of strength and resilience. No longer do the dominant theories view the individual as a passive vessel responding to stimuli; rather, individuals are now seen as decision makers, with choices, preferences, and the possibility of becoming masterful, efficacious, or, in malignant circumstances, helpless and hopeless (Bandura, 1986; Seligman, 1992). Science and practice that rely on this worldview may have the direct effect of preventing much of the major emotional disorders. It may also have two side effects: making the lives of our clients physically healthier, given all that psychologists are learning about the effects of mental well-being on the body. This science and practice will also reorient psychology back to its two neglected missions, making normal people stronger and more productive as well as making high human potential actual....

4

References

Allport, G. W. (1961). *Pattern and growth in personality*. New York: Holt, Rinehart, & Wilson.

Baltes, P. B. & Staudinger, U.M. (2000).Wisdom: A metaheuristic (pragmatic) to orchestrate mind and virtue toward excellence. *American Psychologist, 55*, 122–136.

Bandura, A. (1986). *Social foundations of thoughts and action*. Englewood Cliffs, New Jersey: Prentice-Hall.

Benjamin, L. T. Jr. (Ed.) (1992) The history of American psychology. [Special Issue], *American Psychologist, 47*(2).

Buss, D.M. (2000).The evolution of happiness. *American Psychologist, 47*(2).

Diener, E. (2000). Subjective well-being: The science of happiness, and a proposal for a national index. *American Psychologist, 55*, 34–43.

Hall, G.S. (1922). *Senescence: The last half of life*. New York: Appleton.

James, W. (1958). *Varieties of religious experience*. New York: Mentor. (Original work published 1902)

Jung, C. (1933). *Modern man in search of a soul*. New York, Harcourt.

Jung, C.G. (1969). *The archetypes of the collective unconscious. Vol. 9, The collective works of C.G. Jung*. Princeton, NJ: Princeton University Press. (Original work published 1936)

Kahneman, D. (1999). Objective happiness. In D. Kahneman, E. Diener, & N. Schwartz (Eds.) *Well-Being: The foundations of hedonic psychology* (pp. 3–25). New York: Russell Sage Foundation.

Koch, S. & Leary, D.E. (Eds.) (1985) (Eds.) *A century of psychology as science*. New York: McGraw-Hill.

Larson, R. W. (2000). Toward a psychology of positive youth development. *American Psychologist, 55*, 170–183.

Ledoux, J. & Armony, J. (1999). Can neurobiology tell us anything about human feelings? In D. Kahneman, E. Diener, & N. Schwartz (Eds.) *Well-Being: The foundations of hedonic psychology* (pp.489–499). New York: Russell Sage Foundation.

Lubinski, D. & Benbow, C.P. (2000). States of excellence. *American Psychologist, 55*, 137–150.

Maslow, A. (1971). *The Farthest Reaches of Human Nature*. New York: Viking.

Massimini, F. & Delle Fave, A. (2000) Individual development in a bio-cultural perspective. *American Psychologist, 55*, 24–33.

Myers, D.G. (2000) The funds, friends, and faith of happy people. *American Psychologist, 55*, 56–67.

Peterson, C. (2000). The future of optimism. *American Psychologist, 55*, 68–78.

Ryan, R.M. & Deci, E.L. (2000). Self-determination theory and the facilitation of intrinsic motivation, social development, and well-being. *American Psychologist, 55*, 110–121.

Salovey, P., Rothman, A.J., Detweiler, J.B. & Steward, W.T. (2000). Emotional states and physical health. *American Psychologist, 55*, 110–121.

Schwartz, B. (2000). Self-determination: The tyranny of freedom. *American Psychologist, 55*, 79–88.

Seligman, M. (1992). *Helplessness: On depression, development, and death*. New York: Freeman.

Seligman, M. (1994). *What you can change & what you can't*. New York: Knopf.

Seligman, M. Schulman, P., DeRubeis, R., & Hollon, S. (1999). The prevention of depression and anxiety. *Prevention and Treatment, 2*, Article 8. Available on the World Wide Web: http://journals.apa.org/prevention/volume2/pre0020008a.html

Simonton, D.K. (2000). Creativity: Cognitive, personal, developmental, and social aspects. *American Psychologist, 55*, 151–158.

Smith, R. (1997). *The human sciences*. New York: Norton.

Taylor, S.E., Kemeny, M.E., Reed, G.M., Bower, J.E. & Gruenwald, T.L. (2000). Psychological resources, positive illusions, and health. *American Psychologist, 55*, 99–109.

Terman, L.M. (1939). The gifted student and his academic environment. *School and Society, 49*, 65–73.

Terman, L.M., Buttenweiser, P., Fergusun, L.W., Johnson, W.B., & Wilson, D.P. (1938). *Psychological factors in marital happiness*. New York: McGraw-Hill.

Vaillant, G.E. (2000). Adaptive mental mechanisms: Their role in a positive psychology. *American Psychologist, 55*, 89–98.

Watson, J. (1928). *Psychological care of infant and child*. New York: Norton.

Winner, E. (2000). The origins and ends of giftedness. *American Psychologist, 55*, 159–169.

Editor's note. Martin E.P. Seligman and Mihaly Csikszentmihalyi served as guest editors for the special issue of *American Psychologist*.

* See the special millennial issue of *American Psychologist*, January 2000, for 16 articles on the topic of Positive Psychology.

Author's note. Martin E.P. Seligman, Department of Psychology, University of Pennsylvania; Mihaly Csikszentmihalyi, Department of Psychology, Claremont Graduate University.

Correspondence concerning this article should be addressed to Martin E.P. Seligman, Department of Psychology, University of Pennsylvania, 3813 Walnut Street, Philadelphia, PA 19104–3604. Electronic mail may be sent to seligman@cattell.psych.upenn.edu.

From *American Psychologist*, February 2000, pp. 218–232. © 2000 by the American Psychological Association. Reprinted with permission.

Making Sense of Self-Esteem

Mark R. Leary[1]
Department of Psychology, Wake Forest University, Winston-Salem, North Carolina

Abstract
Sociometer theory proposes that the self-esteem system evolved as a monitor of social acceptance, and that the so-called self-esteem motive functions not to maintain self-esteem per se but rather to avoid social devaluation and rejection. Cues indicating that the individual is not adequately valued and accepted by other people lower self-esteem and motivate behaviors that enhance relational evaluation. Empirical evidence regarding the self-esteem motive, the antecedents of self-esteem, the relation between low self-esteem and psychological problems, and the consequences of enhancing self-esteem is consistent with the theory.

Keywords
self-esteem; self; self-regard; rejection

Self-esteem has been regarded as an important construct since the earliest days of psychology. In the first psychology textbook, William James (1890) suggested that the tendency to strive to feel good about oneself is a fundamental aspect of human nature, thereby fueling a fascination—some observers would say obsession—with self-esteem that has spanned more than a century. During that time, developmental psychologists have studied the antecedents of self-esteem and its role in human development, social psychologists have devoted attention to behaviors that appear intended to maintain self-esteem, personality psychologists have examined individual differences in the trait of self-esteem, and theorists of a variety of orientations have discussed the importance of self-regard to psychological adjust-

ment. In the past couple of decades, practicing psychologists and social engineers have suggested that high self-esteem is a remedy for many psychological and social problems.

Yet, despite more than 100 years of attention and thousands of published studies, fundamental issues regarding self-esteem remain poorly understood. Why is self-esteem important? Do people really have a need for self-esteem? Why is self-esteem so strongly determined by how people believe they are evaluated by others? Is low self-esteem associated with psychological difficulties and, if so, why? Do efforts to enhance self-esteem reduce personal and social problems as proponents of the self-esteem movement claim?

PERSPECTIVES ON THE FUNCTION OF SELF-ESTEEM

Many writers have assumed that people seek to maintain their self-esteem because they possess an inherent "need" to feel good about themselves. However, given the apparent importance of self-esteem to psychological functioning, we must ask why self-esteem is so important and what function it might serve. Humanistic psychologists have traced high self-esteem to a congruency between a person's real and ideal selves and suggested that self-esteem signals people as to when they are behaving in self-determined, autonomous ways. Other writers have proposed that people seek high self-esteem because it facilitates goal achievement. For example, Bednar, Wells, and Peterson (1989) proposed that self-esteem is subjective feedback about the adequacy of the self. This feedback—self-esteem—is positive when the individual copes well with circumstances

but negative when he or she avoids threats. In turn, self-esteem affects subsequent goal achievement; high self-esteem increases coping, and low self-esteem leads to further avoidance.

The ethological perspective (Barkow, 1980) suggests that self-esteem is an adaptation that evolved in the service of maintaining dominance in social relationships. According to this theory, human beings evolved mechanisms for monitoring dominance because dominance facilitated the acquisition of mates and other reproduction-enhancing resources. Because attention and favorable reactions from others were associated with being dominant, feelings of self-esteem became tied to social approval and deference. From this perspective, the motive to evaluate oneself positively reduces, in evolutionary terms, to the motive to enhance one's relative dominance.

One of the more controversial explanations of self-esteem is provided by terror management theory, which suggests that the function of self-esteem is to buffer people against the existential terror they experience at the prospect of their own death and annihilation (Solomon, Greenberg, & Pyszczynski, 1991). Several experiments have supported aspects of the theory, but not the strong argument that the function of the self-esteem system is to provide an emotional buffer specifically against death-related anxiety.

All of these perspectives offer insights into the nature of self-esteem, but each has conceptual and empirical difficulties (for critiques, see Leary, 1999; Leary & Baumeister, in press). In the past few years, a novel perspective—sociometer theory—has cast self-esteem in a somewhat different light as it attempts to address lingering questions about the nature of self-esteem.

SOCIOMETER THEORY

According to sociometer theory, self-esteem is essentially a psychological meter, or gauge, that monitors the quality of people's relationships with others (Leary, 1999; Leary & Baumeister, in press; Leary & Downs, 1995). The theory is based on the assumption that human beings possess a pervasive drive to maintain significant interpersonal relationships, a drive that evolved because early human beings who belonged to social groups were more likely to survive and reproduce than those who did not (Baumeister & Leary, 1995). Given the disastrous implications of being ostracized in the ancestral environment in which human evolution occurred, early human beings may have developed a mechanism for monitoring the degree to which other people valued and accepted them. This psychological mechanism—the *sociometer*—continuously monitors the social environment for cues regarding the degree to which the individual is being accepted versus rejected by other people.

The sociometer appears to be particularly sensitive to changes in relational evaluation—the degree to which others regard their relationship with the individual as valuable, important, or close. When evidence of low relational evaluation (particularly, a decrement in relational evaluation) is detected, the sociometer attracts the person's conscious attention to the potential threat to social acceptance and motivates him or her to deal with it. The affectively laden self-appraisals that constitute the "output" of the sociometer are what we typically call self-esteem.

Self-esteem researchers distinguish between *state self-esteem*—momentary fluctuations in a person's feelings about him- or herself—and *trait self-esteem*—the person's general appraisal of his or her value; both are aspects of the sociometer. Feelings of state self-esteem fluctuate as a function of the degree to which the person perceives others currently value their relationships with him or her. Cues that connote high relational evaluation raise state self-esteem, whereas cues that connote low relational evaluation lower state self-esteem. Trait self-esteem, in contrast, reflects the person's general sense that he or she is the sort of person who is valued and accepted by other people. Trait self-esteem may be regarded as the resting state of

the sociometer in the absence of incoming information relevant to relational evaluation.

SELF-ESTEEM AND ITS RELATIONSHIP TO BEHAVIOR

Sociometer theory provides a parsimonious explanation for much of what we know about self-esteem. Here I examine how sociometer theory answers four fundamental questions about self-esteem raised earlier.

The Self-Esteem Motive

As noted, many psychologists have assumed that people possess a motive or need to maintain self-esteem. According to sociometer theory, the so-called self-esteem motive does not function to maintain self-esteem but rather to minimize the likelihood of rejection (or, more precisely, relational devaluation). When people behave in ways that protect or enhance their self-esteem, they are typically acting in ways that they believe will increase their relational value in others' eyes and, thus, improve their chances of social acceptance.

The sociometer perspective explains why events that are known (or potentially known) by other people have much greater effects on self-esteem than events that are known only by the individual him- or herself. If self-esteem involved only private self-judgments, as many psychologists have assumed, public events should have no greater impact on self-esteem than private ones.

Antecedents of Self-Esteem

Previous writers have puzzled over the fact that self-esteem is so strongly tied to people's beliefs about how they are evaluated by others. If self-esteem is a *self*-evaluation, why do people judge themselves by *other* people's standards? Sociometer theory easily explains why the primary determinants of self-esteem involve the perceived reactions of other people, as well as self-judgments on dimensions that the person thinks are important to significant others. As a monitor of relational evaluation, the self-esteem system is inherently sensitive to real and potential reactions of other people.

Evidence shows that state self-esteem is strongly affected by events

that have implications for the degree to which one is valued and accepted by other people (Leary, Haupt, Strausser, & Chokel, 1998; Leary, Tambor, Terdal, & Downs, 1995). The events that affect self-esteem are precisely the kinds of things that, if known by other people, would affect their evaluation and acceptance of the person (Leary, Tambor, et al., 1995). Most often, self-esteem is lowered by failure, criticism, rejection, and other events that have negative implications for relational evaluation; self-esteem rises when a person succeeds, is praised, or experiences another's love—events that are associated with relational appreciation. Even the mere possibility of rejection can lower self-esteem, a finding that makes sense if the function of the self-esteem system is to warn the person of possible relational devaluation in time to take corrective action.

The attributes on which people's self-esteem is based are precisely the characteristics that determine the degree to which people are valued and accepted by others (Baumeister & Leary, 1995). Specifically, high trait self-esteem is associated with believing that one possesses socially desirable attributes such as competence, personal likability, and physical attractiveness. Furthermore, self-esteem is related most strongly to one's standing on attributes that one believes are valued by significant others, a finding that is also consistent with sociometer theory.

In linking self-esteem to social acceptance, sociometer theory runs counter to the humanistic assumption that self-esteem based on approval from others is false or unhealthy. On the contrary, if the function of self-esteem is to avoid social devaluation and rejection, then the system must be responsive to others' reactions. This system may lead people to do things that are not always beneficial, but it does so to protect their interpersonal relationships rather than their inner integrity.

Low Self-Esteem and Psychological Problems

Research has shown that low self-esteem is related to a variety of psychological difficulties and personal problems, including depression, loneliness, substance abuse, teenage pregnancy, academic failure, and criminal behavior. The evidence in support of the link between low self-esteem and psychological problems has often been overstated; the relationships are weaker and more scattered than typically assumed (Mecca, Smelser, & Vasconcellos, 1989). Moreover, high self-esteem also has notable drawbacks. Even so, low self-esteem tends to be more strongly associated with psychological difficulties than high self-esteem.

From the standpoint of sociometer theory, these problems are caused not by low self-esteem but rather by a history of low relational evaluation, if not outright rejection. As a subjective gauge of relational evaluation, self-esteem may parallel these problems, but it is a coeffect rather than a cause. (In fact, contrary to the popular view that low self-esteem causes these problems, no direct evidence exists to document that self-esteem has any causal role in thought, emotion, or behavior.) Much research shows that interpersonal rejection results in emotional problems, difficulties relating with others, and maladaptive efforts to be accepted (e.g., excessive dependency, membership in deviant groups), precisely the concomitants of low self-esteem (Leary, Schreindorfer, & Haupt, 1995). In addition, many personal problems lower self-esteem because they lead other people to devalue or reject the individual.

Consequences of Enhancing Self-Esteem

The claim that self-esteem does not cause psychological outcomes may appear to fly in the face of evidence showing that interventions that enhance self-esteem do, in fact, lead to positive psychological changes. The explanation for the beneficial effects of programs that enhance self-esteem is that these interventions change people's perceptions of the degree to which they are socially valued individuals. Self-esteem programs always include features that would be expected to increase real or perceived social acceptance; for example, these programs include components aimed at enhancing social skills and interpersonal problem solving, improving physical appearance, and increasing self-control (Leary, 1999).

CONCLUSIONS

Sociometer theory suggests that the emphasis psychologists and the lay public have placed on self-esteem has been somewhat misplaced. Self-esteem is certainly involved in many psychological phenomena, but its role is different than has been supposed. Subjective feelings of self-esteem provide ongoing feedback regarding one's relational value vis-à-vis other people. By focusing on the monitor rather than on what the monitor measures, we have been distracted from the underlying interpersonal processes and the importance of social acceptance to human well-being.

Recommended Reading

Baumeister, R. F. (Ed.). (1993). *Self-esteem: The puzzle of low self-regard.* New York: Plenum Press.

Colvin, C. R., & Block, J. (1994). Do positive illusions foster mental health? An examination of the Taylor and Brown formulation. *Psychological Bulletin, 116,* 3–20.

Leary, M. R. (1999). (See References)

Leary, M. R., & Downs, D. L. (1995). (See References)

Mecca, A. M., Smelser, N. J., & Vasconcellos, J. (Eds.). (1989). (See References)

Note

1. Address correspondence to Mark Leary, Department of Psychology, Wake Forest University, Winston-Salem, NC 27109; e-mail: leary@wfu.edu.

References

Barkow, J. (1980). Prestige and self-esteem: A biosocial interpretation. In D. R. Omark, F. F. Strayer, & D. G. Freedman (Eds.), *Dominance relations: An ethological view of human conflict and social interaction* (pp. 319–332). New York: Garland STPM Press.

Baumeister, R. F., & Leary, M. R. (1995). The need to belong: Desire for interpersonal attachments as a fundamental human motivation. *Psychological Bulletin, 117,* 497–529.

Bednar, R. L., Wells, M. G., & Peterson, S. R. (1989). *Self-esteem: Paradoxes and innovations in clinical theory and practice.* Washington, DC: American Psychological Association.

James, W. (1890). *The principles of psychology* (Vol. 1). New York: Henry Holt.

Leary, M. R. (1999). The social and psychological importance of self-esteem. In R. M. Kowalski & M. R. Leary (Eds.), *The social psychology of emotional and behavioral problems: Interfaces of social and clinical psychology* (pp. 197–221). Washington, DC: American Psychological Association.

Leary, M. R., & Baumeister, R. F. (in press). The nature and function of self-esteem: Sociometer theory. *Advances in Experimental Social Psychology.*

Leary, M. R., & Downs, D. L. (1995). Interpersonal functions of the self-esteem motive: The self-esteem system as a sociometer. In M. H. Kernis (Ed.), *Efficacy, agency, and self-esteem* (pp. 123–144). New York: Plenum Press.

Leary, M. R., Haupt, A. L., Strausser, K. S., & Chokel, J. L. (1998). Calibrating the sociometer: The relationship between interpersonal appraisals and state self-esteem. *Journal of Personality and Social Psychology, 74,* 1290–1299.

Leary, M. R., Schreindorfer, L. S., & Haupt, A. L. (1995). The role of self-esteem in emotional and behavioral problems: Why is low self-esteem dysfunctional? *Journal of Social and Clinical Psychology, 14,* 297–314.

Leary, M. R., Tambor, E. S., Terdal, S. J., & Downs, D. L. (1995). Self-esteem as an interpersonal monitor. The sociometer hypothesis. *Journal of Personality and Social Psychology, 68,* 518–530.

Mecca, A. M., Smelser, N. J., & Vasconcellos, J. (Eds.). (1989). *The social importance of self-esteem.* Berkeley: University of California Press.

Solomon, S., Greenberg, J., & Pyszczynski, T. (1991). A terror management theory of social behavior: The psychological functions of self-esteem and cultural worldviews. *Advances in Experimental Social Psychology, 24,* 93–159.

From *Current Directions in Psychological Science,* February 1999, pp. 32-35. © 1999 by the American Psychological Society. Reprinted by permission of Blackwell Publishers.

Repression tries for experimental comeback

Sigmund Freud and his theoretical heirs have held that people are capable of pushing unwanted memories into a kind of unconscious cold-storage, where they're gone but not forgotten. Many memory researchers view this mental process, called repression, as a fanciful idea lacking empirical support.

In the March 15 NATURE, researchers describe an everyday form of induced forgetting that may provide a scientific footing for Freudian repression.

When people consistently try to forget a memory in the face of reminders, they often succeed rather well at it, say psychologists Michael C. Anderson and Collin Green of the University of Oregon in Eugene. Successful forgetting increases with practice at avoiding a memory, Anderson and Green say.

"Everyday mechanisms of memory inhibition provide a viable model of repression," Anderson says. His view counters that of some clinicians, who hold that repression exists but only as a special process for dealing with traumas.

Anderson's work was inspired by the finding that kids who have been sexually abused by a trusted caregiver forget that experience far more often than do kids abused by a stranger. Children can willingly use indirect reminders, such as the abuser's presence, as cues to avoid thinking about the actual abuse, according to Anderson.

He and Green had 32 college students learn arbitrary word pairs, such as "ordeal-roach." Volunteers then saw a series of single words from those pairs. Words were shown once, eight times, 16 times, or not at all. On each presentation, participants saw a signal to either remember and say aloud the associated word or to avoid thinking about it.

On an ensuing memory test, students recalled nearly all of the words that they had tried to remember. Volunteers recalled progressively fewer other words, the more chances they had to try to forget them. On average, they recalled about 80 percent of words they tried to forget.

Similar findings emerged when participants saw new words and cues intended to jog their memories, such as "insect-r__" to spur recall of "roach." Again, memory suffered for words that students had tried to forget. These findings indicate that volunteers forgot specific words deliberately blocked, not word pairs.

Comparable memory losses emerged for students told that trying to forget a word would make them think about it more. For instance, people told not to think about, say, a white bear, can't think of anything but that white bear.

In Anderson's studies, however, volunteers used cues such as "ordeal" to anticipate and fend off unwanted memories. The white bear never showed its face.

The new data suggest that brain networks that restrain communication "could give rise to the type of repression proposed by Freud to underlie neuroses," says Martin A. Conway of the University of Bristol in England.

Elizabeth F. Loftus of the University of Washington in Seattle notes that memory was still pretty good for those who tried to forget words. She doesn't regard the study as evidence of repression.

Anderson's findings are "broadly consistent" with Freudian repression, remarks Daniel L. Schacter of Harvard University. Still, he cautions, it's too early to conclude that willful forgetting applies to emotionally sensitive experience.

—*B. Bower*

From *Science News,* March 17, 2001, p. 164. © 2001 by the Science Service, 1719 N Street, N.W., Washington, D.C. 20036; www.sciserv.org. Reprinted by permission of Bruce Bower.

Private Lives: Discipline and knowing where to draw the line

Jan Parker and Jan Stimpson

NO MATTER what you do, how hard you try, there may be times when your child behaves appallingly.

Managing these times so that your child's behaviour improves can be difficult and stressful, but leaving the behaviour unchallenged is worse. Only when you show where you draw the line can a child know which side of it she should be on.

To do this constructively, in ways that bring the results you both need without terrifying or crushing your child in the process, you will sometimes need to be gentle, sometimes tough, often both, and always strong enough to stand your ground.

Thinking ahead and considering your options will make it easier to deal calmly with your child's worst moments. Choosing which discipline strategies, if any, best suit your circumstances is also easier if you know the difference between discipline and punishment.

Discipline is an investment. It teaches children what they have done wrong, the consequences of their behaviour and how they could modify it. It encourages self-discipline and motivates them to do better. It is not a soft option, but can be astonishingly effective.

Punishment involves making children suffer for misbehaviour in an attempt to control it. It aims to shame, frighten or otherwise force children into compliance without them necessarily understanding why. It therefore risks teaching children to modify their behaviour for the wrong reasons, such as the risk of being caught.

The distinction between the two is not always clear-cut and some strategies may involve an element of both, but your *ability* to recognise the type and likely outcome of each approach will help you decide how best to proceed.

Effective discipline strategies

As ever, only consider those approaches that feel right for you and are appropriate to your child's age, understanding and temperament. If any strategy does not work as you hoped, or loses its effectiveness, change it.

Learning to challenge

Challenging is a key skill for turning around a child's behaviour. It takes practice. To those who have never tried it, it may sound too "reasonable" to work in the heat of the moment, but both parents and professionals vouch for its *ability* to stop children in their tracks and praise its effectiveness.

It works on the principle that most children will stop behaving unacceptably if they are told in no uncertain terms how it is affecting others and are given the opportunity to change course without loss of face.

Saying no and meaning it

If you mean it, really mean it, your child is much more likely to get the message. If you don't really mean it your child will pick this up in your expression and body *language* and either ignore you or provoke you until you do.

If you do mean "No", say it in a way that increases its effectiveness. Sometimes you may need to be sharp and stern.

To help your child know you mean business, try getting down to her level so you at least have a chance of eye contact.

Try to stay relaxed and say, calmly but firmly: "No. You are to stop that now—no more." This stops you getting drawn into negotiations and keeps you on very certain ground. Children often echo their parents' emotions; staying in control in an otherwise fiery situation may help them follow suit.

Removing the victim, not the culprit

This is especially useful in educating very young children not to hurt others. It denies the aggressor the attention that may fuel her behaviour and also makes the victim feel safer with you than being left alone.

If your child is hurting another, always explain why you do not like that behaviour and how you would like her to behave instead.

Consequences

Helping children understand the natural consequences of their actions is crucial to their improving their behaviour and learning self-control. This approach can also be used when your child is displaying behaviour you need to stop. For example: Parent (firmly and calmly): "Joe, if you throw your toys someone will get hurt, and you don't want that to happen. Play without throwing, or put it down."

This is often all that is needed to help a child *think* through the consequences of an action—and stop. But what happens when you have told your child the natural consequences of an action and she carries on doing it? Or when you have reminded her of a family rule and she still breaks it? To make it very clear where you draw the line, you may have to impose an (artificial) consequence for crossing it. Eg:

The weapons rule

You may have a family rule that no toys are to be used as weapons to hurt or frighten other children. Whenever neces-sary, you remind her of it and tell her the natural consequence of breaking it (ie "You will hurt"). You may even challenge her behaviour. But two minutes later she hits her brother on the head with a drumstick. What next?

Three strikes and it's out

1. Any toy used as a weapon (ie to hurt or frighten others) is immediately removed (for an hour, for the afternoon, for the rest of the day—the older the child the longer the time can be).

2. If it happens again, it is removed again, for longer.

3. If it happens a third time, it is put in the bin.

Standing back

If you react to every misdemeanour you could spend most of your time reining in your child's behaviour, which, by the law of diminishing returns, means she will take less notice and you will become increasingly frustrated and angry.

Liberate yourself by choosing times not to react immediately. At the very least, this will allow you time to assess what you want your child to do and how important it is that they do it, or whether you can let it go. If it is behaviour that you feel you must challenge, a considered response is generally much more effective than a knee-jerk one.

'Raising Happy Children' by Jan Parker and Jan Stimpson (Hodder & Stoughton, pounds 9.99)

Reprinted from *The Independent*, May 3, 1999. © 1999 by Jan Parker and Jan Stimpson.

The Stability of Personality: Observations and Evaluations

Robert R. McCrae and Paul T. Costa, Jr.

"There is an optical illusion about every person we meet," Ralph Waldo Emerson wrote in his essay on "Experience":

In truth, they are all creatures of given temperament, which will appear in a given character, whose boundaries they will never pass: but we look at them, they seem alive, and we presume there is impulse in them. In the moment it seems impulse; in the year, in the lifetime, it turns out to be a certain uniform tune which the revolving barrel of the music-box must play.[1]

In this brief passage, Emerson anticipated modern findings about the stability of personality and pointed out an illusion to which both laypersons and psychologists are prone. He was also perhaps the first to decry personality stability as the enemy of freedom, creativity, and growth, objecting that "temperament puts all divinity to rout." In this article, we summarize evidence in support of Emerson's observations but offer arguments against his evaluation of them.[2]

EVIDENCE FOR THE STABILITY OF ADULT PERSONALITY

Emerson used the term temperament to refer to the basic tendencies of the individual, dispositions that we call personality traits. It is these traits, measured by such instruments as the Minnesota Multiphasic Personality Inventory and the NEO Personality Inventory, that have been investigated in a score of longitudinal studies over the past 20 years. Despite a wide variety of samples, instruments, and designs, the results of these studies have been remarkably consistent, and they are easily summarized.

1. The mean levels of personality traits change with development, but reach final adult levels at about age 30. Between 20 and 30, both men and women become somewhat less emotional and thrill-seeking and somewhat more cooperative and self-disciplined—changes we might interpret as evidence of increased maturity. After age 30, there are few and subtle changes, of which the most consistent is a small decline in activity level with advancing age. Except among individuals with dementia, stereotypes that depict older people as being withdrawn, depressed, or rigid are unfounded.

2. Individual differences in personality traits, which show at least some continuity from early childhood on, are also essentially fixed by age 30. Stability coefficients (test-retest correlations over substantial time intervals) are typically in the range of .60 to .80, even over intervals of as long as 30 years, although there is some decline in magnitude with increasing retest interval. Given that most personality scales have short-term retest reliabilities in the range from .70 to .90, it is clear that by far the greatest part of the reliable variance (i.e., variance not due to measurement error) in personality traits is stable.

3. Stability appears to characterize all five of the major domains of personality—neuroticism, extraver-

sion, openness to experience, agreeableness, and conscientiousness. This finding suggests that an adult's personality profile as a whole will change little over time, and studies of the stability of configural measures of personality support that view.

4. Generalizations about stability apply to virtually everyone. Men and women, healthy and sick people, blacks and whites all show the same pattern. When asked, most adults will say that their personality has not changed much in adulthood, but even those who claim to have had major changes show little objective evidence of change on repeated administrations of personality questionnaires. Important exceptions to this generalization include people suffering from dementia and certain categories of psychiatric patients who respond to therapy, but no moderators of stability among healthy adults have yet been identified.[3]

When researchers first began to publish these conclusions, they were greeted with considerable skepticism—"I distrust the facts and the inferences" Emerson had written—and many studies were designed to test alternative hypotheses. For example, some researchers contended that consistent responses to personality questionnaires were due to memory of past responses, but retrospective studies showed that people could not accurately recall how they had previously responded even when instructed to do so. Other researchers argued that temporal consistency in self-reports merely meant that individuals had a fixed idea of themselves, a crystallized self-concept that failed to keep pace with real changes in personality. But studies using spouse and peer raters showed equally high levels of stability.[4]

The general conclusion that personality traits are stable is now widely accepted. Some researchers continue to look for change in special circumstances and populations; some attempt to account for stability by examining genetic and environmental influences on personality. Finally, others take the view that there is much more to personality than traits, and seek to trace the adult developmental course of personality perceptions or identity formation or life narratives.

These latter studies are worthwhile, because people undoubtedly do change across the life span. Marriages end in divorce, professional careers are started in mid-life, fashions and attitudes change with the times. Yet often the same traits can be seen in new guises: Intellectual curiosity merely shifts from one field to another, avid gardening replaces avid tennis, one abusive relationship is followed by another. Many of these changes are best regarded as variations on the "uniform tune" played by individuals' enduring dispositions.

ILLUSORY ATTRIBUTIONS IN TEMPORAL PERSPECTIVE

Social and personality psychologists have debated for some time the accuracy of attributions of the causes of behavior to persons or situations. The "optical illusion" in person perception that Emerson pointed to was somewhat different. He felt that people attribute behavior to the live and spontaneous person who freely creates responses to the situation, when in fact behavior reveals only the mechanical operation of lifeless and static temperament. We may (and we will!) take exception to this disparaging, if common, view of traits, but we must first concur with the basic observation that personality processes often appear different when viewed in longitudinal perspective: "The years teach much which the days never know."

Consider happiness. If one asks individuals why they are happy or unhappy, they are almost certain to point to environmental circumstances of the moment: a rewarding job, a difficult relationship, a

threat to health, a new car. It would seem that levels of happiness ought to mirror quality of life, and that changes in circumstances would result in changes in subjective well-being. It would be easy to demonstrate this pattern in a controlled laboratory experiment: Give subjects $1,000 each and ask how they feel!

But survey researchers who have measured the objective quality of life by such indicators as wealth, education, and health find precious little association with subjective well-being, and longitudinal researchers have found surprising stability in individual differences in happiness, even among people whose life circumstances have changed markedly. The explanation is simple: People adapt to their circumstances rapidly, getting used to the bad and taking for granted the good. In the long run, happiness is largely a matter of enduring personality traits.[5] "Temper prevails over everything of time, place, and condition, and… fix[es] the measure of activity and of enjoyment."

A few years ago, William Swann and Craig Hill provided an ingenious demonstration of the errors to which too narrow a temporal perspective can lead. A number of experiments had shown that it was relatively easy to induce changes in the self-concept by providing self-discrepant feedback. Introverts told that they were really extraverts rated themselves higher in extraversion than they had before. Such studies supported the view that the self-concept is highly malleable, a mirror of the evaluation of the immediate environment.

Swann and Hill replicated this finding, but extended it by inviting subjects back a few days later. By that time, the effects of the manipulation had disappeared, and subjects had returned to their initial self-concepts. The implication is that any one-shot experiment may give a seriously misleading view of personality processes.[6]

The relations between coping and adaptation provide a final example. Cross-sectional studies show that individuals who use such coping mechanisms as self-blame, wishful thinking, and hostile reactions toward other people score lower on measures of well-being than people who do not use these mechanisms. It would be easy to infer that these coping mechanisms detract from adaptation, and in fact the very people who use them admit that they are ineffective. But the correlations vanish when the effects

of prior neuroticism scores are removed; an alternative interpretation of the data is thus that individuals who score high on this personality factor use poor coping strategies and also have low well-being: The association between coping and well-being may be entirely attributable to this third variable.[7]

Psychologists have long been aware of the problems of inferring causes from correlational data, but they have not recognized the pervasiveness of the bias that Emerson warned about. People tend to understand behavior and experience as the result of the immediate context, whether intrapsychic or environmental. Only by looking over time can one see the persistent effects of personality traits.

THE EVALUATION OF STABILITY

If few findings in psychology are more robust than the stability of personality, even fewer are more unpopular. Gerontologists often see stability as an affront to their commitment to continuing adult development; psychotherapists sometimes view it as an alarming challenge to their ability to help patients;[8] humanistic psychologists and transcendental philosophers think it degrades human nature. A popular account in *The Idaho Statesman* ran under the disheartening headline "Your Personality—You're Stuck With It."

In our view, these evaluations are based on misunderstandings: At worst, stability is a mixed blessing. Those individuals who are anxious, quarrelsome, and lazy might be understandably distressed to think that they are likely to stay that way, but surely those who are imaginative, affectionate, and carefree at age 30 should be glad to hear that they will probably be imaginative, affectionate, and carefree at age 90.

Because personality is stable, life is to some extent predictable. People can make vocational and retirement choices with some confidence that their current interests and enthusiasms will not desert them. They can choose friends and mates with whom they are likely to remain compatible. They can vote on the basis of candidates' records, with some assurance that future policies will resemble past ones. They can learn which co-workers they can depend on, and which they cannot. The personal and social utility of personality stability is enormous.

But it is precisely this predictability that so offends many critics. ("I had fancied that the value of life lay in its inscrutable possibilities," Emerson complained.) These critics view traits as mechanical and static habits and believe that the stability of personality traits dooms human beings to lifeless monotony as puppets controlled by inexorable forces. This is a misunderstanding on several levels.

First, personality traits are not repetitive habits, but inherently dynamic dispositions that interact with the opportunities and challenges of the moment.[9] Antagonistic people do not yell at everyone; some people they flatter, some they scorn, some they threaten. Just as the same intelligence is applied to a lifetime of changing problems, so the same personality traits can be expressed in an infinite variety of ways, each suited to the situation.

Second, there are such things as spontaneity and impulse in human life, but they are stable traits. Individuals who are open to experience actively seek out new places to go, provocative ideas to ponder, and exotic sights, sounds, and tastes to experience. Extraverts show a different kind of spontaneity, making friends, seeking thrills, and jumping at every chance to have a good time. People who are introverted and closed to experience have more measured and monotonous lives, but this is the kind of life they choose.

Finally, personality traits are not inexorable forces that control our fate, nor are they, in psychodynamic language, ego alien. Our traits characterize us; they are our very selves;[10] we act most freely when we express our enduring dispositions. Individuals sometimes fight against their own tendencies, trying perhaps to overcome shyness or curb a bad temper. But most people acknowledge even these failings as their own, and it is well that they do. A person's recognition of the inevitability of his or her one and only personality is a large part of what Erik Erikson called ego integrity, the culminating wisdom of a lifetime.

Notes

1. All quotations are from "Experience," in *Essays: First and Second Series*, R.W. Emerson (Vintage, New York, 1990) (original work published 1844).

2. For recent and sometimes divergent treatments of this topic, see R.R. McCrae and P.T. Costa, Jr., *Personality in Adulthood* (Guilford, New York, 1990); D. C. Funder, R.D. Parke, C. Tomlinson-Keasey and K. Widaman, Eds., *Studying Lives Through Time: Personality and Development* (American Psychological Association, Washington, DC, 1993); T. Heatherton and J. Weinberger, *Can Personality Change?* (American Psychological Association, Washington, DC, 1994).

3. L.C. Siegler, K.A. Welsh, D.V. Dawson, G.G. Fillenbaum, N.L. Earl, E.B. Kaplan, and C.M. Clark, Ratings of personality change in patients being evaluated for memory disorders, *Alzheimer Disease and Associated Disorders, 5*, 240–250 (1991); R.M.A. Hirschfeld, G.L. Klerman, P. Clayton, M.B. Keller, P. McDonald-Scott, and B. Larkin, Assessing personality: Effects of depressive state on trait measurement, *American Journal of Psychiatry, 140*, 695–699 (1983); R.R. McCrae, Moderated analyses of longitudinal personality stability, *Journal of Personality and Social Psychology, 65*, 577–585 (1993).

4. D. Woodruff, The role of memory in personality continuity: A 25 year follow-up, *Experimental Aging Research, 9*, 31–34 (1983); P.T. Costa, Jr., and R.R. McCrae, Trait psychology comes of age, in *Nebraska Symposium on Motivation: Psychology and Aging*, T.B. Sonderegger, Ed. (University of Nebraska Press, Lincoln, 1992).

5. P.T. Costa, Jr., and R.R. McCrae, Influence of extraversion and neuroticism on subjective well-being: Happy and unhappy people, *Journal of Personality and Social Psychology, 38*, 668–678 (1980).

6. The study is summarized in W.B. Swann, Jr., and C.A. Hill, When our identities are mistaken: Reaffirming self-conceptions through social interactions, *Journal of Personality and Social Psychology, 43*, 59–66 (1982). Dangers of single-occasion research are also discussed in J.R. Council, Context effects in personality research, *Current Directions in Psychological Science, 2*, 31–34 (1993).

7. R.R. McCrae and P.T. Costa, Jr., Personality, coping, and coping effectiveness in an adult sample, *Journal of Personality, 54*, 385–405 (1986).

8. Observations in nonpatient samples show what happens over time under typical life circumstances; they do not rule out the possibility that psychotherapeutic interventions can change personality. Whether or not such change is possible, in practice much of psychotherapy consists of helping people learn to live with their limitations, and this may be a more realistic goal than "cure" for many patients. See P.T. Costa, Jr., and R.R. McCrae, Personality stability and its implications for clinical psychology, *Clinical Psychology Review, 6*, 407–423 (1986).

9. A. Tellegen, Personality traits: Issues of definition, evidence and assessment, in *Thinking Clearly About Psychology: Essays in Honor of Paul E. Meehl*, Vol. 2, W. Grove and D. Cicchetti, Eds. (University of Minnesota Press, Minneapolis, 1991).

10. R.R. McCrae and P.T. Costa, Jr., Age, personality, and the spontaneous self-concept, *Journals of Gerontology: Social Sciences*, 43, S177–S185 (1988).

Robert R. McCrae is Research Psychologist and **Paul T. Costa, Jr.**, is Chief, Laboratory of Personality and Cognition, both at the Gerontology Research Center, National Institute on Aging, National Institutes of Health. Address correspondence to Robert R. McCrae, Personality, Stress and Coping Section, Gerontology Research Center, 4940 Eastern Ave., Baltimore, MD 21224.

From *Current Directions in Psychological Science*, December 1994, pp. 173–175. © 1994 by the American Psychological Society. Reprinted by permission of Blackwell Publishers.

How Culture Molds Habits of Thought

By ERICA GOODE

For more than a century, Western philosophers and psychologists have based their discussions of mental life on a cardinal assumption: that the same basic processes underlie all human thought, whether in the mountains of Tibet or the grasslands of the Serengeti.

Cultural differences might dictate what people thought about. Teenage boys in Botswana, for example, might discuss cows with the same passion that New York teenagers reserved for sports cars.

But the habits of thought—the strategies people adopted in processing information and making sense of the world around them— were, Western scholars assumed, the same for everyone, exemplified by, among other things, a devotion to logical reasoning, a penchant for categorization and an urge to understand situations and events in linear terms of cause and effect.

Recent work by a social psychologist at the University of Michigan, however, is turning this long-held view of mental functioning upside down.

In a series of studies comparing European Americans to East Asians, Dr. Richard Nisbett and his colleagues have found that people who grow up in different cultures do not just think about different things: they think differently.

"We used to think that everybody uses categories in the same way, that logic plays the same kind of role for everyone in the understanding of everyday life, that memory, perception, rule application and so on are the same," Dr. Nisbett said. "But we're now arguing that cognitive processes themselves are just far more malleable than mainstream psychology assumed."

A summary of the research will be published next winter in the journal Psychological Review, and Dr. Nisbett discussed the findings Sunday at the annual meetings of the American Psychological Association in Washington.

In many respects, the cultural disparities the researchers describe mirror those described by anthropologists, and may seem less than surprising to Americans who have lived in Asia. And Dr. Nisbett and his colleagues are not the first psychological researchers to propose that thought may be embedded in cultural assumptions: Soviet psychologists of the 1930's posed logic problems to Uzbek peasants, arguing that intellectual tools were influenced by pragmatic circumstances.

But the new work is stirring interest in academic circles because it tries to define and elaborate on cultural differences through a series of tightly controlled laboratory experiments. And the theory underlying the research challenges much of what has been considered gospel in cognitive psychology for the last 40 years.

"If it's true, it turns on its head a great deal of the science that many of us have been doing, and so it's sort of scary and thrilling at the same time," said Dr. Susan Andersen, a professor of psychology at New York University and an associate editor at Psychological Review.

In the broadest sense, the studies—carried out in the United States, Japan, China and Korea—document a familiar division. Easterners, the researchers find, appear to think more "holistically," paying greater attention to context and relationship, relying more on experience-based knowledge than abstract logic and showing more tolerance for contradiction. Westerners are more "analytic" in their thinking, tending to detach objects from their context, to avoid contradictions and to rely more heavily on formal logic.

In one study, for example, by Dr. Nisbett and Takahiko Masuda, a graduate student at Michigan, students from Japan and the United States were shown an animated underwater scene, in which one larger "focal" fish swam among smaller fishes and other aquatic life.

Asked to describe what they saw, the Japanese subjects were much more likely to begin by setting the scene, saying for example, "There was a lake or pond" or "The bottom was rocky," or "The water was green." Americans, in contrast, tended to begin their descriptions with the largest fish, making statements like "There was what looked like a trout swimming to the right."

What Americans notice: the biggest, fastest and shiniest.

Over all, Japanese subjects in the study made 70 percent more statements about aspects of the background environment than Americans, and twice as many statements about the relationships between animate and inanimate objects. A Japanese subject might note, for example, that "The big fish swam past the gray seaweed."

"Americans were much more likely to zero in on the biggest fish, the brightest object, the fish moving the fastest," Dr. Nisbett said. "That's where the money is as far as they're concerned."

But the greater attention paid by East Asians to context and relationship was more than just superficial, the researchers found. Shown the same larger fish swimming against a different, novel background, Japanese participants had more difficulty recognizing it than Americans, indicating that their perception was intimately bound with their perception of the background scene.

When it came to interpreting events in the social world, the Asians seemed similarly sensitive to context, and quicker than the Americans to detect when people's behavior was determined by situational pressures.

Psychologists have long documented what they call the fundamental attribution error, the tendency for people to explain human behavior in terms of the traits of individual actors, even when powerful situational forces are at work. Told that a man has been instructed to give a speech endorsing a particular presidential candidate, for example, most people will still believe that the speaker believes what he is saying.

Yet Asians, according to Dr. Nisbett and his colleagues, may in some situations be less susceptible to such errors, indicating that they do not describe a universal way of thinking, but merely the way that Americans think.

In one study, by Dr. Nisbett and Dr. Incheol Choi, of Seoul National University in Korea, the Korean and American subjects were asked to read an essay either in favor of or opposed to the French conducting atomic tests in the Pacific. The subjects were told that the essay writer had been given "no choice" about what to write. But subjects from both cultures still showed a tendency to "err," judging that the essay writers believed in the position endorsed in the essays.

When the Korean subjects were first required to undergo a similar experience themselves, writing an essay according to instructions, they quickly adjusted their estimates of how strongly the original essay writers believed what they wrote. But Americans clung to the notion that the essay writers were expressing sincere beliefs.

One of the most striking dissimilarities found by the researchers emerged in the way East Asians and Americans in the studies responded to contradiction. Presented with weaker arguments running contrary to their own, Americans were likely to solidify their opinions, Dr. Nisbett said, "clobbering the weaker arguments," and resolving the threatened contradiction in their own minds. Asians, however, were more likely to modify their own position,

acknowledging that even the weaker arguments had some merit.

In one study, for example, Asian and American subjects were presented with strong arguments in favor of financing a research project on adoption. A second group was presented both with strong arguments in support of the project and weaker arguments opposing it.

Both Asian and American subjects in the first group expressed strong support for the research. But while Asian subjects in the second group responded to the weaker opposing arguments by decreasing their support, American subjects increased their endorsement of the project in response to the opposing arguments.

In a series of studies, Dr. Nisbett and Dr. Kaiping Peng of the University of California at Berkeley found that Chinese subjects were less eager to resolve contradictions in a variety of situations than American subjects. Asked to analyze a conflict between mothers and daughters, American subjects quickly came down in favor of one side or the other. Chinese subjects were more likely to see merit on both sides, commenting, for example, that, "Both the mothers and the daughters have failed to understand each other."

Given a choice between two different types of philosophical argument, one based on analytical logic, devoted to resolving contradiction, the other on a dialectical approach, accepting of contradiction, Chinese subjects preferred the dialectical approach, while Americans favored the logical arguments. And Chinese subjects expressed more liking than Americans for proverbs containing a contradiction, like the Chinese saying "Too modest is half boastful." American subjects, Dr. Nisbett said, found such contradictions "rather irritating."

Dr. Nisbett and Dr. Ara Norenzayan of the University of Illinois have also found indications that when logic and experiential knowledge are in conflict, Americans are more likely than Asians to adhere to the rules of formal logic, in keeping with a tradition that in Western societies began with the Ancient Greeks.

For example, presented with a logical sequence like, "All animals with fur hibernate. Rabbits have fur. Therefore rabbits hibernate," the Americans, the researchers found, were more likely to accept the validity of the argument, separating its formal structure, that of a syllogism, from its content, which might or might not be plausible. Asians, in contrast, more frequently judged such syllogisms as invalid based on their implausibility—not all animals with fur do in fact hibernate.

While the cultural disparities traced in the researchers' work are substantial, their origins are much less clear. Historical evidence suggests that a divide between Eastern and Occidental thinking has existed at least since ancient times, a tradition of adversarial debate, formal logical argument and analytic deduction flowering in Greece, while in China an appreciation for context and complexity, dialectical argument and a tolerance for the "yin and yang" of life flourished.

How much of this East-West difference is a result of differing social and religious practices, different languages or even different geography is anyone's guess. But both styles, Dr. Nisbett said, have advantages, and both have limitations. And neither approach is written into the genes: many Asian-Americans, born in the United States, are indistinguishable in their modes of thought from European-Americans.

Dr. Alan Fiske, an associate professor of anthropology at the University of California at Los Angeles, said that experimental research like Dr. Nisbett's "complements a lot of ethnographic work that has been done."

"Anthropologists have been describing these cultures and this can tell you a lot about everyday life and the ways people talk and interact," Dr. Fiske said. "But it's always difficult to know how to make sense of these qualitative judgments, and they aren't controlled in the same way that an experiment is controlled."

Yet not everyone agrees that all the dissimilarities described by Dr.

Nisbett and his colleagues reflect fundamental differences in psychological process.

Dr. Patricia Cheng, for example, a professor of psychology at the University of California at Los Angeles, said that many of the researchers' findings meshed with her own experience. "Having grown up in a traditional Chinese family and also being in Western culture myself," she said, "I do see some entrenched habits of interpretation of the world that are different across the cultures, and they do lead to pervasive differences."

But Dr. Cheng says she thinks that some differences—the Asian tolerance for contradiction, for example—are purely social. "There is not a difference in logical tolerance," she said.

Still, to the extent that the studies reflect real differences in thinking and perception, psychologists may have to radically revise their ideas about what is universal and what is not, and to develop new models of mental process that take cultural influences into account.

From the *New York Times*, August 8, 2000, pp. D1, D4. © 2000 by The New York Times Company. Reprinted by permission.

UNIT 2

Determinants of Behavior: Motivation, Environment, and Physiology

Unit Selections

7. **The Tangled Skeins of Nature and Nurture in Human Evolution**, Paul R. Ehrlich
8. **The Gender Blur**, Deborah Blum
9. **The Personality Genes**, J. Madeleine Nash
10. **Where We Come From**, Nancy Shute
11. **Autism Is Likely to Be Linked to Several Genes**, Hugh McIntosh
12. **The Future of the Brain**, Norbert R. Myslinski
13. **The Biology of Joy**, Jeremiah Creedon
14. **The Tick-Tock of the Biological Clock**, Michael W. Young
15. **Into the Zone**, Jay Tolson
16. **Mind Over Medicine**, Howard Brody

Key Points to Consider

- What evidence do we have that biology is not the only influence on our psychological being? Explain.

- Do you think the environment's influence grows the further we proceed through life? Defend your arguments.

- What is a gene? Why is it important to study heredity? Why is genetic research important to psychologists?

- What brain disorders are being studied with modern scientific techniques? What are some of the modern techniques for mapping the brain?

- What is the biology of joy? What are endorphins? What other biochemical actions influence our moods, emotions, and behaviors? Do you think most moods and emotions are the result of biochemistry?

- Can our minds affect our physical health? How? Offer data to support your position.

 **Links: www.dushkin.com/online/**
These sites are annotated in the World Wide Web pages.

American Psychological Society (APS)
http://www.psychologicalscience.org

Federation of Behavioral, Psychological, and Cognitive Science
http://www.am.org/federation/

Max Planck Institute for Psychological Research
http://www.mpipf-muenchen.mpg.de/BCD/bcd_e.htm

The Opportunity of Adolescence
http://www.winternet.com/~webpage/adolescencepaper.html

Psychology Research on the Net
http://psych.hanover.edu/APS/exponnet.html

Serendip
http://serendip.brynmawr.edu/serendip/

On the front page of every newspaper, in practically every televised newscast, and on many magazine covers the problems of substance abuse in America haunt us. Innocent children are killed when caught in the crossfire of the guns of drug lords or even of their own classmates. Prostitutes selling their bodies for drug money spread the deadly AIDS virus. The white-collar middle manager loses his job because he embezzled company money to support his cocaine habit.

Why do people turn to drugs? Why doesn't the publicity about the ruination of human lives diminish the drug problem? Why can some people consume two cocktails and stop, while others feel helpless against the inebriating seduction of alcohol? Why do some people crave heroin as their drug of choice, while others choose cigarettes or caffeine?

The causes of individual behavior such as drug and alcohol abuse are the focus of this section. If physiology, either biochemistry and the nervous system, or genes, is the determinant of our behavior, then solutions to such puzzles as alcoholism lie in the field of psychobiology, which is the study of behavior in relation to biological processes and in human medicine. However, if experience as a function of our environment and learning creates personality and coping ability and thus causes subsequent behavior, normal or not, then researchers must take a different tack and explore features of the environment that are responsible for certain behaviors. A third explanation is that ability to adjust to change is produced by some complex interaction or interplay between experience and biology. If this interaction accounts for individual differences in personality and ability to cope, scientists then have a very complicated task ahead of them.

Conducting research designed to unravel the determinants of behavior is difficult. Scientists must call upon their best design skills to develop studies that will yield useful and replicable findings. A researcher hoping to examine the role of experience in personal growth and behavior needs to be able to isolate one or two stimuli or environmental features that seem to control a particular behavior. Imagine trying to delimit the complexity of the world sufficiently so that only one or two events stand out as the cause of an individual's alcoholism. Likewise, researchers interested in psychobiology also need refined, technical knowledge. Suppose a scientist hopes to show that a particular form of mental illness is inherited. She cannot merely examine family genetic histories, because family members can also learn maladaptive behaviors from one another. The researcher's ingenuity will be challenged; she must use intricate techniques such as comparing children to their adoptive as well as to their biological parents. Volunteer subjects may be difficult to find, and, even then, the data may be hard to interpret.

The first two articles in this unit offer general information on the interaction of nature and nurture. In the first article, Paul Ehrlich explores the joint interaction of culture and biology. The article discusses the contributions of genes as well as the relative influence of the environment or culture. Ehrlich clearly but succinctly provides a general overview of the nature/nurture controversy. A companion article discusses gender as an exemplar of the nature/nurture issue. From where do gender differences and similarities come? Deborah Blum argues in "The Gender Blur" that the boundaries are becoming less crisp and therefore there are more similar-ities than differences between the two sexes, a situation that makes the study of the origin of gender more complicated.

We next examine the role of nature, in particular of genetics, in determining our behaviors. The first article, "The Personality Genes," assesses how DNA exerts an influence on our developing personalities, one particular aspect of human nature. The article concludes with the understanding that genes do exert significant influence. The next article, "Where We Come From," points out that, through DNA, people can trace their ancestral roots.

A third and companion article, "Autism Is Likely to Be Linked to Several Genes," discusses how such a disorder is usually not tied to the action of a single gene but rather is influenced by multiple genes. The article is also interesting because it divulges information about a baffling and intriguing childhood disorder—autism.

The nervous system is also an important component of the biological determinants of our personal tendencies and behaviors. Three articles provide information about the brain, which is the focal point of the nervous system. In the first article, "The Future of the Brain," the author discusses how special, costly techniques are helping us to better understand the functioning of the brain. Such techniques allow physicians and scientists to conduct research and do surgery on the brain with less damage than older, more invasive methods.

The influence of the brain on the expression of specific aspects of the human psyche is discussed in the next two articles. In the first article, "The Biology of Joy," hormones, neurotransmitters, and particular parts of the brain affect the whole nervous system and thus affect human behavior. Author Jeremiah Creedon discusses the role of biopsychology with regard to one particular and delightful emotion—joy. Psychologists and biologists have discovered certain neurotransmitters related to joy, labeled endorphins, and have found these substances to be secreted during pleasurable events.

A companion article also delves into the role of the brain in regulating our daily lives. Scientists have discovered a biological clock that is controlled by the brain. Knowledge of this regulation and the role that the brain plays in it helps us understand why, for example, heart attacks are more likely during one part of the day than another.

We next turn our attention away from psychobiology to human motivation—an entirely different determinant of human behavior and growth. In "Into the Zone," the author helps us understand that motivation to do something well can sometimes help us overcome biological deficits. By examining "flow," Jay Tolson suggests that highly focused individuals often perform better in sports, in the world of work, and in the theater than unfocused, unmotivated individuals.

In the final article in this unit, we stray far from the laboratory and athletic field but remain within the realm of motivation. In "Mind Over Medicine," author Howard Brody suggests that people are capable of influencing their own health just by the thoughts and motives they possess. New research on the placebo effect is demonstrating that there is in fact a mind-body connection, and that those who believe in the mind's power over the body may indeed be healthier than those who do not so believe.

In summary, this unit covers factors that determine our behavior and thoughts, in other words, factors that are moderated by genes, the nervous system, biochemicals, motives, or some combination of these.

The Tangled Skeins of Nature and Nurture in Human Evolution

By Paul R. Ehrlich

W HEN we think about our behavior as individuals, "Why?" is a question almost always on the tips of our tongues. Sometimes that question is about perceived similarities: why is almost everyone religious; why do we all seem to crave love; why do most of us like to eat meat? But our differences often seem equally or more fascinating: why did Sally get married although her sister Sue did not, why did they win and we lose, why is their nation poor and ours rich? What were the fates of our childhood friends? What kinds of careers did they have; did they marry; how many children did they have? Our everyday lives are filled with why's about differences and similarities in behavior, often unspoken, but always there. Why did one of my closest colleagues drink himself to death, whereas I, who love wine much more than he did, am managing to keep my liver in pretty good shape? Why, of two very bright applicants admitted to our department at Stanford University for graduate work, does one turn out pedestrian science and another have a spectacular career doing innovative research? Why are our natures often so different, and why are they so frequently the same?

The background needed to begin to answer all these *whys* lies within the domain of human biological and cultural evo-

lution, in the gradual alterations in genetic and cultural information possessed by humanity. It's easy to think that evolution is just a process that sometime in the distant past produced the physical characteristics of our species but is now pretty much a matter of purely academic, and local school board, interest. Yet evolution is a powerful, ongoing force that not only has shaped the attributes and behaviors shared by all human beings but also has given every single individual a different nature.

A study of evolution does much more than show how we are connected to our roots or explain why people rule Earth—it explains why it would be wise to limit our intake of beef Wellington, stop judging people by their skin color, concern ourselves about global warming, and reconsider giving our children antibiotics at the first sign of a sore throat. Evolution also provides a framework for answering some of the most interesting questions about ourselves and our behavior.

When someone mentions evolution and behavior in the same breath, most people think immediately of the power of genes, parts of spiral-shaped molecules of a chemical called DNA. Small wonder, considering the marvelous advances in molecular genetics in recent decades. New subdisciplines such as evolutionary medicine and evolutionary psychology have arisen as scientists have come to recognize the importance of evolution in explaining contemporary human beings, the network of life that supports us, and our possible fates. And the mass media have been loaded with stories about real or imagined links between every conceivable sort of behavior and our genes.

Biological evolution—evolution that causes changes in our genetic endowment—has unquestionably helped shape human natures, including human behaviors, in many ways. But numerous commentators expect our genetic endowment to accomplish feats of which it is incapable. People don't have enough genes to program all the behaviors some evolutionary psychologists, for example, believe that genes control. Human beings have something on the order of 100,000 genes, and human brains have more than one *trillion* nerve cells, with about 100–1,000 trillion connections (synapses) between them. That's at least one *billion* synapses per gene, even if each and every gene did nothing but control the production of synapses (and it doesn't). Given that ratio, it would be quite a trick for genes typically to control more than the most general aspects of human behavior. Statements such as "Understanding the genetic roots of personality will help you 'find yourself' and relate better to others" are, at today's level of knowledge, frankly nonsensical.

The notion that we are slaves to our genes is often combined with reliance on the idea that all problems can be solved by dissecting them into ever smaller components—the sort of reductionist approach that has been successful in much of science but is sometimes totally unscientific. It's like the idea that knowing the color of every microscopic dot that makes up a picture of your mother can explain why you love her. Scientific problems have to be approached at the appropriate level of organization if there is to be a hope of solving them.

There are important "coevolutionary" interactions between culture and genetics. For example, our farming practices change our physical environment in ways that alter the evolution of our blood cells.

That combination of assumptions—that genes are destiny at a micro level and that reductionism leads to full understanding—is now yielding distorted views of human behavior. People think that coded into our DNA are "instructions" that control the details of individual and group behavior: that genetics dominates, heredity makes us what we are, and what we are is changeable only over many generations as the genetic endowment of human populations evolves. Such assertions presume, as I've just suggested, that evolution has produced a level

of genetic control of human behavior that is against virtually all available evidence. For instance, ground squirrels have evolved a form of "altruistic" behavior—they often give an alarm call to warn a relative of approaching danger. Evidence does indicate that this behavior is rooted in their genes; indeed, it probably evolved because relatives have more identical genes than do unrelated individuals. But some would trace the "altruistic" behavior of a business executive sending a check to an agency helping famine victims in Africa, or of a devout German Lutheran aiding Jews during the Holocaust, to a genetic tendency as well. In this view, we act either to help relatives or in the expectation of reciprocity—in either case promoting the replication of "our" genes. But experimental evidence indicates that not all human altruistic behavior is self-seeking—that human beings, unlike squirrels, are not hereditarily programmed only to be selfish.

ANOTHER FALSE ASSUMPTION of hereditary programming lies behind the belief that evolution has resulted in human groups of different quality. Many people still claim (or secretly believe), for example, that blacks are less intelligent than whites and women less "logical" than men, even though those claims are groundless. Belief in genetic determinism has even led some observers to suggest a return to the bad old days of eugenics, of manipulating evolution to produce ostensibly more skilled people. Advocating programs for the biological "improvement of humanity"—which in the past has meant encouraging the breeding of supposedly naturally superior individuals—takes us back at least to the days of Plato, more than two millennia ago, and it involves a grasp of genetics little more sophisticated than his.

Uniquely in our species, changes in culture have been fully as important in producing our natures as have changes in the hereditary information passed on by our ancestors. Culture is the nongenetic information (socially transmitted behaviors, beliefs, institutions, arts, and so on) shared and exchanged among us. Indeed, our evolution since the invention of agriculture, about 10,000 years ago, has been overwhelmingly cultural because, as we shall see, cultural evolution can be much more rapid than genetic evolution. There is an unhappy predilection, especially in the United States, not only to overrate the effect of genetic evolution on our current behavior but also to underrate that of cultural evolution. The power of culture to shape human activities can be seen immediately in the diversity of languages around the world. Although, clearly, the ability to speak languages is a result of a great deal of genetic evolution, the specific languages we speak are just as clearly products of cultural evolution. Furthermore, genetic evolution and cultural evolution are not independent. There are important "coevolutionary" interactions between them. To take just one example, our farming practices (an aspect of our culture) change our physical environment in ways that alter the evolution of our blood cells.

Not only is the evolution of our collective nongenetic information critical to creating our natures, but also the rate of that evolution varies greatly among different aspects of human culture. That, in turn, has profound consequences for our behavior and our environments. A major contemporary human problem, for instance, is that the rate of cultural evolution in science and technology has been extraordinarily high in contrast with the snail's pace of change in the social attitudes and political institutions that might channel the uses of technology in more beneficial directions. No one knows exactly what sorts of societal effort might be required to substantially redress that imbalance in evolutionary rates, but it is clear to me that such an effort, if successful, could greatly brighten the human prospect.

Science has already given us pretty good clues about the reasons for the evolution of some aspects of our natures; many other aspects remain mysterious despite a small army of very bright people seeking reasons. Still others (such as why I ordered duck in the restaurant last night rather than lamb) may remain unanswerable—for human beings have a form of free will. But even to *think* reasonably about our natures and our prospects, some background in basic evolutionary theory is essential. If Grace is smarter than Pedro because of her genes, why did evolution provide her with "better" genes? If Pedro is actually smarter than Grace but has been incorrectly evaluated by an intelligence test designed for people of another culture, how did those cultural differences evolve? If I was able to choose the duck for dinner because I have free will, what exactly does that mean? How did I and other human beings evolve that capacity to make choices without being complete captives of our histories? Could I have exercised my free will to eat a cockroach curry had we been in a restaurant that served it (as some in Southeast Asia do)? Almost certainly not—the very idea nauseates me, probably because of an interaction between biological and cultural evolution.

Personality Evolution Core Belief
moral Evolution   Evolution

Trying to separate nature and nurture is like trying to separate the contributions of length and width to the area of a rectangle, which at first seems easy. When you think about it, though, it proves impossible.

Every attribute of *every* organism is, of course, the product of an interaction between its genetic code and its environment. Yes, the number of heads an individual human being possesses is specified in the genes and is the same in a vast diversity of environments. And the language or languages a child speaks (but not her capacity to acquire language) is determined by her environment. But without the appropriate internal environment in the mother's body for fetal development, there would be no head (or infant) at all; and without genetically programmed physical structures in the larynx and in the developing brain, there would be no ca-

pacity to acquire and speak language. Beyond enabling us to make such statements in certain cases, however, the relative contributions of heredity and environment to various human attributes are difficult to specify. They clearly vary from attribute to attribute. So although it is informative to state that human nature is the product of genes interacting with environments (both internal and external), we usually can say little with precision about the processes that lead to interesting behaviors in adult human beings. We can't partition the responsibility for aggression, altruism, or charisma between DNA and upbringing. In many such cases, trying to separate the contributions of nature and nurture to an attribute is rather like trying to separate the contributions of length and width to the area of a rectangle, which at first glance also seems easy. When you think about it carefully, though, it proves impossible.

Diverse notions of inherited superiority or inferiority and of characteristic innate group behaviors have long pervaded human societies: beliefs about the divine right of kings; "natural" attributes that made some people good material for slaves or slave masters; innate superiority of light-skinned people over dark-skinned people; genetic tendencies of Jews to be moneylenders, of Christians to be sexually inhibited, and of Asians to be more hardworking than Hispanics; and so on. Consider the following quote from a recent book titled *Living With Our Genes*, which indicates the tone even among many scientists: "The emerging science of molecular biology has made startling discoveries that show beyond a doubt that genes are the single most important factor that distinguishes one person from another. We come in large part ready-made from the factory. We accept that we *look* like our parents and other blood relatives; we have a harder time with the idea we *act* like them."

In fact, the failure of many people to recognize the fundamental error in such statements (and those in other articles and books based on genetic determinism, such as Richard J. Herrnstein and Charles Murray's famous *The Bell Curve*) is itself an environmental phenomenon—a product of the cultural milieu in which many of us have grown up. Genes do not shout commands to us about our behavior. At the very most, they whisper suggestions, and the nature of those whispers is shaped by our internal environments (those within and between our cells) during early development and later, and usually also by the external environments in which we mature and find ourselves as adults.

How do scientists know that we are not simply genetically programmed automata? First, biological evolution has produced what is arguably the most astonishingly adaptable device that has ever existed—the human nervous system. It's a system that can use one organ, the brain, to plan a marriage or a murder, command muscles to control the flight of a thrown rock or a space shuttle, detect the difference between a 1945 Mouton and a 1961 Latour, learn Swahili or Spanish, and interpret a pattern of colored light on a flat television screen as a three-dimensional world containing real people. It tries to do whatever task the environment seems to demand, and it usually succeeds—and because many of those demands are novel, there is no way that the brain could be preprogrammed to deal with them, even if there were genes enough to do the programming. It would be incomprehensible for evolution to program such a system with a vast number of inherited rules that would reduce its flexibility, constraining it so that it could not deal with novel environments. It would seem equally inexplicable if evolution made some sub-groups of humanity less able than others to react appropriately to changing circumstances. Men and people with white skin have just as much need of being smart and flexible as do women and people with brown skin, and there is every reason to believe that evolution has made white-skinned males fully as capable as brown-skinned women.

A SECOND TYPE OF EVIDENCE that we're not controlled by innate programs is that normal infants taken from one society and reared in another inevitably acquire the behaviors (including language) and competences of the society in which they are reared. If different behaviors in different societies were largely genetically programmed, that could not happen. That culture dominates in creating intergroup differences is also indicated by the distribution of genetic differences among human beings. The vast majority (an estimated 85 percent) is not between "races" or ethnic groups but *between individuals within groups*. Human natures, again, are products of similar (but not identical) inherited endowments interacting with different physical and cultural environments.

Thus, the genetic "make-brain" program that interacts with the internal and external environments of a developing person doesn't produce a brain that can call forth only one type of, say, mating behavior—it produces a brain that can engage in any of a bewildering variety of behaviors, depending on circumstances. We see the same principle elsewhere in our development; for instance, human legs are not genetically programmed to move only at a certain speed. The inherited "make-legs" program normally produces legs that, fortunately, can operate at a wide range of speeds, depending on circumstances. Variation among individuals in the genes they received from their parents produces some differences in that range (in any normal terrestrial environment, I never could have been a four-minute miler—on the moon, maybe). Environmental variation produces some differences, too (walking a lot every day and years of acclimatization enable me to climb relatively high mountains that are beyond the range of some younger people who are less acclimatized). But no amount of training will permit any human being to leap tall buildings in a single bound, or even in two.

Similarly, inherited differences among individuals can influence the range of mental abilities we possess. Struggle as I might, my math skills will never approach those of many professional mathematicians, and I suspect that part of my incapacity can be traced to my genes. But environmental variation can shape those abilities as well. I'm also lousy at learning languages (that may be related to my math incompetence). Yet when I found myself in a professional environment in which it

would have been helpful to converse in Spanish, persistent study allowed me to speak and comprehend a fair amount of the language. But there are no genetic instructions or environmental circumstances that will allow the development of a human brain that can do a million mathematical calculations in a second. That is a talent reserved for computers, which were, of course, designed by human minds.

Are there any behavioral instructions we can be sure are engraved in human DNA? If there are, at least one should be the urge to have as many children as possible. We should have a powerful hereditary tendency to maximize our genetic contributions to future generations, for that's the tendency that makes evolution work. Yet almost no human beings strictly obey this genetic "imperative"; environmental factors, especially cultural factors, have largely overridden it. Most people choose to make smaller genetic contributions to the future—that is, have fewer children—than they could, thus figuratively thwarting the supposed maximum reproduction "ambitions" of their genes.

If genes run us as machines for reproducing themselves, how come they let us practice contraception? We are the only animals that deliberately and with planning enjoy sex while avoiding reproduction. We can and do "outwit" our genes—which are, of course, witless. In this respect, our hereditary endowment made a big mistake by "choosing" to encourage human reproduction not through a desire for lots of children but through a desire for lots of sexual pleasure.

There are environments (sociocultural environments in this case) in which near-maximal human reproduction has apparently occurred. For example, the Hutterites, members of a Mennonite sect living on the plains of western North America, are famous for their high rate of population growth. Around 1950, Hutterite women over the age of 45 had borne an average of 10 children, and Hutterite population growth rates exceeded 4 percent per year. Interestingly, however, when social conditions changed, the growth rate dropped from an estimated 4.12 percent per year to 2.91 percent. Cultural evolution won out against those selfish little genes.

Against this background of how human beings can overwhelm genetic evolution with cultural evolution, it becomes evident that great care must be taken in extrapolating the behavior of other animals to that of human beings. One cannot assume, for example, that because marauding chimpanzees of one group sometimes kill members of another group, selection has programmed warfare into the genes of human beings (or, for that matter, of chimps). And although both chimp and human genetic endowments clearly can interact with certain environments to produce individuals capable of mayhem, they just as clearly can interact with other environments to produce individuals who are not aggressive. Observing the behavior of nonhuman mammals—their mating habits, modes of communication, intergroup conflicts, and so on—can reveal patterns we display in common with them, but those patterns certainly will not tell us which complex behaviors are "programmed" inalterably into our genes. Genetic instructions are of great importance to our natures, but they are not destiny.

THERE are obviously limits to how much the environment ordinarily can affect individual characteristics. No known environment, for example, could have allowed me to mature with normal color vision: like about 8 percent of males, I'm color-blind—the result of a gene inherited from my mother. But the influence on many human attributes of even small environmental differences should not be underestimated. Consider the classic story of the "Siamese twins" Chang and Eng. Born in Siam (now Thailand) on May 11, 1811, these identical twins were joined at the base of their chests by an arm-like tube that in adulthood was five or six inches long and about eight inches in circumference. They eventually ended up in the United States, became prosperous as sideshow attractions, and married sisters. Chang and Eng farmed for a time, owned slaves before the Civil War, and produced both many children and vast speculation about the circumstances of their copulations. They were examined many times by surgeons who, working before the age of X-rays, concluded that it would be dangerous to try to separate them.

From our perspective, the most interesting thing about the twins is their different natures. Chang was slightly shorter than Eng, but he dominated his brother and was quick-tempered. Eng, in contrast, was agreeable and usually submissive. Although the two were very similar in many respects, in childhood their differences once flared into a fistfight, and as adults on one occasion they disagreed enough politically to vote for opposing candidates. More seriously, Chang drank to excess and Eng did not. Partly as a result of Chang's drinking, they developed considerable ill will that made it difficult for them to live together—they were constantly quarreling. In old age, Chang became hard of hearing in both ears, but Eng became deaf only in the ear closer to Chang. In the summer of 1870, Chang suffered a stroke, which left Eng unaffected directly but bound him physically to an invalid. On January 17, 1874, Chang died in the night. When Eng discovered his twin's death, he (although perfectly healthy) became terrified, lapsed into a stupor, and died two hours later, before a scheduled surgical attempt was to have been made to separate the two. An autopsy showed that the surgeons had been correct—the twins probably would not have survived an attempt to separate them.

Chang and Eng demonstrated conclusively that genetic identity does not necessarily produce identical natures, even when combined with substantially identical environments—in this case only inches apart, with no sign that their mother or others treated them differently as they grew up. Quite subtle environmental differences, perhaps initiated by different positions in the womb, can sometimes produce substantially different behavioral outcomes in twins. In this case, in which the dominant feature of each twin's environment clearly was the other twin, the slightest original difference could have led to an escalating reinforcement of differences.

The nature-nurture dichotomy, which has dominated discussions of behavior for decades, is largely a false one—all characteristics of all organisms are truly a result of the simultaneous influences of both. Genes do not dictate destiny in most cases (exceptions include those serious genetic defects that at present cannot be remedied), but they often define a range of possibilities in a given environment. The genetic endowment of a chimpanzee, even if raised as the child of a Harvard professor, would prevent it from learning to discuss philosophy or solve differential equations. Similarly, environments define a range of developmental possibilities for a given set of genes. There is no genetic endowment that a child could get from Mom and Pop that would permit the youngster to grow into an Einstein (or a Mozart or a García Marquez—or even a Hitler) as a member of an isolated rain-forest tribe without a written language.

Attempts to dichotomize nature and nurture almost always end in failure. Although I've written about how the expression of genes depends on the environment in which the genes are expressed, another way of looking at the development of a person's nature would have been to examine the contributions of three factors: genes, environment, *and* gene-environment interactions. It is very difficult to tease out these contributions, however. Even under experimental conditions, where it is possible to say something mathematically about the comparative contributions of heredity and environment, it can't be done completely because there is an "interaction term." That term cannot be decomposed into nature or nurture because the effect of each depends on the contribution of the other.

To construct an artificial example, suppose there were a gene combination that controlled the level of a hormone that tended to make boys aggressive. Further, suppose that watching television also tended to make boys aggressive. Changing an individual's complement of genes so that the hormone level was doubled and also doubling the television-watching time might, then, quadruple some measure of aggressiveness. Or, instead, the two factors might interact synergistically and cause the aggression level to increase fivefold (perhaps television is an especially potent factor when the viewer has a high hormone level). Or the interaction might go the other way—television time might increase aggression only in those with a relatively low hormone level, and doubling both the hormone level and the television time might result in only a doubling of aggression. Or perhaps changing the average *content* of television programming might actually reduce the level of aggressiveness so that even with hormone level and television time doubled, aggressiveness would decline. Finally, suppose that, in addition, these relationships depended in part on whether or not a boy had attentive and loving parents who provided alternative interpretations of what was seen on television. In such situations, there is no way to make a precise statement about the contributions of "the environment" (television, in this case) to aggressiveness. This example reflects the complexity of relationships that has been demonstrated in detailed studies of the ways in which hormones such as testosterone interact with environmental factors to produce aggressive behavior.

The best one can ordinarily do in measuring what genes contribute to attributes (such as aggressiveness, height, or I.Q. test score) is calculate a statistical measure known as heritability. That statistic tells how much, on average, offspring resemble their parents in a particular attribute *in a particular set of environments*. Heritability, however, is a measure that is difficult to make and difficult to interpret. That is especially true in determining heritability of human traits, where it would be unethical or impossible to create the conditions required to estimate it, such as random mating within a population.

Despite these difficulties, geneticists are gradually sorting out some of the ways genes and environments can interact in experimental environments and how different parts of the hereditary endowment interact in making their contribution to the development of the individual. One of the key things they are learning is that it is often very difficult for genetic evolution to change just one characteristic. That's worth thinking about the next time someone tells you that human beings have been programmed by natural selection to be violent, greedy, altruistic, or promiscuous, to prefer certain facial features, or to show male (or white) dominance. At best, such programming is difficult; often it is impossible.

TODAY'S DEBATES about human nature—about such things as the origins of ethics; the meanings of consciousness, self, and reality; whether we're driven by emotion or reason; the relationship between thought and language; whether men are naturally aggressive and women peaceful; and the role of sex in society—trace far back in Western thought. They have engaged thinkers from the pre-Socratic philosophers, Plato, and Aristotle to René Descartes, John Locke, Georg Wilhelm Friedrich Hegel, Charles Sanders Peirce, and Ludwig Wittgenstein, just to mention a tiny handful of those in the Western tradition alone.

What exactly *is* this human nature we hear so much about? The prevailing notion is that it is a single, fixed, inherited attribute—a common property of all members of our species. That notion is implicit in the universal use of the term in singular form. And I think that singular usage leads us astray. To give a rough analogy, *human nature* is to *human natures* as *canyon* is to *canyons*. We would never discuss the "characteristics of canyon." Although all canyons share certain attributes, we always use the plural form of the word when talking about them in general. That's because even though all canyons have more characteristics in common with one another than any canyon has with a painting or a snowflake, we automatically recognize the vast diversity subsumed within the category *canyons*. As with *canyon*, at times there is reason to speak of human nature in the singular, as I sometimes do when referring to what we all share—for example, the ability to communicate in language, the possession of a rich culture, and the capacity to develop complex ethical systems. After all, there are at least *near*-universal aspects of our natures and our genomes (genetic endowments), and the variation within them is small in relation to the differences between, say, human and chimpanzee natures or human and chimpanzee genomes.

I argue, contrary to the prevailing notion, that human nature is not the same from society to society or from individual to individual, nor is it a permanent attribute of *Homo sapiens*. Human natures are the behaviors, beliefs, and attitudes of *Homo sapiens* and the changing physical structures that govern, support, and participate in our unique mental functioning. There are many such natures, a diversity generated especially by the overwhelming power of cultural evolution—the super-rapid kind of evolution in which our species excels. The human nature of a Chinese man living in Beijing is somewhat different from the human nature of a Parisian woman; the nature of a great musician is not identical with that of a fine soccer player; the nature of an inner-city gang member is different from the nature of a child being raised in an affluent suburb; the nature of someone who habitually votes Republican is different from that of her identical twin who is a Democrat; and my human nature, despite many shared features, is different from yours.

The differences among individuals and groups of human beings are, as already noted, of a magnitude that dwarf the differences within any other nondomesticated animal species. Using the plural, *human natures*, puts a needed emphasis on that critical diversity, which, after all, is very often what we want to understand. We want to know why two genetically identical individuals would have different political views; why Jeff is so loud and Barbara is so quiet; why people in the same society have different sexual habits and different ethical standards; why some past civilizations flourished for many centuries and others perished; why Germany was a combatant in two horrendous 20th-century wars and Switzerland was not; why Julia is concerned about global warming and Juliette doesn't know what it is. There is no single human nature, any more than there is a single human genome, although there are features common to all human natures and all human genomes.

But if we are trying to understand anything about human society, past or present, or about individual actions, we must go to a finer level of analysis and consider human nature*s* as actually formed in the world. It is intellectually lazy and incorrect to "explain" the relatively poor school performance of blacks in the United States, or the persistence of warfare, or marital discord, by claiming that nonwhites are "naturally" inferior, that all people are "naturally" aggressive, or that men are "naturally" promiscuous. Intellectual performance, aggression, and promiscuity, aside from being difficult to define and measure, all vary from individual to individual and often from culture to culture. Ignoring that variance simply hides the causative factors—cultural, genetic, or both—that we would like to understand.

Permanence is often viewed as human nature's key feature; after all, remember, "you can't change human nature." But, of course, we *can*—and we do, all the time. The natures of Americans today are very different from their natures in 1940. Indeed, today's human natures everywhere are diverse products of change, of long genetic and, especially, cultural evolutionary processes. A million years ago, as paleoanthropologists, archaeologists, and other scientists have shown, human nature was a radically different, and presumably much more uniform, attribute. People then had less nimble brains, they didn't have a language with fully developed syntax, they had not developed formal strata in societies, and they hadn't yet learned to attach worked stones to wooden shafts to make hammers and arrows.

Human natures a million years in the future will also be un-imaginably different from human natures today. The processes that changed those early people into modern human beings will continue as long as there are people. Indeed, with the rate of cultural evolution showing seemingly continuous acceleration, it would be amazing if the broadly shared aspects of human natures were not quite different even a million *hours* (about a hundred years) in the future. For example, think of how Internet commerce has changed in the past million or so minutes (roughly two years).

As evolving mental-physical packages, human natures have brought not only planetary dominance to our species but also great triumphs in areas such as art, music, literature, philosophy, science, and technology. Unhappily, though, those same packages—human behavioral patterns and their physical foundations—are also the source of our most serious current problems. War, genocide, commerce in drugs, racial and religious prejudice, extreme economic inequality, and destruction of society's life-support systems are all products of today's human natures, too. As Pogo so accurately said, "We have met the enemy, and they is us." But nowhere is it written that those problems have to be products of tomorrow's human natures. It is theoretically possible to make peace with ourselves and with our environment, overcome racial and religious prejudice, reduce large-scale cruelty, and increase economic equality. What's needed is a widespread understanding of the evolutionary processes that have produced our natures, open discourse on what is desirable about them, and conscious collective efforts to steer the cultural evolution of the more troublesome features of our natures in ways almost everyone would find desirable. A utopian notion? Maybe. But considering progress that already has been made in areas such as democratic governance and individual freedom, race relations, religious tolerance, women's and gay rights, and avoidance of global conflict, it's worth a try.

Paul R. Ehrlich is a professor of population studies and of biological sciences at Stanford University. This essay is adapted from his Human Natures: Genes, Cultures, and the Human Prospect, *published by Island Press in August 2000.*

From *The Chronicle of Higher Education,* September 22, 2000, pp. B7-B11. © 2000 by The Chronicle of Higher Education. Reprinted with permission of the author. This article may not be posted, published, or distributed without permission from *The Chronicle.*

The Gender Blur

where does biology end and society take over?

Once there were only two: male and female. Men, mostly, were the big ones, with deep voices and sturdy shoes, sitting with legs splayed. Women, mostly, were the smaller ones, with dainty high heels, legs crossed tightly at the ankle, and painted mouths. It was easy to tell them apart. These days, it's not so easy. Men wear makeup and women smoke cigars; male figure skaters are macho—but Dennis Rodman wears a dress. We can be one gender on the Internet and another in bed. Even science, bastion of the rational, can't prove valid the lines that used to separate and define us. Although researching the biology of gender has answered some old questions, it has also raised important new ones. The consensus? Gender is more fluid than we ever thought. Queer theorists call gender a social construct, saying that when we engage in traditional behaviors and sexual practices, we are nothing but actors playing ancient, empty roles. Others suggest that gender is performance, a collection of masks we can take on and off at will. So are we witnessing the birth of thrilling new freedoms, or the disintegration of the values and behaviors that bind us together? Will we encounter new opportunities for self-realization, or hopeless confusion? Whatever the answers, agreeing that our destinies aren't preordained will launch a search that will profoundly affect society, and will eventually engage us all.   *—The Editors*

By Deborah Blum

I was raised in one of those university-based, liberal elite families that politicians like to ridicule. In my childhood, every human being—regardless of gender—was exactly alike under the skin, and I mean exactly, barring his or her different opportunities. My parents wasted no opportunity to bring this point home. One Christmas, I received a Barbie doll and a softball glove. Another brought a green enamel stove, which baked tiny cakes by the heat of a lightbulb, and also a set of steel-tipped darts and competition-quality dart-board. Did I mention the year of the chemistry set and the ballerina doll?

It wasn't until I became a parent—I should say, a parent of two boys—that I realized I had been fed a line and swallowed it like a sucker (barring the part about opportunities, which I still believe). This dawned on me during my older son's dinosaur phase, which began when he was about 2½. Oh, he loved di-

nosaurs, all right, but only the blood-swilling carnivores. Plant-eaters were wimps and losers, and he refused to wear a T-shirt marred by a picture of a stegasaur. I looked down at him one day, as he was snarling around my feet and doing his toddler best to gnaw off my right leg, and I thought: This goes a lot deeper then culture.

Do the ways that we amplify those early differences in childhood shape the adults we become?

Raising children tends to bring on this kind of politically-incorrect reaction. Another friend came to the same conclusion watching a son determinedly bite

his breakfast toast into the shape of a pistol he hoped would blow away—or at least terrify—his younger brother. Once you get past the guilt part—Did I do this? Should I have bought him that plastic allosaur with the oversized teeth?—such revelations can lead you to consider the far more interesting field of gender biology, where the questions take a different shape: Does love of carnage begin in culture or genetics, and which drives which? Do the gender roles of our culture reflect an underlying biology, and, in turn, does the way we behave influence that biology?

The point I'm leading up to—through the example of my son's innocent love of predatory dinosaurs—is actually one of the most straightforward in this debate. One of the reasons we're so fascinated by childhood behaviors is that, as the old saying goes, the child becomes the man (or woman, of course.) Most girls don't spend their preschool years snarling around the house and pretending to chew off their companion's legs. And they—mostly—don't grow up to be as aggressive as men. Do the ways that we amplify those early differences in childhood shape the adults we become? Absolutely. But it's worth exploring the starting place—the faint signal that somehow gets amplified.

"There's plenty of room in society to influence sex differences," says Marc Breedlove, a behavioral endocrinologist at the University of California at Berkeley and a pioneer in defining how hormones can help build sexually different nervous systems. "Yes, we're born with predispositions, but it's society that amplifies them, exaggerates them. I believe that—except for the sex differences in aggression. Those [differences] are too massive to be explained simply by society."

Aggression does allow a straightforward look at the issue. Consider the following statistics: Crime reports in both the United States and Europe record between 10 and 15 robberies committed by men for every one by a woman. At one point, people argued that this was explained by size difference. Women weren't big enough to intimidate, but that would change, they predicted, with the availability of compact weapons. But just as little girls don't routinely make weapons out of toast, women—even criminal ones—don't seem drawn to weaponry in the same way that men are. Almost twice as many male thieves and robbers use guns as their female counterparts do.

Or you can look at more personal crimes: domestic partner murders. Three-fourths of men use guns in those killings; 50 percent of women do. Here's more from the domestic front: In conflicts in which a woman killed a man, he tended to be the one who had started the fight—in 51.8 percent of the cases, to be exact. When the man was the killer, he again was the likely first aggressor, and by an even more dramatic margin. In fights in which women died, they had started the argument only 12.5 percent of the time.

Enough. You can parade endless similar statistics but the point is this: Males are more aggressive, not just among humans but among almost all species on earth. Male chimpanzees, for instance, declare war on neighboring troops, and one of their strategies is a warning strike: They kill females and infants to terrorize and intimidate. In terms of simple, reproductive genetics, it's an advantage of males to be aggressive: You can muscle your way into dominance, winning more sexual encounters, more offspring, more genetic future. For the female—especially in a species like ours, with time for just one successful pregnancy a year—what's the genetic advantage in brawling?

Thus the issue becomes not whether there is a biologically influenced sex difference in aggression—the answer being a solid, technical "You betcha"—but rather how rigid that difference is. The best science, in my opinion, tends to align with basic common sense. We all know that there are extraordinarily gentle men and murderous women. Sex differences are always generalizations: They refer to a behavior, with some evolutionary rationale behind it. They never define, entirely, an individual. And that fact alone should tell us that there's always—even in the most biologically dominated traits—some flexibility, an instinctive ability to respond, for better and worse, to the world around us.

This is true even with physical characteristics that we've often assumed are nailed down by genetics. Scientists now believe height, for instance, is only about 90 percent heritable. A person's genes might code for a six-foot-tall body, but malnutrition could literally cut that short. And there's also some evidence, in girls anyway, that children with stressful childhoods tend to become shorter adults. So while some factors are predetermined, there's evidence that the prototypical male/female body design can be readily altered.

It's a given that humans, like most other species—bananas, spiders, sharks, ducks, any rabbit you pull out of a hat—rely on two sexes for reproduction. So basic is that requirement that we have chromosomes whose primary purpose is to deliver the genes that order up a male or a female. All other chromosomes are numbered, but we label the sex chromosomes with the letters X and Y. We get one each from our mother and our father, and the basic combinations are these: XX makes female, XY makes male.

There are two important—and little known—points about these chromosomal matches. One is that even with this apparently precise system, there's nothing precise—or guaranteed—about the physical construction of male and female. The other point makes that possible. It appears that sex doesn't matter in the early states of embryonic development. We are unisex at the point of conception.

If you examine an embryo at about six weeks, you see that it has the ability to develop in either direction. The fledgling embryo has two sets of ducts—Wolffian for male, Muellerian for female—an either/or structure, held in readiness for further development. If testosterone and other androgens are released by hormone-producing cells, then the Wolffian ducts develop into the channel that connects penis to testes, and the female ducts wither away.

Without testosterone, the embryo takes on a female form; the male ducts vanish and the Muellerian ducts expand into oviducts, uterus, and vagina. In other words, in humans, anyway (the opposite is true in birds), the female is the default sex. Back in the 1950s, the famed biologist Alfred Jost showed that if you castrate a male rabbit fetus, choking off testosterone, you produce a completely feminized rabbit.

We don't do these experiments in humans—for obvious reasons—but there are naturally occurring instances that prove the same point. For instance: In the fetal testes are a group of cells, called Leydig cells, that make testosterone. In rare cases, the fetus doesn't make enough of these cells (a defect known as Leydig cell hypoplasia). In this circumstance we see the limited power of the XY chromosome. These boys have the right chromosomes and the right genes to be boys; they just don't grow a penis. Obstetricians and parents often think they see a baby girl, and these children are routinely raised as daughters. Usually, the "mistake" is caught about the time of puberty, when menstruation doesn't start. A doctor's examination shows the child to be internally male; there are usually small testes, often tucked within the abdomen. As the researchers put it, if the condition had been known from the beginning, "the sisters would have been born as brothers."

Just to emphasize how tricky all this body-building can get, there's a peculiar genetic defect that seems to be clustered by heredity in a small group of villages in the Dominican Republic. The result of the defect is a failure to produce an enzyme that concentrates testosterone, specifically for building the genitals. One obscure little enzyme only, but here's what happens without it: You get a boy with undescended testes and a penis so short and stubby that it resembles an oversized clitoris.

In the mountain villages of this Caribbean nation, people are used to it. The children are usually raised as "conditional" girls. At puberty, the secondary tide of androgens rises and is apparently enough to finish the construction project. The scrotum suddenly descends, the phallus grows, and the child develops a distinctly male body—narrow hips, muscular build, and even slight beard growth. At that point, the family shifts the child over from daughter to son. The dresses are thrown out. He begins to wear male clothes and starts dating girls. People in the Dominican Republic are so familiar with this condition that there's a colloquial name for it: *guevedoces*, meaning "eggs (or testes) at 12."

It's the comfort level with this slip-slide of sexual identity that's so remarkable and, I imagine, so comforting to the children involved. I'm positive that the sexual transition of these children is less traumatic than the abrupt awareness of the "sisters who would have been brothers." There's a message of tolerance there, well worth repeating, and there are some other key lessons too.

These defects are rare and don't alter the basic male-female division of our species. They do emphasize how fragile those divisions can be. Biology allows flexibility, room to change, to vary and grow. With that comes room for error as well. That it's possible to live with these genetic defects, that they don't merely kill us off, is a reminder that we, male and female alike, exist on a continuum of biological possibilities that can overlap and sustain either sex.

Marc Breedlove points out that the most difficult task may be separating how the brain responds to hormones from how the brain responds to the *results* of hormones. Which brings us back, briefly, below the belt: In this context, the penis is just a result, the product of androgens at work before birth. "And after birth," says Breedlove, "virtually everyone who interacts with that individual will note that he has a penis, and will, in many instances, behave differently than if the individual was a female."

Do the ways that we amplify physical and behavioral differences in childhood shape who we become as adults? Absolutely. But to understand that, you have to understand the differences themselves—their beginning and the very real biochemistry that may lie behind them.

Here is a good place to focus on testosterone—a hormone that is both well-studied and generally underrated. First, however, I want to acknowledge that there are many other hormones and neurotransmitters that appear to influence behavior. Preliminary work shows that fetal boys are a little more active than fetal girls. It's pretty difficult to argue socialization at that point. There's a strong suspicion that testosterone may create the difference.

And there are a couple of relevant animal models to emphasize the point. Back in the 1960s, Robert Goy, a psychologist at the University of Wisconsin at Madison, first documented that young male monkeys play much more roughly than young females. Goy went on to show that if you manipulate testosterone level—raising it in females, damping it down in males—you can reverse those effects, creating sweet little male monkeys and rowdy young females.

Is testosterone the only factor at work here? I don't think so. But clearly we can argue a strong influence, and, interestingly, studies have found that girls with congenital adrenal hypoplasia—who run high in testosterone—tend to be far more fascinated by trucks and toy weaponry than most little girls are. They lean toward rough-and-tumble play, too. As it turns out, the strongest influence on this "abnormal" behavior is not parental disapproval, but the company of other little girls, who tone them down and direct them toward more routine girl games.

And that reinforces an early point: If there is indeed a biology to sex differences, we amplify it. At some point—when it is still up for debate—we gain a sense of our gender, and with it a sense of "gender-appropriate" behavior.

Some scientists argue for some evidence of gender awareness in infancy, perhaps by the age of 12 months. The consensus seems to be that full-blown "I'm a girl" or "I'm a boy" instincts arrive between the ages of 2 and 3. Research shows that if a family operates in a very traditional, Beaver Cleaver kind of environment, filled with awareness of and association with "proper" gender behaviors, the "boys do trucks, girls do dolls" attitude seems to come very early. If a child grows up in a less traditional family, with an emphasis on partnership and sharing—"We all do the dishes, Joshua"—children maintain a more flexible sense of gender roles until about age 6.

In this period, too, relationships between boys and girls tend to fall into remarkably strict lines. Interviews with children find that 3-year-olds say that about half their friendships are with the opposite sex. By the age of 5, that drops to 20 percent. By 7, almost no boys or girls have, or will admit to having, best friends of the opposite sex. They still hang out on the same playground, play on the same soccer teams. They may be friendly, but the real friendships tend to be boy-to-boy or girl-to-girl.

There's some interesting science that suggests that the space between boys and girls is a normal part of development; there are periods during which children may thrive and learn from hanging out with peers of the same sex. Do we, as parents, as a culture at large, reinforce such separation? Is the pope Catholic? One of my favorite studies looked at little boys who asked for toys. If they asked for a heavily armed action figure, they got the soldier about 70 percent of the time. If they asked for a "girl" toy, like a baby doll or a Barbie, their parents purchased it maybe 40 percent of the time. Name a child who won't figure out how to work *that* system.

How does all this fit together—toys and testosterone, biology and behavior, the development of the child into the adult, the way that men and women relate to one another?

> *Will that wonderful, unpredictable, flexible biology that we've been given allow a shift, so that one day, we will literally be far more alike?*

Let me make a cautious statement about testosterone: It not only has some body-building functions, it influences some behaviors as well. Let's make that a little less cautious: These behaviors include rowdy play, sex drive, competitiveness, and an in-your-face attitude. Males tend to have a higher baseline of testosterone than females—in our species, about seven to ten times as much—and therefore you would predict (correctly, I think) that all of those behaviors would be more generally found in men than in women.

But testosterone is also one of my favorite examples of how responsive biology is, how attuned it is to the way we live our lives. Testosterone, it turns out, rises in response to competition and threat. In the days of our ancestors, this might have been hand-to-hand combat or high-risk hunting endeavors. Today, scientists have measured testosterone rise in athletes preparing for a game, in chess players awaiting a match, in spectators following a soccer competition.

If a person—or even just a person's favored team—wins, testosterone continues to rise. It falls with a loss. (This also makes sense in an evolutionary perspective. If one was being clobbered with a club, it would be extremely unhelpful to have a hormone [under] one to battle on.) Testosterone also rises in the competitive world of dating, settles down with a stable and supportive relationship, climbs again if the relationship starts to falter.

It's been known for years that men in high-stress professions—say, police work or corporate law—have higher testosterone levels than men in the ministry. It turns out that women in the same kind of strong-attitude professions have higher testosterone than women who choose to stay home. What I like about this is the chicken-or-egg aspect. If you argue that testosterone influenced the behavior of those women, which came first? Did they have high testosterone and choose the law? Or did they choose the law, and the competitive environment ratcheted them up on the androgen scale? Or could both be at work?

And, returning to children for a moment, there's an ongoing study by Pennsylvania researchers, tracking that question in adolescent girls, who are being encouraged by their parents to engage in competitive activities that were once for boys only. As they do so, the researchers are monitoring, regularly, two hormones: testosterone and cortisol, a stress hormone. Will these hormones rise in response to this new, more traditionally male environment? What if more girls choose the competitive path; more boys choose the other? Will female testosterone levels rise, male levels fall? Will that wonderful, unpredictable, flexible biology that we've been given allow a shift, so that one day, we will literally be far more alike?

We may not have answers to all those questions, but we can ask them, and we can expect that the answers will come someday, because science clearly shows us that such possibilities exist. In this most important sense, sex differences offer us a paradox. It is only through exploring and understanding what makes us different that we can begin to understand what binds us together.

Deborah Blum is a Pulitzer Prize-winning science writer, a professor of journalism at the University of Wisconsin-Madison, and author of Sex on the Brain: The Biological Differences Between Men and Women (*Penguin, 1997*).

From *Utne Reader*, September/October 1998, pp. 44–48. Reprinted by permission of International Creative Management, Inc. © 1998 by Deborah Blum.

THE PERSONALITY
GENES

Does DNA shape behavior?
A leading researcher's behavior is a case in point

By J. MADELEINE NASH

MOLECULAR BIOLOGIST DEAN Hamer has blue eyes, light brown hair and the goofy sense of humor of a stand-up comic. He smokes cigarettes, spends long hours in a cluttered laboratory at the National Institutes of Health, and in his free time clambers up cliffs and points his skis down steep, avalanche-prone slopes. He also happens to be openly, matter-of-factly gay.

What is it that makes Hamer who he is? What, for that matter, accounts for the quirks and foibles, talents and traits that make up anyone's personality? Hamer is not content merely to ask such questions; he is trying to answer them as well. A pioneer in the field of molecular psychology, Hamer is exploring the role genes play in governing the very core of our individuality. To a remarkable extent, his work on what might be called the gay, thrill-seeking and quit-smoking genes reflects his own genetic predispositions.

That work, which has appeared mostly in scientific journals, has been gathered

into an accessible and quite readable form in Hamer's provocative new book, *Living with Our Genes* (Doubleday; $24.95). "You have about as much choice in some aspects of your personality," Hamer and coauthor Peter Copeland write in the introductory chapter, "as you do in the shape of your nose or the size of your feet."

Until recently, research into behavioral genetics was dominated by psychiatrists and psychologists, who based their most compelling conclusions about the importance of genes on studies of identical twins. For example, psychologist Michael Bailey of Northwestern University famously demonstrated that if one identical twin is gay, there is about a 50% likelihood that the other will be too. Seven years ago, Hamer picked up where the twin studies left off, homing in on specific strips of DNA that appear to influence everything from mood to sexual orientation.

Hamer switched to behavioral genetics from basic research; after receiving his

Ph.D. from Harvard, he spent more then a decade studying the biochemistry of metallothionein, a protein that cells use to metabolize heavy metals like copper and zinc. As he was about to turn 40, however, Hamer suddenly realized he had learned as much about metallothionein as he cared to. "Frankly, I was bored," he remembers, "and ready for something new."

Instrumental in Hamer's decision to switch fields was Charles Darwin's *The Descent of Man, and Selection in Relation to Sex*. "I was fascinated to learn that Darwin seemed so convinced that behavior was partially inherited," he remembers, "even though when he was writing, genes had not been discovered, let alone DNA." Homosexual behavior, in particular, seemed ripe for exploration because few scientists had dared tackle such an emotionally and politically charged subject. "I'm gay," Hamer says with a shrug, "but that was not a major motivation. It was more of a question of intellectual curios-

Nature or Nurture?

Many aspects of personality may have a genetic component—such as sexual orientation, anxiety, a tendency to take chances and ...

ILLUSTRATIONS FOR TIME BY SCOTT MENCHIN

ity—and the fact that no one else was doing this sort of research."

The results of Hamer's first foray into behavioral genetics, published by the journal *Science* in 1993, ignited a furor that has yet to die down. According to Hamer and his colleagues, male homosexuality appeared to be linked to a stretch of DNA at the very tip of the X chromosome, the chromosome men inherit from their mothers. Three years later, in 1996, Hamer and his collaborators at NIH seconded an Israeli group's finding that linked a gene on chromosome 11 to the personality trait psychologists called novelty seeking. That same year Hamer's lab helped pinpoint another gene, this time on chromosome 17, that appears to play a role in regulating anxiety.

Unlike the genes that are responsible for physical traits, Hamer emphasizes, these genes do not cause people to become homosexuals, thrill-seeking rock climbers or anxiety-ridden worrywarts. The biology of personality is much more complicated than that. Rather, what genes appear to do, says Hamer, is subtly bias the psyche so that different individuals react to similar experiences in surprisingly different ways.

Intriguing as these findings are, other experts caution that none has been unequivocally replicated by other research teams. Why? One possibility is that, despite all of Hamer's work, the links between these genes and these particular personality traits do not, in fact, exist. There is, however, another, more tantalizing possibility. Consider the genes that give tomatoes their flavor, suggests Hamer's colleague Dr. Dennis Murphy of the National Institute of Mental Health. Even a simple trait like acidity is controlled not by a single gene but by as many as 30 that operate in concert. In the same way, he speculates, many genes are involved in setting up temperamental traits and psychological vulnerabilities; each gene contributes just a little bit to the overall effect.

Hunting down the genes that influence personality remains a dauntingly difficult business. Although DNA is constructed out of a mere four chemicals—adenine, guanine, cytosine, thymine—it can take as many as a million combinations to spell out a single human gene. Most of these genes vary from individual to individual by only one chemical letter in a thousand, and it is precisely these minute differences that Hamer and his colleagues are trying to identify. Of particular interest are variations that may affect the operation of such brain chemicals as dopamine and serotonin, which are well-known modulators of mood. The so-called novelty-seeking gene, for example, is thought to affect how efficiently nerve cells absorb dopamine. The so-called anxiety gene is postulated to affect serotonin's action.

How can this be? After all, as Hamer and Copeland observe in their book, "… genes are not switches that say 'shy' or 'outgoing' or 'happy' or 'sad.' Genes are simply chemicals that direct the combination of more chemicals." What genes do is order up the production of proteins in organs like the kidney, the skin and also the brain. Thus, Hamer speculates, one version of the novelty-seeking gene may make a protein that is less efficient at absorbing dopamine. Since dopamine is the chemical that creates sensations of pleasure in response to intense experiences, people who inherit this gene might seek to stimulate its production by seeking out thrills.

Still, as critics emphasize and Hamer himself acknowledges, genes alone do not control the chemistry of the brain. Ultimately, it is the environment that determines how these genes will express themselves. In another setting, for example, it is easy to imagine that Hamer might have become a high school dropout rather than a scientist. For while he grew up in an affluent household in Montclair, N.J., he was hardly a model child. "Today," he chuckles, "I probably would have been diagnosed with attention-deficit disorder and put on Ritalin." In his senior year in high school, though, Hamer discovered organic chemistry and went from being an unruly adolescent to a first-rate student. What people are born with, Hamer says, are temperamental traits. What they can acquire through experience is the ability to control these traits by exercising that intangible part of personality called character.

Over the coming decade, Hamer predicts, scientists will identify thousands of genes that directly and indirectly influence behavior. A peek inside the locked freezer in the hallway outside his own lab reveals a rapidly expanding stash of plastic tubes that contain DNA samples from more than 1,760 volunteers. Among them: gay men and their heterosexual brothers, a random assortment of novelty seekers and novelty avoiders, shy children and now a growing collection of cigarette smokers.

Indeed, while Hamer has maintained a professional distance from his studies, it is impossible to believe he is not also driven by a desire for self-discovery. Soon, in fact, his lab will publish a paper about a gene that makes it harder or easier for people to stop smoking. Judging by the pack of cigarettes poking out of his shirt pocket, Hamer would seem to have drawn the wrong end of that genetic stick. He has tried to stop smoking and failed, he confesses, dozens of times. "If I quit," he says, "it will be an exercise of character." And not, it goes without saying, of his genes.

From *Time*, April 27, 1998, pp. 60–61. © 1998 by Time Inc. Magazine Company. Reprinted by permission.

Where We Come From

Recent advances in genetics are starting to illuminate the wanderings of early humans

BY NANCY SHUTE

Andy Carvin is a pioneer on the strange frontier of DNA genealogy. The 29-year-old Internet policy analyst had built his family tree back to ancestors in Busk, Ukraine, but that's where the trail went cold. Then he read about research tracing the Y sex chromosome, which is passed intact from father to son, all the way back to the time of Aaron, the single progenitor of the priestly *cohen* caste 3,000 years ago. More than once, his father had told him their family was *cohanim*. "I was really curious," Carvin says, "to see if there was even a small possibility that the oral tradition was true."

On the Internet, Carvin located Family Tree DNA, a small Houston firm created to answer such questions. He mailed in a sample of his DNA, gathered by swabbing the inside of his cheek, and waited. In late October, he got a call from Bennett Greenspan, president of Family Tree DNA. Not only did his Y chromosome have the *cohanim* markers—small genetic variations—but other markers matched with those of another man in the database, making it likely that they share a forefather within the past 250 years.

So, just before Thanksgiving, Carvin set off on a DNA-induced family reunion. He took the train from his home in Washington, D.C., to Philadelphia and met Bill Swersky, a 59-year-old federal official. "We immediately hit it off," says Carvin. "I felt like I was visiting one of my uncles." Over smoked whitefish and bagels, they paged through family photos. Andy's dad looks like Bill's father. Bill's son looks like Andy when he was younger. "He's a hell of a lot better looking than I am," Swersky says of his new relative. "I'm jealous."

It's exceedingly unusual to find such treasure in the genetic attic. Humans are very much alike genetically, with most of the variation within—rather than between—ethnic groups. Carvin and Swersky struck gold because they're part of the small *cohanim* group, which is itself a subset of an insular group, Jews. Finns, Sardinians, and Basques are among other groups with small founding populations that also have highly distinctive genetic pedigrees. By contrast, most people of European origin are so genetically mixed that it's impossible to tell German from Frenchman, Bosnian from Serb.

But the tools of biotechnology have become so powerful that it's now possible to deduce ancient human history from a drop of blood or a few shed skin cells. This molecular view of the past is already being employed to trace the cause of ailments such as cancer and heart disease, as well as aiding individuals like Carvin in tracking their roots. Most significantly for scientists studying past human life and culture, it offers the best insight yet into the abiding mystery of how modern *Homo sapiens* arose out of archaic hominids who first left Africa about 1.7 million years ago. "It's a very exciting time," says Colin Renfrew, a professor of archaeology at the University of Cambridge. "In the next 10 years the whole course of early human history is going to become very much clearer."

Indeed, in recent months, two groups of geneticists have published sweeping chronicles of the peopling of Europe, one tracing maternal DNA lineages, the other, paternal. These findings portray the majority of European forebears arriving from the Middle East as hunter-gatherers 25,000 to 40,000 years ago. During the last Ice Age, these first Europeans fled south to Iberia, Ukraine, and the Balkans. As the ice retreated, the Ice Age survivors spread out and flourished. The last major migration from the East 9,000 years ago brought agriculture and domestic animals but did not displace the earlier settlers, as some researchers had thought.

Genetic clock. The European studies are among the first to capitalize on a new ability to compare the migrations of males and females, which don't always follow the same path through history. Over the past 20 years, researchers have been able to track women's wanderings through mitochondria—tiny energy-producing bodies that cluster by the hundreds in human cells. Mitochondria have very odd DNA. They contain genetic material only from the maternal line, unlike the cell nucleus, which is a mix of DNA from both parents. This means that all children, male and female, carry copies of their mother's mitochondrial DNA.

That peculiarity gave geneticists a key tool for learning the movements of ancient populations. That's because as mitochondrial DNA is passed along, tiny, harmless mutations occur. By comparing the mutations among people, it's possible to calculate how closely they're related. And by calculating the mutation rate, researchers can deduce how far back in time different groups split apart. Douglas Wallace, director of the center for molecular medicine at Emory University Medical School, says: "You literally have a genetic clock." Wallace proved that point in 1980, when he was able to differentiate people from Europe, Asia, and Africa by comparing their DNA.

The realization that there is a map and a clock of human history in every cell completely transformed the small, highly technical field of population genetics. Scientists had been searching for human history in the genes at least since World War I, when two Polish immunologists discovered that different armies had very different proportions of various blood types.(Type B blood, for example, is more common in East Asians and Africans than it is in Europeans. Since blood type is hereditary, controlled by a single gene, a blood type can be used as a crude form of genealogy.) Blood types were used to prove that the Romany, or Gypsies, were correct when they claimed they originally came from the Indian subcontinent, not Europe.

But although researchers kept cataloging genetic markers in blood proteins, the number identified was far fewer than the millions of inherited mutations that must exist. "There just weren't enough data to answer the interesting questions," says Kenneth Kidd, a genetics professor at Yale University School of Medicine. Times changed. Since the mid-1980s, technology has unleashed a flood of new data, so much that researchers struggle to keep pace. Restriction enzymes allow scientists to snip DNA into tiny, easy-to-read bits. The 1983 invention of the polymerase chain reaction, or PCR, made it possible to make unlimited copies of a DNA strand in a test tube. PCR made it possible to decode the human genome. And for students of human history, it is opening the window to the past further than anyone imagined.

Enter Eve. In 1987, Allan Wilson, Rebecca Cann, and Mark Stoneking, researchers at the University of California-Berkeley, catapulted mitochondrial DNA into the headlines worldwide when they announced that they had traced it back 200,000 years to the oldest female ancestor of living humans—an African woman quickly dubbed Eve. Eve's debut rocked the archaeological community, which had been arguing for decades over whether modern humans evolved on more than one continent or instead swept out of Africa to replace more archaic hominids around the world. Wilson's group was attacked for sloppy science, and in fact there were problems with the original calculations. But genetic data from dozens of researchers have since almost universally supported the "Out of Africa" theory. "History has made a pretty consistent stamp on populations," says Lynn

Jorde, a geneticist at the University of Utah, who has found African roots in nuclear DNA as well as in mitochondria and the Y. "Looking at more and more of the nuclear DNA is going to clarify the picture."

Questions remain about the nature of the early human diaspora. For instance, lively debate continues over whether Neanderthals and modern humans mated [box, "Ancient History in the DNA"]. And some remain skeptical about the Out of Africa theory itself. This month researchers at Australian National University published the results of mitochondrial DNA testing on a 60,000-year-old skeleton called Lake Mungo 3. The DNA didn't match that of living humans, suggesting that the Mungo lineage evolved in Australia, not Africa. But it could simply mean that the Mungo lineage went extinct, as have many others.

Indeed, there have been many Adams, and many Eves. The genetic record reflects only those whose offspring survived and reproduced. For instance, the earliest forefather identified so far is 20,000 to 30,000 years younger than Eve. "It's rather distressing to find that Eve could not be the wife of Adam," says Luigi Luca Cavalli-Sforza, a professor emeritus at Stanford University and pioneer of population genetics. The bulk of the genetic data suggests that a small population of modern humans, as few as 10,000, left Africa 100,000 or so years ago, wandering into the Middle East and on to Asia and Europe. Their genetic footprints lead all the way to Tierra del Fuego.

Emory's Wallace has spent the past decade tracking mitochondrial markers from Africa to Asia and the Americas—and fueling a robust dispute over just when humans first arrived in the New World. For much of the past 50 years, archaeologists thought that people tramped across the Bering Land Bridge and through a gap in the glaciers about 14,000 years ago. But Wallace thinks there were other migrations, one as early as 30,000 years ago. Archaeological sites in Pennsylvania, Virginia, and Chile support this earlier migration, although the notion remains hotly contested.Wallace's newest and most surprising discovery is a set of genetic markers found only in the Ojibwa and other tribes living near the Great Lakes; the markers are not found in any other native Americans or in Asia. "We just don't know how it got there," Wallace says, "but it's clearly related to the European population." The simple answer would be that the DNA arrived with European colonists, but the strain is different enough from the existing European lineage that it must have left the Old World long before Columbus. The lineage could have passed through Asia and later died out there. But Dennis Stanford, a paleoarchaeologist at the Smithsonian Institution, says this mystery strain, dubbed Haplogroup X, bolsters his theory that a hardy band of Europeans left Iberia and navigated the North Atlantic ice pack 15,000 years ago."During colder time periods the sea ice was as far south as the Bay of Biscay," Stanford says, adding that the ice edge would have been ideal for hunting and fishing, just as it is in the Arctic today.

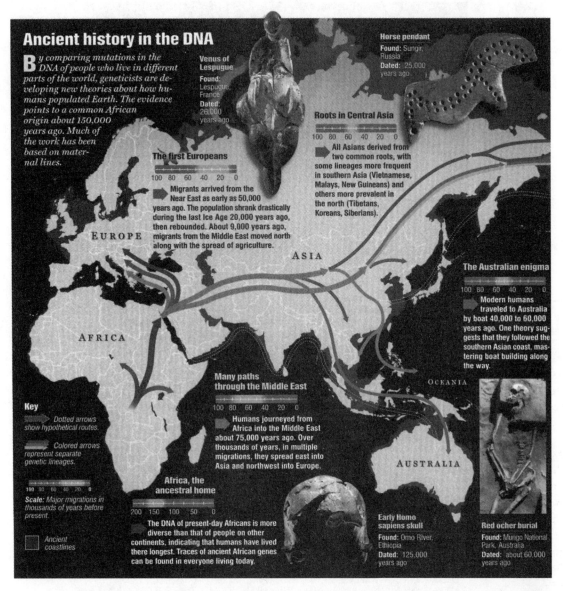

Ancient history in the DNA

By comparing mutations in the DNA of people who live in different parts of the world, geneticists are developing new theories about how humans populated Earth. The evidence points to a common African origin about 150,000 years ago. Much of the work has been based on maternal lines.

Venus of Lespugue
Found: Lespugue, France
Dated: 26,000 years ago

Horse pendant
Found: Sungir, Russia
Dated: 25,000 years ago

The first Europeans

100 80 60 40 20 0

Migrants arrived from the Near East as early as 50,000 years ago. The population shrank drastically during the last Ice Age 20,000 years ago, then rebounded. About 9,000 years ago, migrants from the Middle East moved north along with the spread of agriculture.

Roots in Central Asia

100 80 60 40 20 0

All Asians derived from two common roots, with some lineages more frequent in southern Asia (Vietnamese, Malays, New Guineans) and others more prevalent in the north (Tibetans, Koreans, Siberians).

EUROPE

ASIA

AFRICA

The Australian enigma

100 80 60 40 20 0

Modern humans traveled to Australia by boat 40,000 to 60,000 years ago. One theory suggests that they followed the southern Asian coast, mastering boat building along the way.

OCEANIA

Many paths through the Middle East

100 80 60 40 20 0

Humans journeyed from Africa into the Middle East about 75,000 years ago. Over thousands of years, in multiple migrations, they spread east into Asia and northwest into Europe.

AUSTRALIA

Key

Dotted arrows show hypothetical routes.

Colored arrows represent separate genetic lineages.

100 80 60 40 20 0

Scale: Major migrations in thousands of years before present.

Ancient coastlines

Africa, the ancestral home

200 150 100 50 0

The DNA of present-day Africans is more diverse than that of people on other continents, indicating that humans have lived there longest. Traces of ancient African genes can be found in everyone living today.

Early Homo sapiens skull
Found: Omo River, Ethiopia
Dated: 125,000 years ago

Red ocher burial
Found: Mungo National Park, Australia
Dated: about 60,000 years ago

CLOCKWISE FROM TOP LEFT: SCALA /ART RESOURCE; KENNETH GARRETT—NATIONAL GEOGRAPHIC IMAGE COLLECTION; J.M. MCAVOY—NOTTTOWAY RIVER SURVEY; KENNETH GARRETT—NATIONAL GEOGRAPHIC IMAGE COLLECTION; AUSTRALIAN NATIONAL UNIVERSITY/REUTERS/ARCHIVE; DAVID L. BRILL

While Wallace and others were finding remarkable stories in mitochondrial DNA, scientists seeking similar tales in the Y chromosome were met with silence. It was particularly frustrating because the Y—passed intact from father to son—seemed like an ideal tool for tracking human origins. But unlike mitochondrial DNA, the male chromosome shows little variation, and searching for markers was excruciating work. Michael Hammer, a geneticist at the University of Arizona who first identified key Y markers, started looking for a *cohanim* marker in 1995, after he got a call from Karl Skorecki, an Israeli physician. Skorecki was wondering if the very different looking men he saw reading the Torah in shul could possibly all be sons of Aaron, as the Bible said. Intrigued, Hammer started searching the DNA of Skorecki and other Jewish men who according to oral tradition were *cohanim*, the priest caste. Hammer identified markers that are often shared by men who think they are *cohanim*, including Andy Carvin and Bill Skwersky. By comparing the variations, Hammer determined that the *cohanim* had a common male ancestor 84 to 130 generations ago—which includes the time of the exodus from Egypt and the original *cohen*, Aaron.

Brothers and enemies. Since then, other researchers have used the *cohanim* markers to ascertain that the Lemba, a Bantu-speaking people in Southern Africa who have traditionally claimed Jewish ancestry, do indeed have Semitic roots. And last June, Hammer published results showing that although Palestinian and Jewish men may be political foes, they are also brethren, so closely related as to be genetically indistinguishable.

The Y chromosome is starting to yield other intriguing tales as well. Last November, Peter Underhill, a Stanford

Stone tools
Found: Cactus Hill, Virginia
Dated: 15,000 to 18,000 years ago

Land bridge between continents

The X factor
A small group of Indians near the Great Lakes has a lineage (haplogroup "X") unlike those of other American Indians, but related to a European strain. Some archaeologists think that the colonists came from Iberia about 15,000 years ago, crossing the North Atlantic ice pack to Greenland. Others believe the X factor is the remnant of a vanished Asian lineage.

A bridge to the New World

100 80 60 40 20 0

The first inhabitants of the New World migrated from central Siberia 20,000 to 30,000 years ago along the Bering land bridge. They may have been joined by a second migration 15,000 years ago that skirted the coast. Na-Dene people, who include the Athabascans, Apaches, and Navajos, are genetically distinct from the first American Indians, and came from northern Siberia about 9,000 years ago. Eskimos and Aleuts arrived 4,000 to 6,000 years later.

NORTH AMERICA

For most of the past 65,000 years, sea levels have been lower than today. During the last Ice Age 20,000 years ago, sea levels were about 400 feet lower.

Along the Andes to Tierra del Fuego

100 80 60 40 20 0

The earliest migration swept from Siberia to Tierra del Fuego, traveling along the Andes. Another route curved farther east, to present-day Brazil.

SOUTH AMERICA

Throwing stone
Found: Monte Verde, Chile
Dated: 14,800 years ago

Sources: Douglas Wallace, Michael Brown, and Marie Lott, Emory University; David Anderson, Paula Dunbar, NOAA; Theodore Schurr, Southwest Foundation for Biomedical Research; The Human Career

SOURCES: DOUGLAS WALLACE, MICHAEL BROWN, AND MARIE LOTT, EMORY UNUVERSITY; DAVID ANDERSON, PAULA DUNBAR, NOAA; THEODORE SCHURR, SOUTHWEST FOUNDATION FOR BIOMEDICAL RESEARCH; *THE HUMAN CAREER*

University researcher, published a list of 87 new Y markers, which he used to draw a tree that sorts all the world's men into just 10 branches. Indeed, men's lineages have much crisper divisions than women's, perhaps because men move into an area and kill or expel the men already there. "You get this alpha male effect," Underhill says.

Women, by contrast, move because they've married into a new family and village. Generation after generation, daughters marry and move out, while sons stay put, making women's DNA often more well traveled than men's. People living near Medellín, Colombia, have almost exclusively Native American mitochondrial DNA and European—specifically, Spanish—Y chromosome DNA. The story is familiar, and tragic: The Spanish colonists killed or supplanted the native men and married the native women.

For all its dazzle—or perhaps because of it—molecular anthropology is not without critics. "The molecular stuff has been very important," says Milford Wolpoff, an anthropology professor at the University of Michigan and a leading critic of the Out of Africa theory of human origins. "But in the end it has the same problem fossils have—the sample size is very small." Earlier this month, the journal *Science* published a Wolpoff study of early human skulls, which suggests that Africans may have mixed with earlier hominids rather than supplanting them. The small number of living humans sampled by geneticists, Wolpoff says, and the effects of natural selection over the millennia, make it foolhardy to say with assurance that Out of Africa is right. The geneticists, for their part, readily admit that they need more samples, more markers, and more precise calculations. But they also say that even with today's imperfect science, the DNA is right. And in places like India and China, where the fossil record is scanty, the genetic history will be the only history. "Genetics is moving so fast," says Chris Stringer, a paleoanthropologist at the Natural History Museum in London. "It's well ahead of the fossil and historical record."

Gene-based anthropology also struggles with the specter of racism. Australia has banned researchers from publishing work involving Aboriginal DNA, and India bars the export of its citizens' genetic matter. Geneticists are dismayed by these attitudes; if there's one thing the genes show, they say, it is that there is no such thing as race. The external differences that most people would use in defining race—skin color, eye shape, height—are genetically inconsequential, minor variations that evolved in response to the environment, the genetic equivalent of a sunburn. For instance, a change in just one gene accounts for Northern Europeans' fair skin,which may have developed to better absorb sunlight and synthesize vitamin D. "We are all brothers," says Stanford's Underhill, "and we're all different."

Genealogy by the genes

For-profit genetic genealogy services are springing up, but they can answer only limited questions.

•**Family Tree** DNA (713-828-4200, *www.familytreedna.com*) helps connect distantly related "genetic cousins."

•**GeneTree** (888-404-4363, *www.genetree.com*) tests whether families with the same surname are related.

•**Oxford Ancestors** (*www.oxfordancestors.com*) groups people into ancient maternal and paternal lineages.

Custom medicine. The differences may be minor, but they matter a lot to medical researchers. African-Americans are more apt to get sickle-cell anemia; some people with Eastern European roots have a gene that confers resistance to AIDS; women with Scottish ancestry are predisposed to one form of breast cancer. So researchers are using molecular anthropology to seek the origins of disease and then using that knowledge to create customized treatments. They're looking increasingly at nuclear DNA—the DNA of genes and inherited traits—which mingles with every generation. "Go back five generations," says Yale's Kidd. "You have 32 ancestors. At each nuclear locus you may have a gene from a different set of two of those ancestors." Thus nuclear DNA paints a much fuller picture of the past than mitochondrial and Y, which represent only two ancestors in any generation. Kidd is now studying nuclear DNA in 33 populations around the world, seeking a better understanding of schizophrenia, Tourette's syndrome, and alcoholism. Science is far from being able to simply scan the human genome to find the

causes of complex diseases like these. But the day will come, and soon, when it will be possible to pinpoint the genetic roots of disease without the geographic history. "Who cares where patients come from?" asks Aravinda Chakravarti, head of the institute of genetic medicine at Johns Hopkins University. "We'll be looking at what kind of diabetes is there, not whether they came from Timbuktu or Thailand or Towson."

NEANDERTHAL MYSTERY

Did early man mix it up?

Humans have been arguing about Neanderthals ever since an unusual skeleton with a beetled brow was dug up in a quarry by Germany's River Neander in 1856. Were these the bones of ancestors of modern *Homo sapiens*? More recent evidence that humans and Neanderthals both lived in Europe up to 26,000 years ago raised a more startling question: Did Neanderthals and humans have sex?

Since 1997, researchers have managed to extract mitochondrial DNA from three Neanderthal skeletons. The genes appear to have diverged from the modern human lineage about 500,000 years ago, way too early for Stone Age whoopee.

But in 1998, the skeleton of a child with human and Neanderthal features was found in Lagar Velho, Portugal. Washington University anthropologist Erik Trinkaus who is researching the find, says the 24,500-year-old bones are clear evidence of admixture. Both geneticists and archaeologists could be right with any mixed DNA lost by chance over the millennia. "We can't say anything about sexual practices in the Pleistocene." says Svante Pääbo, the geneticist at the Max Planck Institute for Evolutionary Anthropology in Leipzig who analyzed the Neanderthal DNA.

The thought of Neanderthal-human hybrids fascinates more than a few humans. Three years after the Lagar Velho find, Trinkaus still gets E-mails from people writing: "That explains Uncle George." –*N.S.*

But for some people, knowing where they came from matters a lot. Alice Petrovilli, a 71-year-old Aleut living in Anchorage, says she was eager to participate in a University of Kansas study on Aleut origins, even though other Aleut elders refused. "I think it's important. People always acted like because we were so far away we were a substandard species. It proves we were out here for a long, long time." Her DNA helps establish the Aleuts as people who migrated through Alaska and arrived in the Aleutian Islands 4,000 to 6,000 years ago and are genetically related to the Chukchi of northeast Russia.

Pearl Duncan is also interested in where her genes have been.The 51-year-old Jamaica-born writer had exhaustively researched her family history through genealogical records and traced several nicknames to Ghanaian dialects. But the trail ended there, lost in the Middle Passage when her slave ancestors were brought from Africa to the New World. So she tested her father's Y against DNA she gathered from members of Ghanaian churches in New York, where she lives, and found a match. "I really traced a cultural voice that is missing from the African-American narrative," says Duncan, who is writing a book about her search. She is incorporating her Ghanaian history with that of John Smellie, her Scottish ancestor 12 generations back.

No lifeguards. But geneticists fear that for every Pearl Duncan who boldly dives into the gene pool, at home with her mixed racial history, other more naive searchers may be dismayed at what they find. "Five percent of the people in America are sending Father's Day cards to the wrong guy," says Martin Tracey, a professor of genetics at Florida International University in Miami. What's more, mitochondrial and Y DNA reveal just a tiny slice of family history. Only one out of four great-grandfathers is represented on the Y, for instance, and only one great-grandmother in mitochondrial DNA. Go back just five generations, and only one of 16 forefathers is revealed. Thus someone seeking African roots could have DNA tests come back purely European, even though the person has largely African ancestors. "It's really dangerous to market a single locus as a statement of identity," says Emory's Wallace, who counsels patients with devastating genetic diseases. "I don't want to say to someone, 'I believe you're a Native American, but your mitochondria are European.'"

Indeed, few genetic genealogists will experience the same thrill as Adrian Targett, a schoolteacher in Cheddar, England, who discovered through DNA testing that he's a blood relative of Cheddar Man, a 9,000-year-old skeleton found in a nearby cave. But some people, those who seek answers to very specific questions, say they get their money's worth (box, "Genealogy by the Genes"). Doug Mumma, a 65-year-old retired nuclear physicist in Livermore, Calif., searched out strangers with his surname all over the world and paid $170 per sample to have their Y chromosomes tested. Many turned out to have no genetic link to Mumma, but he did locate several blood relatives in Germany. Mumma says, "To me it's cheap for what I want to do."

From *U.S. News & World Report*, January 29, 2001, pp. 34-41. © 2001 by U.S. News & World Report, L.P. Reprinted by permission.

Autism is likely to be linked to several genes

*Researchers are close to identifying several genes
that influence different aspects of autism.*

By Hugh McIntosh

Ever since a study revealed that if one identical twin had autism, the other was likely to have it too, researchers have been searching for genes that cause autism. Now, after 20 years of looking, scientists believe they're closing in on a handful of genes and chromosomal "hot spots" that may be responsible for different aspects of the disorder.

Identification of specific autism-related genes would reveal the proteins the genes produce—knowledge that will boost researchers' ability to diagnose autism and to discover more effective treatments for the disorder, which is characterized by communication problems, social impairment, and unusual or repetitive behaviors.

The discovery of such genes has been hampered by the complex nature of autism. Because the symptoms of people with autism vary dramatically in degree and form, researchers believe the condition might involve two or more of a large number of genes. In fact, a person with autism may have mutations in several of perhaps 20 possible genes. Thus, two people with the disorder might have mutations in two completely different sets of genes.

In the past two years, scientists have identified several candidate genes. Some might alter the effects on the brain of neurotransmitters, others might compromise the immune system enough to allow viral infections that may cause autism, and another may influence embryonic development of the nervous system.

Chromosome 15

Among the most promising findings, say experts, are reports that an autism gene may be on the long arm of chromosome 15, near the centromere—an indented point that holds the two sides of a chromosome together. This region is a well-known spot for genetic abnormalities, including duplications of parts of the chromosome's DNA. Short duplications cause no apparent harm. But

longer duplications are associated with about a 50 percent risk for autism.

Last year, the research team of child psychiatrist Edwin Cook, MD, of the University of Chicago, reported that the autism risk associated with longer duplications appears to come through the mother.

In the past two years, scientists have identified several candidate genes. Some might alter the effects on the brain of neurotransmitters, others might compromise the immune system enough to allow viral infections that may cause autism, and another may influence embryonic development of the nervous system.

Cook suspects that genes in this region of chromosome 15, which encode receptors for the neurotransmitter gamma-amino butyric acid (GABA), might be involved with autism. In fact, three genes for three GABA receptor subunits all are good candidates because they are associated with seizures and anxiety, which are common among autistic children, Cook says.

His team found moderately strong evidence for an association between one GABA subunit and autism—about one of every 70 children studied had a chromosome 15 duplication including this gene. Their study is published in the *American Journal of Human Genetics* (Vol. 62, No. 5, p. 1077–1083).

Duke University researchers say an autism gene might be a little farther away from chromosome 15's centromere, just beyond the GABA receptor genes. A genetic screening of about 50 families with autistic children turned up three positive markers in this area, says molecular geneticist John Gilbert, PhD. An autism susceptibility gene may lie between these markers and the GABA receptor genes. Exactly what that gene might do is still unknown.

To examine the link between chromosome 15 duplications and autism more closely, researchers at the University of California, Los Angeles, hope next year to launch a nationwide study of 100 children with these duplications. Researchers will look for molecular differences that might explain why half the people with this duplication have autism and half do not, says geneticist Carolyn Schanen, MD, PhD. They will also try to determine whether autistic children with this duplication are more likely to have severe language problems.

"In the kids that I know… it essentially wipes out language to have this extra piece," Schanen says. In the study, a psychologist will travel around the country to assess the children's phenotype, as well as to collect blood samples for genetic analysis.

A serotonin transporter gene?

Researchers have long found that many autistic persons have elevated blood levels of the neurotransmitter serotonin. This finding suggests that people with autism have a defect in the gene that produces serotonin transporter—a substance that sweeps serotonin from the space between two nerve cells, thus ending its effect on the cells.

In the general population, the transporter gene occurs in either a long or a short form. Last year Cook and his colleagues reported finding that children with autism inherited the short form more frequently than expected, based on typical inheritance patterns. This pattern of inheritance, called "preferential transmission," suggests that the gene is a susceptibility gene—one that plays a role in whether a person gets the disorder.

Research groups in France and Germany, however, found preferential transmission of the long form. Though conflicting, these results represent some of the stronger evidence to date for a genetic role in autism.

However, Yale University neurochemist George Anderson, PhD, says that, to him, the findings of the three studies suggest that the serotonin transporter gene may not be a susceptibility gene. Rather, it may be a "quantitative trait locus," which affects the degree of a genetic trait in someone who already has the disorder.

Cook agrees with that possibility but offers another explanation for the findings: The three samples studied may have contained different mixes of autism subtypes. The two other studies, he says, may have enrolled higher proportions of children referred for treatment of severe behavior problems such as aggression. In contrast, his group's sample contained a high proportion of people

referred for communication or socialization problems rather than severe behavior problems. To test this possibility, his group has begun collecting data about aggression in people in their sample.

Nervous-system genes

Another autism candidate gene may lie among the genes involved with early development of the nervous system. This idea emerged from a Swedish study of 100 people whose mothers had taken thalidomide during pregnancy.

The study found that five of the 15 people exposed to thalidomide during days 20 to 24 of gestation had autism, says embryologist Patricia Rodier, PhD, of the University of Rochester. This suggests that the damage leading to autism occurred during the development of the hindbrain, long before the cortex and other parts of the forebrain developed. These and other findings have led Rodier and her colleagues to look for mutations in several well-known developmental genes.

"If you have mutations in some of these genes that are critical in the early stages of the development of the nervous system, that in itself may be sufficient to cause the kinds of neuroanatomical changes that we think underlie autism," Rodier says. "But it could also be that that just makes you more sensitive to environmental agents at that time."

For example, the investigators hypothesize that embryonic environmental factors—such as the presence of thalidomide—may act during early embryonic development on the genes being studied.

Immune deficiency?

Gene-environment interaction is the idea behind another candidate autism gene, called C4B, on the short arm of chromosome 6. This gene produces complement C4 protein, which works with the antibody immunoglobulin A to fight viruses. Deficiencies in either of these substances reduce the immune system's ability to respond to viral infection.

"Autistic children are chronically ill, which is an indication that they have a deficiency in their immune system," says immunologist Roger Burger, PhD, at Utah State University in Logan.

Immune deficiency might contribute to some cases of autism by allowing a virus to damage the brain or trigger an auto-immune response that causes brain injury, Burger says. Damage might also occur in utero if the mother has an immune deficiency. People with autism have an unusually high frequency of a form of the C4B gene that produces no protein.

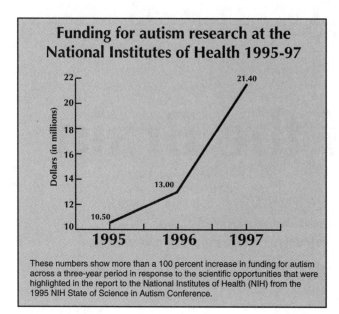

Funding for autism research at the National Institutes of Health 1995-97

These numbers show more than a 100 percent increase in funding for autism across a three-year period in response to the scientific opportunities that were highlighted in the report to the National Institutes of Health (NIH) from the 1995 NIH State of Science in Autism Conference.

ANGELA E. TERRY

Working together

While the University of Utah research team and others follow interesting leads, the National Institutes of Health (NIH) is funding five major collaborative groups to conduct genome screens of families with autism. Earlier this year, one of these consortiums reported in the journal *Human Molecular Genetics* (Vol. 7, No. 3, p. 571–578) that they'd found a hot spot on chromosome 7.

"We think it's a susceptibility gene," says geneticist Anthony Monaco, MD, PhD, of the University of Oxford. "But what gene… or what type of gene, we really have no idea." The suspect region includes genes expressed in the brain during development.

Supporting their finding is evidence from another collaborative group headquartered at Duke University. The researchers screened about 50 families and turned up "a number of interesting regions" on chromosome 7, says Duke geneticist Margaret Pericak-Vance, PhD.

A group at the University of Iowa has evidence for a link between autism and chromosome 13. The group is also exploring the idea that there is a broad autism phenotype that includes people with milder autism-like symptoms, as well as those with classic autistic disorder.

"We're seeing some pretty large pedigrees where there are maybe two autistic kids and an autistic first cousin, and then in between a lot of people who we think have the broad phenotype," says child psychiatrist Joseph Piven, MD. "These pedigrees… look more like single-gene disorders" than multigene disorders.

Although a single gene might explain autism in one family, the number of tantalizing prospects turning up from the genome screens suggests several genes are involved in autism, says Marie Bristol-Power, PhD, coordinator of the NIH autism network. She notes that the five collaborative groups together are expected to enroll more than 1,000 families with autistic children, generating plenty of statistical power to root out the genetics of this complex disorder.

Hugh McIntosh is a writer in Chicago.

From *APA Monitor*, November 1998, p. 13. © 1998 by the American Psychological Association. Reprinted by permission.

The Future of the Brain

The pairing of innovative technologies with scientific discoveries about the brain opens new ways of handling information, treating diseases, and possibly creating robots with human characteristics.

Norbert R. Myslinski

*For I dipp'd into the future,
far as human eye could see,
Saw the Vision of the world,
and all the wonder that would be.*

—*Alfred, Lord Tennyson*

An understanding of the brain helps us understand our nature. Over the course of evolution, the brain has acquired greater functions and higher consciousness. The reptilian brain, for instance, exerts control over vegetative functions, such as eating, sleeping, and reproduction. Development of the mammalian brain added the ability to express emotions. The human brain has the additional powers of cognition—such as reasoning, judgment, problem solving, and creativity. The latter functions, which are controlled by an area of the brain called the prefrontal cortex (located behind the forehead), distinguish us from other forms of life and represent the flower of our humanity. They have allowed us to re-create ourselves and decide our destiny.

Besides these long-term changes, our brains undergo short-term modifications during our lifetime. Not only does the brain control behavior, but one's behavior leads to changes in the brain, in terms of both structure and function. Subjective experiences play a major role in brain functions and the manifestation of one's mind, consciousness, and personal values. Thus the brain adapts to each individual's changing world.

Modern society and technology have given us the time, protection, and freedom to focus on the higher powers of the brain. As individual freedoms and the free enterprise system are extended around the world, we will see a continuing rise of innovative ventures and scientific exploration. In addition, our success at eliminating brain diseases and expanding brain functions will depend on the uniquely human characteristics of the brain. Given the finances and technology, we will need vision and creativity.

But modern technology also raises a number of questions about our future. For instance, how will the continuing information explosion challenge the powers of our brains? What does the next century have in store for us regarding memory drugs, brain surgery, brain regeneration, and other treatments for brain disorders? How will the relationships between mind and body or brain and machine evolve? More im-portant, are we prepared to handle such challenges, socially, psychologically, and ethically?

The Information Explosion

Information technologies have been increasingly successful in helping us acquire and communicate large new areas of knowledge. But the same success challenges the brain's capacity. How will the brain continue to cope with this information explosion? It will probably employ the same techniques it always has: filtering, organizing, and selective forgetting [see "Sherlock Holmes' Lesson," THE WORLD & I, June 2000, p. 316].

Our brains allow us to exert such uniquely human powers as reasoning, judgment, problem solving, and creativity—thereby guiding our own development and destiny.

Already, the brain filters out more than 99 percent of all sensory input before it reaches consciousness. In the future, it will be even more important to filter out the repetitive, boring, and unnecessary, and retain the novel, relevant, and necessary information. Actually, the brain is not good at remembering isolated facts but is great at organizing and associating thoughts and ideas. This ability will help it handle new information without suffering overload.

As the human genome is mapped, scientists hope to find cures for many genetically linked diseases, including those that affect the brain.

Just as important as the biology inside the brain is the technology outside. First with the introduction of books, and now computers, we have become increasingly reliant on artificial means of storing information. Thus the relative need for long-term (storage) memory in the brain and the time span for storage have decreased. As this trend continues, we will make greater use of our working memory and less use of our storage memory [see "Now Where Did I Put Those Keys?" THE WORLD & I, November 1998, p. 160].

Help for our memories may also come in the form of a pill. Research related to Alzheimer's disease has already produced a drug that can improve normal memory in small, healthy animals.

Furthermore, the rate at which we access and share information will most likely continue to accelerate. As a result, our brains will be challenged to think faster and make decisions more quickly. Anything less will be inefficient. Bureaucracy and red tape will be our enemies. We may be compelled to place greater emphasis on intuition and "gut feelings."

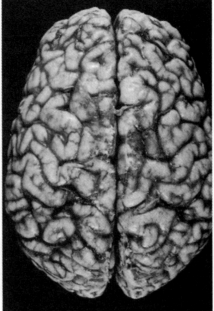

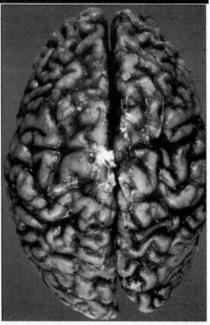

BOTH IMAGES COURTESY OF THE NATIONAL INSTITUTE OF NEUROLOGICAL DISORDERS AND STROKE/NIH

Convolutions in the brain of an Alzheimer's patient show considerable shrinkage (bottom) compared with those in a normal brain (top). Cures for Alzheimer's and other brain diseases may be found through such approaches as genetic engineering or neural cell regeneration.

Treating hereditary brain disorders

In living organisms, another type of memory occurs in the form of ge-

netic material known as DNA (deoxyribonucleic acid). It is the blueprint for the body and the chemical memory for traits that are passed down from generation to generation. The DNA representing the human genome (complete set of genetic information) consists of over 3 billion subunits (base pairs) and contains the coding for anywhere between 40,000 and 100,000 genes.

Scientists are already tackling the ambitious goal of determining the sequence of base pairs and mapping the genes of the entire human genome. Two groups—a publicly funded, international consortium (whose work is known as the Human Genome Project) and the private company Celera Genomics Corporation (based in Rockville, Maryland)—have just recently submitted "working drafts," with the promise of more detailed, high-quality results in the near future.

The human genetic map will help locate biomarkers for the diagnosis and treatment of hereditary disorders, including those affecting the brain. One type of treatment, known as gene therapy, is directed toward replacing defective genes with undamaged ones [see "Doctoring Genes to Beat Disease," THE WORLD & I, December 1997, p. 178]. But the many gene therapy trials conducted over the past 10 years have met with a low success rate, indicating the need for further refinements to the technique. In the meantime, a promising new strategy called *chimeraplasty*, in which the cell is stimulated to repair its own defective genes, has emerged [see "The Promise of Genetic Cures," THE WORLD & I, May 2000, p. 147]. Either approach may also be used to fight noninherited disorders by increasing the body's production of substances (such as interleukin or interferon) that protect the body.

The genetic information will probably lead to tests performed *in utero* or early in life to detect markers that suggest predispositions to such conditions as obesity and alcoholism, or such diseases as schizophrenia and Alzheimer's. People would then have the opportunity to get genetic counseling and design a lifestyle that integrates medical surveillance to stay healthy. At the same time, however, we need to improve our system of laws to prevent discrimination against people—particularly in employment and insurance coverage—based on this information. In February this year, President Clinton prohibited federal employers from requiring or requesting genetic tests as a condition of being hired or receiving benefits.

Environment and behavior can alter our brains; free will can influence our behavior.

Moreover, knowledge of a person's genotype (gene structure and organization) will not necessarily enable us to predict his phenotype (body structure), which is the manifestation of not only the genetic information but environmental influences and life experiences as well. The phenotype for a brain disease, for example, could range anywhere from no symptoms to total disability. Even identical twins are not 100 percent concordant for most brain disorders. The health and character of the human brain (and the rest of the body) are neither predetermined nor inevitable. Environment and behavior can alter our brains; free will can influence our behavior.

It is also possible that a treatment that alters one gene may affect many traits, even those that we do not wish to change. The same gene linked to a brain disorder might also influence intelligence or creativity. The risk involved in altering a gene is especially great for disorders associated with multiple genes.

Vaccines, drugs, surgery, and brain regeneration

We have grown up in a world of miracle drugs, but most alleviate just the symptoms. The next century will focus on prevention and cures. Scien-

tists are already working on oral vaccines that would attack the pathological plagues and tangles of Alzheimer's disease, decrease brain damage after a stroke or seizure, and lower the number of seizures in epileptics. We will be able to administer specific substances (called trophic factors) that will stimulate brain cells to multiply and replace cells degenerating because of brain diseases such as Parkinson's and Huntington's.

The trial-and-error method of finding effective drugs is now being replaced by the use of computers to design molecules that will precisely fit into specific receptors for the purpose of treating diseases. In the future, we will also be able to manufacture and use larger quantities of disease-fighting chemicals—such as interleukins, interferon, and brain trophic factors—that occur naturally in the body.

One strategy for making large quantities of specific antibodies is called the monoclonal antibody technique. Antibodies of a particular type are produced in large quantities by fusing the specific antibody-producing cells with tumor cells that grow and proliferate indefinitely. We could even piggyback drugs onto antibodies that target specific parts of the brain, thereby reducing the drug dosage and minimizing side effects.

Another approach currently being pursued is genetically engineering plants to produce pharmaceuticals. Until recently, efforts have been directed at protecting crops and improving their taste and nutritional value. About two dozen companies are now working to enhance the availability and lower the cost of drugs by genetically engineering plants to produce them. Some of the drugs may be ingested by simply eating the plant food.

With the improvement of brain imaging and robotics, brain surgery will improve and become less invasive. The brain is ideally suited for robotic surgery. It is enclosed in a firm skull that's appropriate for mounting instruments and provid-

ing fixed reference points by which to navigate the brain. Robotics and microscopic brain imaging will be used for higher precision, fewer mistakes, and minimally invasive surgical techniques.

On Being Human

According to futurist Alvin Toffler, the new millennium will challenge our understanding of what it means to be human. The fusion of computer technology, genetic engineering, and research on the brain will allow us to control our own evolution. For instance, electronic microchips may be placed in our brains to repair lost functions or create new ones. Scientists can now make microchips that are part organic. What about computers that are part protoplasm? When do we stop calling them machines and start calling them life?

There is currently a debate about the ethics of producing human clones or designer babies with "better" abilities. Can we also modify the genes of animals to give them human intelligence? Or can we create robots that take on human characteristics, such as human behavior or even self-replication? If so, should they be considered part human?

Whatever the answers may turn out to be, our differing views of what it means to be human are likely to polarize society because of conflicting causes taken up by political, religious, and scientific groups. We may experience a moral divide that could exceed that seen with slavery or abortion.

—*N.R.M.*

While pharmacological and surgical treatments improve, another approach that's gaining in importance is the regeneration of neural tissue. This approach has become possible because of recent research on stem cells and trophic factors, along with the discovery that adult brain cells can divide and multiply. Neural regeneration is the hope for those who suffer from such disorders as paralysis, Lou Gehrig's disease (amyotrophic lateral sclerosis), Down syndrome, retina degeneration, and Parkinson's disease.

The mind-body relationship

Charles Schultz, the beloved creator of Charlie Brown and author of the comic strip *Peanuts* for 50 years, died this year on the very day that his farewell strip was published. It was as if he stayed alive just long enough to see it end. Was that just a coincidence?

Warm, loving relationships, as well as isolation, can influence longevity and the will to live. How often have we heard of a person dying soon after his spouse dies? The body is not a biological machine operating independently of the mind. Even Hippocrates proposed that health was a balance of mind and body in the proper environment.

Robotics and microscopic brain imaging will be used for higher precision, fewer mistakes, and minimally invasive surgical techniques.

The mind has a powerful effect on our physical health by influencing our immune, cardiovascular, and endocrine systems. It can change the levels of such body substances as cortisol, adrenaline, and natural killer cells. Happy people get sick less often. Angry people have more health problems. Stress, anger, depression, and loneliness suppress the immune system, overexert the heart, raise blood pressure, enhance blood clotting, increase bone loss, harden the arteries, and increase cholesterol and abdominal fat. These factors can increase the incidence and severity of cancer, heart disease, stroke, arthritis, and even the common cold.

Western medicine, however, has underappreciated this mind-body relationship. Now that brain imaging can be used to observe the effect of the mind on the body, we will see the medical establishment embrace this concept as the basis of a legitimate form of therapy. Support groups, meditation, and relaxation therapy will be prescribed to ward off disease and dampen its devastating effects.

Research has shown that people who derive strength and comfort from religion live healthier and longer lives [see "Is Religion Good for Your Health?" THE WORLD & I, February 1996, p. 291]. The benefits of religion go beyond social contact or the encouragement of healthier habits. It can be a mechanism to help cope with life and stressful situations. Faith in a Higher Being has been shown to be an important part of the successful Twelve Steps program of Alcoholics Anonymous—a program that has been extended to treat other addictions, such as gambling and overeating [see "Spirituality in Healing," THE WORLD & I, May 2000, p. 153]. Doctors will use it to increase the compliance of patients with the treatments prescribed for a wide range of acute and chronic medical problems.

People get better because they believe they will. This is called the placebo effect. A patient's belief that he is receiving effective medicine will alleviate his symptoms. The stronger his belief, the stronger the relief. This effect has been known and used by doctors for many years. It must be taken into account when testing new medicines and therapies.

The placebo effect is based on the brain's ability to anticipate the future and prepare for it. For example, the brain analyzes trajectories of objects in motion and predicts their future location, or it analyzes environmental temperatures and predicts the body's future temperature. Also, our senses are notorious for seeing what we hope to see and tasting what we expect to taste. The brain produces a placebo effect by stimulating cells

and releasing hormones that start the healing process in anticipation of getting better.

Brain Doctors

Technology will enable drugs to be more selective and surgeries to be more exact. But what about the doctors? How will they change? Their early training will involve greater use of virtual reality and less use of animals. They will emphasize prevention and cure rather than the treatment of symptoms. They will have to be genetic counselors and focus on the whole person rather than symptoms. They must put humanity back into medicine.

Today's neurologists tend to be technicians more than healers. They are trained primarily to diagnose and fix defective brains. Their success is determined by how effective they are at minimizing symptoms, restoring functions, and curing diseases. Although most patients are grateful, many find the doctor's help to be insufficient or lacking. Substituting a side effect for a symptom, or prolonging a life of pain and distress, may not be an improvement in the patient's quality of life.

In addition, the psychological and spiritual needs of the patient often go unattended. Patients need someone to appreciate their distress and relate to them on a human level. Recognizing these needs, medical education is now increasing its emphasis on treating the whole person. Doctors are realizing that the way to a healthy body is through the mind.

—*N.R.M.*

The brain-machine connection

Over the past century, we have aided our vision and hearing with lenses and amplifiers. During the next century, we will probably replace eyes and ears with light and sound detectors and computer chips that send signals to the brain.

Every year, the International NAISO Congress on Information Science Innovations holds a Robot Soccer Competition. Winners are those who create robots that can "see" with greater acuity, "think" more perceptively, and move faster and with greater agility. Software companies are already making advertising claims that their programs can "think." Will molecular electronics and nanotechnology, combined with genetic engineering, give us the power to create sentient robots?

We need to find ways to understand consciousness and how the brain is involved in the powers of reasoning, creativity, and love.

If so, a modern-day Pandora's box is being opened. Unlike scientific breakthroughs of the past, the robots and engineered organisms of the future could have the potential for self-replication. While the uncontrolled replication of mischievous programs on the Internet—as seen with the "Melissa" and "I Love You" viruses—can cause a lot of damage, the uncontrolled replication of sentient robots may pose a threat to our humanity. Will this evolution come suddenly, like the news about cloning the first mammal, or gradually, so that we will get used to it? Or will modern-day Luddites have the courage and foresight to say no and steer us in another direction?

We began the twentieth century looking at the brain's structure through a simple microscope and ended by examining its functions with such techniques as PET (positron emission tomography) and

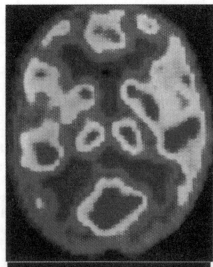
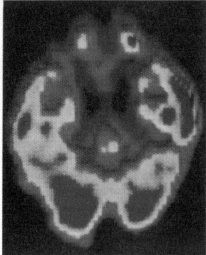

COURTESY OF THE NATIONAL INSTITUTE OF NEURO-LOGICAL DISORDERS AND STROKE/NIH

Just as current PET scans (above) reveal general activity in the brain, future techniques may show microscopic details Top: The brain of a young man listening intently to a story uses a great deal of glucose in the auditory cortex (gray areas near the ears). Bottom: An image at a different level of the same brain shows activity in the hippocampus (gray spots at short distances in from the sides), where short-term learning is converted to long-term memory.

MRI (magnetic resonance imaging). We went through the stages of neuroanatomy, neurophysiology, and neurochemistry. We learned how the brain controls movement and processes sensory information. We scratched the surface in our attempts to clarify intelligence and emotions. Among the challenges of the new century will be to find ways to understand consciousness and how the brain is involved in the powers of reasoning, creativity, and love.

Speculating about the future, however, is daunting, even for experts. In a 1987 survey, medical scientists predicted that by the year 2000 we would probably have a cure for two-thirds of all cancers, AIDS would be eliminated, and coronary bypass surgery would be replaced by less invasive techniques.

Distinguishing between fact and fiction is difficult even today. On the first day of my neuroscience course in graduate school, our instructor told us that half of what he would teach us that semester would eventually prove to be wrong—the problem was, he could not tell which half was wrong. Since then, I have repeatedly witnessed the truth of that statement. Revisions of our knowledge will continue in the twenty-first century. We must keep testing our view of the world, and if it fails, replace it with a better one. We must remain flexible in our beliefs, just as our brains remain flexible in their structure and function.

Norbert R. Myslinski is associate professor of neuroscience at the University of Maryland and director of Maryland Brain Awareness Week.

This article appeared in the August 2000 issue of *The World & I*, pp. 152-159. *The World & I* is a publication of The Washington Times Corporation. © 2000.

THE BIOLOGY OF *Joy*

Scientists are unlocking the secrets of pleasure— and discovering what poets already knew

By Jeremiah Creedon

Pleasure, like fire, is a natural force that from the beginning humans have sought to harness and subdue. We've always sensed that pleasure is somehow crucial to life, perhaps the only tangible payoff for its hardships. And yet many have discovered that unbridled pleasure can also be dangerous, even fatal. Since ancient times, philosophers and spiritual leaders have debated its worth and character, often comparing it unfavorably to its more stable sibling, happiness. No one, however, saint or libertine, has ever doubted which of the pair would be the better first date.

Happiness is a gift for making the most of life. Pleasure is born of the reckless impulse to forget life and give yourself to the moment. Happiness is partly an abstract thing, a moral condition, a social construct: The event most often associated with happiness, some researchers say, is seeing one's children grow up to be happy themselves. How nice. Pleasure, pure pleasure, is a biological reflex, a fleeting "reward" so hot and lovely you might sell your children to get it. Witness the lab rat pressing the pleasure bar until it collapses. Or the sad grin of the crack addict as the molecules of mountain shrub trip a burst of primal gratitude deep in a part of the human brain much like a rat's. Both know all too well that pleasure, uncaged, can eat you alive.

Some scientists claim they're close to knowing what pleasure is, biologically speaking. Their intent is to solve the riddle of pleasure much as an earlier generation unleashed the power of the atom. Splitting pleasure down to its very molecules will have many benefits, they say, including new therapies for treating drug abuse and mental illness. Others note that research on the biology of pleasure is part of a wider trend that's exploding old ideas about the human brain, if not the so-called "Western biomedical paradigm" in general, with its outmoded cleaving of body from mind.

The assumption is that somehow our lives will be better once this mystery has been unraveled. Beneath that is the enduring belief that we can conquer pleasure as we've conquered most everything else, that we can turn it into a docile beast and put it to work. That we've never been able to do so before, and yet keep trying, reveals a lot about who we are, as creatures of a particular age—and species.

Of all the animals that humans have sought to tame, pleasure most resembles the falcon in its tendency to revert to the wild. That's why we're often advised to keep it hooded. The Buddha warned that to seek pleasure is to chase a shadow; it only heightens the unavoidable pain of life, which has to be accepted. Nevertheless, most have chosen to discover that for themselves. The early Greek hedonists declared pleasure the ultimate good, then immediately began to hedge. Falling in love, for instance, wasn't really a pleasure, given the inevitable pain of falling out of it. The hedonists thought they could be masters of pleasure, not its slaves; yet their culture's literature is a chronicle of impetuous, often unspeakable pleasures to be indulged at any cost.

When the Christians crawled out of the catacombs to make Rome holy, they took revenge on pagan pleasure by sealing it in—then pretended for centuries not to hear its muffled protests. Eclipsed was the Rose Bowl brilliance of the Roman circus, where civic pleasure reached a level of brutal spectacle unmatched until the advent of *Monday Night Football*. Pleasure as a public function seemed to vanish.

The end of the Dark Ages began with the Italian poet Dante, who, for all his obsession with the pains of hell, endures as one of the great, if ambivalent, students of pleasure. His *Inferno* is but a portrait of the enjoyments of his day turned inside out, like a dirty sock. For every kind of illicit bliss possible in the light of the world above, Dante created a diabolically fitting punishment in his theme-park hell below. We can only guess what terrible eternity he has since devised for his countryman, the pleasure-loving Versace, felled in what Dante would have considered the worst of ways—abruptly, without a chance to confess his sins. At the very least he's doomed to wear Armani.

Sensuous LIKE ME

How I got back in my body through my nose

Some mornings my head is like a little dog panting, whimpering, and straining at his leash. *Let's go, let's go, let's go!* My head gets me up and leads me around all day. Sometimes it's dinnertime before I remember that I have a body.

And the idea that this body can give me pleasure—well, that's a really hard one. I used to think that because I read hip French books about sexual ecstasy I had somehow escaped my Calvinist heritage—the idea that the body is shameful and only a narcissistic lazybones would pay any attention to it. No such luck. My version of Calvinist body-denial was compulsive reading, and the more I read about French people's ecstasies, which are usually pretty cerebral anyway—the more I hid out from my own body. A body that, let's face it, is plumper, paler, and more easily winded than I would prefer.

Falling in love changed things. Intimacy with a woman who was learning to accept and even love her body gave me new eyes to see (and new nerve endings to feel) my own. I started—just started—to think of my body as a means of communication with the world, not a sausage case for Great Thoughts. I wanted to go further.

It was my wife who found Nancy Conger, professor of the five senses. A slender young woman with apparently bottomless reserves of energy and optimism, she lives in an old farmhouse in western Wisconsin, plays the violin, and teaches people how to get out of debt, simplify their lives, and use their senses for entertainment and joy. She even teaches a one-night class called "Sensuous Living." Laurie and I enrolled.

A class in sensuousness. An idea not without irony, amazing that we actually have to study this stuff. Five perfectly sensible-looking adults perched on plastic chairs in a drab little classroom in Minneapolis, with Nancy presiding in a sleeveless black jumpsuit. On two tables toward the front: nasturtiums in a vase, a strip of fur, a piece of sandpaper, a twig, a violin, a seashell.

"Lick your forearm," said Nancy, "and smell yourself."

Lick my forearm and smell myself?

I looked around me. The matronly woman in the purple blouse and matching shoes was licking her forearm. So was the shy, 40ish guy with the salt-and-pepper beard, and the thin, Italian-looking young woman with the big braid. Finally, feeling uncomfortably canine, I licked myself. I sniffed ("Little, short sniffs, like perfumers use," said Nancy). Hmm. A faintly metallic aroma. Sniff, sniff. Beneath it, something breadlike.

Like a wine, I had a bouquet.

Then Nancy got us out of our chairs to wander around and "smell what doesn't seem to have a smell." I put my nose right up next to a big pad of paper on an easel. Faint wheaty aroma like my school tablets in fifth grade. All the sunshiny, chalk-dusty, gentle boredom of elementary school came back, like a tune.

A brick gave off a mysterious musty tang, charged with the past. A quarter smelled sour, a metal door bitter and somehow sad.

"Smell detours right around your thinking brain, back to the limbic system at the bottom of the brain, where memory is," Nancy told us. She also explained that smell can be hugely improved, made more subtle and precise, if you keep sniffing. "Smell dishes. Smell clothes. Smell everything," she exhorted.

I did want to keep on smelling, but we were on to a trust-and-touch experiment. We paired off (I went with the big-braid woman) and took turns blindfolding and leading each other. I put my partner's hand on a brick, a door, a seashell, a twig.

Then I put on the blindfold (it smelled powdery and lusciously feminine), and she led me. Without any visual clues to tell me what things were supposed to feel like, I met each surface with a small thrill of tactile freshness. A metal door, I discovered, was studded with sharp little grains. A twig was as rough as sandpaper, and the sandpaper itself practically made me jump out of my skin. With most of the objects, I enjoyed a few wonderful seconds of pure sensation before the thinking brain clicked in and gave the thing a name. But click in it did; and that's when the magic ended.

The evening concluded with experiments in sound (Nancy played her violin very near each of us so we could feel the vibration in our bodies) and taste (we passed around a loaf of focaccia), but as we drove home I was still hung up on the smell and touch thing.

My nose, which I had mostly used as a passive receiver of pretty large and often alarming signals (skunk crushed on an Iowa road, underarms needing immediate attention, and so on) felt amazingly discriminating, having actually sniffed the difference between a door and a quarter. My fingers still tingled with the thrill of sandpaper and brick and (blessed relief!) fur.

The part of my head that names, makes distinctions, and is vigilant against stupidities pointed out that five middle-class white folks in a certain demographic had just spent three hours rubbing, if not exactly gazing at, their navels.

The honorable side of my Calvinism (as a kid I lived on Calvin Avenue in Grand Rapids, Michigan, just down the street from Calvin College) bridled at the idea of stroking my nerve endings like some French decadent poet, while an entire society—an entire world—splits along economic fault lines.

A third part of me rejoiced: I had discovered the cleverest answer yet to television. It was the exquisite entertainment technology of a body—my body. Anyone's body. It is—or could be—an immediate rebuke and alternative to the technologies of consumerism, which coarsen, obscure, jack up, deny, extend beyond reason, and in general do numbing violence to the subtle, noble equipment for receiving the joys of life that we were all issued at birth.

Anyone can sniff a leaf or reach out to the rough bark of a tree. Anyone can listen for a little while to the world. And anyone can do it now, at the kitchen table, in the schoolroom, at the racetrack, in the hospital bed. And we can keep doing it until we believe again in the wondrous beauty of our own equipment (absolutely no amplification from Sony required).

—Jon Spayde

Dante's ability to find a certain glee in the suffering of others—not to mention in the act of writing—goes to the heart of the problem of pleasure. Let's face it: Pleasure has a way of getting twisted. Most people, most of the time, are content with simple pleasures: a walk on the beach, fine wine, roses, cuddling, that sort of thing. But pleasure can also be complicated, jaded, and sick. The darker aspects of pleasure surely lie dormant in many of us, like the Minotaur in the heart of the labyrinth waiting for its yearly meal of pretty flesh. In the words of the Mongol ruler Genghis Khan, "Happiness lies in conquering one's enemies, in driving them in front of oneself, in taking their property, in savoring their despair, in outraging their wives and daughters." He meant pleasure, of course, not happiness—but *you* tell him.

In the Age of Reason, the vain hope that humans could reason with pleasure returned. Thinkers like Jeremy Bentham took up the old Greek idea of devising a "calculus" of pleasure—complex equations for estimating what pleasure really is, in light of the pain often caused by the quest for it. But the would-be moral engineers, rational to a fault, found the masses oddly attached to the older idea of pleasure being a simple sum of parts, usually private parts. As for the foundlings thus multiplied, along with certain wretched venereal ills, well, who would have figured?

The first "scientists of mind" were pretty sure that the secrets of pleasure, and the emotions in general, lay locked beyond their reach, inside our heads. Throughout the 19th century, scientists could only speculate about the human brain and its role as "the organ of consciousness." Even more galling, the era's writers and poets clearly speculated so much better—especially those on drugs.

Two of them, Samuel Taylor Coleridge and Thomas De Quincey, both opium addicts, also may have been early explorers of the brain's inner geography. Images of a giant fountain gushing from a subterranean river in Coleridge's most famous poem—"Kubla Khan; or, A Vision in a Dream" bear an odd resemblance to modern models of brain function, especially brains steeped in mind-altering chemicals. Writing in *The Human Brain* (BasicBooks, 1997), Susan A. Greenfield, professor of pharmacology at Oxford University, describes the "fountainlike" nerve-cell structures that arise in the brain stem and release various chemical messengers into the higher brain areas. As Greenfield notes, and Coleridge perhaps intuited, these geysers of emotion are "often the target of mood-modifying drugs."

De Quincey describes a similar terrain in *Confessions of an English Opium Eater (1821)*. He even suggests that the weird world he envisioned while he was on the drug might have been his own fevered brain projected, a notion he fears will seem "ludicrous to a medical man." Not so. Sherwin B. Nuland, National Book Award winner and clinical professor of surgery at Yale, expresses an updated version of that concept in *The Wisdom of the Body* (Knopf, 1997). In Nuland's view, we may possess an "awareness" distinct from rational thought, a kind of knowledge that rises up from our cells to "imprint itself" on how we interpret the world. "It is by this means that our lives… and even our culture come to be influenced by, and are the reflection of, the conflict that exists within cells," he writes.

Maybe De Quincey really could see his own brain. Maybe that's what many artists see. Think of Dante's downward-spiraling hell, or the Minotaur in the labyrinth, even the cave paintings at Altamira and Lascaux. The first known labyrinth was built in Egypt nearly 4,000 years ago, a convoluted tomb for both a pharaoh's remains and those of the sacred crocodiles teeming in a nearby lake. It's an odd image to find rising up over and over from the mind's sunless sea, of subterranean passages leading ever deeper to an encounter with… the Beast. In an age when high-tech imaging devices can generate actual images of the brain at work, it's intriguing to think that artists ventured to the primordial core of that process long ago. And left us maps.

Today, Paul D. MacLean, National Institute of Mental Health scientist and author of *The Triune Brain in Evolution* (Plenum, 1990), describes a similar geography. He theorizes that the human brain is "three-brains-in-one," reflecting its "ancestral relationship to reptiles, early mammals, and recent mammals." Peter C. Whybrow, director of the Neuropsychiatric Institute at UCLA, uses this model to explain what he calls "the anatomical roots of emotion." Writing in *A Mood Apart* (BasicBooks, 1997), his study of depression and other "afflictions of the self," Whybrow notes: "The behavior of human beings is more complicated than that of other animals… but nonetheless we share in common with many creatures such behaviors as sexual courtship, pleasure-seeking, aggression, and the defense of territory. Hence it is safe to conclude that the evolution of human behavior is, in part, reflected in the evolution and hierarchical development of other species."

Deciphering the code of art into the language of modern science took most of two centuries. One discipline after another tried to define what feelings like pleasure were, and from where they arose, only to fall short. Darwin could sense that emotions were important in his evolutionary scheme of things, but he was limited to describing how animals and humans expressed them on the outside, using their bodies, especially faces. William James, in a famous theory published in 1884, speculated that the brain only translates various sensations originating below the neck into what we think of as, say, joy and fear. Others saw it the other way around—emotions begin in the brain and the bodily reactions follow. Without knowing what pleasure actually is, Freud could see that the inability to feel it is a kind of disease, or at least a symptom, that he traced to (you guessed it) neurotic conflict.

By then, though, many people were fed up with all the talking. The study of mind had reached that point in the movie where the gung-ho types shove aside the hostage negotiator and shout, *"We're going in."* And with scalpels drawn, they did. In 1872, Camillo Golgi, a young doctor working at a "home for incurables" in an Italian village, discovered the basic component of brain tissue, the neuron. During the 1920s, German scientist Otto Loewi, working with frog hearts, first identified neurotransmitters: chemical messengers that carry information across the gap between the neurons—the synapse—to receptors on the other side. Meanwhile, the Canadian neurosurgeon Wilder Penfield, operating on conscious patients with severe epilepsy, managed to trigger various emotions and dreamlike memories by electrically stimulating their brains. Such work gave rise to the idea that various mental functions might be "localized" in particular brain areas.

In 1954, psychologists James Olds and Peter Milner made a remarkable breakthrough—by accident. While researching the

THE NEW *Pleasure* PRINCIPLE

This just in: Pain is not the route to happiness

Don't worry. Be happy.

The philosophy is simple, but living it is not, especially in our achievement-oriented society. According to Los Angeles-based therapist Stella Resnick, that's because we focus on the pain in our lives—getting through it, around it, or over it. Pleasure, the "visceral, body-felt experience of well-being," is a better path to growth and happiness, she contends in her book *The Pleasure Zone* (Conari Press, 1997). If only we knew how to feel it.

Resnick had to learn, too. Her childhood was unpleasant; her father left when she was 5, and, for 10 years, she endured beatings from her stepfather. She hung out on street corners and dated a gang leader. By age 32, she'd had two brief marriages and was involved in another stormy relationship. Although she'd built a successful San Francisco therapy practice, she was lonely and miserable. Nothing helped: not yoga, nor meditation, nor exercise, nor a vegetarian diet. "I was a very unhappy young woman," she recalls. "I'd had the best therapy from the best therapists, but even with all the work I had done on myself, something was missing."

What was missing, she discovered, was the ability to enjoy herself. At 35, after she lost her mother to cancer, she moved to a small house in the Catskill Mountains, where she lived alone for a year and, for the first time, paid attention to what felt good. At first she cried and felt sorry for herself. But by year's end, she was dancing to Vivaldi and the Temptations, and finding creativity in cooking and chopping wood.

She soon realized that most of her patients shared the same pleasure deprivation. "Our whole society diminishes the value of pleasure," she writes. "We think of it as fun and games, an escape from reality—rarely a worthwhile end in itself. Amazingly, we don't make the connection between vitality—the energy that comes from feeling good—and the willingness to take pleasure in moment-by-moment experience."

Therapy too often concentrates on pain and what the mind thinks; Resnick focused on pleasure and what the body feels. But when she first published her ideas in 1978, epithets were hurled: "narcissist," "hedonist," "icon for the Me Decade." It wasn't until research on the positive effects of pleasure and the negative effects of stress began to accumulate in the '80s that people became more receptive. "This is not about creating a society of me-first people,"

she says of her work. "There's no joy in hoarding all the goodies for our lonesome."

To help people understand pleasure, Resnick divides it into eight "core" categories: primal (the feeling of floating); pain relief (being touched and soothed); elemental (childlike laughter, play, movement, and voice); mental (the fun of learning); emotional (the feeling of love); sensual (the five senses, plus imagination); sexual (arousal, eroticism, orgasm); and spiritual (empathy, morality, and altruism).

Her prescription is body-based and simple. Listen to a fly buzz. Float on your back. Tell a dream. Her number-one tip for falling and staying in love is… breathe. Conscious breathing enhances relationships, she claims, because it allows us to let go in sweet surrender, rather than fighting or resisting ourselves or each other.

Experiencing pleasure opens the body, releasing enormous energy, says Resnick. Ironically, this flow is what scares us, causing us to tense up and shut down, because we don't know what to do with it. We can miss the healing power of great sex, for example, by wanting to release the energy as soon as we get turned on. She advises allowing the excitement to build and circulate so that "it's something you feel in your heart. And in your big toes."

Repressing one's desire for pleasure was once considered virtuous, a sign of moral superiority. But Resnick questions whether it's good to continue in that vein. "We have poor race relations, poor man-woman relations, whole segments of society that have problems with parents and institutions," she says. "Could we do better if we enjoyed our relationships more, if people knew how to encourage and inspire themselves instead of being motivated by shame, guilt, and other negative emotions?"

Resnick doesn't advocate always succumbing to immediate gratification—there's pleasure in yearning—or fear and anger, which can inform and protect us. But using negative means to pursue positive ends simply doesn't work. "The secret to success in all things—business, creativity, art, relationships, family, spirituality—is to be relaxed during challenging times," she says. "Don't hold yourself in, or brace yourself for what might go wrong." And if you don't get it at first, don't worry. Even Resnick has to remind herself to breathe.

—*Cathy Madison*

---

alerting mechanism in rat brains, they inadvertently placed an electrode in what they soon identified as a rat's pleasure-and-reward center: the so-called limbic system deep inside the brain. When the rats were later wired in a way that let them press a lever and jolt themselves, they did so as many as 5,000 times an hour.

This became the basis for current research on the "biology of reward." Scientists like Kenneth Blum have linked what they call reward deficiency syndrome to various human behavioral disorders: alcoholism, drug abuse, smoking, compulsive eating and gambling. Blum traces these disorders to genetically derived flaws in the neurotransmitters and receptors now associated with pleasure, including the pathways tied to the brain

chemicals serotonin and dopamine, and the endorphins. Other researchers aren't so sure.

We all know by now that endorphins are the "body's own natural morphine." The discovery of endorphins in the early '70s marked the start of what some have declared the golden age of modern neuroscience. The impact was clear from the beginning to Candace B. Pert, whose work as a young scientist was crucial to the discovery. A few years earlier, she had helped identify the receptors that the endorphins fit into, as a lock fits a key, thus popping the lid of pleasure. According to Pert, "it didn't matter if you were a lab rat, a First Lady, or a dope addict—everyone had the exact same mechanism in the brain for creating bliss and expanded consciousness." As she recounts in

Molecules of Emotion (Scribner, 1997), her early success led to a career at the National Institute of Mental Health identifying other such messenger molecules, now known as neuropeptides.

Pert's interest in the natural opiates soon took her into uncharted territory—sexual orgasm. Working with Nancy Ostrowski, a scientist "who had left behind her desire to become a nun and gone on instead to become an expert on the brain mechanisms of animal sex," Pert turned her clinical gaze on the sexual cycle of hamsters. "Nancy would inject the animals with a radioactive opiate before copulation, and then, at various points in the cycle, decapitate them and remove the brains," Pert writes. "We found that blood endorphin levels increased by about 200 percent from the beginning to the end of the sex act." She doesn't say what happened to their own endorphin levels while they watched—but Dante has surely kept a log.

Modern students of pleasure and emotion have their differences. Pert, for instance, having worked so much with neuropeptides, doesn't buy the idea that emotions are localized in certain brain areas. "The hypothalamus, the limbic system, and the amygdala have all been proposed as the center of emotional expression," she writes. "Such traditional formulations view only the brain as important in emotional expressivity, and as such are, from the point of view of my own research, too limited. From my perspective, the emotions are what link body and mind into bodymind."

This apparent reunion of body and mind is, in one sense, Pert's most radical conjecture. And yet, oddly, it's the one idea that many modern researchers do seem to share, implicitly or otherwise, to varying degrees. Most would agree that the process of creating human consciousness is vastly complex. It is also a "wet" system informed and modulated by dozens of neurochemical messengers, perhaps many more, all moving at incredible speeds. Dare we call it a calculus? Not on your life. Any analogy of the brain that summons up a computer is definitely uncool. For now.

There also seems to be a shared sense, not always stated, that some sort of grand synthesis may be, oh, 20 minutes away. In other words, it's only a matter of time before the knowledge of East and West is melded back into oneness, a theory that reunifies body and mind—and, as long as we're at it, everything else. That may be. But given that a similar impulse seems so prevalent throughout the culture, could it be that what we're really seeing is not purely science, but a case of primal yearning, even wishful thinking? A generation of brilliant scientists, their sensibilities formed in the psychedelic '60s, could now be looking back to the vision of mystical union they experienced, or at least heard about over and over again, in their youth. Perhaps they long to reach such a place, abstract though it is, for the same reason a salmon swims to the placid pool where its life began. We, like all creatures, are driven by the hope of an ultimate reward, a pleasure that has no name, a pleasure that in fact may not be ours to feel. Thus, we never conquer pleasure; pleasure conquers us. And for its own reasons, both wondrous and brutal.

None of which makes the alleged new paradigm any less real. As the poets of our day, for better or worse, the modern scientists of mind have already shaped our reality with their words and concepts. Who hasn't heard of the endorphin-driven runner's high, or traced a pang of lover's jealousy to their reptilian brain? On *Star Trek Voyager*, a medical man of the future waves his magic wand over a crewmate emerging from a trance and declares, "His neuropeptides have returned to normal!"

You didn't have to be a Darwin to see that the news gave Captain Janeway a certain... pleasure.

Jeremiah Creedon is a senior editor of Utne Reader.

From *Utne Reader*, November/December 1997, pp. 66–71, 106. © 1997 by Jeremiah Creedon. Reprinted by permission.

The Tick-Tock of the Biological Clock

Biological clocks count off 24-hour intervals in most forms of life. Genetics has revealed that related molecular timepieces are at work in fruit flies, mice and humans

by Michael W. Young

You have to fight the urge to fall asleep at 7:00 in the evening. You are ravenous at 3 P.M. but have no appetite when suppertime rolls around. You wake up at 4:00 in the morning and cannot get back to sleep. This scenario is familiar to many people who have flown from the East Coast of the U.S. to California, a trip that entails jumping a three-hour time difference. During a week long business trip or vacation, your body no sooner acclimatizes to the new schedule than it is time to return home again, where you must get used to the old routine once more.

Nearly every day my colleagues and I put a batch of *Drosophila* fruit flies through the jet lag of a simulated trip from New York to San Francisco or back. We have several refrigerator-size incubators in the laboratory: one labeled "New York" and another tagged "San Francisco." Lights inside these incubators go on and off as the sun rises and sets in those two cities. (For consistency, we schedule sunup at 6 A.M. and sundown at 6 P.M. for both locations.) The temperature in the two incubators is a constant, balmy 77 degrees Fahrenheit.

The flies take their simulated journey inside small glass tubes packed into special trays that monitor their movements with a narrow beam of infrared light. Each time a fly moves into the beam, it casts a shadow on a phototransistor in the tray, which is connected to a computer that records the activity. Going from New York to San Francisco time does not involve a five-hour flight for our flies: we simply disconnect a fly-filled tray in one incubator, move it to the other one and plug it in.

We have used our transcontinental express to identify and study the functions of several genes that appear to be the very cogs and wheels in the works of the biological clock that controls the day-night cycles of a wide range of organisms that includes not only fruit flies but mice and humans as well. Identifying the genes allows us to determine the proteins they encode—proteins that might serve as targets for therapies for a wide range of disorders, from sleep disturbances to seasonal depression.

The main cog in the human biological clock is the suprachiasmatic nucleus (SCN), a group of nerve cells in a region at the base of the brain called the hypothalamus. When light hits the retinas of the eyes every morning, specialized nerves send signals to the SCN, which in turn controls the production cycle of a multitude of biologically active substances. The SCN stimulates a nearby brain region called the pineal gland, for instance. According to instructions from the SCN, the pineal rhythmically produces melatonin, the so-called sleep hormone that is now available in pill form in many health-food stores. As day progresses into evening, the pineal gradually begins to make more melatonin. When blood levels of the hormone rise, there is a modest decrease in body temperature and an increased tendency to sleep.

The Human Clock

Although light appears to "reset" the biological clock each day, the day-night, or circadian, rhythm continues to operate even in individuals who are deprived of light, indicating that the activity of the SCN is innate. In the early 1960s Jürgen Aschoff, then at the Max Planck Institute of Behavioral Physiology in Seewiesen, Germany, and his colleagues showed that volunteers who lived in an isolation bunker—with no natural light, clocks or other clues about time—nevertheless maintained a roughly normal sleep-wake cycle of 25 hours.

More recently Charles Czeisler, Richard E. Kronauer and their colleagues at Harvard University have determined that the human circadian

THE BASICS

THE BIOLOGICAL CLOCK
THE AUTHOR ANSWERS SOME KEY QUESTIONS

Where is the biological clock? In mammals the master clock that dictates the day-night cycle of activity known as circadian rhythm resides in a part of the brain called the suprachiasmatic nucleus (SCN). But cells elsewhere also show clock activity.

What drives the clock? Within individual SCN cells, specialized clock genes are switched on and off by the proteins they encode in a feedback loop that has a 24-hour rhythm.

Is the biological clock dependent on the normal 24-hour cycle of light and darkness? No. The molecular rhythms of clock-gene activity are innate and self-sustaining. They persist in the absence of environmental cycles of day and night.

What role does light play in regulating and resetting the biological clock? Bright light absorbed by the retina during the day helps to synchronize the rhythms of activity of the clock genes to the prevailing environmental cycle. Exposure to bright light at night resets circadian rhythms by acutely changing the amount of some clock-gene products.

How does the molecular clock regulate an individual's day-night activity? The fluctuating proteins synthesized by clock genes control additional genetic pathways that connect the molecular clock to timed changes in an animal's physiology and behavior.

rhythm is actually closer to 24 hours—24.18 hours, to be exact. The scientists studied 24 men and women (11 of whom were in their 20s and 13 of whom were in their 60s) who lived for more than three weeks in an environment with no time cues other than a weak cycle of light and dark that was artificially set at 28 hours and that gave the subjects their signals for bedtime.

They measured the participants' core body temperature, which normally falls at night, as well as blood concentrations of melatonin and of a stress hormone called cortisol that drops in the evening. The researchers observed that even though the subjects' days had been abnormally extended by four hours, their body temperature and melatonin and cortisol levels continued to function according to their own internal 24-hour circadian clock. What is more, age seemed to have no effect on the ticking of the clock: unlike the results of previous studies, which had suggested that aging disrupts circadian rhythms, the body-temperature and hormone fluctuations of the older subjects in the Harvard study were as regular as those of the younger group.

As informative as the bunker studies are, to investigate the genes that underlie the biological clock scientists had to turn to fruit flies. Flies are ideal for genetic studies because they have short life spans and are small, which means that researchers can breed and interbreed thousands of them in the laboratory until interesting mutations crop up. To speed up the mutation process, scientists usually expose flies to mutation-causing chemicals called mutagens.

The first fly mutants to show altered circadian rhythms were identified in the early 1970s by Ron Konopka and Seymour Benzer of the California Institute of Technology. These researchers fed a mutagen to a few fruit flies and then monitored the movement of 2,000 of the progeny, in part using a form of the same apparatus that we now use in our New York to San Francisco experiments. Most of the flies had a normal 24-hour circadian rhythm: the insects were active for roughly 12 hours a day and rested for the other 12 hours. But three of the flies had mutations that caused them to break the pattern. One had a 19-hour cycle, one had a 28-hour cycle, and the third fly appeared to have no circadian rhythm at all, resting and becoming active seemingly at random.

Time Flies

In 1986 my research group at the Rockefeller University and another led by Jeffrey Hall of Brandeis University and Michael Rosbash of the Howard Hughes Medical Institute at Brandeis found that the three mutant flies had three different alterations in a single gene named *period*, or *per*, which each of our teams had independently isolated two years earlier. Because different mutations in the same gene caused the three behaviors, we concluded that *per* is somehow actively involved both in producing circadian rhythm in flies and in setting the rhythm's pace.

After isolating *per*, we began to question whether the gene acted alone in controlling the day-night cycle. To find out, two postdoctoral fellows in my laboratory, Amita Sehgal and Jeffrey Price, screened more than 7,000 flies to see if they could identify other rhythm mutants. They finally found a fly that, like one of the *per* mutants, had no apparent circadian rhythm. The new mutation turned out to be on chromosome 2, whereas *per* had been mapped to the X chromosome. We knew this had to be a new gene, and we named it *timeless*, or *tim*.

But how did the new gene relate to *per*? Genes are made of DNA, which contains the instructions for making proteins. DNA never leaves the nucleus of the cell; its molecular recipes are read out in the form of messenger RNA, which leaves the nucleus and enters the cytoplasm, where proteins are made. We used the *tim* and *per* genes to make PER and TIM proteins in the laboratory. In collaboration with Charles Weitz of Harvard Medical School, we observed that when we mixed the two proteins, they stuck to each other, suggesting that they might interact within cells.

In a series of experiments, we found that the production of PER and TIM proteins involves a clock-like feedback loop. The *per* and *tim* genes are active until concentrations of their proteins become high

CLOCKS EVERYWHERE
THEY ARE NOT JUST IN THE BRAIN

Most of the research on the biological clocks of animals has focused on the brain, but that is not the only organ that observes a day-night rhythm.

Jadwiga Giebultowicz of Oregon State University has identified PER and TIM proteins—key components of biological clocks—in the kidneylike malpighian tubules of fruit flies. She has also observed that the proteins are produced according to a circadian cycle, rising at night and falling during the day. The cycle persists even in decapitated flies, demonstrating that the malpighian cells are not merely responding to signals from the insects' brains.

In addition, Steve Kay's research group at the Scripps Research Institute in La Jolla, Calif., has uncovered evidence of biological clocks in the wings, legs, oral regions and antennae of fruit flies. By transferring genes that direct the production of fluorescent PER proteins into living flies, Kay and his colleagues have shown that each tissue carries an independent, photoreceptive clock. The clocks even continue to function and respond to light when each tissue is dissected from the insect.

And the extracranial biological clocks are not restricted to fruit flies. Ueli Schibler of the University of Geneva showed in 1998 that the *per* genes of rat connective-tissue cells called fibroblasts are active according to a circadian cycle.

The diversity of the various cell types displaying circadian clock activity suggests that for many tissues correct timing is important enough to warrant keeping track of it locally. The findings might give new meaning to the term "body clock."—*M.W.Y.*

---

enough that the two begin to bind to each other. When they do, they form complexes that enter the nucleus and shut down the genes that made them. After a few hours enzymes degrade the complexes, the genes start up again, and the cycle begins anew.

Moving the Hands of Time

Once we had found two genes that functioned in concert to make a molecular clock, we began to wonder how the clock could be reset. After all, our sleep-wake cycles fully adapt to travel across any number of time zones, even though the adjustment might take a couple of days or weeks.

That is when we began to shuttle trays of flies back and forth between the "New York" and "San Francisco" incubators. One of the first things we and others noticed was that whenever a fly was moved from a darkened incubator to one that was brightly lit to mimic daylight, the TIM proteins in the fly's brain disappeared—in a matter of minutes.

Even more interestingly, we noted that the direction the flies "traveled" affected the levels of their TIM proteins. If we removed flies from "New York" at 8 P.M. local time, when it was dark, and put them into "San Francisco," where it was still light at 5 P.M. local time, their TIM levels plunged. But an hour later, when the lights went off in "San Francisco," TIM began to reaccumulate. Evidently the flies' molecular clocks were initially stopped by the transfer, but after a delay they resumed ticking in the pattern of the new time zone.

In contrast, flies moved at 4 A.M. from "San Francisco" experienced a premature sunrise when they were placed in "New York," where it was 7 A.M. This move also caused TIM levels to drop, but this time the protein did not begin to build up again because the molecular clock was advanced by the time-zone switch.

We learned more about the mechanism behind the different molecular responses by examining the timing of the production of *tim* RNA. Levels of *tim* RNA are highest at about 8 P.M. local time and lowest between 6 A.M. and 8 A.M. A fly moving at 8 P.M. from "New York" to "San Francisco" is producing maximum levels of *tim* RNA, so protein lost by exposure to light in "San Francisco" is easily replaced after sunset in the new location. A fly traveling at 4 A.M. from "San Francisco" to "New York," however, was making very little *tim* RNA before departure. What the fly experiences as a premature sunrise eliminated TIM and allows the next cycle of pro-

duction to begin with an earlier schedule.

Not Just Bugs

Giving flies jet lag has turned out to have direct implications for understanding circadian rhythm in mammals, including humans. In 1997 researchers led by Hajime Tei of the University of Tokyo and Hitoshi Okamura of Kobe University in Japan—and, independently, Cheng Chi Lee of Baylor College of Medicine—isolated the mouse and human equivalents of *per*. Another flurry of work, this time involving many laboratories, turned up mouse and human forms of *tim* in 1998. And the genes were active in the suprachiasmatic nucleus.

Studies involving mice also helped to answer a key question: What turns on the activity of the *per* and *tim* genes in the first place? In 1997 Joseph Takahashi of the Howard Hughes Medical Institute at Northwestern University and his colleagues isolated a gene they called *Clock* that when mutated yielded mice with no discernible circadian rhythm. The gene encodes a transcription factor, a protein that in this case binds to DNA and allows it to be read out as messenger RNA.

Shortly thereafter a fly version of the mouse *Clock* gene was isolated, and various research teams began to introduce combinations of the *per, tim* and *Clock* genes into mammalian and fruit fly cells. These experiments revealed that the CLOCK protein targets the *per* gene in mice and both the *per* and *tim* genes in flies. The system had come full circle: in flies, whose clocks are the best understood, the CLOCK protein—in combination with a protein encoded by a gene called *cycle*—binds to and activates the *per* and *tim* genes, but only if no PER and TIM proteins are present in the nucleus. These four genes and their proteins constitute the heart of the biological clock in flies, and with some modifications they appear to form a mechanism governing circadian rhythms throughout the animal kingdom, from fish to frogs, mice to humans.

Recently Steve Reppert's group at Harvard and Justin Blau in my laboratory have begun to explore the specific signals connecting the mouse and fruit fly biological clocks to the timing of various behaviors, hormone fluctuations and other functions. It seems that some output genes are turned on by a direct interaction with the CLOCK protein. PER and TIM block the ability of CLOCK to turn on these genes at the same time as they are producing the oscillations of the central feedback loop—setting up extended patterns of cycling gene activity.

An exciting prospect for the future involves the recovery of an entire system of clock-regulated genes in organisms such as fruit flies and mice. It is likely that previously uncharacterized gene products with intriguing effects on behavior will be discovered within these networks. Perhaps one of these, or a component of the molecular clock itself, will become a favored target for drugs to relieve jet lag, the side effects of shift work, or sleep disorders and related depressive illnesses. Adjusting

BODY CHANGES OVER 24-HOUR PERIOD

1:00 A.M.
- Pregnant women are most likely to go into labor.
- Immune cells called helper T lymphocytes are at their peak.

2:00 A.M.
- Levels of growth hormones are highest.

4:00 A.M.
- Asthma attacks are most likely to occur.

6:00 A.M.
- Onset of menstruation is most likely.
- Insulin levels in the bloodstream are lowest.
- Blood pressure and heart rate begin to rise.
- Levels of the stress hormone cortisol increase.
- Melatonin levels begin to fall.

7:00 A.M.
- Hay fever symptoms are worst.

8:00 A.M.
- Risk for heart attack and stroke is highest.
- Symptoms of rheumatoid arthritis are worst.
- Helper T lymphocytes are at their lowest daytime level.

Noon
- Level of hemoglobin in the blood is at its peak.

3:00 P.M.
- Grip strength, respiratory rate and reflex sensitivity are highest.

4:00 P.M.
- Body temperature, pulse rate and blood pressure peak.

6:00 P.M.
- Urinary flow is highest.

9:00 P.M.
- Pain threshold is lowest.

11:00 P.M.
- Allergic responses are most likely

to a trip from New York to San Francisco might one day be much easier.

Further Information

THE MOLECULAR CONTROL OF CIRCADIAN BEHAVIORAL RHYTHMS AND THEIR ENTRAINMENT IN *DROSOPHILA*. Michael W. Young in *Annual Review of Biochemistry*, Vol. 67, pages 135–152; 1998.

MOLECULAR BASES FOR CIRCADIAN CLOCKS. Jay C. Dunlap in *Cell*, Vol. 96, No. 2, pages 271–290; January 22, 1999.

TIME, LOVE, MEMORY: A GREAT BIOLOGIST AND HIS QUEST FOR THE ORIGINS OF BEHAVIOR. J. Weiner. Alfred Knopf, 1999.

A tutorial on biological clocks—including ideas for home and classroom activities—can be found on the National Science Foundation's Science and Technology Center for Biological Timing's site at http://cbt4pc.bio.virginia.edu/tutorial/TUTORIALMAIN.html on the World Wide Web.

MICHAEL W. YOUNG is a professor and head of the Laboratory of Genetics at the Rockefeller University. He also directs the Rockefeller unit of the National Science Foundation's Science and Technology Center for Biological Timing, a consortium that connects laboratories at Brandeis University, Northwestern University, Rockefeller, the Scripps Research Institute in La Jolla, Calif., and the University of Virginia. After receiving a Ph.D. from the University of Texas in 1975, Young took a postdoctoral fellowship at the Stanford University School of Medicine to study gene and chromosome structure. In 1978 he joined the faculty of Rockefeller, where members of his research group have isolated and deciphered the functions of four of the seven genes that have been linked to the fruit fly biological clock.

Reprinted with permission from *Scientific American*, March 2000, pp. 64–71. © 2000 by Scientific American, Inc. All rights reserved.

Into the Zone

The kind of mental conditioning that makes athletes into superstars also helps ordinary folks become extraordinary

By Jay Tolson

Sometimes you have to kill the thing you love. Pop-psych 101? To be sure. But Tiger Woods's Shermanesque march through the 2000 U.S. Open at Pebble Beach gave new force and meaning to the phrase. It's not just that Woods mowed down some of his nearest and dearest competitors, though that he certainly did. Nor is it only that he brought one of his favorite courses–and one of golf's hardest–to its knees. He also seemed to subdue the game itself: to beat it into submission.

"Kill them," Kultida Woods used to say when her young son went off to face the competition. It was oddly predatory counsel coming from a Thai-born mother who at other times imparted Buddhist wisdom about inner peace. But if Woods was ever confused by these seemingly dissonant messages, he didn't show it at the Open. He killed 'em, every one, with almost transcendent calm, posting the biggest margin of victory in the history of golf's four "major" annual tournaments. "He's so focused every time," said an amazed Ernie Els, who tied for a distant second place. "That hunger for winning a major championship, it's like 110 percent. To be honest with you, I don't feel like that every week when I'm playing. He's just differ-

ent. I'm not sure there's a lot of players out here like that."

Focus. Control. Flow. In the zone. Think of any other synonym for mental mastery, and it applies to the level of play that Woods achieved in the Open. And while this state of internal calm and power has different names, it boils down to this: When the body is brought to peak condition and the mind is completely focused, even unaware of what it's doing, an individual can achieve the extraordinary.

But this is not a game of chance. Psychologists and physiologists say ordinary people can achieve this state by inducing changes in physiology, including brain-wave patterns and even heart rates, through focusing and relaxation techniques. These might include breathing exercises or using verbal cues or developing rituals (bouncing the ball exactly three times before you take the foul shot). It also might involve visualizing successful outcomes before you make the swing or jump shot, without thinking about the mechanics of the action. The "stay in the present" focus that enables Woods to sink almost routinely those deadly 8- and 10-foot putts for par came in part from what his father, Earl Woods–his best personal sports psychol-

ogist–taught him about having a mental picture of the ball rolling into the hole.

Today, Americans of all stripes are using mental conditioning not just as a means to a better golf swing but also to make them better corporate competitors, more creative artists, and, some argue, better human beings. "When you're in the zone, it's so quiet, it's so peaceful," says Harriet Ross, a potter from Hartsdale, N.Y., who uses the lessons of Zen to relax and focus. Julio Bocca, who has been a ballet prodigy since he was 4 years old in Argentina, worried about a decline as his 30s approached. Instead, he has been dancing to acclaim around the world–an achievement reached, he believes, through mental focus.

Winning a high-speed car race or coming out on top in a corporate takeover isn't just a matter of skill; it's also about how people handle pressure. The intangible factor, not knowing who's going to buckle or who's going to hit the last-second field goal, is what makes these pursuits exciting–or terrifying. The same week that Woods breezed through the Open, for example, Yankee second baseman Chuck Knoblauch, who has become phobic about routine throws, made three errors in a single game. Golfer John Daly, whose physical gifts nearly match

Woods's, took 14 strokes on Pebble Beach's 18th hole and quit the Open after the first round.

Many athletes speak of choking as a failure to be "in the zone." That state is not unlike the "flow" defined by the Hungarian-American psychologist Mihaly Csikszentmihalyi. He began his career-long interest in the early 1960s studying a group of artists for his thesis on creativity. Struck by how so many became oblivious to their surroundings while they worked, he went on to investigate whether other activities and even jobs produced such absorption, such flow. What he found was that any pursuit was an "autotelic activity" if the doing, and not the goal, was the end in itself and if it involved such things as intense concentration, clarity of goals, quick feedback, and a fine balance of skills and challenges. Which is what works for Bocca. "When I do a solo–that's the moment you have to be 100 percent there– my mind is just in the character. I've been doing this for so many years, I don't have to think about what to do with my body. I don't think 'now is my pirouette, now is my jump.'"

Practitioners of Zen, yoga, and many Eastern forms of martial arts have experienced the truth behind these principles without having had them explained scientifically, as Csikszentmihalyi and other proponents of flow-and-peak states well realize. Indeed, the scientists have learned a great deal from those and other premodern disciplines. Folklore about the mental dimension of sport is as old as the games themselves, but the scientific study of that dimension did not begin until the late 19th century, primarily in Germany and France. Throughout most of the first half of the 20th century, researchers concentrated on the description of the character types and personalities of athletes and paid almost no attention to performance. A rare exception was German psychiatrist Johannes Heinrich Schultz (1884–1970), who developed "autogenic training," a form of self-hypnosis that was supposed to boost relaxation. Yet not even Schultz believed that his research into the links between emotional and bodily states should serve to enhance athletic performance.

The coaches of the East bloc nations, including East Germany, are often cred-

---

IN FINE FETTLE
Braving the 'bod pod'

ORLANDO—At LGE Performance Systems, the road to an "ideal performance state" starts with a 75-question survey: Are you pessimistic? Competitive? Do you think "me" or "we"? Self-introspection alone isn't enough: The questionnaire must also be completed by five people who know you best—a coach, say, or a secretary.

That heavy navel-gazing comes before you even arrive at the sprawling training camp. Which is good, because at LGE, it doesn't matter who you are—fine physical specimen of a professional football player, flabby *Fortune* 500 executive, or hard-bodied housewife. Everyone here is poked, prodded, and rebuilt from the outside in by an infuriatingly fit, impossibly relaxed team of psychologists, physiologists, trainers, and nutritionists. The three-day program, which runs around $4,000, begins with a battery of high-tech exams, including the terrifying "bod pod," an egg-shaped contraption that gauges body-fat percentage.

The goals here come straight from basic psychology: to unearth who you really are, to decide who you want to be, and to take action. Clients are taught to alternate periods of intense stress with periods of relaxation or release, in fitness and in life. "In the corporate world, people are trained to be linear," says Terry Lyles, a resident clinical psychologist. "They start the day and don't take breaks." He explains that an emotional and mental shift down—a rolling pattern as opposed to a straight line—will allow executives to come back and be totally refreshed.

"Last year, my mind was a barrier; it was holding me back," says Adrienne Johnson, 26, a guard for the Orlando Miracle, the local WNBA team, who found herself warming the bench all last season. She started working with LGE, and this season she's a starter, averaging 30 minutes a game—and double-digit points.
—*Carolyn Kleiner*

---

ited with being the first to use psychology to supercharge their athletes. (Sports historian John Hoberman contends this is largely a Cold War myth, based partly on a desire of Western observers to see athletes from communist countries as programmed robots.) The perception that psychology lay behind the success of East bloc athletes prompted curiosity in the West–and even, according to some leading American sports psychologists, a desire to venture into the field themselves.

Such was at least partly the case with Jim Loehr. Founder of a leading sports and motivational training center, LGE Performance Systems, in Orlando, Fla., Loehr began his career in the early 1970s as the head of a mental health center in southern Colorado. But the experience of successfully treating two professional athletes–albeit "under the cover of darkness"–changed his plans. It was not long before he decided to launch his own sports psychology practice in Denver, a decision greeted by derision from his peers.

Holy Grail. Some of the challenges he faced continue to plague the field. Prominent among them was Americans' tendency to associate psychology with the treatment of weakness or disorders, even though Loehr was concerned with improving performance, not in administering therapy. Undaunted, Loehr developed his own version of the peak performance state that has come to be the Holy Grail of the larger American sports psychology industry–the "ideal performance state" (IPS), he prefers to call it, or "mental toughness."

"The mind and the body are one," says Loehr. "Mental toughness is not just something you can sit in a room and visualize and all of a sudden you're mentally tough. The ability to handle physical stress takes us right into the ability to handle mental and emotional stress."

The center that he founded in Orlando in the early 1990s quickly became a mecca for a wide assortment of people who have one thing in common: the desire to be the best they can possibly be. Last week, for example, you could find retired tennis champ Jim Courier (getting in shape for his new career as a commentator), a dozen executives from Macy's department store, a 600-pound sumo wrestler, and various amateur athletes wandering the LGE grounds (box, Braving the 'bod pod'). They came to improve their performance on the playing field, in the boardroom, or in life in general–and what they got is an intense workout for both the mind and the muscles.

"When there's no time left on the clock, you're 2 points down and on the foul line, what is that person thinking about before they shoot the shot? If they have one mental thought that says, 'If I miss this shot we lose'… within moments, they are secreting negative brain chemistry," says Terry Lyles, LGE psychologist. It's all about taking yourself out of the moment, he explains, about using rituals to transport yourself before the shot or point. "They have to go from the mental side to tap into the emotional side next, which takes them to the physical part, which will be to shoot the foul shot. They've shot thousands of foul shots, but the issue is not shooting the foul shot, the issue is screaming fans, no time on the clock, and your whole team is looking for you to perform. The issue is focus."

"All of corporate America has its own form of stress, the same way the athlete has stress," says Rudy Borneo, vice chairman of Macy's West, who was visiting LGE last week. "It's really how you use that stress, how you build a format to make it positive rather than negative, how you can turn it into a growth factor."

Tony DiCicco became head of the U.S. Women's World Cup soccer team in 1994; a year later, he hired sports psychologist Colleen Hacker. He knew that coaches often talk about the importance of the mental game but rarely give it time commensurate with its importance. He is certain that hiring Hacker strengthened both individual and team performance. DiCicco points out that he is not alone in a growing appreciation of the value of sports psychologists: The U.S. Olympic team had only one in 1988, but it had 100 by 1996. There are now over 100 academic programs specializing in sports psychology, at least three academic journals, and over 1,000 members listed by the Association for the Advancement of Applied Sports Psychology. And elite professional and amateur teams and athletes seem to be increasingly using their services.

The business. These specialists are taking the lessons of great athletes and coaches and shaping them into techniques that aspiring peak performers can learn to use. Sports Publishing Inc. of Champaign, Ill., whose books discuss how athletes get in the zone, plans to release 112 titles this year, about double last year's number. In the past few years, Simon & Schuster has published and reissued such titles as *Golf is a Game of Confidence* and *Executive Trap: How to Play Your Personal Best on the Golf Course and On the Job*. Many professional sports teams have psychologists on call, but that's a largely reactive, therapeutic approach. But another approach is spreading. Baseball's Cleveland Indians have a three-man performance-enhancement program that costs about $300,000 a year and deserves some credit for five straight American League Central Division titles since 1995, two of which led to World Series appearances.

Bob Troutwine, a psychologist in Liberty, Mo., has helped 18 NFL teams decide which players to recruit and how to use them. In 1998, Troutwine urged the Indianapolis Colts to draft Tennessee's Peyton Manning over another quarterback with similar statistics, Washington State's Ryan Leaf. A personality test showed that Manning was confident, but not brash, and Troutwine liked the fact that he was the son of former NFL quarterback Archie Manning. Troutwine was vindicated: Manning did well with the Colts, and Leaf, who was drafted by the San Diego Chargers, has flailed as a quarterback, insulted fans, and wants to leave the team. "In general you want competitive players," says Troutwine, who also consults for such corporate clients as Ford Motor Co. and Sprint Co., "but if a team is in a building phase, a hypercompetitive player may not handle losing very well."

The trend in hiring sports psychologists has yet to trickle down to the lower levels of sport, according to Albert J. Figone of California's Humboldt State University. But that's in large part because coaches view motivation and the mental game as their prerogative, even if they usually give it too little attention. Stanford University's Jim Thompson, director of the Positive Coaching Alliance, thinks it's absurd to use this stuff on kids. "All the sports psychology in the world isn't going to help the average kid unless he has tremendous skills as well," Thompson points out. "The danger is that parents might think, gee, if I could get my kid a good sports psychologist, he could be Tiger Woods. Well, no."

Kid stuff. But back in Orlando, Neil Clausen is on the court for his daily tennis lesson, nailing one perfect backhand after another. Just 10 years old, this pint-size player already has a clear idea of his goals ("I'm here because I'm trying to go to Wimbledon") and an even more pronounced conception of what it's going to take to get there: "I need to work on my racket preparation, but things like concentration are very important [too]. I see players throwing their racket around… and I just don't think it really works, I don't think its very nice." His mother brings him to LGE six days a week. "We will go to matches and whether it's professionals or 12-year-olds, you have some incredible athletes, physically blessed people, who are just not able to pull it off during a match, all because their mental strength lets them down, or they couldn't focus, or they got distracted," she says. Neil is a quick study. In a pretend match, in between points, he quietly, solemnly goes through his own rituals: He adjusts strings on his racket, for one thing, and works on his breathing.

In an interview last year with *Psychology Today*, Richard Suinn, who in 1972 became the first sports psychologist to serve on the U.S. Olympic sports medicine team, listed the mental skills that modern sports psychology focuses on, including "stress management, self-regulation, visualization, goal setting, concentration, focus, even relaxation." Sound good? It's clear why so many who are outside sports respond to what sports psychology offers. "If you attack work, family, spiritual life the way you attack a game, it all works the same way," says Peter Cathey, chief operating officer of XPO Network Inc., a start-up interactive marketing company. Cathey has faced several challenges recently–moving across the country to start a new company, dealing with his mother's death, and putting his father in the hospital. But he says he's never felt more mentally fit, thanks to skills acquired at LGE. "There's no emotional hit in the face I can't deal with."

"If Tiger goes out to play and doesn't take a good relaxing breath or relax once in two hours, then that tension shows up as a bogey," explains stay-at-home mother Caryn Rohrbaugh, of Lemoyne, Pa. Rohrbaugh went through LGE so that she could perform better in the home and enjoy her time there. "For me, two hours of not taking a breath, not eating right, not being in the right mind-set turns up as impatience, forgetting to schedule something, a general feeling of being overwhelmed. It's still a bogey, though."

There is no question that the mental toughness developed by world-class athletes has pulled them through trials off the playing field as well as on–another reason why so many people are drawn to the peak performance ideal. Perhaps no sport is more mentally demanding than competitive cycling, and champion Lance Armstrong demonstrated some of the mental grit he acquired over years of fierce competitive racing by struggling back from testicular cancer. Diagnosed with the disease in 1996, he not only survived the surgery and debilitating chemo treatments but came back to win the Tour de France in 1999, a story recounted in his book, *It's Not About the Bike*.

The most honest, articulate, and (not coincidentally) influential specialists will tell you forthrightly that they are drawing on the collective wisdom of the best proven minds in the field–the great coaches of past and present. Many of them are or have been coaches themselves, and most are athletes, former or active. Bob Rotella, former director of the sports psychology program at the University of Virginia and now a full-time consultant to golf professionals and other athletes, says that so much of the formal psychology that he read in graduate school focused on dysfunction and problems that he "turned to people like Vince Lombardi or [UCLA's] John Wooden and studied their philosophies."

Rotella has taught what he calls "learned effectiveness" for years, which means, he says, "teaching about being in the best state of mind, basing your thinking on where you want to go, not where you've been." Doing so, Rotella found himself in strong sympathy with the work of at least one theoretical psychologist, the great turn-of-the-century thinker William James. James, whose work is making a strong comeback these days because of its emphasis on the conscious mind and the will, spoke clearly to Rotella. "He seemed to fit with what I learned from the coaches." That might sound like a dubious distinction to some intellectuals, but James probably would have taken it as a compliment. The power of the mind to shape reality was one of his lasting beliefs.

Just as James is the quintessential American thinker for having created a serious philosophy of human potential, so the best sports psychologists, and not just Rotella, extend that philosophy in popular form, often in an eloquent popular literature that includes books by Rotella himself (many written with Bob Cullen) and such modern classics as Michael Murphy's *Golf in the Kingdom*.

Obsession. Proponents of peak performance see it as laudably consistent with the American dream of self-betterment and the pursuit of happiness. "To me, pursuing excellence is why we came to America," says Rotella. But John Hoberman, a University of Texas professor who has written often about the dehumanization of sports, sees the emphasis on performance as part of the contemporary obsession with competitiveness, an obsession that crowds out other human and civilized values, "including," he says, "moderation and balance."

But do critics like Hoberman ignore the possibility that peak performance might entail leading a richer, more balanced life, one that can allow more attention to others, including family, friends, and community? Being in the zone or the flow may be in fact a supremely human value, particularly if it is, as many sports psychologists contend, a state in which our peak capacities are exercised almost without thinking. After all, competition is a reality that cannot be wished away; why not learn to manage it as best as one can? As Woods commented after he'd won, "I had a–a weird feeling this week–it's hard to describe–a feeling of tranquillity, calmness."

Csikszentmihalyi, who now directs the Quality of Life Research Center at Claremont Graduate University, sees peak performance state as a concept or ideal that can approach his notion of flow, but only with difficulty. "In my work," he explains, "I'm trying to understand how to make life better as it goes. The question is, why are you experiencing the peak performance state–for its own sake or in order to win? If winning, the goal, takes over, the pleasure of the doing fades."

In other words, if the peak performance state becomes merely an instrument, its resemblance to true flow will vanish. But there is no guarantee, of course, that this will not happen in any discipline or undertaking that one pursues, whether it be the making of pottery in the spirit of Zen or the playing of the piano in the spirit of the heck of it. When and if peak performance ceases to be the kind of activity that another quintessential American, Robert Frost, writes about in his poem "Two Tramps in Mud Time," then it might well become a lesser thing. Listen to the poet describe the state that he aimed for, and consider its possible relevance to our peak performance culture:

> But yield who will to their separation,
> My object in living is to unite
> My avocation and my vocation
> As my two eyes make one in sight.
> Only where love and need are one,
> And the work is play for mortal stakes,
> Is the deed ever really done
> For Heaven and the future's sakes.

With Carolyn Kleiner and David L. Marcus

From *U.S. News & World Report*, July 3, 2000, pp. 38–45. © 2000 by U.S. News & World Report, L.P. Reprinted by permission.

MindoverMedicine

Diseases and disorders are hardly ever "all in your head," but often, the power to heal is. Howard Brody, M.D., Ph.D., reveals how we can tap into our "inner pharmacy" to stay healthy and recover more rapidly from illness

By Howard Brody, M.D., Ph.D.

We begin and end with a mystery—a mystery of healing. So it seems appropriate to lead off with a riddle: What do the following people have in common?

Albert consults his physician about a bothersome cold. Because the condition is viral, his doctor knows antibiotics won't help. But Albert—a bit of a hypochondriac—is sure the cold is turning into pneumonia, although it shows no medical signs of doing so, and he pleads for antibiotics. His physician writes him a prescription for what he says is a potent antibiotic. In reality, it is a simple sugar pill—100% medically ineffective. Yet once Albert begins taking the "antibiotic," his cold disappears almost overnight.

Beatrice, who strongly believes in herbal remedies, purchases a new and much-touted organic food supplement at a health food store. After taking it for several weeks, she feels considerably more energized—despite the lack of any recognized scientific evidence that the supplement can physiologically affect the body.

Charles develops cancer and undergoes the standard surgery and chemotherapy. As he believes strongly in the healing powers of the mind, he also begins practicing meditation, thinking positive thoughts and forgiving all the people against whom he harbored grudges. He also stops blaming himself for contracting the disease, realizing it was a bad break but hardly his fault. Not only does he feel better and enjoy life more, he also remains in remission after several years.

Just what is it that Albert, Beatrice and Charles have in common? At first glance, you'd probably say, "Nothing at all." Not me. I'd suggest, by contrast, that it's that mysterious phenomenon of the mind working in tandem with the body to enhance healing: the placebo response. What I mean by that phrase is that when a certain set of circumstances are present, ill persons seem to improve greatly in what at first seems an inexplicable way.

The placebo response occurs when we receive certain types of messages or signals from the environment around us. These messages work in some fashion, at some level, to alter the meaning of our state of health or illness. What does the body do with these messages? The best way to summarize what science has taught us about the placebo response is to visualize an "inner pharmacy," which we all possess.

Our bodies are capable of producing many substances which can heal a wide variety of illnesses, and make us feel generally healthier and more energized. When the body simply secretes these substances on its own, we have what is often termed "spontaneous healing." Some of the time, our bodies seem slow to react, and a message from outside can serve as a wake-up call to our inner pharmacy. The placebo response can thus be seen as the reaction of our inner pharmacies to that wake-up call— the message of new meaning.

One of the most often-repeated stories about the placebo response is a case reported by a colleague to Dr. Bruno Klopfer and published by Klopfer in 1957. As a single incident, it must be interpreted with skepticism; but the facts are so intriguing, it's difficult to discount. Klopfer's colleague was the personal physician of a patient, known as "Mr. Wright," who was suffering from cancer of the lymph system and had developed large tumors throughout his body that could easily be felt by his doctors.

At the time, a group of physicians was studying a new chemical formula called krebiozen, which was being widely touted by the media as a miracle cure for cancer— although the medical establishment was less convinced. Wright's cancer was so far advanced that the physicians gave him the drug only as a compassionate exception— not because they expected any response. What happened next truly seemed like a miracle. Wright gained weight, looked and felt better, and his tumors shrank so drastically, they could hardly be detected.

Wright's improvement continued until newspapers began reporting krebiozen was not the great advance they had thought. After reading the negative coverage, Wright became discouraged, immediately began to lose weight, and his tumors grew once more.

Assuming that the power of suggestion had been largely responsible for Wright's response to the medication, the physicians decided to tell him that the first batches of krebiozen had not been at full potency. The lab had corrected the problem, they assured him, and the new, stronger batch of the drug would soon be on its way. They continued to encourage Wright's hopes, finally announcing that the big day was here—the new batch of the drug had arrived. They then proceeded to give Wright injections just as before—using sterile water.

Wright showed the same dramatic improvements that had occurred with the krebiozen. His remission lasted until, for a second time, the newspapers undermined the physicians—stating unequivocally, "AMA reports that krebiozen is worthless against cancer." Mr. Wright once again began to sink, his tumors grew massive, and shortly thereafter, he died.

THE FLIP SIDE OF THE COIN

What happens when a sick person like Mr. Wright attaches a negative rather than a positive meaning to the attempt at treatment? This negative mindset can be so strong, it's been given its own name: the nocebo response.

One of the more compelling case reports of the nocebo response was recorded by renowned cardiologist Dr. Bernard Lown.

Early in his career, Dr. Lown was working under a very distinguished senior cardiologist, who in turn was taking care of a woman, Mrs. S., with a non-life-threatening heart valve condition called tricuspid stenosis. She also suffered from a mild degree of congestive heart failure, which was successfully controlled with medication. At the time of the precipitating event, Mrs. S. was in the hospital to have some tests done, and was in her usual stable condition.

One day, the senior cardiologist came into her room, accompanied by a bevy of residents, interns and medical students. The group talked among themselves—excluding her from their conversation. Before turning on their heels and filing out of the room, the senior physician announced, "This woman has TS"—employing an abbreviation for tricuspid stenosis.

Dr. Lown came back shortly thereafter and was stunned to find Mrs. S. anxious, frightened and breathing very rapidly. Her lungs, which had been perfectly clear, now displayed the most crackling noises in the lower portions which portended worsening of the congestive heart failure. When Lown asked Mrs. S. what was the matter, she replied, "That doctor said I was going to die for sure."

Lown protested that his senior couldn't possibly have made such a statement. "I heard him," Mrs. S. replied firmly. "He said I had TS. I know that means 'terminal situation.' You doctors never tell us the truth straight out. But I know what he meant."

> ## After a heart patient thought she heard doctors say she would die—she did—later that same day, despite the total lack of evidence that anything had changed in her heart condition.

Despite Lown's attempts to clear up the misunderstanding, Mrs. S. continued to slide into progressively worse heart failure, despite the total lack of objective evidence that anything fundamental had changed in her underlying heart condition. She passed away later that same day.

Historically, medicine first discovered the effect of symbolic significance on health by seeing improvement in patients who were given bread pills, sugar pills or other dummy medicines that could exert only a symbolic power. Today, we need not be limited by that history. We realize that virtually every time a healer administers a treatment to a person with an illness, or every time an individual treats herself for an illness with some healing substance or process, he or she receives messages from the environment that may trigger a placebo response.

By defining our terms in such a way that the placebo response does not depend in any way on administering placebos, we have cleared the path for completely ethical, nondeceptive communications between the healer and the patient.

In terms of deception, physicians had assumed for centuries that if sugar pills worked, they could work only because the patient did not know what they really were. No one could conceive of handing a patient sugar pills, saying, "This is a bottle of sugar pills," and still see the patient get better.

Two psychiatrists, Lee Park and Lino Covi, decided in the early 1960s to study truth-telling in the use of placebos. They were doing research on psychiatric patients who suffered from what at the time was generally termed "neurosis." The patients had quite a number of different bodily symptoms which were thought to be part of their condition, and Park and Covi were using a detailed symptom checklist to keep track of total symptoms over time. The authors used the symptom checklist scores to determine which treatment or set of treatments worked best at reducing symptoms. Some studies had involved placebo control groups, and as expected, a number of patients got noticeably better while taking placebos. In those studies, no subject knew whether he was receiving a placebo or the study drug.

Now Park and Covi enrolled a group of 15 new patients in trials with neither an "active" drug group nor psychotherapy, as they had done in the past. Instead, after the patients went through the symptom checklist process, they were given a bottle of pills. The experimenters told them frankly, "These are sugar pills, which contain no active medicine." Then they added that despite that fact, many patients had gotten better after taking one of the pills three times a day for a week. A checkup visit was to be held at the end of that week.

Some study subjects taking placebos were so convinced that the pills contained medication that they reported experiencing a number of side effects.

When 14 of the 15 subjects returned a week later, the new symptom checklists showed that 13 of those 14 had significantly reduced symptoms. From their conversations with the subjects, Park and Covi learned, first of all, that not all their subjects had believed them about what was being prescribed. In fact, the 14 subjects could be divided into three roughly equivalent groups. The first group took the scientists at their word and assumed they were taking sugar pills. The second group decided you simply couldn't trust psychiatry researchers and believed the pills were really some kind of tranquilizer—and that they'd been lied to, possibly to make the study more accurate or because there would be less chance of their getting hooked on the drug. The third group was merely unsure of what they had received.

Park and Covi then asked the "certain-placebo" subjects how they could account for their having gotten better. Despite the limited size of the group, their answers give us some of the most important clues about what physicians must do to trigger a placebo response in their patients. About half of these subjects said that they got better because they took the placebo, while the other half claimed they improved because somehow they had drawn upon their own innate abilities to cope.

One woman reported that every time she took one of the placebos, she reminded herself that she really could do something to better her own condition. Some other subjects also testified that they appreciated the fact that they were not getting an "active" drug, and so were spared the likely side effects and risks of addiction.

By contrast, the "certain-real drug" group explained that, because they thought they were getting an active drug, they saw their symptoms improving. The improvement served to reinforce their views that the pills were genuine medicine. Some people even reported a number of side effects they had felt throughout the week.

By the mid-1960s, most physicians believed that the placebo response hinged on patients' expectations of a cure. But few physicians imagined that their own expectations could be equally powerful when disclosed to the patient.

That's what Dr. E. H. Uhlenhuth and his colleagues at the Johns Hopkins University Department of Psychiatry had to deal with when they sat down to analyze the data from a double-blind randomized study of two tranquilizers compared to placebo for psychiatric clinic patients with anxiety. These tranquilizers are generally viewed as effective for anxiety symptoms, and so the investigators naturally expected to show in their study that they did better than the placebo. When their data did not show this, they knew that something must have gone wrong. It occurred to them to analyze the data according to which of the two psychiatrists the patients had seen when they were being given their capsules.

The psychiatrists were supposed to treat all patients identically, and they claimed to have done so. But if you considered only the half of the patients who had seen psychiatrist A, there was no difference between either of the tranquilizers and the placebo. If you considered only those patients seeing psychiatrist B, however, one of the drugs was better than placebo. When the data were combined, the lack of effect on the A side obscured the effect on the B side so that overall there was no statistical difference between the medication and the control groups.

It turned out that Dr. A was a younger physician who seemed rather noncommittal to patients, and in his own mind doubted that any of the drugs actually made a difference. Dr. B, by contrast, was older and appeared more fatherly to the patients; his own thinking was that one of the drugs, meprobamate, was definitely superior to placebo, though he was not so convinced about the other "active" drug.

Neither A nor B was consciously aware of having transmitted his personal views to any of the experimental subjects. We can only speculate what sorts of signals A and B could have transmitted to their patients' inner pharmacies. Whatever it was, the experimental results were virtually identical to the unexpressed expectations of the two physicians.

As you can see from these research findings, there seems to be a consistent thread of "mind over matter"— the ability of the body to undergo a healing change because the mind expects it to happen. In the case of the Uhlenhuth experiment, the expectancy lay perhaps more in the mind of the physician than in that of the patient, but it still worked. One case report showed a small child to be affected by the healing expectations of the parent. In an older study, patients improved more on placebos than on tranquilizers when the medicine was administered by nurses who strongly disapproved of giving "drugs" to these patients.

One patient became 100% convinced that his two-colored capsules would not work unless he swallowed them green-end first.

Other bits of data that seem to support the expectancy theory are findings about which placebos work most effectively, and for what conditions. Many investigators have found that capsules work better than drugs taken by mouth, and that injections that sting work better than painless injections. Surgery can be an especially powerful placebo stimulus. Placebos taken four times a day seem to be more effective than placebos taken twice a day. When placebos (or drugs, for that matter) are in the form of colored capsules or coated tablets, blue, green and purple ones seem to work especially well as sedatives and sleeping pills, while red, yellow and orange seem to work best as stimulants or energy-boosters. All of these effects seem to go along with the natural expectancy of the average person. One patient, unlike the average person, became 100% convinced that his two-colored capsules would not work unless he swallowed them green-end first. Needless to say, what he expected ended up happening.

Psychologists add depth to the expectancy theory by tying it to an evolutionary view of human behavior. According to this view, the body's reaction to a message from the outside world will be a combination of two factors: the "bottom-up" processing of the incoming information, in which the higher centers of the brain analyze the new information in detail; and a "top-down" response, in which the brain quickly scans its existing inventory of behavior patterns for something that seems to match the overall pattern of the new information. The bottom-up process may take a long time, so the human body is hard-wired to respond to some situations from the top-down reaction—a sort of "shoot first, ask questions later" mode. The top-down process is most likely to be triggered in situations where the mind-body unity regards itself as being in significant danger, and where the extra time required for a full bottom-up analysis might be too risky.

For example, you see something in the grass at your feet that might be a snake. The top-down reaction is basically, "Snake!", which produces a rapid jump backward,

as well as stress responses such as faster heart rate, increased blood pressure and higher muscle tone. The bottom-up reaction is, "Let's look at this more carefully. It's long and thin and brown, so it could be a snake. But it's not moving, and it's pretty straight.... Maybe it's actually a stick. Let me reach down carefully and touch it—yup, it's a stick." The evolutionary part of the theory proposes that for most of its history, the human race had a much better survival chance if the top-down response was the first to kick in. So natural selection favored our minds' developing and retaining a number of top-down response patterns.

The placebo response might be just such a top-down reaction. Since illness is a threat to the organism, the brain may well have stored in its memory files certain pathways of healing: signals that can be sent to the inner pharmacy to stimulate the release of healing chemicals. If a message is then received that resembles in its outward form something that the person expects to be associated with healing, that might be enough to trigger one of the stored top-down reaction pathways, leading to a release from the inner pharmacy, followed by bodily healing. That can occur even if a more careful analysis would have shown that the message was a fraud—that the pill was a sugar pill and not a chemically powerful substance.

Science has yet to discover a single pathway—a term scientists use to describe a series of causes and effects—that accounts for the placebo response. Our inner pharmacies, it would seem, have quite an array of different biochemical substances on their shelves. There are at least three known mind-body healing pathways.

Endorphins: We have a strong suspicion that at least some placebo pain relief, and perhaps the effects placebos have on anxiety and shortness of breath, occur because placebos stimulate the release of endorphins, a morphine-like drug produced by the body.

Stress/Relaxation Response: Many diseases, including hypertension, memory loss and chronic fatigue syndrome, are associated with elevated levels of stress hormones, such as cortisol. Placebos may trigger the body's lowering of these stress hormones in a transaction known as the "relaxation response." Strong social support plays an important role in heightening this response, much as a support group relaxes and fortifies its members.

Psychoneuroimmune Pathways: While this area of research is relatively new, my impression is that it has proven, beyond a reasonable doubt, that mental and emotional changes can alter the immune system, influencing the manufacture and function of immune cells. It stands to reason, then, that a person's emotional state or behavior may be linked to disease. In this pathway, placebos positively influence a person's emotional state or behavior, and thereby boost his or her immune system.

You can use all of these various pathways to invoke the placebo response—and take charge of your own health. Some key elements for stimulating your own inner pharmacy are: constructing a meaningful "story" about the condition you may be suffering from, being open to alternative and traditional medicine, finding a physician with whom you can form a healing partnership, and maintaining positive social connections.

At this point, it's easy to be optimistic. I've seen the processes we've discussed work, as have countless physicians and scientists. These means of healing don't often produce results as dramatic as, say, the faith healings at Lourdes. No, the paralyzed may not throw down their crutches and walk away unaided. Nonetheless, the processes are effective at the level where most good medicine functions: People suffer less from the symptoms of their illness, discover they can do more despite their illness, and realize that, even with illness, their lives are meaningful.

When all this happens, I know that I am in the presence of healing. Just how and why it happens may remain a mystery. That it happens is as certain as anything can be in the practice of medicine.

READ MORE ABOUT IT

The Placebo Effect, Anne Harrington, Ed. (Harvard University Press, 1999)
The Power of Hope: A Doctor's Perspective, Howard M. Shapiro, M.D. (Yale University Press, 1998)

Excerpted from The Placebo Response *by Howard Brody, M.D., Ph.D., with permission from HarperCollins (June 2000). Brody is Director of the Center for Ethics and Humanities in the Life Sciences at Michigan State University.*

SWEET SABOTAGE How Sugar Pills Compromise Drug Trials

By Joseph Arpaia, M.D.

The placebo effect can work wonders for your body, but its powerful influence renders drug trials misleading and unreliable. How can a simple sugar pill sabotage a test of powerful medication?

The problem arises in "double-blind" studies—the gold standard for testing new medications—in which neither researchers nor subjects know who is getting the medication and who is getting placebo. While the "double-blind system is supposed to guard against the bias that the placebo effect can cause, it fails miserably. Noticeable sensations from the medication easily distinguish the drug takers from placebo takers, effectively removing the blindfold and allowing bias to shine through.

Reports began surfacing in the 1950s that the double-blind design was not as scientifically objective as originally assumed. In 1993, Seymour Fisher, Ph.D., and Roger P. Greenberg, Ph.D., raised radical questions about the methodology when their investigation of previous reviews of antidepressant literature, as one sample of drug trials, turned up only the most modest evidence of the drugs' therapeutic power. They were surprised to find that even the most positive research reviews indicated that 30% to 40% of antidepressant studies showed that there was no significant difference in response to drug versus placebo.

Patients learn to discriminate between drug and placebo largely from bodily sensations and symptoms—or lack thereof. Studies suggest that 70% to 80% of study subjects correctly guess which pill they're taking. And since the more open to bias a drug trial is, the greater the apparent superiority of the drug over placebo, the result is an industry-sanctioned drug test that systematically overestimates the power of drugs, especially those with noticeable side effects!

Imagine that a new antidepressant that is being tested causes side effects such as insomnia, dizziness, weight gain and sexual dysfunction (which many do), and that it doesn't actually relieve depression. Participants in a "double-blind" study who experience those marked symptoms will most likely conclude that they are taking "real" medication, rather than placebo, since no sugar pill would produce such side effects. Just knowing they are taking "real" medication produces a powerful healing effect, which makes the drug being tested look extremely beneficial. The placebo effect is so powerful that it could even make a medication that produces a mild depression appear to be an effective antidepressant—as long as the drug produces noticeable side effects. Conversely, if another antidepressant—one that actually has a small beneficial effect—does not cause marked side effects, drug trial participants might conclude that they're not getting any medicine. In that case, the placebo effect would not kick in, and the drug would not seem as beneficial as the one with side effects.

In this way, the double-blind study may actually select for drugs that are toxic—and potentially less effective—over their gentler, more subtle cousins. This carries an immense personal and economic cost.

Last year, the *Journal of the American Medical Association* reported that adverse drug effects may be the fourth leading cause of death in hospitalized patients, killing 100,000 people a year. The fact is, we are more likely to die from a medication than from most diseases.

(continued)

Such faulty testing techniques have yielded a new batch of antidepressants, so-called selective serotonin reuptake inhibitors (SSRIs), that can end up making people more depressed and even suicidal, according to a report in the May 1998 *Clinical Psychiatry News*. Worse, internal Food & Drug Administration documents show that these drugs can also cause hypomania/mania—a severe psychotic disorder involving extreme overactivity, insomnia, racing thoughts, frantic outbursts, paranoia and suicide—in 1% of users. That means 1,000 of every million Americans taking one of the newer antidepressants will likely develop manic reactions. The figures could be even more disastrous, since FDA drug trials excluded patients already at risk of psychotic mania. The drugs' manic effect is even more pronounced in children. In *Reclaiming Our Children*, psychiatrist Peter R. Breggin, M.D., cites research indicating a 6% rate of mania and an even higher rate of behavioral problems—including violence—in children taking these antidepressants.

The problem is not limited to antidepressants: It affects every medication, including those for pain, digestion and blood pressure, anti-inflammatory drugs and others. The drug Rezulin, used to treat diabetes, was recently recalled because it was causing liver failure. The anti-heartburn drug Propulsid was pulled from the shelves because it was causing cardiac arrest, and 80 people had died from taking it.

After the double-blind design botches drug trials, thanks to the placebo effect, aggressive marketing of the resulting FDA-approved medications creates a one-two punch. With glossy, full-page magazine ads touting the sweeping promises of happier days, it is easy to understand how a drug like Prozac, for example, gained its popularity, though studies have shown that most of its benefit can be attributed to the placebo effect. In fact, an article in the *British Journal of Psychiatry* in 1998 pointed out that in seven out of nine studies reviewed, subjects taking an antidepressant did no better than those taking a substance that was not an antidepressant, but that had similar noxious side effects. This phenomenon has been called the "active placebo" effect, in which side effects convince all subjects that they are getting "strong" or "real" medicine, heightening their positive response to the pills. The research team, led by Joanna Moncrieff of the Institute of Psychiatry in London, concluded, "The ef-fects of antidepressants may be smaller than generally believed, with placebo accounting for more of the clinical improvement… than is known to be the case."

The studies pharmaceutical companies claim "prove effectiveness," therefore, actually prove nothing. The drug companies have been so stymied by their inability to show that psychiatric drugs are better than placebos that they recently held a conference that focused on how to get around the placebo effect. This past May, in Chicago, eight major pharmaceutical companies joined several research institutes and the Johns Hopkins School of Medicine to explore ways of improving clinical trial design and conduct for successful drug development. It was a researcher from Eli Lilly Laboratories who led the featured panel discussion on "minimizing the placebo response."

The way we test drugs may select for ones that are toxic, and perhaps less effective, over their gentler cousins.

The medical profession is not off the hook, either. Current thinking holds that every condition requires one or more pills to treat it. But doctors would do well to realize that many of the drugs they prescribe today are no more effective than the drugs of 30 years ago.

Being a physician means offering knowledge and hope, not just drugs. Doctors must remember that the most powerful therapeutic intervention is the patient's own internal healing response, which they can stimulate by educating, motivating and encouraging the patient to engage in healthy patterns of behavior—something that is nearly impossible to do in today's seven-minute office visit.

We would do well to place our faith instead in our own internal healing abilities. That would reduce our dependence on marginally effective drugs, reign in growing health care costs, and prevent thousands of people from dying unnecessarily of side effects.

Joseph Arpaia, M.D., is a psychiatrist and medical director of the Cascades Wellness Center. He also teaches in the psychology department at the University of Oregon.

Reprinted from *Psychology Today*, July/August 2000, pp. 60–67. Excerpted from *The Placebo Response*. © 2000 by Howard Brody. Reprinted by permission of HarperCollins Publishers, Inc.

UNIT 3
Problems Influencing Personal Growth

Unit Selections

17. **The Seven Stages of Man**, Constanza Villalba
18. **Fetal Psychology**, Janet L. Hopson
19. **Four Things You Need to Know About Raising Baby**, Joanna Lipari
20. **What Ever Happened to Play?** Walter Kirm with Wendy Cole
21. **Parenting: The Lost Art**, Kay S. Hymowitz
22. **Disarming the Rage**, Richard Jerome, Ron Arias, Mary Boone, and Lauren Comander
23. **A World of Their Own**, Sharon Begley
24. **The Road Ahead: A Boomer's Guide to Happiness**, Barbara Kantrowitz
25. **Live to 100? No Thanks**, Susan L. Crowley
26. **Start the Conversation**, *Modern Maturity*

Key Points to Consider

- Individuals face challenges at every phase of development. What are some of the phases or stages of development?

- What are the various factors that can influence fetal development?

- What other factors besides drugs and alcohol influence prenatal life? Are there times when a child can overcome even the most traumatic and debilitating prenatal experiences? How so?

- Are parents necessary to child development? What other individuals do you think have an impact on a child's development?

- Why do you think there has been an epidemic of violence in our high schools? What is bullying; when does it occur?

- Are teens today different from teens of their parents' generation? How so? If you believe that today's teens are different, to what aspects of society can you point to explain these differences?

- Why is the topic of death so stigmatized in American society?

 **Links: www.dushkin.com/online/**
These sites are annotated in the World Wide Web pages.

Adolescence: Changes and Continuity
http://www.personal.psu.edu/faculty/n/x/nxd10/adolesce.htm

Ask NOAH About: Mental Health
http://www.noah-health.org/english/illness/mentalhealth/mental.html

Facts for Families
http://www.aacap.org/info_families/index.htm

Mental Health Infosource: Disorders
http://www.mhsource.com/disorders/

Mental Health Risk Factors for Adolescents
http://education.indiana.edu/cas/adol/mental.html

Suicide Awareness: Voices of Education
http://www.save.org

At each stage of development from infancy to old age, humans are faced with new challenges. The infant has the rudimentary sensory apparatus for seeing, hearing, and touching but needs to begin coordinating stimuli into meaningful information. For example, early in life the baby begins to recognize familiar and unfamiliar people and usually becomes attached to the primary caregivers. As a toddler, the same child must master the difficult skills of walking, talking, and toilet training. This energetic, mobile, and sociable child also needs to learn the boundaries set on his or her behavior by others. As the child matures, not only do physical changes continue to take place, but the family composition may change when siblings are added, parents divorce, or mother and father work outside the home. Playmates become more influential, and others in the community, such as day-care workers and teachers, have an increasing influence on the child. The child may eventually spend more time at school than at home. The demands in this new environment require that the child sit still, pay attention, learn, and cooperate with others for long periods of time—behaviors perhaps never before extensively demanded of him or her.

In adolescence the body changes noticeably. Peers may pressure the individual to indulge in new behaviors such as using illegal drugs or engaging in premarital sex. Some older teenagers are said to be faced with an identity crisis when they must choose among career, education, and marriage. The pressures of work and family life exact a toll on less mature youths, while others are satisfied with the workplace and home.

Adulthood, middle age, and old age may bring contentment or turmoil as individuals face career peaks, empty nests, advancing age, and perhaps the death of loved ones, such as parents or spouses. Again, some individuals cope more effectively with these events than do others.

At any step in the developmental sequence, unexpected stressors challenge individuals. These stressors include major illnesses, accidents, natural disasters, economic recessions, and family or personal crises. It is important to remember, however, that an event need not be negative to be stressful. Any major life change may cause stress. As welcome as weddings, new babies, and job promotions may be, they, too, can be stressful because of the changes in daily life that they demand. Each challenge and each change must be met and adjusted to if the individual is going to move successfully to the next stage of development. Some individuals continue along their paths unscathed; others do not fare so well.

This unit of the book examines problems in various stages of life from before birth to death. The first article commences with and forecasts our chronological look at issues of development. In "The Seven Stages of Man," Costanza Villalba offers an overview of what can go right or wrong for both males and females in various life eras.

We next look at several developmental stages in more detail. In "Fetal Psychology," Janet Hopson reveals why fetal life is so important and so delicate. Drugs, alcohol, and other substances can adversely affect the fetus. As the article suggests, problems for our development exist even before birth.

We next turn to early childhood. In "Four Things You Need to Know About Raising Baby," Joanna Lepau explains that babies are not passive recipients of sensory information. Babies, in fact, are far more capable than we believed at first. Lepau tackles myths about infancy by enlisting scientific evidence to the contrary.

In the next article, authors Walter Kim and Wendy Cole question what has happened to childhood in America. Children used to have lots of free time to play. Today, parents seem to involve their children in too many planned activities; leisure time play, which the authors view as natural and normal, has fallen by the wayside.

Continuing our developmental theme, we next focus on the parents, rather than the children. Parenting apparently is a "lost art," according to Kay Hymowitz. Hymowitz claims that parents today would rather be friends or peers of their children rather than parents who discipline, set boundaries, and act as adults around their children. Hymowitz suggests that this is why schools and parents are often at odds about the child's behavior.

We move next to adolescence. A timely issue of great importance is school violence by American adolescents. Recent studies have linked violence to students who are isolated and bullied by their peers. The article, "Disarming the Rage," reveals why bullying occurs and what the sad consequences are. Schools and parents are provided with tips to help reduce or prevent bullying and therefore the violent aftermath.

A companion article about adolescents, "A World of Their Own," explores other features of peer pressure in teens. Sharon Begley discusses why teens today are so different from past generations. Many of the differences are blamed on the modern media and on technology, especially the Internet.

Middle age is the next developmental milestone undertaken in this unit. As the baby boomers swell the ranks of the middle aged, some are bound to be disappointed in midlife while others will be content. In "The Road Ahead: A Boomer's Guide to Happiness," the author discusses what issues face boomers and how the masses of boomers can find happiness at midlife.

Old age is the central issue in "Live to 100? No Thanks." Do people seek the fountain of youth? How long can we really live? What factors induce people to live to older ages? Do people really want to live to 100? The answer is a resounding "no." In a survey of elderly individuals, results demonstrate that people prefer a better quality of life over longevity.

The ultimate developmental stage is death. Death is a topic that both fascinates and frightens most of us. In "Start the Conversation," the veil of stigma that surrounds the issue of death is lifted. The article is designed to help people come to grips with their own fears and thus accept their own or another's death more comfortably.

The Seven Stages of Man

Men are often portrayed as big boys, differing from their younger selves only in the sums of money they spend on their toys. Indeed, because men can reproduce well into old age, and do not experience cyclical hormonal changes, their health is regarded as fairly static. But medical experts are learning that between the boy and the man stand a variety of genetic, biological and social changes. Understanding these factors may help men prepare for the stages that await them.

CONSTANZA VILLALBA

INFANCY

At the precise moment when a single sperm wiggles its way into an awaiting egg, the sex of the developing baby is defined. If that sperm carries a portly X chromosome, the egg turned embryo will give rise to a baby girl. If that sperm carries a diminutive Y chromosome, the baby will be a boy. With the blueprint for the male architecture, however, come several, often unfortunate genetic predispositions: hemophilia and Duchenne's Muscular Dystrophy afflict boys and men almost exclusively, while boys are more likely than girls to suffer from Fragile-X Syndrome, the nation's leading cause of mental retardation.

But being born a boy also comes with perks. Baby boys are an animated lot who display a marked curiosity about the world. Compared with girls, they are more alert and emotionally interactive with caretakers. They begin suppressing their emotions later in life, suggesting that masculine stoicism is learned, not hard-wired.

BOYHOOD

Once in school, boys tend to excel at mathematics and other tasks controlled by the brain's right side, or hemisphere. These natural aptitudes may be strengthened by the spike of testosterone that infant boys experience before and right after birth. But the biological machinery that gives boys an advantage in math and spatial tasks may predispose them to learning and developmental disorders: that is, in boys the left brain hemisphere, which controls language and facilitates socialization, may be underdeveloped.

On the playground, school-age boys resist playing with girls. They enjoy rough-and-tumble play and have inherent skill at games involving hit-the-target motor and navigational challenges. This time spent among other boys relays lessons—not all of them healthy—about what it means to be male. Chase and target games, for example, may be an evolutionary throwback to when men had to be good hunters.

ADOLESCENCE

Testosterone's effects on boys' development become most obvious during adolescence. As their soprano voices morph into tenors, boys squawk. Muscles begin replacing baby fat. Male hormones are also responsible for teen-age boys' novel interest in sex. Unfortunately, this interest is not always coupled with mature attitudes about safety and promiscuity. Data show that adolescents account for one-quarter of the 12 million cases of sexually transmitted diseases reported each year. The good news is that teen-agers may be getting the message. Gonorrhea among adolescent boys has been decreasing over the last seven years.

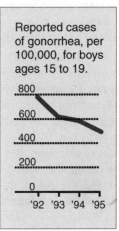

Reported cases of gonorrhea, per 100,000, for boys ages 15 to 19.

800
600
400
200
0
'92 '93 '94 '95

But boys' interest in girls is not purely sexual. Compared with previous generations, teen-age boys are more likely to have Platonic relationships with girls and to agree with survey statements like "Boys and girls should both be allowed to express feelings."

The hormones that pique boys' interest in sex goad them toward risky and aggressive behavior. At the same time, parental and societal expectations about masculinity may prevent them from expressing confusion or fear about the changes befalling them. These factors make teen-age boys 2.5 times more likely than girls to die of an unintentional injury and 5 times more likely to die from a homicide or suicide.

YOUNG ADULTHOOD

Men are physically in their prime. This period is characterized by a drive for achievement and by the re-alization that the foolhardiness of youth has unavoidable conse-quences. Fatherhood gives men the opportunity to redefine masculinity in a healthful way for themselves and their children.

Bad habits, like smoking, become less appealing but more difficult to shake; more than 80 percent of adults who ever smoked began do-ing so before age 18. Still, men are smoking less than they did and the incidence of lung cancer in men is falling. Although the incidence of smoking—28.8 percent for black men, 27.1 percent for white men—is similar, black men are at much higher risk of lung cancer than white men.

H.I.V. infection, the leading cause of death among men between ages 25 and 44, is often contracted during adolescence, when boys are experi-menting with sex and are oblivious to the risks of infection. But with ad-vances in drug therapies, the inci-dence of H.I.V.-related deaths has declined over the last four years.

MIDDLE AGE

Beginning in their early 40's, men experience a decline in testosterone of 1 percent each year. These reduc-tions coincide with increased de-pressive symptoms, including anxiety and sexual dissatisfaction. While some doctors consider this stage tantamount to "male meno-pause," others argue that the hor-monal changes are too subtle to account for these symptoms. They note, too, that impotence and other

conditions associated with middle age can be caused by ailments that tend to strike men in this age group, like diabetes.

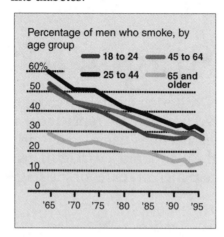

The risk of heart disease, hyperten-sion and diabetes is exacerbated by obesity, and middle age is when men are likely to be overweight. They lose 3 percent to 5 percent of their muscle mass for every decade after age 25. Reduced muscle mass and physical activity conspire to decrease men's resting metabolic rate. As men age, then, they burn less energy while resting and can gain weight even without changing their eating habits. And they do gain—2 to 3 pounds for every year over age 30.

Heart disease continues to be the leading cause of death for men in the United States. But the rate of heart disease-related deaths among men has decreased more than 50 percent since 1950; those who die of heart disease are dying later in life.

EARLY OLD AGE

Because men continue to produce testosterone throughout life, they are protected from—though not immune to—conditions like Alzheimer's Dis-ease and osteoporosis. Their larger bone size also helps protect against this bone-weakening illness. Men can further maintain their mental acuity by engaging in intellectual activities.

They can strengthen their bones and stem bone loss by undertaking weight-bearing exercise. The contin-ued production of testosterone, how-ever, can also adversely affect men. Testosterone aggravates hair loss and stimulates growth of the prostate gland. Noncancerous enlargement of the prostate occurs in more than half of men in their 60's and up to 90 per-cent of men in their 70's and 80's. At the same time, 80 percent of all pros-tate cancer cases occur in men age 65 and over.

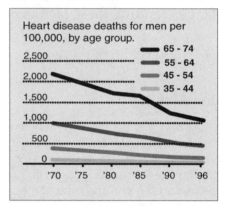

LATER OLD AGE

Studies indicate that men are less likely than women to have difficulty maintaining normal routines, like bathing, dressing and using the toi-let, as they age.

Still, the trend among the elderly in general is that they become less active, and so need fewer calories. Their appetites diminish, yet their nutritional needs increase because their bodies have lost the ability to synthesize and absorb important vi-tamins and nutrients. Their skin, for example, no longer easily synthe-sizes vitamin D when exposed to the sun. The benefits of avoiding poten-tially harmful foods, such as those high in cholesterol, lessen with age. Maintaining weight and making sure the right nutrients are present in the diet become more important.

From the *New York Times*, February 17, 1999. © 1999 by The New York Times Company. Reprinted by permission.

FETAL PSYCHOLOGY

Behaviorally
speaking, there's little
difference between a newborn
baby and a 32-week-old fetus.
A new wave of research suggests
that the fetus can feel, dream, even
enjoy *The Cat in the Hat*. **The
abortion debate may never
be the same**.

By Janet L. Hopson

The scene never fails to give goose bumps: the baby, just seconds old and still dewy from the womb, is lifted into the arms of its exhausted but blissful parents. They gaze adoringly as their new child stretches and squirms, scrunches its mouth and opens its eyes. To anyone watching this tender vignette, the message is unmistakable. Birth is the beginning of it all, ground zero, the moment from which the clock starts ticking. Not so, declares Janet DiPietro. Birth may be a grand occasion, says the Johns Hopkins University psychologist, but "it is a trivial event in development. Nothing neurologically interesting happens."

Armed with highly sensitive and sophisticated monitoring gear, DiPietro and other researchers today are discovering that the real action starts weeks earlier. At 32 weeks of gestation—two months before a baby is considered fully prepared for the world, or "at term"—a fetus is behaving almost exactly as a newborn. And it continues to do so for the next 12 weeks.

A fetus spends hours in the rapid eye movement sleep of dreams.

As if overturning the common conception of infancy weren't enough, scientists are creating a startling new picture of intelligent life in the womb. Among the revelations:

• By nine weeks, a developing fetus can hiccup and react to loud noises. By the end of the second trimester it can hear.

• Just as adults do, the fetus experiences the rapid eye movement (REM) sleep of dreams.

• The fetus savors its mother's meals, first picking up the food tastes of a culture in the womb.

• Among other mental feats, the fetus can distinguish between the voice of Mom and that of a stranger, and respond to a familiar story read to it.

• Even a premature baby is aware, feels, responds, and adapts to its environment.

• Just because the fetus is responsive to certain stimuli doesn't mean that it should be the target of efforts to enhance development. Sensory stimulation of the fetus can in fact lead to bizarre patterns of adaptation later on.

The roots of human behavior, researchers now know, begin to develop early—just weeks after conception, in fact. Well before a woman typically knows she is pregnant, her embryo's brain has already begun to bulge. By five weeks, the organ that looks like a lumpy inchworm has already embarked on the most spectacular feat of human development: the creation of the deeply creased and convoluted cerebral cortex, the part of the brain that will eventually allow the growing person to move, think, speak, plan, and create in a human way.

At nine weeks, the embryo's ballooning brain allows it to bend its body, hiccup, and react to loud sounds. At week ten, it moves its arms, "breathes" amniotic fluid in and out, opens its jaw, and stretches. Before the first trimester is over, it yawns, sucks, and swallows as well as feels and smells. By the end of the second trimester, it can hear; toward the end of pregnancy, it can see.

FETAL ALERTNESS

Scientists who follow the fetus' daily life find that it spends most of its time not exercising these new abilities but sleeping. At 32 weeks, it drowses 90 to 95% of the day. Some of these hours are spent in deep sleep, some in REM sleep, and some in an indeterminate state, a product of the fetus' immature brain that is different from sleep in a baby, child, or adult. During REM sleep, the fetus' eyes move back and forth just as an adult's eyes do, and many researchers believe that it is dreaming. DiPietro speculates that fetuses dream about what they know—the sensations they feel in the womb.

Closer to birth, the fetus sleeps 85 to 90% of the time, the same as a newborn. Between its frequent naps, the fetus seems to have "something like an awake alert period," according to developmental psychologist William Fifer, Ph.D., who with his Columbia University colleagues is monitoring these sleep and wakefulness cycles in order to identify patterns of normal and abnormal brain development, including potential predictors of sudden infant death syndrome. Says Fifer, "We are, in effect, asking the fetus: 'Are you paying attention? Is your nervous system behaving in the appropriate way?' "

FETAL MOVEMENT

Awake or asleep, the human fetus moves 50 times or more each hour, flexing and extending its body, moving its head, face, and limbs and exploring its warm wet compartment by touch. Heidelise Als, Ph.D., a developmental psychologist at Harvard Medical School, is fascinated by the amount of tactile stimulation a fetus gives itself. "It touches a hand to the face, one hand to the other hand, clasps its feet, touches its foot to its leg, its hand to its umbilical cord," she reports.

Als believes there is a mismatch between the environment given to preemies in hospitals and the environment they would have had in the womb. She has been working for years to change the care given to preemies so that they can curl up, bring their knees together, and touch things with their hands as they would have for weeks in the womb.

By 15 weeks, a fetus has an adult's taste buds and may be able to savor its mother's meals.

Along with such common movements, DiPietro has also noted some odder fetal activities, including "licking the uterine wall and literally walking around the womb by pushing off with its feet." Laterborns may have more room in the womb for such maneuvers than first babies. After the initial pregnancy, a woman's uterus is bigger and the umbilical cord longer, allowing more freedom of movement. "Second and subsequent children may develop more motor experience in utero and so may become more active infants," DiPietro speculates.

Fetuses react sharply to their mother's actions. "When we're watching the fetus on ultrasound and the mother starts to laugh, we can see the fetus, floating upside down in the womb, bounce up and down on its head, bum-bum-bum, like it's bouncing on a trampoline," says DiPietro. "When mothers watch this on the screen, they laugh harder, and the fetus goes up and down even faster. We've wondered whether this is why people grow up liking roller coasters."

FETAL TASTE

Why people grow up liking hot chilies or spicy curries may also have something to do with the fetal environment. By 13 to 15 weeks a fetus' taste buds already look like a mature adult's, and doctors know that the amniotic fluid that surrounds it can smell strongly of curry, cumin, garlic, onion and other essences from a mother's diet. Whether fetuses can taste these flavors isn't yet known, but scientists have found that a 33-week-old preemie will suck harder on a sweetened nipple than on a plain rubber one.

"During the last trimester, the fetus is swallowing up to a liter a day" of amniotic fluid, notes Julie Mennella, Ph.D., a biopsychologist at the Monell Chemical Senses Center in Philadelphia. She thinks the fluid may act as a "flavor bridge" to breast milk, which also carries food flavors from the mother's diet.

FETAL HEARING

Whether or not a fetus can taste, there's little question that it can hear. A very premature baby entering the world at 24 to 25 weeks responds to the sounds around it, observes Als, so its auditory apparatus must already have been functioning in the womb. Many pregnant women report a fetal jerk or sudden kick just after a door slams or a car backfires.

Even without such intrusions, the womb is not a silent place. Researchers who have inserted a hydrophone into the uterus of a pregnant woman have picked up a noise level "akin to the background noise in an apartment," according to DiPietro. Sounds include the whooshing of blood in the mother's vessels, the gurgling and rumbling of her stomach and intestines, as well as the tones of her voice filtered through tissues, bones, and fluid, and the voices of other people coming through the amniotic wall. Fifer has found that fetal heart rate slows when the mother is speaking, suggesting that the fetus not only hears and recognizes the sound, but is calmed by it.

FETAL VISION

Vision is the last sense to develop. A very premature infant can see light and shape; researchers presume that a fetus has the same ability. Just as the womb isn't com-

What's the Impact on Abortion?

Though research in fetal psychology focuses on the last trimester, when most abortions are illegal, the thought of a fetus dreaming, listening and responding to its mother's voice is sure to add new complexity to the debate. The new findings undoubtedly will strengthen the convictions of right-to-lifers—and they may shake the certainty of pro-choice proponents who believe that mental life begins at birth.

Many of the scientists engaged in studying the fetus, however, remain detached from the abortion controversy, insisting that their work is completely irrelevant to the debate.

"I don't think that fetal research informs the issue at all," contends psychologist Janet DiPietro of Johns Hopkins University. "The essence of the abortion debate is: When does life begin? Some people believe it begins at conception, the other extreme believes that it begins after the baby is born, and there's a group in the middle that believes it begins at around 24 or 25 weeks, when a fetus can live outside of the womb, though it needs a lot of help to do so.

"Up to about 25 weeks, whether or not it's sucking its thumb or has personality or all that, the fetus cannot survive outside of its mother. So is that life, or not? That is a moral, ethical, and religious question, not one for science. Things can behave and not be alive. Right-to-lifers may say that this research proves that a fetus is alive, but it does not. It cannot."

"Fetal research only changes the abortion debate for people who think that life starts at some magical point," maintains Heidelise Als, a psychologist at Harvard University. "If you believe that life begins at conception, then you don't need the proof of fetal behavior." For others, however, abortion is a very complex issue and involves far more than whether research shows that a fetus hiccups. "Your circumstances and personal beliefs have much more impact on the decision," she observes.

Like DiPietro, Als realizes that "people may use this research as an emotional way to draw people to the pro-life side, but it should not be used by belligerent activists." Instead, she believes, it should be applied to helping mothers have the healthiest pregnancy possible and preparing them to best parent their child. Columbia University psychologist William Fifer, Ph.D., agrees. "The research is much more relevant for issues regarding viable fetuses—preemies."

Simply put, say the three, their work is intended to help the babies that live—not to decide whether fetuses should.—*Camille Chatterjee*

pletely quiet, it isn't utterly dark, either. Says Fifer: "There may be just enough visual stimulation filtered through the mother's tissues that a fetus can respond when the mother is in bright light," such as when she is sunbathing.

A fetus prefers hearing Mom's voice over a stranger's—speaking in her native, not a foreign tongue—and being read aloud familiar tales rather than new stories.

Japanese scientists have even reported a distinct fetal reaction to flashes of light shined on the mother's belly. However, other researchers warn that exposing fetuses (or premature infants) to bright light before they are ready can be dangerous. In fact, Harvard's Als believes that retinal damage in premature infants, which has long been ascribed to high concentrations of oxygen, may actually be due to overexposure to light at the wrong time in development.

A six-month fetus, born about 14 weeks too early, has a brain that is neither prepared for nor expecting signals from the eyes to be transmitted into the brain's visual cortex, and from there into the executive-branch frontal lobes, where information is integrated. When the fetus is forced to see too much too soon, says Als, the accelerated stimulation may lead to aberrations of brain development.

FETAL LEARNING

Along with the ability to feel, see, and hear comes the capacity to learn and remember. These activities can be rudimentary, automatic, even biochemical. For example, a fetus, after an initial reaction of alarm, eventually stops responding to a repeated loud noise. The fetus displays the same kind of primitive learning, known as habituation, in response to its mother's voice, Fifer has found.

But the fetus has shown itself capable of far more. In the 1980s, psychology professor Anthony James DeCasper, Ph.D., and colleagues at the University of North Carolina at Greensboro, devised a feeding contraption that allows a baby to suck faster to hear one set of sounds through headphones and to suck slower to hear a different set. With this technique, DeCasper discovered that within hours of birth, a baby already prefers its mother's voice to a stranger's, suggesting it must have learned and remembered the voice, albeit not necessarily consciously, from its last months in the womb. More recently, he's found that a newborn prefers a story read to it repeatedly in the womb—in this case, *The Cat in the Hat*—over a new story introduced soon after birth.

DeCasper and others have uncovered more mental feats. Newborns can not only distinguish their mother from a stranger speaking, but would rather hear Mom's voice, especially the way it sounds filtered through amniotic fluid rather than through air. They're xenophobes, too: they prefer to hear Mom speaking in her native language than to hear her or someone else speaking in a foreign tongue.

By monitoring changes in fetal heart rate, psychologist Jean-Pierre Lecanuet, Ph.D., and his colleagues in Paris have found that fetuses can even tell strangers' voices apart. They also seem to like certain stories more than others. The fetal heartbeat will slow down when a familiar French fairy tale such as *"La Poulette"* ("The Chick") or *"Le Petit Crapaud"* ("The Little Toad"), is read near the mother's belly. When the same reader delivers another unfamiliar story, the fetal heartbeat stays steady.

The fetus is likely responding to the cadence of voices and stories, not their actual words, observes Fifer, but the conclusion is the same: the fetus can listen, learn, and remember at some level, and, as with most babies and children, it likes the comfort and reassurance of the familiar.

FETAL PERSONALITY

It's no secret that babies are born with distinct differences and patterns of activity that suggest individual temperament. Just when and how the behavioral traits originate in the womb is now the subject of intense scrutiny.

In the first formal study of fetal temperament in 1996, DiPietro and her colleagues recorded the heart rate and movements of 31 fetuses six times before birth and compared them to readings taken twice after birth. (They've since extended their study to include 100 more fetuses.) Their findings: fetuses that are very active in the womb tend to be more irritable infants. Those with irregular sleep/wake patterns in the womb sleep more poorly as young infants. And fetuses with high heart rates become unpredictable, inactive babies.

"Behavior doesn't begin at birth," declares DiPietro. "It begins before and develops in predictable ways." One of the most important influences on development is the fetal environment. As Harvard's Als observes, "The fetus gets an enormous amount of 'hormonal bathing' through the mother, so its chronobiological rhythms are influenced by the mother's sleep/wake cycles, her eating patterns, her movements."

The hormones a mother puts out in response to stress also appear critical. DiPietro finds that highly pressured mothers-to-be tend to have more active fetuses—and more irritable infants. "The most stressed are working pregnant women," says DiPietro. "These days, women tend to work up to the day they deliver, even though the implications for pregnancy aren't entirely clear yet. That's our cultural norm, but I think it's insane."

Als agrees that working can be an enormous stress, but emphasizes that pregnancy hormones help to buffer both mother and fetus. Individual reactions to stress also matter. "The pregnant woman who chooses to work is a different woman already from the one who chooses not to work," she explains.

She's also different from the woman who has no choice but to work. DiPietro's studies show that the fetuses of poor women are distinct neurobehaviorally—less active, with a less variable heart rate—from the fetuses of middle-class women. Yet "poor women rate themselves as less stressed than do working middle-class women," she notes. DiPietro suspects that inadequate nutrition and exposure to pollutants may significantly affect the fetuses of poor women.

Stress, diet, and toxins may combine to have a harmful effect on intelligence. A recent study by biostatistician Bernie Devlin, Ph.D., of the University of Pittsburgh, suggests that genes may have less impact on IQ than previously thought and that the environment of the womb may account for much more. "Our old notion of nature influencing the fetus before birth and nurture after birth needs an update," DiPietro insists. "There is an antenatal environment, too, that is provided by the mother."

Parents-to-be who want to further their unborn child's mental development should start by assuring that the antenatal environment is well-nourished, low-stress, drug-free. Various authors and "experts" also have suggested poking the fetus at regular intervals, speaking to it through a paper tube or "pregaphone," piping in classical music, even flashing lights at the mother's abdomen.

Does such stimulation work? More importantly: Is it safe? Some who use these methods swear their children are smarter, more verbally and musically inclined, more physically coordinated and socially adept than average. Scientists, however, are skeptical.

"There has been no defended research anywhere that shows any enduring effect from these stimulations," asserts Fifer. "Since no one can even say for certain when a fetus is awake, poking them or sticking speakers on the mother's abdomen may be changing their natural sleep patterns. No one would consider poking or prodding a newborn baby in her bassinet or putting a speaker next to her ear, so why would you do such a thing with a fetus?"

Als is more emphatic: "My bet is that poking, shaking, or otherwise deliberately stimulating the fetus might alter its developmental sequence, and anything that affects the development of the brain comes at a cost."

Gently talking to the fetus, however, seems to pose little risk. Fifer suggests that this kind of activity may help parents as much as the fetus. "Thinking about your fetus, talking to it, having your spouse talk to it, will all help prepare you for this new creature that's going to jump into your life and turn it upside down," he says—once it finally makes its anti-climactic entrance.

Reprinted with permission from *Psychology Today*, September/October 1998, pp. 44-48, 76. © 1998 by Sussex Publishers, Inc.

FOUR THINGS YOU NEED TO KNOW ABOUT RAISING BABY

New thinking about the newborn's brain, feelings and behavior are changing the way we look at parenting

BY JOANNA LIPARI, M.A.

Bookstore shelves are crammed with titles purporting to help you make your baby smarter, happier, healthier, stronger, better-behaved and everything else you can imagine, in what I call a shopping-cart approach to infant development. But experts are now beginning to look more broadly, in an integrated fashion, at the first few months of a baby's life. And so should you.

Psychological theorists are moving away from focusing on single areas such as physical development, genetic inheritance, cognitive skills or emotional attachment, which give at best a limited view of how babies develop. Instead, they are attempting to synthesize and integrate all the separate pieces of the infant-development puzzle. The results so far have been enlightening, and are beginning to suggest new ways of parenting.

The most important of the emerging revelations is that the key to stimulating emotional and intellectual growth in your child is your own behavior—what you do, what you don't do, how you scold, how you reward and how you show affection. If the baby's brain is the hardware, then you, the parents, provide the software. When you understand the hardware (your baby's brain), you will be better able to design the software (your own behavior) to promote baby's well-being.

The first two years of life are critical in this regard because that's when your baby is building the mental foundation that will dictate his or her behavior through adulthood. In the first year alone, your baby's brain grows from about 400g to a stupendous 1000g. While this growth and development is in part predetermined by genetic force, exactly how the brain grows is dependent upon emotional interaction, and that in-

volves you. "The human cerebral cortex adds about 70% of its final DNA content after birth," reports Allan N. Schore, Ph.D., assistant clinical professor of psychiatry and biobehavioral sciences at UCLA Medical School, "and this expanding brain is directly influenced by early environmental enrichment and social experiences."

Failure to provide this enrichment during the first two years can lead to a lifetime of emotional disability, according to attachment theorists. We are talking about the need to create a relationship and environment that allows your child to grow up with an openness to learning and the ability to process, understand and experience emotion with compassion, intelligence and resilience. These are the basic building blocks of emotional success.

Following are comparisons of researchers' "old thinking" and "new thinking." They highlight the four new insights changing the way we view infant development. The sections on "What To Do" then explain how to apply that new information.

1 FEELINGS TRUMP THOUGHTS

It is the emotional quality of the relationship you have with your baby that will stimulate his or her brain for optimum emotional and intellectual growth.

OLD THINKING: In this country, far too much emphasis is placed on developing babies' cognitive abilities. Some of this push came out of the promising results of the Head Start program. Middle-class families reasoned that if a little stimulation in an under-endowed home environment is beneficial, wouldn't "more" be better? And the race to create the "superbaby" was on.

Gone are the days when parents just wished their child were "normal" and could "fit in" with other kids. Competition for selective schools and the social pressure it generates has made parents feel their child needs to be "gifted." Learning exercises, videos and educational toys are pushed on parents to use in play with their children. "Make it fun," the experts say. The emphasis is on developing baby's cognitive skills by using the emotional reward of parental attention as a behavior-training tool.

THE NEW THINKING: Flying in the face of all those "smarter" baby books are studies suggesting that pushing baby to learn words, numbers, colors and shapes too early forces the child to use lower-level thinking processes, rather than develop his or her learning ability. It's like a pony trick at the circus: When the pony paws the ground to "count" to three, it's really not counting; it's simply performing a stunt. Such "tricks" are not only not helpful to baby's learning process, they are potentially harmful. Tufts University child psychologist David Elkind, Ph.D., makes it clear that putting pressure on a child to learn information sends the message that he or she needs to "perform" to gain the parents' acceptance, and it can dampen natural curiosity.

Instead, focus on building baby's emotional skills. "Emotional development is not just the foundation for important capacities such as intimacy and trust," says Stanley Greenspan, M.D., clinical professor of psychiatry and pediatrics at George Washington University Medical School and author of the new comprehensive book *Building Healthy Minds*. "It is also the foundation of intelligence and a wide variety of cognitive skills. At each stage of development, emotions lead the way, and learning facts and skills follow. Even math skills, which appear [to be] strictly an impersonal cognition, are initially learned through the emotions: 'A lot' to a 2-year-old, for example, is more than he would expect, whereas 'a little' is less than he wants."

It makes sense: Consider how well you learn when you are passionate about a subject, compared to when you are simply required to learn it. That passion is the emotional fuel driving the cognitive process. So the question then becomes not "what toys and games should I use to make my baby smarter?" but "how should I interact with my baby to make him 'passionate' about the world around him?"

WHAT TO DO: When you read the baby "milestone" books or cognitive development guides, keep in mind that the central issue is your baby's *emotional* development. As Greenspan advises, "Synthesize this information about milestones and see them with emotional development as the central issue. This is like a basketball team, with the coach being our old friend, emotions. Because emotions tell the child what he wants to do—move his arm, make a sound, smile or frown. As you look at the various 'milestone components'—motor, social and cognitive skills—look to see how the whole mental team is working together."

Not only will this give you more concrete clues as to how to strengthen your emotional relationship, but it will also serve to alert you to any "players" on the team that are weak or injured, i.e., a muscle problem in the legs, or a sight and hearing difficulty.

2 NOT JUST A SCREAMING MEATLOAF: BIRTH TO TWO MONTHS It's still largely unknown how well infants understand their world at birth, but new theories are challenging the traditional perspectives.

OLD THINKING: Until now, development experts thought infants occupied some kind of presocial, precognitive, preorganized life phase that stretched from birth to two months. They viewed newborns' needs as mainly physiological—with sleep-wake, day-night and hunger-satiation cycles, even calling the first month of life "the normal autism" phase, or as a friend calls it, the "screaming meatloaf" phase. Certainly, the newborn has emotional needs, but researchers thought they were only in response to basic sensory drives like taste, touch, etc.

THE NEW THINKING: In his revolutionary book, *The Interpersonal World of the Infant*, psychiatrist Daniel Stern, Ph.D., challenged the conventional wisdom on infant development by proposing that babies come into this world as social beings. In research experiments, newborns consistently demonstrate that they actively seek sensory stimulation, have distinct preferences and, from birth, tend to form hypotheses about what is occurring in the world around them. Their preferences are emotional ones. In fact, parents would be unable to establish the physiological cycles like wake-sleep without the aid of such sensory, emotional activities as rocking, touching, soothing, talking and singing. In turn, these interactions stimulate the child's brain to make the neuronal connections she needs in order to process the sensory information provided.

WHAT TO DO: "Take note of your baby's own special biological makeup and interactive style," Greenspan advises. You need to see your baby for the special individual he is at birth. Then, "you can deliberately introduce the world to him in a way that maximizes his delight and minimizes his frustrations." This is also the time to learn how to help your baby regulate his emotions, for example, by offering an emotionally overloaded baby some soothing sounds or rocking to help him calm down.

3 THE LOVE LOOP: BEGINNING AT TWO MONTHS At approximately eight weeks, a miraculous thing occurs—your baby's vision improves and for the first time, she can fully see you and can make direct eye contact. These beginning visual experiences of your baby play an important role in social and emotional development. "In particular, the mother's emotionally expressive face is, by far, the most potent visual stimulus in the infant's environment," points out UCLA's Alan Schore, "and the child's intense interest in her face, especially in her eyes, leads him/her to track it in space to engage in periods of intense mutual gaze." The result: Endorphin levels rise in the baby's brain, causing pleasurable feelings of joy and excitement. But the key is for this joy to be interactive.

OLD THINKING: The mother pumps information and affection into the child, who participates only as an empty receptacle.

THE NEW THINKING: We now know that the baby's participation is crucial to creating a solid attachment bond. The loving gaze of parents to child is reciprocated by the baby with a loving gaze back to the parents, causing their endorphin levels to rise, thus completing a closed emotional circuit, a sort of "love loop." Now, mother (or father) and baby are truly in a dynamic, interactive system. "In essence, we are talking less about what the mother is doing to the baby and more about how the mother is being with the baby and how the baby is learning to be with the mother," says Schore.

The final aspect of this developing interactive system between mother and child is the mother's development of an "emotional synchronization" with her child. Schore defines this as the mother's ability to tune into the baby's internal states and respond accordingly. For example: Your baby is quietly lying on the floor, happy to take in the sights and sounds of the environment. As you notice the baby looking for stimulation, you respond with a game of "peek-a-boo." As you play with your child and she responds with shrieks of glee, you escalate the emotion with bigger and bigger gestures and facial expressions. Shortly thereafter, you notice the baby turns away. The input has reached its maximum and you sense your child needs you to back off for awhile as she goes back to a state of calm and restful inactivity. "The synchronization between the two is more than between their behavior and thoughts; the synchronization is on a biological level—their brains and nervous systems are linked together," points out Schore. "In this process, the mother is teaching and learning at the same time. As a result of this moment-by-moment matching of emotion, both partners increase their emotional connection to one another. In addition, the more the mother fine-tunes her activity level to the infant during periods of play and interaction, the more she allows the baby to disengage and recover quietly during periods of nonplay, before initiating actively arousing play again."

Neuropsychological research now indicates that this attuned interaction—engaged play, disengagement and restful nonplay, followed by a return to play behavior—is especially helpful for brain growth and the development of cerebral circuits. This makes sense in light of the revelation that future cognitive development depends not on the cognitive stimulation of flashcards and videos, but on the attuned, dynamic and emotional interactions between parent and child. The play periods stimulate baby's central nervous system to excitation, followed by a restful period of alert inactivity in which the developing brain is able to process the stimulation and the interaction.

In this way, you, the parents, are the safety net under your baby's emotional highwire; the act of calming her down, or giving her the opportunity to calm down, will help her learn to handle ever-increasing intensity of stimulation and thus build emotional tolerance and resilience.

WHAT TO DO: There are two steps to maximizing your attunement ability: spontaneity and reflection. When in sync, you and baby will both experience positive emotion; when out of sync, you will see negative emotions. If much of your interactions seem to result in negative emotion, then it is time to reflect on your contribution to the equation.

In these instances, parents need to help one another discover what may be impeding the attunement process. Sometimes, on an unconscious level, it may be memories of our own childhood. For example, my friend sings nursery rhymes with a Boston accent, even though she grew up in New York, because her native Bostonian father sang them to her that way. While the "Fah-mah in the Dell" will probably not throw baby into a temper tantrum, it's a good example of how our actions or parenting style may be problematic without our realizing it.

But all parents have days when they are out of sync with baby, and the new perspective is that it's not such a bad thing. In fact, it's quite valuable. "Misattunement" is not a bioneurological disaster if you can become attuned again. The process of falling out of sync and then repairing the bond actually teaches children resilience, and a sense of confidence that the world will respond to them and repair any potential hurt.

Finally, let your baby take the lead. Schore suggests we "follow baby's own spontaneous expression of himself," which lets the child know that another person, i.e., mom or dad, can understand what he is feeling, doing, and even thinking. Such experiences, says Schore, assist in the development of the prefrontal area, which controls "empathy, and therefore that which makes us most 'human.'"

4 THE SHAME TRANSACTION Toward the end of the first year, as crawling turns to walking, a shift occurs in the communication between child and parents. "Observational studies show that 12-month-olds receive more positive responses from mothers, while 18-month-olds receive more instructions and directions," says Schore. In one study, mothers of toddlers expressed a prohibition—basically telling the child "no"—approximately every nine minutes! That's likely because a mobile toddler has an uncanny knack for finding the most dangerous things to explore!

Yesterday, for example, I walked into the living room to find my daughter scribbling on the wall with a purple marker. "NO!" shot out of my mouth. She looked up at me with stunned shock, then realized what she had done. Immediately, she hung her head, about to cry. I babbled on a bit about how markers are only for paper, yada-yada and then thought, "Heck, it's washable." As I put my arm around my daughter, I segued into a suggestion for another activity: washing the wall! She brightened and raced to get the sponge. We had just concluded a "shame transaction."

OLD THINKING: Researchers considered all these "no's" a necessary byproduct of child safety or the socialization process. After all, we must teach children to use the potty rather than wet the bed, not to hit another child when mad, to behave properly in public. Researchers did not consider the function of shame vis-à-vis brain development. Instead, they advised trying to limit situations in which the child would feel shame.

NEW THINKING: It's true that you want to limit the shame situations, but they are not simply a necessary evil in order to civilize your baby. Neurobiological studies indicate that episodes of shame like the one I described can actually stimulate the development of the right hemisphere, the brain's source of creativity, emotion and sensitivity, as long as the shame period is short and followed by a recovery. In essence, it's not the experience of shame that can be damaging, but rather the inability of the parent to help the child recover from that shame.

WHAT TO DO: It's important to understand "the growth-facilitating importance of small doses of shame in the socialization process of the infant," says Schore. Embarrassment (a component of shame) first emerges around 14 months, when mom's "no" results in the child lowering his head and looking down in obvious sadness. The child goes from excited (my daughter scribbling on the wall) to sudden deflation (my "NO!") back to excitement ("It's okay, let's wash the wall together"). During this rapid process, various parts of the brain get quite a workout and experience heightened connectivity, which strengthens these systems. The result is development of the orbitofrontal cortex (cognitive area) and limbic system (emotional area) and the ability for the two systems to interrelate emotional resiliency in the child and the ability to self-regulate emotions and impulse control.

What is important to remember about productive shame reactions is that there must be a quick recovery. Extended periods of shame result in a child learning to shut down, or worse, become hyperirritable, perhaps even violent. It's common sense: Just think how you feel when someone embarrasses you. If that embarrassment goes on without relief, don't you tend to either flee the situation or rail against it?

From these new research findings, it's clear that successful parenting isn't just about intuition, instinct and doing what your mother did. It's also not about pushing the alphabet, multiplication tables or violin lessons. We now believe that by seeing the newborn as a whole person—as a thinking, feeling creature who can and should participate in his own emotional and cognitive development—we can maximize the nurturing and stimulating potential of our relationship with a newborn baby.

Joanna Lipari is pursuing a Psy.D. at Pepperdine University in Los Angeles.

READ MORE ABOUT IT

The Irreducible Needs of Children: What Every Child Must Have to Grow, Learn and Flourish, T. Berry Brazelton, M.D., and Stanley Greenspan, M.D. (Perseus Books, 2000).

Building Healthy Minds, Stanley Greenspan, M.D. (Perseus Books, 1999).

Reprinted with permission from *Psychology Today*, July/August 2000, pp. 38-43. © 2000 by Sussex Publishers, Inc.

What Ever Happened To
PLAY?

Kids are spending less time
frolicking freely, though fun is one
of the best things for them

By WALTER KIRN with WENDY COLE

Theresa Collins lives next to a park, but her kids don't play there all that often. For one thing, all three of her children lead busy lives, what with school, piano lessons, soccer practice and the constant distraction of the home computer. What's more, she fears that the park is dangerous. "I've heard of people exposing themselves there," says Theresa, a 42-year-old special-education teacher in Sarasota, Fla. And while she's not sure if the scary stories are true, she would rather be safe than sorry, like so many other contemporary parents. Her daughter Erica, 9, isn't allowed to visit the park without her brother Christopher, 11, who wasn't permitted to play alone there until about a month ago. As for Matthew, 16, who might have supervised Christopher, he avoids the park by choice. He favors video games. "It's a shame," says Theresa. So why doesn't she take the kids to the park? "It's boring. And I don't have time," she says.

"When I'm home, I have a lot to do here."

No wonder America's swing sets are feeling lonely. With so many roving flashers to elude, so many high-tech skills to master, so many crucial tests to pass and so many anxious parents to reassure, children seem to be playing less and less these days. Even hassled grown-ups are starting to notice. "We're taking away childhood," says Dorothy Sluss, a professor of early-childhood education at East Tennessee State University. "We don't value play in our society. It has become a four-letter word."

Statistics back her up. In 1981, according to University of Michigan researchers, the average school-age child had 40% of the day for free time—meaning hours left over after sleeping, eating, studying and engaging in organized activities. By 1997, the figure was down to 25%.

The very existence of research studies on play suggests that ours is a serious society that can take the fun out of almost anything, including the issue of fun itself. That's why any list of the enemies of play must begin with adults, who make the rules. If play is endangered, it's parents who have endangered it, particularly those who feel that less goofing off in the name of youthful achievement is a good thing. See Dick run. Well, that's fine for little Dick, but wouldn't most parents rather raise a Jane who sits still, studies and gets into Harvard?

If so, they're shortsighted, say the experts on play. Alvin Rosenfeld, co-author of *The Over-Scheduled Child: Avoiding the Hyper-Parenting Trap*, holds an old-fashioned view of play: it's joyful and emotionally nourishing. Stuart Brown, a retired psychiatrist and founder of the Institute for Play in Carmel Valley, Calif., believes that too little play may have a dark side. What Brown calls "play deprivation" can lead, he says, to depression, hostility and the loss of "the things that make us human beings."

Play doesn't just make kids happy, healthy and human. It may also make them smarter, says Rosenfeld. Today's mania for raising young Einsteins, he observes, might have destroyed the real Einstein—a notorious dreamer who earned poor grades in school but somewhere in his frolics divined the formula for the relationship between matter and energy. Play refreshes and stimulates the mind, it seems. And "frequent breaks may actually make kids more interested in learning," according to Rhonda Clements, a Hofstra University professor of physical education.

The case for play is simple and intuitive, which is what makes the decline of play a mystery. If Dick can run wild and get into Princeton too, then why isn't he out there running his little head off? That play has real value won't surprise most parents. That their kid horses around less than they did when they were young probably doesn't shock them either. The puzzle is, Where did all the playtime go?

Millie Wilcox, 60, thinks she knows. The retired nurse and mother of two grown boys (one of them being this writer) doesn't have a Ph.D. in child psychology, just a memory of her own Ohio childhood picking elderberries in the alley and once—imagine doing this today—playing house inside a cardboard box set smack dab in the middle of the street. "There wasn't so much traffic back then," says Wilcox, "and it seems like every neighborhood had a vacant lot. Vacant lots were important. Plus, our mothers were around during the day, and they knew everyone on the block, so they weren't scared for us."

There's common sense behind Wilcox's nostalgia for her old stamping grounds. After all, play needs to happen somewhere—preferably somewhere safe and open and not entirely dominated by grownups—but those idyllic somewheres are growing scarce. "In the huge rush to build shopping malls and banks," says Clements, "no one is thinking about where kids can play. That doesn't generate tax revenue."

What about those inviting vacant lots? "There's practically no such thing

anymore," laments urban planner Robin Moore, a former president of the International Association for the Child's Right to Play. Thanks to sidewalk-free subdivisions, congested roads and ubiquitous commercial developments, "all the free space has been spoken for," says Moore. Roger Hart, an environmental psychologist at the City University of New York, cites a general "disinvestment in public space" as one reason children are playing less outdoors. Even public sandboxes are vanishing. Says Hart: "People have become paranoid about animal waste." What's more, as the average family size gets smaller and suburban houses are built farther apart, "kids have a harder time finding each other than they used to," Moore says.

Parental fear is also a factor. Fear of molesters, bacteria, zooming SUVS. Neighbors who own guns. Neighbors who let their kids eat refined sugar. The list is as lengthy as last Sunday's newspaper, and it grows longer with every new edition. "It used to be," Hart says, "that in the presence of one another, kids formed a critical mass to keep each other safe. Gone are the days when children make any of their own plans." Their fearful, ambitious parents made plans for them, but these plans don't always mesh, unfortunately. A suburban Chicago mom who wishes to remain anonymous called up a school friend of her daughter's to arrange a play date. The kindergartner was booked solid. "It seems like kids today are always on the way to somewhere," complains the disillusioned mom

One place kids keep rushing to is Chuck E. Cheese, the chain of video game–crammed pizzerias where families can frolic in air-conditioned safety, separated by turnstiles from the Big Bad Wolf. Such enterprises fill the play vacuum with something far more modern and secure—"edutainment." It's a growing industry. Randy White is CEO of White Hutchinson Leisure & Learning Group in Kansas City, Mo. His company develops cavernous play facilities, up to 30,000 sq. ft. in area, that are Xanadus of prefabricated diversion, offering art projects, costumes, blocks and even simulated fishing. "We're reintroducing free play to families," says White. Free play at a price, that is. His facilities charge up

to $10 a head. "Parents feel that if they're not paying much for an experience, it's not worth it educationally," he says.

> ## Screen Time
> THESE DAYS, when kids do play, it's often indoors and with machines, limiting their opportunities for free exploration

When young fun has to prove itself in educational terms—when it's not sufficient that play be just playful—the world has reached a dreary spot. Yet here we are. Consider this: since the 1980s, with the rise of the academic-standards movement, hundreds of American elementary schools have eliminated recess. The Atlanta schools have dropped recess system-wide, and other districts are thinking of following suit. Does a no-recess day raise test scores or aid kids' mental performance? There's no evidence for it. There is plenty of evidence, however, that unbroken classwork drives children slightly batty, as Atlanta teachers are starting to note. Multiple studies show that when recess time is delayed, elementary-school kids grow increasingly inattentive. Goodbye recess, hello Ritalin.

Rebecca Lamphere, 25, of Virginia Beach, Va., is a play activist, to coin an awkward phrase. Her mission began three years ago after she noticed that the school playground adjacent to her house was always empty. School officials later instituted a "recess substitute" program called Walk 'n Talk that involved having children circle four orange cones set up on the grounds after lunchtime. "It was considered social time," Lamphere says, "but they all had to go in one direction and keep their voices down." Lamphere wasn't pleased—her daughter Charleen was about to start kindergarten—so she launched a protest. She circulated a petition, sought out experts in child development and ultimately attracted statewide attention. Last April, Virginia Beach mandated daily recess, and the state followed five months later.

Is that what we've come to—obligatory play? The defenders of unfettered recreation have a way of making it sound like broccoli, wholesome and vitamin packed but unenticing. "Kids need to learn how to navigate themselves and keep their bodies safe," says Richard Cohen, a child-development expert and play-programs manager at Brookfield Zoo outside Chicago. What fun! At their grimmest, the play scholars sound like Stuart Brown recounting a study of Texas prison inmates that found a common element in their childhoods. "They didn't engage in rough-and-tumble play," he says, offering anxious parents yet one more reason to live in mortal fear of almost everything.

Fear—the natural enemy of play. The fear that a French lesson missed is a Yale acceptance letter lost. The fear that sending junior outside to roam will end in reporting him missing to the police. Do we now have to add to these fears—some of them neurotic, others real—the fear that "play deprivation" will stunt kids' spirits, shrink their brains and even land them in jail? Such protective obsessing seems to be the problem, and doing more of it offers no solution. Parents should probably just tell kids that fooling around is bad for them, open the door and follow them outside. All work and no play can make adults dull too—sometimes even a little paranoid.

From *Time*, April 30, 2001, pp. 56-58. © 2001 by Time Inc. Reprinted by permission.

PARENTING: THE LOST ART

BY KAY S. HYMOWITZ

LAST FALL the Federal Trade Commission released a report showing what most parents already knew from every trip down the aisle of Toys R Us and every look at prime time television: Entertainment companies routinely market R-rated movies, computer games, and music to children. The highly publicized report detailed many of the abuses of these companies—one particularly egregious example was the use of focus groups of 9- and 10-year-olds to test market violent films—and it unleashed a frenzied week of headlines and political grandstanding, all of it speaking to Americans' alarm over their children's exposure to an increasingly foul-mouthed, vicious, and tawdry media.

But are parents really so alarmed? A more careful reading of the FTC report considerably complicates the fairy tale picture of big, bad wolves tempting unsuspecting, innocent children with ads for *Scream* and *Doom* and inevitably raises the question: "Where were the parents?" As it turns out, many youngsters saw the offending ads not when they were reading *Nickelodeon Magazine* or watching *Seventh Heaven* but when they were leafing through *Cosmo Girl*, a junior version of Helen Gurley Brown's sex manual *Cosmopolitan*, or lounging in front of *Smackdown!*—a production of the World Wrestling Federation where wrestlers saunter out, grab their crotches, and bellow "Suck It!" to their "ho's" standing by. Other kids came across the ads when they were watching the WB's infamous teen sex soap opera *Dawson's Creek* or MTV, whose most recent hit, "Undressed," includes plots involving whipped cream, silk teddies, and a tutor who agrees to strip every time her student gets an answer right. All of these venues, the report noted without irony, are "especially popular among 11- to 18-year-olds." Oh, and those focus groups of 9- and 10-year-olds? It turns out that all of the children who attended the meetings had permission from their parents. To muddy the picture even further, only a short time before the FTC report, the Kaiser Family Foundation released a study entitled *Kids and Media: The New Millennium*

showing that half of all parents have no rules about what their kids watch on television, a number that is probably low given that the survey also found that two-thirds of American children between the ages of eight and eighteen have televisions in their bedrooms; and even more shocking, one-third of all under the age of seven.

In other words, one conclusion you could draw from the FTC report is that entertainment companies are willing to tempt children with the raunchiest, bloodiest, crudest media imaginable if it means expanding their audience and their profits. An additional conclusion, especially when considered alongside *Kids and the Media*, would be that there are a lot of parents out there who don't mind enough to do much about it. After all, protesting that your 10-year-old son was subjected to a trailer for the R-rated *Scream* while watching *Smackdown!* is a little like complaining that he was bitten by a rat while scavenging at the local dump.

Neither the FTC report nor *Kids and the Media* makes a big point of it, but their findings do begin to bring into focus a troubling sense felt by many Americans—and no one more than teachers—that parenting is becoming a lost art. This is not to accuse adults of being neglectful or abusive in any conventional sense. Like always, today's boomer parents love their children; they know their responsibility to provide for them and in fact, as *Kids and the Media* suggests, they are doing so more lavishly than ever before in human history. But throughout that history adults have understood something that perplexes many of today's parents: That they are not only obliged to feed and shelter the young, but to teach them self-control, civility, and a meaningful way of understanding the world. Of course, most parents care a great deal about their children's social and moral development. Most are doing their best to hang on to their sense of what really matters while they attempt to steer their children through a dizzyingly stressful, temptation-filled, and in many ways unfamiliar world. Yet these parents know they often cannot count on the support of their peers. The parents of their 10-year-old's friend let the girls watch an R-rated movie until 2 a.m. during a sleepover; other parents are nowhere to be found when beer is passed around at a party attended by their 14-year-old. These AWOL parents have redefined the meaning of the term. As their children gobble down their own microwaved dinners, then go on to watch their own televisions or surf the Internet on their own computers in wired bedrooms where they set their own bedtimes, these parents and their children seem more like housemates and friends than experienced adults guiding and shaping the young. Such parent-peers may be warm companions and in the short run effective advocates for their children, but they remain deeply uncertain about how to teach them to lead meaningful lives.

If anyone is familiar with the fallout from the lost art of parenting, it is educators. About a year ago, while researching an article about school discipline, I spoke to teachers, administrators, and school lawyers around the country and asked what is making their job more difficult today. Their top answer was almost always the same: parents. Sometimes they describe overworked, overburdened parents who have simply checked out: "I work 10 hours a day, and I can't come home and deal with this stuff. He's *your* problem," they might say. But more often teachers find parents who rather than accepting their role as partners with educators in an effort to civilize the next generation come in with a "my-child-right-or-wrong" attitude. These are parent-advocates.

Everyone's heard about the growing number of suspensions in middle and high schools around the country. Now the state of Connecticut has released a report on an alarming increase in the number of young children—first-graders, kindergartners, and *preschoolers*—suspended for persistent biting, kicking, hitting, and cursing. Is it any wonder? Parent-advocates have little patience for the shared rules of behavior required to turn a school into a civil community, not to mention those who would teach their own children the necessary limits to self-expression. "'You and your stupid rules.' I've heard that a hundred times," sighs Cathy Collins, counsel to the School Administrators of Iowa, speaking not, as it might sound, of 16-year-olds, but of their parents. Even 10 years ago when a child got into trouble, parents assumed the teacher or principal was in the right. "Now we're always being second-guessed," says a 25-year veteran of suburban New Jersey elementary schools. "I know my child, and he wouldn't do this," or, proudly, "He has a mind of his own," are lines many educators repeat hearing.

In the most extreme cases, parent-advocates show (and teach their children) their contempt for school rules by going to court. Several years ago, a St. Charles, Mo., high schooler running for student council was suspended for distributing condoms on the day of the election as a way of soliciting votes. His family promptly turned around and sued on the grounds that the boy's free speech rights were being violated because other candidates had handed out candy during student council elections without any repercussions. Sometimes principals are surprised to see a lawyer trailing behind an angry parent arriving for a conference over a minor infraction. Parents threaten teachers with lawsuits, and kids repeat after them: "I'll sue you," or "My mother's

going to get a lawyer." Surveys may show a large number of parents in favor of school uniforms, but for parent-advocates, dress codes that limit their child's self-expression are a particular source of outrage. In Northumberland County, Pa., parents threatened to sue their children's *elementary* school over its new dress code. "I have a little girl who likes to express herself with how she dresses," one mother of a fourth-grader said. "They ruined my daughter's first day of school," another mother of a kindergartner whined.

Parent-advocates may make life difficult for teachers and soccer coaches. But the truth is things aren't so great at home either. Educators report parents of second- and third-graders saying things like: "I can't control what she wears to school," or "I can't make him read." It's not surprising. At home, parent-advocates aspire to be friends and equals, hoping to maintain the happy affection they think of as a "good relationship." It rarely seems to happen that way. Unable to balance warmth with discipline and affirmation with limit-setting, these parents are puzzled to find their 4-year-old ordering them around like he's Louis XIV or their 8-year-old screaming, "I hate you!" when they balk at letting her go to a sleepover party for the second night in a row. These buddy adults are not only incapable of helping their children resist the siren call of a sensational, glamorous media; in a desperate effort to confirm their "good relationship" with their kids, they actively reinforce it. They buy them their own televisions, they give them "guilt money," as market researchers call it, to go shopping, and they plan endless entertainments. A recent article in *Time* magazine on the Britney Spears fad began by describing a party that parents in Westchester, N.Y., gave their 9-year-old complete with a Britney impersonator boogying in silver hip-huggers and tube top. Doubtless such peer-parents tell themselves they are making their children happy and, anyway, what's the harm. They shouldn't count on it. "When one of our teenagers comes in looking like Britney Spears, they carry with them an attitude," one school principal was quoted as saying. There's a reason that some of the clothing lines that sell the Britney look adopt names such as "Brat" or "No Boundaries."

Of course, dressing like a Las Vegas chorus girl at 8 years old does not automatically mean a child is headed for juvenile hall when she turns 14. But it's reasonable to assume that parent-friends who don't know how to get their third-graders to stop calling them names, never mind covering their midriffs before going to school, are going to be pretty helpless when faced with the more serious challenges of adolescence. Some parents simply give up. They've done all they can, they say to themselves; the kids have to figure it out for themselves. "I feel if [my son] hasn't learned the proper values by 16, then we haven't done our job," announces the mother of a 16-year-old in a fascinating 1999 *Time* magazine series, "Diary of a High School." Others continue the charade of peer friendship by endorsing their adolescent's risk-taking as if they were one of the in-crowd. In a recent article in *Education Week*, Anne W. Weeks, the director of college guidance at a Maryland high school, tells how when police broke up a party on the field of a nearby college, they discovered that most of the kids were actually local high schoolers. High school officials called parents to express their concern, but they were having none of it; it seems parents were the ones providing the alcohol and dropping their kids off at what they knew to be a popular (and unchaperoned) party spot. So great is the need of some parents to keep up the pretense of their equality that they refuse to heed their own children's cry for adult help. A while back, the *New York Times* ran a story on Wesleyan University's "naked dorm" where, as one 19-year-old male student told the reporter: "If I feel the need to take my pants off, I take my pants off," something he evidently felt the need to do during the interview. More striking than the dorm itself—after all, when kids are in charge, as they are in many colleges, what would we expect?—was the phone call a worried female student made to her parents when she first realized she had been assigned to a "naked dorm." She may have been alarmed, but her father, she reports, simply "laughed."

Perhaps more common than parents who laugh at naked dorms or who supply booze for their kids' parties, are those who dimly realize the failure of their experiment in peer-parenting. These parents reduce their role to exercising damage control over kids they assume "are going to do it anyway." For them, there is only one value left they are comfortable fighting for: safety. One mother in *Time*'s "Diary of a High School" replenishes a pile of condoms for her own child and his friends once a month, doubtless congratulating herself that she is protecting the young. Safety also appears to be the logic behind the new fad of co-ed sleepover parties as it was described recently in the *Washington Post*. "I just feel it's definitely better than going to hotels, and this way you know all the kids who are coming over, you know who they are with," explains the mother of one high schooler. Kids know exactly how to reach a generation of parents who, though they waffled on whether their 8-year-old could call them "idiot," suddenly became tyrants when it came to seat belts and helmets. The article describes how one boy talked his parents into allowing him to give a co-ed sleepover party. "It's too dangerous for us to be out late at night with all the drunk drivers. Better that we are home. It's better than us lying about where we are and renting some sleazy motel room." The father found the "parental logic," as the reporter puts it, so irresistible that he allowed the boy to have not one, but two co-ed sleepover parties.

NOTHING GIVES a better picture of the anemic principles of peer-parenting—and their sorry impact on kids—than a 1999 PBS *Frontline* show entitled "The Lost Children of Rockdale County." The occasion for the show was an outbreak of syphilis in an affluent Atlanta suburb that ultimately led health officials to treat 200 teenagers. What was so remarkable was not that 200 teenagers in a large suburban area were having sex and that they have overlapping partners. It was the way they were having sex. This was teen sex as *Lord of the Flies* author William Golding might have imagined it—a heart of darkness tribal rite of such degradation that it makes a collegiate "hook up" look like splendor in the grass. Group sex was commonplace, as were 13-year-old participants. Kids would gather together after school and watch the Playboy cable TV channel, making a game of imitating everything they saw. They tried almost every permutation of

sexual activity imaginable—vaginal, oral, anal, girl-on-girl, several boys with a single girl, or several girls with a boy. During some drunken parties, one boy or girl might be "passed around" in a game. A number of the kids had upwards of 50 partners.

To be sure, the Rockdale teens are the extreme case. The same could not be said of their parents. As the *Frontline* producers show them, these are ordinary, suburban soccer moms and dads, more affluent than most, perhaps, and in some cases overly caught up in their work. But a good number were doing everything the books tell you to do: coaching their children's teams, cooking dinner with them, going on vacations together. It wasn't enough. Devoid of strong beliefs, seemingly bereft of meaningful experience to pass on to their young, these parents project a bland emptiness that seems the exact inverse of the meticulous opulence of their homes and that lets the kids know there are no values worth fighting for. "They have to make decisions, whether to take drugs, to have sex," the mother of one of the boys intones expressionlessly when asked for her view of her son's after-school activity. "I can give them my opinion, tell them how I feel. But they have to decide for themselves." These lost adults of Rockdale County have abdicated the age-old distinction between parents and children, and the kids know it. "We're pretty much like best friends or something," one girl said of her parents. "I mean I can pretty much tell 'em how I feel, what I wanna do and they'll let me do it." Another girl pretty well sums up the persona of many contemporary parents when she says of her own mother. "I don't really consider her a mom all that much. She takes care of me and such, but I consider her a friend more."

So what happened to the lost art of parenting? Why is it that so many adults have reinvented their traditional role and turned themselves into advocates, friends, and copious providers of entertainment?

For one thing, this generation of parents has grown up in a culture that devotedly worships youth. It's true that America, a nation of immigrants fleeing the old world, has always been a youthful country with its eye on the future. But for the "I-hope-I-die-before-I-get-old" generation, aging, with its threat of sexual irrelevance and being out of the loop, has been especially painful. Boomers are the eternal teenagers—hip, sexy, and aware—and when their children suggest otherwise, they're paralyzed with confusion. In an op-ed published in the *New York Times* entitled "Am I a Cool Mother?" Susan Borowitz, co-creator of *Fresh Prince of Bel-Air*, describes her struggle with her role as parent-adult that one suspects is all too common. On a shopping expedition, she is shocked when her 10-year-old daughter rolls her eyes at the outfits she has chosen for her. "There is nothing more withering and crushing," she writes. "I stood there stunned. 'This can't be happening to me. I'm a cool mom.'" Determined to hang on to her youthful identity, she buys a pair of bell-bottom pants to take her daughter to DJ Disco Night at her school where she spots other "cool moms... pumping their fist and doing the Arsenio woof." Finally Borowitz comes to her senses. "This was a party for the kids. I am not a kid. I am a mom." No one could quarrel with her there, but the telling point is that it took 10 years for her to notice.

The Parent as Career Coach

There is one exception to today's parents' overall vagueness about their job description: They *know* they want their children to develop impressive résumés. This is what William Doherty, professor of family science at the University of Minnesota, calls "parenting as product development."

As early as the preschool years, parent-product developers begin a demanding schedule of gymnastics, soccer, language, and music lessons. In New York City, parents take their children to "Language for Tots," beginning at six months—that is, before they can even speak. Doherty cites the example of one Minnesota town where, until some cooler—or more sleep-deprived—heads prevailed, a team of 4-year-olds was scheduled for hockey practice the only time the rink was available—at 5 A.M. By the time children are ready for Little League, some parents hire hitting and pitching coaches from companies like Grand Slam USA. So many kids are training like professionals in a single sport instead of the more casual three or four activities of childhood past that doctors report a high rate of debilitating and sometimes even permanent sports injuries.

Of course, there's nothing wrong with wanting to enrich your children's experience by introducing them to sports and the arts. But as children's list-worthy achievements take on disproportionate and even frenzied significance, parents often lose sight of some of the other things they want to pass down—such as kindness, moral clarity, and a family identity. One Manhattan nursery school director reports that if a child receives a high score on the ERB (the IQ test required to get into private kindergarten), parents often conclude that the child's brilliance excuses him or her from social niceties. "If he can't pass the juice or look you in the eye, it's 'Oh, he's bored.'" Douglas Goetsch, a teacher at Stuyvesant High School, the ultra-competitive school in New York City, recently wrote an article in the school newspaper about the prevalence of cheating; in every case, he says, cheating is related to an "excessively demanding parent." Other educators are seeing even young children complaining about stress-related headaches and stomachaches.

Katherine Tarbox, a Fairfield, Conn., teen, describes all this from the point of view of the child-product in her recently published memoir *Katie.com*. At 13, Katie was an "A" student, an accomplished pianist who also sang with the school choir, and a nationally ranked swimmer. Impressive as they were, Katie's achievements loomed too large. "I always felt like my self-worth was determined by how well I placed. And I think my parents felt the same way—their status among the team parents depended on how well their child placed." Like many middle-class children today, the combination of school, extracurricular activities, and her parents' work schedule reduced family time so much that, "Home was a place I always felt alone." Aching to be loved for herself rather than her swim times and grade point average, she develops an intense relationship with a man on the Internet who very nearly rapes her when they arrange to meet at an out-of-town swim meet.

Even after their daughter's isolation stands revealed, Katie's parents are so hooked on achievement they still don't really notice their daughter. Katie complains to her therapist that her mother is always either at the office or working on papers at home. The woman has a helpful suggestion that epitomizes the overly schematized, hyper-efficient lives that come with parenting as product development: She suggests that Katie schedule appointments with her mother.

Related to this youth worship is the boomer parents' intense ambivalence about authority. The current generation of parents came of age at a time when parents, teachers, the police, and the army represented an authority to be questioned and resisted. Authority was associated with *Father Knows Best*, the Vietnam War, Bull Connor, and their own distant fathers. These associations linger in boomer parents' subconscious minds and make them squirm uncomfortably when their own children beg for firm guidance. Evelyn Bassoff, a Colorado therapist, reports that when she asks the women in her mothers' groups what happens when they discipline their daughters, they give answers such as "I feel mean," "I feel guilty," and "I quake all over; it's almost like having dry heaves inside." A survey by Public Agenda confirms that parents feel "tentative and uncertain in matters of discipline and authority." And no wonder. Notice the way *Time* describes the dilemma faced by parents of Britney Spears wannabes; these parents, the writers explain, are "trying to walk the line between fashion and fascism." The message is clear; the opposite of letting your child do what she wants is, well, becoming Hitler.

It would be difficult to overstate how deep this queasiness over authority runs in the boomer mind. Running so hard from outmoded models of authority that stressed absolute obedience, today's parents have slipped past all recognition of the child's longing for a structure he can believe in. In some cases, their fear not only inhibits them from disciplining their children, it can actually make them view the rebellious child as a figure to be respected. (Oddly enough, this is true even when, as is almost always the case these days, that rebellion takes the form of piercings and heavy metal music vigorously marketed by entertainment companies.) It's as if parents believe children learn individuality and self-respect in the act of defiance, or at the very least through aggressive self-assertion. Some experts reinforce their thinking. Take Barbara Mackoff, author of *Growing a Girl* (with a chapter tellingly entitled "Make Her the Authority"). Mackoff approvingly cites a father who encourages a child "to be comfortable arguing or being mad at me. I figure if she has lots of practice getting mad at a six-foot-one male, she'll be able to say what she thinks to anyone." The author agrees; the parent who tells the angry child "calm down, we don't hit people," she writes, "is engaging in silencing." In other words, to engage in civilization's oldest parental task—teaching children self-control—is to risk turning your child into an automaton ripe for abuse.

But the biggest problem for boomer peer-parents is that many of them are not really sure whether there are values important enough to pursue with any real conviction. In his book *One Nation After All*, the sociologist Alan Wolfe argues that although Americans are concerned about moral decline, they are also opposed to people who get too excited about it. This inherent contradiction—people simultaneously judge and refuse to judge—explains how it is that parents can both dislike their children watching *Smackdown!* on TV, talking back to them, drinking, or for that matter, engaging in group sex, but also fail to protest very loudly. Having absorbed an ethos of nonjudgmentalism, the parents' beliefs on these matters have been drained of all feeling and force. The Rockdale mother who blandly repeats "her opinion" about drugs and sex to her son is a perfect example; perhaps she is concerned about moral decline, but because her concern lacks all gravity or passion, it can't possibly have much effect. All in all, Wolfe seems to find the combination of concern and nonjudgmentalism a fairly hopeful state of affairs—and surely he is right that tolerance is a key value in a pluralistic society—but refusing to judge is one thing when it comes to your neighbor's divorce and quite another when it comes to your 13-year-old child's attitudes toward, say, cheating on a test or cursing out his soccer coach.

W HEN PARENTS fail to firmly define a moral universe for their children, it leaves them vulnerable to the amoral world evoked by their peers and a sensational media. As the Rockdale story makes clear, the saddest consequences appear in the sex lives of today's teenagers. Recently in an iVillage chat room, a distraught mother wrote to ask for advice after she learned that her 15-year-old daughter had sex with a boy. The responses she got rehearsed many of the principles of peer-parenting. Several mothers stressed safety and told the woman to get her daughter on the pill. Others acted out the usual boomer uneasiness over the power they have with their children. "Let your daughter know you trust her to make the 'right' decision when the time comes," wrote one. "Tell her that you are not 'giving your permission,'" another suggested, "but that you are also very aware that she will not 'ask for permission' either when the time comes." But it was the one teenager who joined in that showed how little these apparently hip mothers understood about the pressures on kids today; when she lost her virginity at 14, the girl writes: "it was because of a yearning to be loved, to be accepted." Indeed, the same need for acceptance appears to be driving the trend among middle-schoolers as young as seventh grade engaging in oral sex. According to the December 2000 *Family Planning Perspectives*, some middle school girls view fellatio as the unpleasant price they have to pay to hang on to a boyfriend or to seem hip and sophisticated among their friends. The awful irony is that in their reluctance to evoke meaningful values, parent advocates and peers have produced not the free-thinking, self-expressive, confident children they had hoped, but kids so conforming and obedient they'll follow their friends almost anywhere.

And so in the end, it is children who pay the price of the refusal of parents to seriously engage their predicament in a media-saturated and shadowy adult world. And what a price it is. When parenting becomes a lost art, children are not only deprived of the clarity and sound judgment they crave. They are deprived of childhood.

Kay S. Hymowitz, a senior fellow at the Manhattan Institute and contributing editor at City Journal, *is the author of* Ready or Not: What Happens When We Treat Children as Small Adults *(Encounter Books, 2000).*

From *American Educator*, Spring 2001, pp. 4-9. © 2001 by American Educator, the quarterly journal of the American Federation of Teachers. Reprinted by permission.

DISARMING THE RAGE

Across the country, thousands of students stay home from school each day, terrified of humiliation or worse at the hands of bullies. In the wake of school shootings—most recently in California and Pennsylvania—parents, teachers and lawmakers are demanding quick action

Richard Jerome

In the rigid social system of Bethel Regional High School in Bethel, a remote town in the tundra of southwest Alaska, Evan Ramsey was an outcast, a status earned by his slight frame, shy manner, poor grades and broken family. "Everybody had given me a nickname: Screech, the nerdy character on *Saved by the Bell*," he recalls. "I got stuff thrown at me, I got spit on, I got beat up. Sometimes I fought back, but I wasn't that good at fighting." Taunted throughout his years in school, he reported the incidents to his teachers, and at first his tormentors were punished. "After a while [the principal] told me to just start ignoring everybody. But then you can't take it anymore."

On the morning of Feb. 19, 1997, Ramsey, then 16, went to school with a 12-gauge shotgun, walked to a crowded common area and opened fire. As schoolmates fled screaming, he roamed the halls shooting randomly— mostly into the air. Ramsey would finally surrender to police, but not before killing basketball star Josh Palacios, 16, with a blast to the stomach, and principal Ron Ed-

wards, 50, who was shot in the back. Tried as an adult for murder, Ramsey was sentenced to 210 years in prison after a jury rejected a defense contention that he had been attempting "suicide by cop," hoping to be gunned down but not intending to kill anyone. Still, Ramsey now admits in his cell at Spring Creek Correctional Center in Seward, Alaska, "I felt a sense of power with a gun. It was the only way to get rid of the anger."

Unfortunately Ramsey is not alone. Children all over the country are feeling fear, hopelessness and rage, emotions that turn some of them into bullies and others into their victims. Some say that is how it has always been and always will be—that bullying, like other adolescent ills, is something to be endured and to grow out of. But that view is changing. At a time when many parents are afraid to send their children to school, the wake-up call sounded by the 13 killings and 2 suicides at Columbine High School in Colorado two years ago still reverberates. It is now clear that Columbine shooters Dylan Klebold and

Eric Harris felt bullied and alienated, and in their minds it was payback time.

In recent months there have been two other horrifying shooting incidents resulting, at least in part, from bullying. On March 5, 15-year-old Charles "Andy" Williams brought a .22-cal. pistol to Santana High School in Santee, Calif., and shot 15 students and adults, killing 2. He was recently certified to stand trial for murder as an adult. His apparent motive? Lethal revenge for the torment he had known at the hands of local kids. "We abused him pretty much, I mean verbally," concedes one of them. "I called him a skinny faggot one time."

Two days after the Williams shooting, Elizabeth Bush, 14, an eighth grader from Williamsport, Pa., who said she was often called "idiot, stupid, fat, ugly," brought her father's .22-cal. pistol to school and shot 13-year-old Kimberly Marchese, wounding her in the shoulder. Kimberly, one of her few friends, had earned Elizabeth's ire by allegedly turning on her and joining in with the taunters. Bush admitted her guilt and offered apologies. A ward of the court until after she turns 21, she is now in a juvenile psychiatric facility. Kimberly, meanwhile, still has bullet fragments in her shoulder and is undergoing physical therapy.

As school enrollment rises and youths cope with the mounting pressures of today's competitive and status-conscious culture, the numbers of bullied children have grown as rapidly as the consequences. According to the National Education Association, 160,000 children skip school each day because of intimidation by their peers. The U.S. Department of Education reports that 77 percent of middle and high school students in small midwestern towns have been bullied. And a National Institutes of Health study newly released in the *Journal of the American Medical Association* reveals that almost a third of 6th to 10th graders—5.7 million children nationwide—have experienced some kind of bullying. "We are talking about a significant problem," says Deborah Prothrow-Stith, professor of public health practice at Harvard, who cites emotional alienation at home as another factor in creating bullies. "A lot of kids have grief, loss, pain, and it's unresolved."

Some experts see bullying as an inevitable consequence of a culture that rewards perceived strength and dominance. "The concept of power we admire is power over someone else," says Jackson Katz, 41, whose Long Beach, Calif., consulting firm counsels schools and the military on violence prevention. "In corporate culture, in sports culture, in the media, we honor those who win at all costs. The bully is a kind of hero in our society." Perhaps not surprisingly, most bullies are male. "Our culture defines masculinity as connected to power, control and dominance," notes Katz, whose work was inspired in part by the shame he felt in high school when he once stood idly by while a bully beat up a smaller student.

As for the targets of bullying, alienation runs like a stitch through most of their lives. A study last fall by the

U.S. Secret Service found that in two-thirds of the 37 school shootings since 1974, the attackers felt "persecuted, bullied, threatened, attacked or injured." In more than three-quarters of the cases, the attacker told a peer of his violent intentions. William Pollack, a clinical psychologist and author of *Real Boys' Voices,* who contributed to the Secret Service study, said that several boys from Columbine described bullying as part of the school fabric. Two admitted to mocking Klebold and Harris. "Why don't people get it that it drives you over the edge?" they told Pollack. "It isn't just Columbine. It is everywhere."

That sad fact is beginning to sink in, as the spate of disturbing incidents in recent years has set off desperate searches for answers. In response, parents have begun crusades to warn and educate other families, courts have seen drawn-out legal battles that try to determine who is ultimately responsible, and lawmakers in several states—including Texas, New York and Massachusetts—have struggled to shape anti-bullying legislation that would offer remedies ranging from early intervention and counseling to the automatic expulsion of offenders.

One of the most shocking cases of victimization by bullies took place near Atlanta on March 28, 1994. That day, 15-year-old Brian Head, a heavyset sophomore at suburban Etowah High School, walked into his economics class, pulled out his father's 9-mm handgun and pressed it to his temple. "I can't take this anymore," he said. Then he squeezed the trigger. Brian had been teased for years about his weight. "A lot of times the more popular or athletic kids would make him a target," his mother, Rita, 43, says of her only child, a sensitive boy with a gift for poetry [see box at right]. "They would slap Brian in the back of the head or push him into a locker. It just broke him." Not a single student was disciplined in connection with his death. After his suicide, Rita, a magazine copy editor, and her husband, Bill, 47, counseled other parents and produced a video for elementary school students titled *But Names Will Never Hurt Me* about an overweight girl who suffers relentless teasing.

Georgia residents were stunned by a second child's death on Nov. 2, 1998. After stepping off a school bus, 13-year-old Josh Belluardo was fatally punched by his neighbor Jonathan Miller, 15, who had been suspended in the past for bullying and other infractions. In that tragedy's wake Georgia Gov. Roy Barnes in 1999 signed an anti-bullying law that allows schools to expel any student three times disciplined for picking on others.

On the other side of the continent, Washington Gov. Gary Locke is pressing for anti-bullying training in schools, following two high-profile cases there. Jenny Wieland of Seattle still cannot talk of her only child, Amy Ragan, shot dead at age 17 more than eight years ago, without tearing up. A soccer player and equestrian in her senior year at Marysville-Pilchuck High School, Amy was heading to the mall on the night of Nov. 20, 1992, when she stopped at a friend's apartment. There, three schoolmates had gathered by the time Trevor Oscar Turner showed up. Then 19, Turner was showing off a .38-cal. revolver, holding it to kids' heads, and when he got to Amy, the weapon went off. Turner pleaded guilty to first-degree manslaughter and served 27 months of a 41-month sentence.

"I can't help but wonder what Amy's life would be like if she was still alive," says Wieland today. "I wonder about her career and if she'd be in love or have a baby." Wieland turned her grief into action. In 1994 she helped start Mothers Against Violence in America (MAVIA), an activist group patterned after Mothers Against Drunk Driving. She left her insurance job to become the program's director and speaks annually at 50 schools. In 1998 she became the first director of SAVE (Students Against Violence Everywhere), which continues to grow, now boasting 126 student chapters nationwide that offer schools anti-harassment and conflict-resolution programs. "People ask how I can stand to tell her story over and over," she says. "If I can save just one child, it's well worth the pain."

Not long after Amy Ragan's death, another bullying scenario unfolded 50 miles away in Stanwood, Wash. Confined to a wheelchair by cerebral palsy, Calcutta-born Taya Haugstad was a fifth grader in 1993, when a boy began calling her "bitch" and "retard." The daily verbal abuse led to terrible nightmares. By middle school, according to a lawsuit Taya later filed, her tormentor—a popular athlete—got physical, pushing her wheelchair into the wall and holding it while his friends kicked the wheels. Eventually Taya was diagnosed with posttraumatic stress disorder. "Imagine that you can't run away or scream," says her psychologist Judith McCarthy. "Not only was she traumatized, she's handicapped. She felt terribly unsafe in the world." Her adoptive parents, Karrie and Ken Haugstad, 48 and 55, complained to school authorities and went to court to get a restraining order against the bully, but it was never issued. Taya sued the school district and the boy in 1999. The judge awarded her $300,000 last year, ruling that the school was negligent in its supervision, thus inflicting emotional distress. (The ruling is under appeal.) Taya, now 19 and a high school junior, hopes to study writing in college. She says she holds no grudge against her nemesis, who received undisclosed punishment from the school. "I don't think about him," she says.

But Josh Sneed may never forgive the boys he refers to as the Skaters. It was in 1996, late in his freshman year at Powell High School in Powell, Tenn., when, he says, a group of skateboarders began to terrorize him. With chains clinking and baseball bats pounding the pavement, he claims, they chased him and threatened to beat him to death. Why Josh? He was small and "a country boy," says his homemaker mother, Karen Grady, 41. "They made fun of him for that. They told him he was poor and made fun of him for that."

Then on Oct. 17, 1996, "I just snapped," her son says. As Jason Pratt, known as one of the Skaters, passed him in the cafeteria, Sneed whacked him on the head with a tray. "I figured if I got lucky and took him out, all the other non-

Lost in the Shadows

BRIAN HEAD, 15

After years of being tormented at school, this Georgia teen who loved music and video games ended his life with a gunshot. Later, his parents found this poem among his belongings.

As I walk in the light, the shadow draws me closer,
with the ambition and curiosity of a small boy
and the determination of a man.
The shadow is sanctuary, a place to escape the light.
In the light they can see me,
in the light they can see all.
Although the light is wide in its spread,
they still cannot see the pain in my face.
The pain that their eyes bring to bear when
they look upon me.
They see me as an insignificant "thing,"
Something to be traded, mangled and mocked.
But in the shadows I know they would not,
nor could not, see such a lie.
In the shadows, their evil eyes cannot stare
my soul into oblivion.
In the dark, I am free to move without their
judgmental eyes on me.
In the shadows, I can sleep without dreams of
despair and deception.
In the shadows I am home.

sense would stop." But after a few punches, Josh slipped on a scrap of food, hit his head on the floor and lost consciousness as Pratt kneed him in the head several times. Finally a football player leapt over two tables and dragged Sneed away, likely saving his life. Four titanium plates were needed to secure his shattered skull, and he was so gravely injured that he had to relearn how to walk and talk. Homeschooled, Sneed eventually earned his GED, but he hasn't regained his short-term memory. Assault charges against both him and Pratt were dismissed, but Pratt (who declined to comment) was suspended from school for 133 days.

Grady sued the county, claiming that because the school knew Josh was being terrorized but never disciplined the tormentors, they effectively sanctioned the conditions that led to the fight. Her attorney James A. H. Bell hopes the suit will have national implications. "We tried to make a statement, holding the school system accountable for its failure to protect," he says. In February Sneed and Grady were awarded $49,807 by a judge who found the county partly at fault. A tractor buff who once aspired to own a John Deere shop, Josh now lives on his grandfather's farm, passing his days with cartoons, video games and light chores. "Everybody's hollering that they need to get rid of guns, but it's not that," he says. "You need to find out what's going on in school."

Around the country, officials are attempting to do precisely that, as many states now require a safe-school plan that specifically addresses bullying. Most experts agree that metal detectors and zero-tolerance expulsions ignore the root of the problem. Counseling and fostering teamwork seem most effective, as evidenced by successful programs in the Cherry Creek, Colo., school district and DeKalb County, Ga. "We create an atmosphere of caring—it's harder to be a bully when you care about someone," says John Monferdini, head counselor at the DeKalb Alternative School, which serves 400 county students, most of whom have been expelled for bullying and violent behavior. Apart from academics, the school offers conflict-resolution courses and team-oriented outdoor activities that demand cooperation. "Yeah, I'm a bully," says Chris Jones, 15. "If I'm with friends and we see someone coming along we can jump on, we do it. It's like, you know, an adrenaline rush." But a stint in DeKalb is having a transformative effect. "When I came here, it was because we beat up a kid so badly—sticking his head in the bleachers—and the only thing I wished was that we'd had a chance to hurt him worse before we got caught. That's not the way I am now."

One wonders if intervention might have restrained the bullies who tormented Evan Ramsey. Ineligible for parole until 2066, when he'll be 86, Ramsey, now 20, spends most days working out, playing cards, reading Stephen King novels and studying for his high school diploma. He also has plenty of time to reflect on the horrible error in judgment he made. "The worst thing is to resort to violence," he says. "I'd like to get letters from kids who are getting problems like I went through. I could write back and help them." His advice: "If they're being messed with, they have to tell someone. If nothing's done, then they have to go [to] higher and higher [authority] until it stops. If they don't get help, that's when they'll lose it and maybe do something bad—really bad. And the pain of doing that never really stops."

Ron Arias in Seward, **Mary Boone** in Seattle, **Lauren Comander** in Chicago, **Joanne Fowler** in New York City, **Maureen** Harrington in Stanwood, **Ellen Mazo** in Jersey Shore, Pa., **Jamie Reno** in Santee, **Don Sider** in West Palm Beach and **Gail Cameron Wescott** in Atlanta

BULLIES 101

How can parents tell when their child is being bullied—or bullying others?

In 1993 a panel of experts in the Cherry Creek School District in Englewood, Colo., published Bully-Proofing Your School, *a manifesto designed to stop bullying at an early age. One of its coauthors, Dr. William Porter, 55, a clinical psychologist, offers the following guidelines for parents.*

•**What is a bully?**
A bully is a child who takes repeated hostile actions against another child and has more power than the individual he targets. Bullies tend to be very glib and don't accept responsibility for their behavior.

•**How do I know if my child is being bullied?**
He or she may show an unwillingness to go to school and may have bruises or damage to belongings that can't be explained. Children who are being bullied tend to keep silent about it and may become withdrawn, depressed and feel no one can help.

•**What do I do if my child is being bullied?**
Listen to your child and express confidence that the problem can be solved. Keep trying until you find someone at the school to help. Practice with your child such protective skills as avoiding the confrontation or using humor to deflate a tense moment.

•**What if my child is a bully?**
Set clear and consistent expectations of behavior, and work with the school on follow-up. Don't let the child talk his or her way out of the behavior, and find positive ways for him or her to get attention.

From *People Weekly*, June 4, 2001, pp. 54-61. © 2001 by Richard Jerome. Reprinted by permission. All rights reserved.

A World of Their Own

They're spiritual, optimistic and ambitious. How teens want to shape the future.

By Sharon Begley

THE TEMPTATION, OF COURSE, IS to seek The Teen, the one who can stand as a symbol of this generation, who exemplifies in a single, still-young life the aspirations, the values, the habits and outlook of the 22 million other Americans 13 to 19. Who, then, shall we offer up? Perhaps Vanesa Vathanasombat, 17, of Whittier, Calif., who spends her free time going to the beach and hanging at malls with friends. "You are who you hang around with," she says. "Before, parents made you who you are. Now, teens are pretty much defined by their friends. I see my mom maybe an hour a day and not at all on weekends." Or maybe Zoe Ward, 15, of Shoreline, Wash., who takes road trips with a friend (they sleep in the car) and sells her poetry on the street: "I can't decide if I want to be famous or if I want to go live in the mountains. That's what it's like for a lot of high-school kids: we don't know how to get there, what it's really going to be like." Or, finally, Marcus Ruopp, 16, of Newton, Mass., who would like to be an engineer or maybe a teacher after the Peace Corps, in order to "give back to the community."

No one teen incorporates all the attitudes and characteristics that the teachers who teach them, the parents who raise them, the researchers who study them and the kids who *are* them name as the identifying marks of this generation. In large part that is because "today's teens may have less in common with each other than those in generations past," says psychologist William Damon of Stanford University. "[Some] are absolutely on track: they're bright-eyed, genuine and ambitious. But a significant number are drifting or worse." Innumerable teens, then, will not recognize themselves in the portraits that follow. Yes, of course there are teens for whom adults are a strong presence, and teens who seldom volunteer. There are teens who are emotional wrecks, or even mentally ill. There are teens to whom "Instant Message" means Mom's telling them right away who

phoned while they were out. And there are teens who belong to no clique—or "tribe." But, according to a new NEWSWEEK Poll as well as sociologists who have studied tens of thousands of the kids born between 1981 and 1987, those teens are the exceptions. As much as is possible when you are talking about 22 million human beings, a portrait of the millennial generation is emerging.

Style counts
Teen cliques are more fluid than adults think, but each has its own distinctive tribal markings, from hippie chic to body art to buttoned-down prep

They were born at a time when the very culture was shifting to accommodate them—changing tables in restrooms, BABY ON BOARD signs and minivans. Yet, as a group, they lead lives that are more "adult-free" than those of previous generations. "Adolescents are not a tribe apart because *they* left *us*, as most people assume," says Patricia Hersch, author of the 1998 book "A Tribe Apart." "We left them. This generation of kids has spent more time on their own than any other in recent history."

When today's teens are not with their friends, many live in a private, adult-free world of the Web and videogames. Aminah McKinnie, 16, of Madison, Miss., attends church, loves gospel hip-hop and hopes to work in the computer industry. She doesn't "hang out," she says. "I shop on the Internet and am looking for a job on the Internet. I do homework, research, e-mail and talk to my friends on the Internet." She is not unusual. Data released last year from the Alfred P. Sloan Study of Youth and Social Development found that teens spend 9 percent of their waking hours outside school with friends. They spend 20 percent of their waking hours alone. "Teens are isolated to an extent that has never been possible before," says Stanford's Damon. "There is an ethic among adults that says, 'Kids want to be autonomous; don't get in their face.' "

A Snapshot of a Generation

In the Internet age, teens seem to be coming of age ever earlier. A recent NEWSWEEK Poll explores what concerns today's youth and asks if their parents have a clue.

• Stress: Do teens today face more problems than their parents did as teens?		• Family: Do your parents spend enough time with you?	
	TEENS		TEENS
More	70%	Enough	61%
Fewer	5	Too little	24
Same	24	Too much	5

• **48% of teens say they use a computer almost every day at home**

• **21% have looked at something on the Internet that they wouldn't want their parents to know about**

• **Identity: How much peer pressure from friends do you feel (does your teen feel) today to do the following?**

THOSE RESPONDING A LOT	TEENS	PARENTS
Have sex	10%	20%
Grow up too fast	16	34
Steal or shoplift	4	11
Use drugs or abuse alcohol	10	18
Defy parents or teachers	9	16
Be mean to kids who are different	11	14

• **If you had to choose between fitting in with friends or becoming outstanding in some way, which would you (your teen) choose?**

	TEENS	PARENTS
Fitting in	26%	43%
Becoming outstanding	69	50

• **Worries: How concerned are you about the following?**

THOSE RESPONDING A LOT	TEENS	PARENTS
Not having enough money to buy the things you (they) want	34%	35%
The cost of your (their) college education	54	68
Violence in society	59	82
Not being sure about your (their) future job opportunities	43	49
Your (their) getting into trouble with drugs	25	66
Your (their) drinking or abusing alcohol	26	64
Sexual permissiveness in society	33	72
Sexually transmitted diseases	58	75

• Hostility: Many teens these days feel a lot of anger. How angry are you?		• Faith: How important is religion in your life today?	
	TEENS		TEENS
Very	3%	Very	43%
Somewhat	25	Somewhat	35
Not too	43	Not too	14
Not at all	29	Not at all	8

• **17% of teens and 37% of parents say they worry a lot about safety at school**

• **21% of teenagers polled say that most of the teens they know have already had sex**

FOR THIS SPECIAL NEWSWEEK POLL, PRINCETON SURVEY RESEARCH ASSOCIATES INTERVIEWED A NATIONAL SAMPLE OF TEENS 13–19 AND 509 PARENTS OF SUCH TEENS BY TELEPHONE APRIL 20–28. THE MARGIN OF ERROR IS +/–5 PERCENTAGE POINTS FOR PARENTS; +/– 6 FOR ALL TEENS; COPYRIGHT 2000 BY NEWSWEEK, INC.

This generation is strongly peer-driven. "This is much more a team-playing generation," says William Strauss, coauthor of the 1997 book "The Fourth Turning." "Boomers may be bowling alone, but Millennials are playing soccer in teams." That makes belonging so crucial that it can be a matter of life and death. In Littleton, Colo., a year ago, the two teenage shooters stood apart, alienated from the jock culture that infused Columbine High School. Yet in a landmark study of 7,000 teens, researchers led by Barbara Schneider of the University of Chicago found that teen social groups are as fluid and hard to pin down as a bead of mercury. "Students often move from one group to another, and friendships change over a period of a few weeks or months," they write in "The Ambitious Generation." "Best friends are few." As a group, today's teens are also infused with an optimism not seen among kids in decades (it doesn't hurt to have grown up in a time of relative peace and the longest economic expansion in U.S. history). "I think a lot of adolescents now are being taught that they can make a difference," says Sophie Mazuroski, 15, of Portland, Maine. "Children of our generation want to. I am very optimistic." Still the law of teenage angst is still on the books: 4.3 percent of ninth graders make suicide attempts serious enough to require medical treatment.

Sound and Fury
"There's a lot of anger in my generation. You can hear it in the music. Kids are angry for a lot of reasons, but mostly because parents aren't around."

Robertino Rodriquez, 17

This generation of teens is more spiritual than their parents, but often less conventionally so. Many put together their own religious canon as they would a salad from a salad bar. Yet despite their faith, teens, as well as those who study them, say that "lying and cheating are standard behavior," as Trisha Sandoval, 17, of Santa Fe Springs, Calif., puts it—more so than for earlier generations. Elsewhere on the values front, teens today are less likely than those in 1992 "to get somebody pregnant, drive drunk or get into fights," says Kevin Dwyer, president of the National Association of School Psychologists. And teens, says Strauss, "had harsher opinions about the Clinton-Lewinsky scandal than any other group." Coming of age in a time of interracial marriages, many eschew the old notions of race; maturing at Internet speed, they are more connected than any generation. Both may bode well for tolerance. "Prejudice against homosexuals, bisexuals, African-Americans, Latinos—this is a big issue," says Kathryn Griffin, 18, of Palo Alto, Calif., who hopes to make a career in advertising or marketing. "It's insane that people have these feelings [about other people] when they don't even know them."

What do they want out of life? Schneider and coauthor David Stevenson found that today's teens "are the most occupationally and educationally ambitious generation" ever. Most plan to attend college, and many aspire to work as professionals. A majority identify "happiness" as a goal, along with love and a long and enjoyable life. But many doubt that marriage and career will deliver that, so they channel their energies more broadly. About half of teens perform community service once a month by, for instance, delivering meals to the homeless or reading to the elderly. But does their volunteer work reflect real compassion, or meeting a school requirement?

In Living Colors
"We don't care about skin, man. I know a lot about my heritage, about who I am. I'm more than just some black dude who is good at sports. I'm the future."

Marcus Robinson, 17

Regardless of what their terrified parents suspect, the belief that today's teens "are more sexual, rebellious and inebriated is flat-out wrong," says pediatrician Victor Strasburger of the University of New Mexico. In 1997, 48 percent of high-school students had had sexual intercourse, compared with 54 percent in 1991, according to the CDC. More are smoking (36 percent, compared with 28 percent in 1991), but the percentage who are drinking alcohol remains at 51 percent. The social surround, though, may be different now. "A lot of my friends are into drinking a lot," says Marcus Ruopp. "Kids don't see it as a big problem. It's a regular thing, not like they're rebelling. There is no pressure to drink."

Some sociologists believe that each generation assumes the societal role of the generation that is dying, as if something in the Zeitgeist whispers to the young what is being lost, what role they can fill. Those now passing away are the children of the Depression and of World War II. They were tested, and they emerged with optimism, and purpose, and a commitment to causes larger than themselves. As Trisha Sandoval puts it, "We want to accomplish something with our lives." Teens today, with their tattoos and baggy shorts, could not seem more different from their grandparents. But every generation has a chance at greatness. Let this one take its shot.

With PAT WINGERT *in Washington,* HOPE WHITE SCOTT *in Boston,* ANA FIGUEROA *in Los Angeles and* DEVIN GORDON, SUSANNAH MEADOWS *and* MICHAEL CRONIN *in New York*

From *Newsweek,* May 8, 2000, pp. 53-56. © 2000 by Newsweek, Inc. All rights reserved. Reprinted by permission.

The Road Ahead:
A Boomer's Guide to Happiness

THE NEW MIDDLE AGE: The baby boom has always made its own rules, and now it's redefining growing old. From work to family to money, here's how boomers are writing the next chapter.

BY BARBARA KANTROWITZ

THE 50 THING STARTED HITTING Kate Donohue at 49.5. "I don't want to be that old," says the San Francisco psychologist. "It's a half century." But when the big day came in January, Donahue decided to see it as a chance to fix the things in her life she didn't like. She made three resolutions: to worry less, to "make more space" for herself by not being so busy and to be more adventurous—more like the woman she was in her 20s and 30s when she routinely set off on solo trekking and biking trips. In August, she will head off to Africa to learn more about West African dance, a longtime passion. Procrastination is not an option. Her 83-year-old father is in the advanced stages of Parkinson's disease; her mother, 79, is active but suffers from a heart condition and glaucoma. "Seeing my parents get so tiny is the way it hits me," Donohue says. "How many more years do I have?"

For so long, the generation born between 1946 and 1964 (an estimated 78 million Americans) has been in collective denial as the years added up. Boomers couldn't be getting older—although, amazingly, everyone else seemed to. But while they're still inclined to moments of self-delusion ("No one would ever guess that I'm 50"), they can no longer escape intimations of their own mortality. The oldest boomers will turn 55 next year, an age when many people begin thinking seriously about retirement. Even the youngest

members of this overchronicled cohort are on the cusp of Grecian Formula time.

Their own parents are aging and dying, making many of them the elders in their families. "There's the feeling that you're the next in line, and there's nothing between you and the abyss," says Linda Waite, director of the Center on Aging at the University of Chicago. When they look in the mirror, they see gray hair and wrinkles. Their bodies are beginning to creak and they're worried that all those years of avoiding the gym and stuffing their faces with Big Macs may add up.

At work, they're feeling the threat of a new generation fluent in technology and willing to work 24/7. Corporate America seems to value experience less, and has come to view older workers in the same way investors view Old Economy stocks: sure, they perform at a steady pace, but these younger, untested companies/employees have so much *potential*.

But don't expect boomers to go quietly into boring and predictable senescence. They're likely to transform the last decades of life just as they have already demolished other conventional milestones. There are 50-year-olds lugging toddlers and 40-year-olds retiring early after cashing out piles of dot-com stock. Settling down is anathema. Boomers switch jobs, and even careers (not to mention spouses) in a never-ending search for fulfillment. "The first generation to grow up with remote controls, we invented channel-surfing and attention-deficit

living," says journalist Michael Gross in his new book, "My Generation." "That taught us to be infinitely adaptable, even in the baby-boom cliché of 'diminished expectations.'"

It helps that they're better educated and richer than previous generations and, as their parents die, expected to benefit from the largest transfer of inherited wealth in history. In a new Heinz Family Philanthropies/NEWSWEEK Poll, nearly half of all boomers said their personal financial situation was "good" or "excellent." Unlike their parents, they don't have to rely on Social Security or limited pensions. A healthy economy and a strong stock market give them new options as they phase out of full-time employment. They may decide to freelance, work part time or start their own companies.

At the same time, they're likely to embrace their more spiritual side, motivated by a need to give back—an echo of the anti-materialism of the '60s. Marialice Harwood, 53, a marketing executive with the Minneapolis Star Tribune, had her moment of reckoning three years ago when her brother, then 51, died of a heart attack. "My faith is more important to me," says Harwood, a Roman Catholic. "I care about different things." She's downsized to a town house now that her kids are grown and, although she intends to work until she's 65, "when I retire, I don't see myself in a resort community. I see myself in the

By the Numbers: A Boomer's Life

The front line of this much-analyzed cohort hits 55 next year. Where have they been, and what's in store? A look at the stats that define this trendsetting generation.

  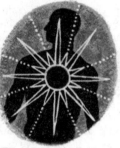  

Your job

■ **71%** of boomer households had both spouses working in 1998. In 23% of the households, only the husband worked; in 4%, only the wife.

■ **32%** of boomers age 35 to 44 worked at home in 1997, as did 27% of those 45 to 54.

■ **39%** of boomer households made $60,000 or more in 1997

Median income, in thousands, of boomers 35 to 44 in 1997

[line graph showing Men and Women from 1980 to 1995, y-axis $0 to $50]

Your money

Average annual spending, in thousands, of households, 1997

	AGE 35–44	45–54
Housing	$13.4	$13.9
Transp.	7.3	8.7
Food	5.7	6.0
Taxes	4.3	4.9
Entertain.	2.1	2.4
Apparel	2.1	2.1
Health care	1.6	1.9

■ **71%** of boomers owned their homes in 1998

■ **92%** of boomers 35 to 44 had financial assets averaging $11,600 in 1995; 92% of those 45 to 54 had more than double the assets at $24,800

■ **$90,500** was the net worth of householders 45 to 54 in 1995

Your health

■ **37%** of boomers polled in 1992 said they suffer from muscle aches and pains, 37% from headaches, 28% from fatigue and 18% from anxiety

■ **21%** of men and 33% of women 30 to 39 said in 1995 that they rarely or never exercise

■ **27%** of men and 41% of women 40 to 49 said they rarely or never exercise

Adults who say they are in excellent health

AGE	1976	1996
18–29	44%	36%
30–39	41	35
40–49	27	32
50–59	23	30
60–69	18	23
70+	17	17

Your parents

Those who, at age 16, were living with both their parents

AGE NOW		1996
18–24		60%
25–34		60
35–44		74
45–54		76
55–64		71
65–74		70
75+		74

■ **6%** of male boomers lived with their parents in 1998; 3% of female boomers did

■ **19%** of boomers were raised by their mothers only; 5% were raised only by their fathers

■ **65%** of boomers 45 to 54 still had their mothers living in 1994; 34% had fathers living

Your kids

■ **36%** of married boomers in 1998 had no children under 18 living at home; 14% had three or more children at home

■ **63%** of Hispanic boomer households had children at home in 1998, compared with 50% of whites and 46% of blacks

■ **12%** of male boomers lived alone in 1997; 9% of female boomers lived alone

Boomer households with children at home by age of child, 1998

Any age		61%
under 18		50
under 12		32
under 6		14
under 1		2

SOURCE: "The Baby Boom, Americans aged 35 to 54," Cheryl Russell

inner city working with kids. That's my dream."

California gerontologist Ken Dychtwald, who has written extensively about boomers, says many "will age rebelliously," resisting stereotypes and convention. Paul Fersen celebrated turning 50 by getting a tattoo and putting down a deposit on a Harley. "I always wanted a tattoo and I got one, a striped bass," says Fersen, a marketing manager for Orvis, the fly-fishing outfitters based in Manchester, Vt. But that's just one of the changes he sees in his

future. "Some people say my job could be voted best on the planet," Fersen says, given that he gets paid for fishing all over the country. But, he says, "I'm still working for somebody else." He has a quieter, more independent vision for his future: "There's a little country store in the next town. It's got two gas pumps and it's a deer weigh-in station. It's the main focal point of the town. I'd like to finish out my days by owning that store."

While their parents—seared by the Depression and war—craved security,

boomers have always embraced the new and the unknown. Boomer women, in particular, have learned to march ahead without a road map. "Ours was the generation that broke the rules," says Jeanne Giordano, 51, an urban planner in Manhattan. "Anything was possible. You could speak back to your parents. You didn't have to get married." She found meaning in her work, including designing the master plan for the restoration of Grand Central Terminal. Now, like many boomers, she's thinking closer to home. "What I would

Future Imperfect

With 78 million members in their generation, boomers have wielded a lot of economic and social power. Here's what they had to say in a recent Heinz/NEWSWEEK Poll.

- **69%** are satisfied with their current standard of living
- **69%** have some form of health insurance for all members of their families; 30% have one or more family members uninsured

Nonretirees: are you saving enough for retirement?

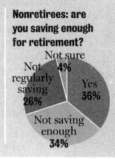

Not sure 4%

Not regularly saving 26%

Yes 36%

Not saving enough 34%

- **47%** of boomers believe that, in their communities, moral and ethical standards are sinking even lower
- **60%** believe we should have a third major political party in this country

- **62%** of boomers are concerned about having to care for an aging parent or relative
- **64%** worry about being able to afford health care for a family member who becomes sick

Over the past five years, have you or your family ...?

	ANSWERING "YES"
Felt stressed out from too much debt	46%
Been unable to pay loans	34
Maxed out your credit cards	27
Declared personal bankruptcy	9

ILLUSTRATIONS BY JAMES STEINBERG

FOR THIS SPECIAL HEINZ FAMILY PHILANTROPIES/NEWSWEEK POLL, PRINCETON SURVEY RESEARCH ASSOCIATES INTERVIEWED A RANDOM NATIONAL SAMPLE OF 1,501 ADULTS BY TELEPHONE IN ENGLISH OR SPANISH FEB 18–MARCH 5, 2000. THE MARGIN OF ERROR IS +/-3 PERCENTAGE POINTS, +/-4 POINTS FOR 617 IN THE 35-54 BOOMER AGE GROUP. COPYRIGHT © 2000 BY NEWSWEEK, INC.

'Nick at Twilight'

An imaginary guide to classic boomer TV, at midlife. **By Mark O'Donnell**

Lassie: After Large Timmy buries the seventh Lassie, he's gripped by a sudden sense of his own mortality and halfheartedly plans to visit Tibet. Guest appearance by, amazingly, June Lockhart. Large Timmy's trophy wife: Jennifer Lopez. Lassie Eight: a shiny red Lamborghini.

Robbie McClaran—SABA, Foto Fantasies

like is to have a relationship that takes me into my final chapters," she says. "I no longer look at it as an imposition. The one thing I haven't done is rely on someone, trust someone to be a part of my life."

Unfinished business is a persistent theme. Dreams interrupted or delayed, regrets about relationships that fizzled. Staring at the abyss, many boomers are reordering their priorities. "You recog-nize that life is really very short," says Terry Patten, 49. In 1998 he sold his company, Tools for Exploration, and he's now working out of his house in Marin County, Calif., writing a book on improving intelligence. His marriage of 22 years broke up three years ago but he's committed to a new, "wonderful, loving" relationship. He's doing yoga, lifting weights and running. Like many boomers, he's also a prodigious consumer of products that claim to extend life and takes 25 supplements, including DHEA. Says Patten, "I'm just trying to optimize my quality of life as I embrace the inevitable." In other words, going out with a bang—and just a little bit of a whimper.

With PATRICIA KING *in San Francisco,* SARAH DOWNEY *in Chicago and* HOPE WHITE SCOTT *in Boston*

From *Newsweek,* April 3, 2000, pp. 56–60. © 2000 by Newsweek, Inc. All rights reserved. Reprinted by permission.

Live to 100? No thanks

Most people opt for quality, not quantity, in later years

BY SUSAN L. CROWLEY

Despite stunning medical advances that can extend life, most Americans do not want to live to be 100. They fear the disabilities, impoverishment and isolation commonly thought to accompany old age.

The finding emerged in a wide-ranging AARP survey on attitudes toward longevity. When asked how long they want to live, 63 percent of the 2,032 respondents opted for fewer than 100 years.

"What this says to me," notes Constance Swank, director of research at AARP, "is that people are more interested in the quality of their lives than the length. They don't want to be encumbered by poor health and financial worries in their older years."

Survey respondents reported they would like to live to an average of about 91 years, but expect to live to 80. According to the U.S. Census Bureau, the life expectancy for a child born in 1997 is 76.5 years. A person turning 65 in 1997 could expect to live another 17.6 years.

The telephone survey, conducted from April 9 to 14 for AARP by Market Facts, Inc. of McLean, Va., also found that a huge majority of people are aware that their behavior and habits can affect how well they age.

This was "the real take-home message for me," says Terrie Wetle, deputy director of the National Institute on Aging. "It was very good news that more than 90 percent recognized that they had some control over how they age."

Harvard neuropsychologist Margery Hutter Silver, who is associate director of the New England Centenarian Study, agrees: "Just the fact of thinking you have control is going to have tremendous impact."

Over eight out of 10 respondents reported doing things to stay healthy. Seventy percent said they exercise, 33 percent watch their diets, 10 percent watch their weight and 10 percent maintain a positive attitude.

Most Americans are also optimistic that life will be better for the typical 80-year-old in 2050 and that medical advances will lead to cures for cancer, heart disease, AIDS and Alzheimer's disease.

Yet, even though they are taking steps to age well and are upbeat about the future, most people are still leery of what might befall them if they live to be 100.

That shouldn't come as a surprise, people of all ages told the Bulletin. "Our society bases its economy on young stars and young entrepreneurs," says Lynda Preble, 28, who works for a public relations firm in San Francisco. "I'm sure most people don't understand where they fit in once they are older."

"I was not surprised," says writer and publicist Susan Hartt, 57, of Baltimore. "As the saying goes, 'Old age is not for sissies.'"

Even though disability rates among the old are declining, chronic health problems and poverty are still more likely to appear in advanced age, Wetle says, and "people know that."

"I'm going to hang it up when I'm restricted to bed," say Marion Ballard, 59, a former software company owner in Bethesda, Md.

"A slow mental decline scares me the most," says Lilavati Sinclair, a 32-year-old mother in Bothell, Wash. For Peter Winkert, 47, a sales executive in Cazenovia, N.Y., "running out of income is my biggest concern."

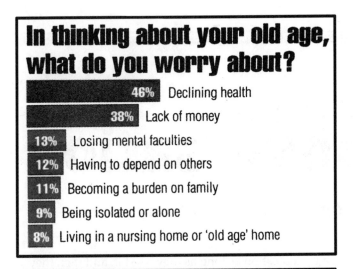

In thinking about your old age, what do you worry about?

- **46%** Declining health
- **38%** Lack of money
- **13%** Losing mental faculties
- **12%** Having to depend on others
- **11%** Becoming a burden on family
- **9%** Being isolated or alone
- **8%** Living in a nursing home or 'old age' home

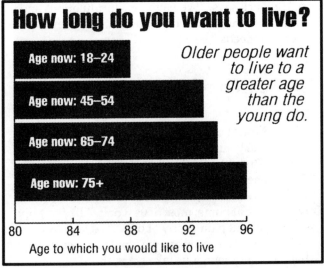

How long do you want to live?

Older people want to live to a greater age than the young do.

- Age now: 18–24
- Age now: 45–54
- Age now: 65–74
- Age now: 75+

80   84   88   92   96
Age to which you would like to live

AARP SURVEY BY MARKET FACTS, INC. MCLEAN, VA.

Others express fear of being alone, burdening their families, living in a nursing home or, as one person puts it, "losing my joy and will to keep on living."

How old a person is tends to influence his or her views on age and aging. Among those ages 18 to 24, a person is "old" at 58, according to the survey, while those 65 or older think "old" starts at 75.

"I used to think I would be dead at 30," jokes one woman who just turned 30. "Now that I know I'll be around a while, I want to enjoy life as long as possible."

Not unexpectedly, older people hope and expect to live to greater ages than the young. Survey respondents 75 and older want to live to 96, but for 18- to 24-year-olds, 88 is enough.

Julie Vermillion, 24, who is a public affairs assistant in Washington, D.C., and Erin Laughlin, 23, a dog trainer in Sebastopol, Calif., say that living to 85 is about right.

Yet 85-year-old Lucille Runkel of Cochranton, Pa., is still in good shape and still active. "I wouldn't mind living to be 100 if I'm in good health," she says, "but I don't want to be dependent on my children."

"If I feel well enough," says lawyer Lester Nurick, 84, of Potomac, Md., "I could go on forever...but I would never put a number on it."

"Young people deal with the mythology instead of the reality of aging," says AARP's Swank. "Older people are living it, and many embrace the challenges, the joys. No one wants to be debilitated, but for many, the later years are highly satisfying. So why walk away from it?"

Older people have also witnessed the development of life-saving vaccines, drugs and surgical techniques and are more confident of continuing medical breakthroughs. "What we see here," Swank says, "is the wisdom of age."

Writer Hartt says she wouldn't mind putting up with some infirmities to achieve such wisdom. "So what was adolescence—a day at the beach?"

Lack of information helps fuel the myths of old age. For example, only 28 percent of survey respondents know that the 85-plus age group is the fastest-growing segment of the population.

And many people don't know that most Americans over 65 live independently, with fewer than 5 percent in nursing homes, adds Harvard's Silver.

Other survey highlights:

• On average, people with a college education hope to live longer (to age 92) than those with a high-school education (to 89).

• Fifty-two percent of those with a yearly household income of over $50,000 worry about poor health in old age, compared to 41 percent among those with incomes lower than $50,000.

• Those who say they are doing things to stay healthy and active expect to live to 81, while others expect to live to 76.

Given new findings about centenarians—whose numbers in the United States grew to more than 62,000 by 1998 and by some estimates could reach 1 million by 2050—aiming for the century mark is not unreasonable.

Living to 100 doesn't mean you'll be in poor health, says Silver, who is co-author with Thomas T. Perls, M.D., of "Living to 100" (Basic Books, 1999). To the contrary, centenarians are often healthier than people in their 80s.

But there's a trick, according to their book: "One must stay healthy the vast majority of one's life in order to live to 100."

Some think it's a worthy goal.

"It would be cool to live for over a century, just because of the history involved," says one 30-something. "I can't even guess what will come."

From the *AARP Bulletin*, July/August 1999, pp. 6-7. © 1999 by the American Association of Retired Persons. Reprinted by permission.

Start the Conversation

The MODERN MATURITY guide to end-of-life care

The Body Speaks

Physically, dying means that "the body's various physiological systems, such as the circulatory, respiratory, and digestive systems, are no longer able to support the demands required to stay alive," says Barney Spivack, M.D., director of Geriatric Medicine for the Stamford (Connecticut) Health System. "When there is no meaningful chance for recovery, the physician should discuss realistic goals of care with the patient and family, which may include letting nature take its course. Lacking that direction," he says, "physicians differ in their perception of when enough is enough. We use our best judgment, taking into account the situation, the information available at the time, consultation with another doctor, or guidance from an ethics committee."

Without instructions from the patient or family, a doctor's obligation to a terminally ill person is to provide life-sustaining treatment. When a decision to "let nature take its course" has been made, the doctor will remove the treatment, based on the patient's needs. Early on, the patient or surrogate may choose to stop interventions such as antibiotics, dialysis, resuscitation, and defibrillation. Caregivers may want to offer food and fluids, but those can cause choking and the pooling of dangerous fluids in the lungs. A dying patient does not desire or need nourishment; without it he or she goes into a deep sleep and dies in days to weeks. A breathing machine would be the last support: It is uncomfortable for the patient, and may be disconnected when the patient or family finds that it is merely prolonging the dying process.

The Best Defense Against Pain

Pain-management activists are fervently trying to reeducate physicians about the importance and safety of making patients comfortable. "In medical school 30 years ago, we worried a lot about creating addicts," says Philadelphia internist Nicholas Scharff. "Now we know that addiction is not a problem: People who are in pain take pain medication as long as they need it, and then they stop." Spivack says, "We have new formulations and delivery systems, so a dying patient should never have unmet pain needs."

In Search of a Good Death

If we think about death at all, we say that we want to go quickly, in our sleep, or, perhaps, while fly-fishing. But in fact only 10 percent of us die suddenly. The more common process is a slow decline with episodes of organ or system failure. Most of us want to die at home; most of us won't. All of us hope to die without pain; many of us will be kept alive, in pain, beyond a time when we would choose to call a halt. Yet very few of us take steps ahead of time to spell out what kind of physical and emotional care we will want at the end.

The new movement to improve the end of life is pioneering ways to make available to each of us a good death—as we each define it. One goal of the movement is to bring death through the cultural process that childbirth has achieved; from an unconscious, solitary act in a cold hospital room to a situation in which one is buffered by pillows, pictures, music, loved ones, and the solaces of home. But as in the childbirth movement, the real goal is choice—here, to have the death you want. Much of death's sting can be averted by planning in advance, knowing the facts, and knowing what options we all have. Here, we have gathered new and relevant information to help us all make a difference for the people we are taking care of, and ultimately, for ourselves.

In 1999, the Joint Commission on Accreditation of Healthcare Organizations issued stern new guidelines about easing pain in both terminal and nonterminal patients. The movement intends to take pain seriously:

to measure and treat it as the fifth vital sign in hospitals, along with blood pressure, pulse, temperature, and respiration.

The best defense against pain, says Spivack, is a combination of education and assertiveness. "Don't be afraid to speak up," he says. "If your doctor isn't listening, talk to the nurses. They see more and usually have a good sense of what's happening." Hospice workers, too, are experts on physical comfort, and a good doctor will respond to a hospice worker's recommendations. "The best situation for pain management," says Scharff, "is at home with a family caregiver being guided by a hospice program."

The downsides to pain medication are, first, that narcotics given to a fragile body may have a double effect: The drug may ease the pain, but it may cause respiratory depression and possibly death. Second, pain medication may induce grogginess or unconsciousness when a patient wants to be alert. "Most people seem to be much more willing to tolerate pain than mental confusion," says senior research scientist M. Powell Lawton, Ph.D., of the Philadelphia Geriatric Center. Dying patients may choose to be alert one day for visitors, and asleep the next to cope with pain. Studies show that when patients control their own pain medication, they use less.

Final Symptoms

Depression This condition is not an inevitable part of dying but can and should be treated. In fact, untreated depression can prevent pain medications from working effectively, and antidepressant medication can help relieve pain. A dying patient should be kept in the best possible emotional state for the final stage of life. A combination of medications and psychotherapy works best to treat depression.

Anorexia In the last few days of life, anorexia—an unwillingness or inability to eat—often sets in. "It has a protective effect, releasing endorphins in the system and contributing to a greater feeling of well-being," says Spivack. "Force-feeding a dying patient could make him uncomfortable and cause choking."

Dehydration Most people want to drink little or nothing in their last days. Again, this is a protective mechanism, triggering a release of helpful endorphins.

Drowsiness and Unarousable Sleep In spite of a coma-like state, says Spivack, "presume that the patient hears everything that is being said in the room."

Agitation and Restlessness, Moaning and Groaning The features of "terminal delirium" occur when the patient's level of consciousness is markedly decreased; there is no significant likelihood that any pain sensation can reach consciousness. Family members and other caregivers may interpret what they see as "the patient is in pain" but as these signs arise at a point very close to death, terminal delirium should be suspected.

Hospice: The Comfort Team

Hospice is really a bundle of services. It organizes a team of people to help patients and their families, most often in the patient's home but also in hospice residences, nursing homes, and hospitals:

- Registered nurses who check medication and the patient's condition, communicate with the patient's doctor, and educate caregivers.
- Medical services by the patient's physician and a hospice's medical director, limited to pain medication and other comfort care.
- Medical supplies and equipment.
- Drugs for pain relief and symptom control.
- Home-care aides for personal care, homemakers for light housekeeping.
- Continuous care in the home as needed on a short-term basis.
- Trained volunteers for support services.
- Physical, occupational, and speech therapists to help patients adapt to new disabilities.
- Temporary hospitalization during a crisis.
- Counselors and social workers who provide emotional and spiritual support to the patient and family.
- Respite care—brief noncrisis hospitalization to provide relief for family caregivers for up to five days.
- Bereavement support for the family, including counseling, referral to support groups, and periodic check-ins during the first year after the death.

Hospice Residences Still rare, but a growing phenomenon. They provide all these services on-site. They're for patients without family caregivers; with frail, elderly spouses; and for families who cannot provide at-home care because of other commitments. At the moment, Medicare covers only hospice services; the patient must pay for room and board. In many states Medicaid also covers hospice services (see How Much Will It Cost?). Keep in mind that not all residences are certified, bonded, or licensed; and not all are covered by Medicare.

Getting In A physician can recommend hospice for a patient who is terminally ill and probably has less than six months to live. The aim of hospice is to help people cope with an illness, not to cure it. All patients entering hospice waive their rights to curative treatments, though only for conditions relating to their terminal illness. "If you break a leg, of course you'll be treated for that," says Karen Woods, executive director of the Hospice Association of America. No one is forced to accept a hospice referral, and patients may leave and opt for curative care at any time. Hospice programs are listed in the Yellow Pages. For more information, see Resources.

The Ultimate Emotional Challenge

Adying person is grieving the loss of control over life, of body image, of normal physical functions, mobility and strength, freedom and independence, security, and the illusion of immortality. He is also grieving the loss of an earthly future, and reorienting himself to an unknowable destiny.

At the same time, an emotionally healthy dying person will be trying to satisfy his survival drive by adapting to this new phase, making the most of life at the moment, calling in loved ones, examining and appreciating his own joys and accomplishments. Not all dying people are depressed; many embrace death easily.

Facing the Fact

Doctors are usually the ones to inform a patient that he or she is dying, and the end-of-life movement is training physicians to bring empathy to that conversation in place of medspeak and time estimates. The more sensitive doctor will first ask how the patient feels things are going. "The patient may say, 'Well, I don't think I'm getting better,' and I would say, 'I think you're right,' " says internist Nicholas Scharff.

At this point, a doctor might ask if the patient wants to hear more now or later, in broad strokes or in detail. Some people will need to first process the emotional blow with tears and anger before learning about the course of their disease in the future.

"Accept and understand whatever reaction the patient has," says Roni Lang, director of the Geriatric Assessment Program for the Stamford (Connecticut) Health System, and a social worker who is a longtime veteran of such conversations. "Don't be too quick with the tissue. That sends a message that it's not okay to be upset. It's okay for the patient to be however she is."

Getting to Acceptance

Some patients keep hoping that they will get better. Denial is one of the mind's miracles, a way to ward off painful realities until consciousness can deal with them. Denial may not be a problem for the dying person, but it can create difficulties for the family. The dying person could be leaving a lot of tough decisions, stress, and confusion behind. The classic stages of grief outlined by Elisabeth Kübler-Ross—denial, anger, bargaining, depression, and acceptance—are often used to describe post-death grieving, but were in fact delineated for the process of accepting impending loss. We now know that these states may not progress in order. "Most people oscillate between anger and sadness, embracing the prospect of death and unrealistic episodes of optimism," says Lang. Still, she says, "don't place demands on them

Survival Kit for Caregivers

A study published in the March 21, 2000, issue of **Annals of Internal Medicine** shows that caregivers of the dying are twice as likely to have depressive symptoms as the dying themselves.

No wonder. Caring for a dying parent, says social worker Roni Lang, "brings a fierce tangle of emotions. That part of us that is a child must grow up." Parallel struggles occur when caring for a spouse, a child, another relative, or a friend. Caregivers may also experience sibling rivalry, income loss, isolation, fatigue, burnout, and resentment.

To deal with these difficult stresses, Lang suggests that caregivers:

•Set limits in advance. How far am I willing to go? What level of care is needed? Who can I get to help? Resist the temptation to let the illness always take center stage, or to be drawn into guilt-inducing conversations with people who think you should be doing more.
•Join a caregiver support group, either disease-related like the Alzheimer's Association or Gilda's Club, or a more general support group like The Well Spouse Foundation. Ask the social services department at your hospital for advice. Telephone support and online chat rooms also exist (see Resources).
•Acknowledge anger and express it constructively by keeping a journal or talking to an understanding friend or family member. Anger is a normal reaction to powerlessness.
•When people offer to help, give them a specific assignment. And then, take time to do what energizes you and make a point of rewarding yourself.
•Remember that people who are critically ill are self-absorbed. If your empathy fails you and you lose patience, make amends and forgive yourself.

to accept their death. This is not a time to proselytize." It is enough for the family to accept the coming loss, and if necessary, introduce the idea of an advance directive and health-care proxy, approaching it as a "just in case" idea. When one member of the family cannot accept death, and insists that doctors do more, says Lang, "that's the worst nightmare. I would call a meeting, hear all views without interrupting, and get the conversation around to what the patient would want. You may need another person to come in, perhaps the doctor, to help 'hear' the voice of the patient."

What Are You Afraid Of?

The most important question for doctors and caregivers to ask a dying person is, What are you afraid of? "Fear aggravates pain," says Lang, "and pain aggravates fear." Fear of pain, says Spivack, is one of the most common problems, and can be dealt with rationally. Many people do not know, for example, that pain in dying is not inevitable. Other typical fears are of being separated from loved ones, from home, from work; fear of being a burden, losing control, being dependent, and leaving things undone. Voicing fear helps lessen it, and pinpointing fear helps a caregiver know how to respond.

How to Be With a Dying Person

Our usual instinct is to avoid everything about death, including the people moving most rapidly toward it. But, Spivack says, "In all my years of working with dying people, I've never heard one say 'I want to die alone.' " Dying people are greatly comforted by company; the benefit far outweighs the awkwardness of the visit. Lang offers these suggestions for visitors:

• Be close. Sit at eye level, and don't be afraid to touch. Let the dying person set the pace for the conversation. Allow for silence. Your presence alone is valuable.

• Don't contradict a patient who says he's going to die. Acceptance is okay. Allow for anger, guilt, and fear, without trying to "fix" it. Just listen and empathize.

• Give the patient as much decision-making power as possible, as long as possible. Allow for talk about unfinished business. Ask: "Who can I contact for you?"

• Encourage happy reminiscences. It's okay to laugh.

• Never pass up the chance to express love or say goodbye. But if you don't get the chance, remember that not everything is worked through. Do the best you can.

Taking Control Now

Sixty years ago, before the invention of dialysis, defibrillators, and ventilators, the failure of vital organs automatically meant death. There were few choices to be made to end suffering, and when there were—the fatal dose of morphine, for example—these decisions were made privately by family and doctors who knew each other well. Since the 1950s, medical technology has been capable of extending lives, but also of prolonging dying. In 1967, an organization called Choice in Dying (now the Partnership for Caring: America's Voices for the Dying; see Resources) designed the first advance directive—a document that allows you to designate under what conditions you would want life-sustaining treatment to be continued or terminated. But the idea did not gain popular understanding until 1976, when the parents of Karen Ann Quinlan won a long legal battle to disconnect her from respiratory support as she lay for months in a vegetative state. Some 75 percent of Americans are in favor of advance directives, although only 30–35 percent actually write them.

Designing the Care You Want

There are two kinds of advance directives, and you may use one or both. A Living Will details what kind of life-sustaining treatment you want or don't want, in the event of an illness when death is imminent. A durable power of attorney for health care appoints someone to be your decision-maker if you can't speak for yourself. This person is also called a surrogate, attorney-in-fact, or health-care proxy. An advance directive such as Five Wishes covers both.

Most experts agree that a Living Will alone is not sufficient. "You don't need to write specific instructions about different kinds of life support, as you don't yet know any of the facts of your situation, and they may change," says Charles Sabatino, assistant director of the American Bar Association's Commission on Legal Problems of the Elderly.

The proxy, Sabatino says, is far more important. "It means someone you trust will find out all the options and make a decision consistent with what you would want." In most states, you may write your own advance directive, though some states require a specific form, available at hospital admitting offices or at the state department of health.

When Should You Draw Up a Directive?

Without an advance directive, a hospital staff is legally bound to do everything to keep you alive as long as possible, until you or a family member decides otherwise. So advance directives are best written before emergency status or a terminal diagnosis. Some people write them at the same time they make a will. The process begins with discussions between you and your family and doctor. If anybody is reluctant to discuss the subject, Sabatino suggests starting the conversation with a story. "Remember what happened to Bob Jones and what his family went through? I want us to be different...." You can use existing tools—a booklet or questionnaire (see Resources)—to keep the conversation moving. Get your doctor's commitment to support your wishes. "If you're asking for something that is against your doctor's conscience" (such as prescribing a lethal dose of pain medication or removing life support at a time he considers premature), Sabatino says, "he may have an obligation to transfer you to another doctor." And make sure the person you name as surrogate agrees to act for you and understands your wishes.

Filing, Storing, Safekeeping...

An estimated 35 percent of advance directives cannot be found when needed.

• Give a copy to your surrogate, your doctor, your hospital, and other family members. Tell them where to find the original in the house—not in a safe deposit box where it might not be found until after death.

Five Wishes

Five Wishes is a questionnaire that guides people in making essential decisions about the care they want at the end of their life. About a million people have filled out the eight-page form in the past two years. This advance directive is legally valid in 34 states and the District of Columbia. (The other 16 require a specific state-mandated form.)

The document was designed by lawyer Jim Towey, founder of Aging With Dignity, a nonprofit organization that advocates for the needs of elders and their caregivers. Towey, who was legal counsel to Mother Teresa, visited her Home for the Dying in Calcutta in the 1980s. He was struck that in that haven in the Third World, "the dying people's hands were held, their pain was managed, and they weren't alone. In the First World, you see a lot of medical technology, but people die in pain, and alone." Towey talked to MODERN MATURITY about his directive and what it means.

What are the five wishes? Who do I want to make care decisions for me when I can't? What kind of medical treatment do I want toward the end? What would help me feel comfortable while I am dying? How do I want people to treat me? What do I want my loved ones to know about me and my feelings after I'm gone?

Why is it so vital to make advance decisions now? Medical technology has extended longevity, which is good, but it can prolong the dying process in ways that are almost cruel. Medical schools are still concentrating on curing, not caring for the dying. We can have a dignified season in our life, or die alone in pain with futile interventions. Most people only discover they have options when checking into the hospital, and often they no longer have the capacity to choose. This leaves the family members with a guessing game and, frequently, guilt.

What's the ideal way to use this document? First you do a little soul searching about what you want. Then discuss it with people you trust, in the livingroom instead of the waiting room—before a crisis. Just say, "I want a choice about how I spend my last days," talk about your choices, and pick someone to be your health-care surrogate.

What makes the Five Wishes directive unique? It's easy to use and understand, not written in the language of doctors or lawyers. It also allows people to discuss comfort dignity, and forgiveness, not just medical concerns. When my father filled it out, he said he wanted his favorite afghan blanket in his bed. It made a huge difference to me that, as he was dying, he had his wishes fulfilled.

For a copy of Five Wishes in English or Spanish, send a $5 check or money order to Aging With Dignity, PO Box 1661, Tallahassee, FL 32302. For more information, visit www.agingwithdignity. org.

•Some people carry a copy in their wallet or glove compartment of their car.

•Be aware that if you have more than one home and you split your time in several regions of the country, you should be registering your wishes with a hospital in each region, and consider naming more than one proxy.

•You may register your Living Will and health-care proxy online at uslivingwillregistry.com (or call 800-548-9455). The free, privately funded confidential service will instantly fax a copy to a hospital when the hospital requests one. It will also remind you to update it: You may want to choose a new surrogate, accommodate medical advances, or change your idea of when "enough is enough." M. Powell Lawton, who is doing a study on how people anticipate the terminal life stages, has discovered that "people adapt relatively well to states of poor health. The idea that life is still worth living continues to readjust itself."

Assisted Suicide: The Reality

While advance directives allow for the termination of life-sustaining treatment, assisted suicide means supplying the patient with a prescription for life-ending medication. A doctor writes the prescription for the medication; the patient takes the fatal dose him- or herself. Physician-assisted suicide is legal only in Oregon (and under consideration in Maine) but only with rigorous preconditions. Of the approximately 30,000 people who died in Oregon in 1999, only 33 received permission to have a lethal dose of medication and only 26 of those actually died of the medication. Surrogates may request an end to life support, but to assist in a suicide puts one at risk for charges of homicide.

Good Care: Can You Afford It?

The ordinary person is only one serious illness away from poverty," says Joanne Lynn, M.D., director of the Arlington, Virginia, Center to Improve Care of the Dying. An ethicist, hospice physician, and health-services researcher, she is one of the founding members of the end-of-life-care movement. "On the whole, hospitalization and the cost of suppressing symptoms is very easy to afford," says Lynn. Medicare and Medicaid will help cover that kind of acute medical care. But what is harder to afford is at-home medication, monitoring, daily help with eating and walking, and all the care that will go on for the rest of the patient's life.

"When people are dying," Lynn says, "an increasing proportion of their overall care does not need to be done by doctors. But when policymakers say the care is nonmedical, then it's second class, it's not important, and nobody will pay for it."

Bottom line, Medicare pays for about 57 percent of the cost of medical care for Medicare beneficiaries.

Another 11 percent is paid by Medicaid, 20 percent by the patient, 10 percent from private insurance, and the rest from other sources, such as charitable organizations.

Medi-what?

This public-plus-private network of funding sources for end-of-life care is complex, and who pays for how much of what is determined by diagnosis, age, site of care, and income. Besides the private health insurance that many of us have from our employers, other sources of funding may enter the picture when patients are terminally ill.
•**Medicare** A federal insurance program that covers health-care services for people 65 and over, some disabled people, and those with end-stage kidney disease. Medicare Part A covers inpatient care in hospitals, nursing homes, hospice, and some home health care. For most people, the Part A premium is free. Part B covers doctor fees, tests, and other outpatient medical services. Although Part B is optional, most people choose to enroll through their local Social Security office and pay the monthly premium ($45.50). Medicare beneficiaries share in the cost of care through deductibles and co-insurance. What Medicare does not cover at all is outpatient medication, long-term nonacute care, and support services.
•**Medicaid** A state and federally funded program that covers health-care services for people with income or assets below certain levels, which vary from state to state.
•**Medigap** Private insurance policies covering the gaps in Medicare, such as deductibles and co-payments, and in some cases additional health-care services, medical supplies, and outpatient prescription drugs.

Many of the services not paid for by Medicare can be covered by private long-term-care insurance. About 50 percent of us over the age of 65 will need long-term care at home or in a nursing home, and this insurance is an extra bit of protection for people with major assets to protect. It pays for skilled nursing care as well as non-health services, such as help with dressing, eating, and bathing. You select a dollar amount of coverage per day (for example, $100 in a nursing home, or $50 for at-home care), and a coverage period (for example, three years—the average nursing-home stay is 2.7 years). Depending on your age and the benefits you choose, the insurance can cost anywhere from around $500 to more than $8,000 a year. People with pre-existing conditions such as Alzheimer's or MS are usually not eligible.

How Much Will It Cost?

Where you get end-of-life care will affect the cost and who pays for it.
•**Hospital** Dying in a hospital costs about $1,000 a day. After a $766 deductible (per benefit period), Medicare reimburses the hospital a fixed rate per day, which varies by region and diagnosis. After the first 60 days in a hospital, a patient will pay a daily deductible ($194) that goes up (to $388) after 90 days. The patient is responsible

for all costs for each day beyond 150 days. Medicaid and some private insurance, either through an employer or a Medigap plan, often help cover these costs.
•**Nursing home** About $1,000 a week. Medicare covers up to 100 days of skilled nursing care after a three-day hospitalization, and most medication costs during that time. For days 21–100, your daily co-insurance of $97 is usually covered by private insurance—if you have it. For nursing-home care not covered by Medicare, you must use your private assets, or Medicaid if your assets run out, which happens to approximately one-third of nursing-home residents. Long-term-care insurance may also cover some of the costs.
•**Hospice care** About $100 a day for in-home care. Medicare covers hospice care to patients who have a life expectancy of less than six months. (See Hospice: The Comfort Team.) Such care may be provided at home, in a hospice facility, a hospital, or a nursing-home. Patients may be asked to pay up to $5 for each prescription and a 5 percent co-pay for in-patient respite care, which is a short hospital stay to relieve caregivers. Medicaid covers hospice care in all but six states, even for those without Medicare.

About 60 percent of full-time employees of medium and large firms also have coverage for hospice services, but the benefits vary widely.
•**Home care without hospice services** Medicare Part A pays the full cost of medical home health care for up to 100 visits following a hospital stay of at least three days. Medicare Part B covers home health-care visits beyond those 100 visits or without a hospital stay. To qualify, the patient must be homebound, require skilled nursing care or physical or speech therapy, be under a physician's care, and use services from a Medicare-participating home-health agency. Note that this coverage is for medical care only; hired help for personal nonmedical services, such as that often required by Alzheimer's patients, is not covered by Medicare. It is covered by Medicaid in some states.

A major financial disadvantage of dying at home without hospice is that Medicare does not cover out-patient prescription drugs, even those for pain. Medicaid does cover these drugs, but often with restrictions on their price and quantity. Private insurance can fill the gap to some extent. Long-term-care insurance may cover payments to family caregivers who have to stop work to care for a dying patient, but this type of coverage is very rare.

Resources

MEDICAL CARE

For information about pain relief and symptom management:
Supportive Care of the Dying (503-215-5053; careofdying.org).

For a comprehensive guide to living with the medical, emotional, and spiritual aspects of dying:

Handbook for Mortals by Joanne Lynn and Joan Harrold, Oxford University Press.

For a 24-hour hotline offering counseling, pain management, downloadable advance directives, and more:

The Partnership for Caring (800-989-9455; www.partnershipforcaring.org).

EMOTIONAL CARE

To find mental-health counselors with an emphasis on lifespan human development and spiritual discussion:
American Counseling Association (800-347-6647; counseling.org).

For disease-related support groups and general resources for caregivers:
Caregiver Survival Resources (caregiver911.com).

For AARP's online caregiver support chatroom, access **America Online** every Wednesday night, 8:30–9:30 EST (keyword: AARP).

Education and advocacy for family caregivers:
National Family Caregivers Association (800-896-3650; nfcacares.org).

For the booklet,
Understanding the Grief Process (D16832, EEO143C), e-mail order with title and numbers to member@aarp.org or send postcard to AARP Fulfillment, 601 E St NW, Washington DC 20049. Please allow two to four weeks for delivery.

To find a volunteer to help with supportive services to the frail and their caregivers:
National Federation of Interfaith Volunteer Caregivers (816-931-5442; nfivc.org).

For information on support to partners of the chronically ill and/or the disabled:
The Well Spouse Foundation (800-838-0879; www.wellspouse.org).

LEGAL HELP

AARP members are entitled to a free half-hour of legal advice with a lawyer from **AARP's Legal Services Network**. (800-424-3410; www.aarp.org/lsn).

For **Planning for Incapacity,** *a guide to advance directives in your state,* send $5 to Legal Counsel for the Elderly, Inc., PO Box 96474, Washington DC 20090-6474. Make out check to LCE Inc.

For a **Caring Conversations** *booklet on advance-directive discussion:*
Midwest Bioethics Center (816-221-1100; midbio.org).

For information on care at the end of life, online discussion groups, conferences:
Last Acts Campaign (800-844-7616; lastacts.org).

HOSPICE

To learn about end-of-life care options and grief issues through videotapes, books, newsletters, and brochures:
 Hospice Foundation of America (800-854-3402; hospicefoundation.org).

For information on hospice programs, FAQs, and general facts about hospice:
National Hospice and Palliative Care Organization (800-658-8898; nhpco.org).

For **All About Hospice: A Consumer's Guide** (202-546-4759; www.hospice-america.org).

FINANCIAL HELP

For **Organizing Your Future,** *a simple guide to end-of-life financial decisions,* send $5 to Legal Counsel for the Elderly, Inc., PO Box 96474, Washington DC 20090-6474. Make out check to LCE Inc.

For **Medicare and You 2000** *and a* **2000 Guide to Health Insurance for People With Medicare** (800-MEDICARE [633-4227]; medicare.gov).

To find your State Agency on Aging: **Administration on Aging, U.S. Department of Health and Human Services** (800-677-1116; aoa.dhhs.gov).

GENERAL

For information on end-of-life planning and bereavement: (www.aarp.org/endoflife/).

For health professionals and others who want to start conversations on end-of-life issues in their community:
Discussion Guide: On Our Own Terms: Moyers on Dying, based on the PBS series, airing September 10–13. The guide provides essays, instructions, and contacts. From PBS, www.pbs.org/onourownterms Or send a postcard request to On Our Own Terms Discussion Guide, Thirteen/WNET New York, PO Box 245, Little Falls, NJ 07424-9766.

Funded with a grant from The Robert Wood Johnson Foundation, Princeton, N.J. *Editor* Amy Gross; *Writer* Louise Lague; *Designer* David Herbick

Reprinted from *Modern Maturity*, September/October 2000. © 2000 by American Association for Retired Persons (AARP).

UNIT 4
Relating to Others

Unit Selections

27. **Friendships and Adaptation Across the Life Span**, Willard W. Hartup and Nan Stevens
28. **Emotional Intelligence**, Casey D. Cobb and John D. Mayer
29. **Nurturing Empathy**, Julia Glass
30. **What's in a Face?** Beth Azar
31. **How to Spot a Liar**, James Geary
32. **Shyness: The New Solution**, Bernardo Carducci
33. **Revealing Personal Secrets**, Anita E. Kelly
34. **Welcome to the Love Lab**, John Gottman and Sybil Carrere
35. **Finding Real Love**, Carey Barbor
36. **Prescription for Passion**, David M. Buss

Key Points to Consider

- What is a friend? Do friendships change as we mature? How so? What kinds of people attract us to them? How is mental health related to friendship?

- What is emotional intelligence? How does it develop? How can we tell if we possess it? How do people with EQ differ from people without it? Do you have EQ? If not, can you do anything to cultivate it? Explain.

- What is empathy? Why is it important? Can empathy be nurtured in children? How? Is empathy the same as EQ?

- How do you feel when you know that someone has lied to or deceived you? Can you spot a liar? How? Are humans the only creatures who use deception? How do other species use and detect deception?

- Why are some people painfully shy? How can shyness be overcome?

- How do scientists study marriage? What makes a marriage high quality? How do happy couples and unhappy couples differ in their interactions? Can we predict whose marriage will end in divorce? What are some of the signs of an unhappy marriage? Do you think such marriages can be saved? Under what circumstances?

- Are there situations in which we sabotage intimate relationships? When and why do we do this? Do you think a subverted relationship can be salvaged? How?

- What is jealousy? Is jealousy normal or not? Do you think jealousy is a necessary part of romance and intimacy? Can jealousy ever promote positive emotions or passion in couples?

 **Links: www.dushkin.com/online/**
These sites are annotated in the World Wide Web pages.

CYFERNET-Youth Development
http://www.cyfernet.mes.umn.edu/youthdev.html
Hypermedia, Literature, and Cognitive Dissonance
http://www.uncg.edu/~rsginghe/metastat.htm
Emotional Intelligence Discovery
http://www.cwrl.utexas.edu/~bump/Hu305/3/3/3/
The Personality Project
http://personality-project.org

People can be seen everywhere in groups: couples in love, parents and their children, teachers and students, gatherings of friends, church groups, theatergoers. People have much influence on one another when they congregate in groups.

Groups spend a great deal of time communicating with members and nonmembers. The communication can be intentional and forceful, such as when protesters demonstrate against a totalitarian regime in a far-off land. Or communication can be more subtle, for example, when fraternity brothers reject a prospective brother who refuses to wear the symbols of membership.

In some groups, the reason a leader emerges is clear—perhaps the most skilled individual in the group is elected leader by the group members. In other groups, for example, during a spontaneous nightclub fire, the qualities of the rapidly emerging, perhaps self-appointed, leader are less apparent. Nonetheless, the followers flee unquestioningly in the leader's direction. Even in dating couples, one person may lead or be dominant over the other.

Some groups, such as formalized business corporations, issue formal, written rules; discipline for rule breaking is also formalized. Other groups, families or friends, for example, possess fewer and less formalized rules and disciplinary codes, but their rules are still quickly learned by and are important to all unit members.

Some groups are large but seek more members, such as nationalized labor unions. Other groups seek to keep their groups small and somewhat exclusive, such as teenage cliques. Groups exist that are almost completely adversarial with other groups. Conflict between youth gangs is receiving much media attention today. Other groups pride themselves on their ability to remain cooperative, such as neighbors who band together in a community crime watch.

Psychologists are so convinced that interpersonal relationships are important to the human experience that they have intensively studied them. There is ample evidence that contact with other people is a necessary part of human existence. Research has shown that most individuals do not like being isolated from other people. In fact, in laboratory experiments in which subjects experience total isolation for extended periods, they begin to hallucinate the presence of others. In prisons, solitary confinement is often used as a form of punishment because of its aversive effect. Other research has shown that people who must wait under stressful circumstances prefer to wait with others, even if the others are total strangers, rather than wait alone.

This unit examines smaller and therefore fairly interpersonal relationships such as those among friends, dating partners, and married couples. The next unit examines the effects of larger groups, specifically, society at large.

The first article provides a general introduction to the unit. In "Friendship and Adaptation Across the Life Span," the authors discuss why friendship is vitally important. They also disclose how friendship is construed differently by children and adults. The authors explain why we are attracted to various types of individuals. It is no surprise that we are most attracted to competent, mentally healthy individuals.

In the next two articles, various factors that color our relationships are discussed. The very first article reviews a fairly new and important concept—emotional intelligence or EQ. Emotional intelligence relates to our ability to get along with and be sensitive to other people's needs and emotions. Emotional intelligence may be more important to our success in life than any other aspect of our being. In fact, there exists research that indicates that EQ may be more predictive of our life trajectory than IQ or intelligence.

A related article concerns empathy, the ability to actually experience someone else's emotions. Parents who wish to promote empathy in their children may want to read "Nurturing Empathy."

An important avenue to understanding others' emotions, moods, and behaviors is to watch their faces. In "What's in a Face?" Beth Azar discusses the face as a mirror of another person's emotions. How to "read" faces and therefore know more about others is the focus of this important article.

Another concept related to the importance of the face is the ability to detect deception on the part of others. In "How to Spot a Liar," James Geary examines how nature has provided various species with a way for members to deceive others. Similarly, nature usually also provides clues that point to these very same deceptions in order to help the deceived detect the delusion. In the human, the face is one of the best lie detectors.

While those with EQ, empathy, and the ability to read others thrive in social situations, others are not so fortunate. Shyness overwhelms them and sometimes prevents them from making and keeping friends. Bernardo Carducci writes about shyness or social anxiety and how to overcome it in "Shyness: The New Solution." He explains, for example, that the Internet offers an opportunity to meet and interact with others without being overwhelmed by social anxiety.

The next few articles are about special types of interpersonal relationships. In "Revealing Personal Secrets" the author discloses why and when we tell others our secrets. The article would not be complete, though, without reference to the secrets we decide to keep to ourselves and why.

We then cover some very close and intimate interpersonal relationships. "Welcome to the Love Lab" is an article that discusses research by renowned expert John Gottman (with coauthor Sybil Carrere). Gottman contends that he can detect which relationships are headed for trouble even at their beginning.

In a companion piece, "Finding Real Love," Cary Barbor suggests that we sometimes sabotage intimate relationships; we actually make our situation worse with someone we supposedly love. Barbor claims that when our intimate lovers and friends remind us of a disliked parent, we are bound to derail the relationship.

In the last article, "Prescription for Passion," the author discusses jealousy, an emotion that can signal problems in a romantic relationship. David Buss takes the approach that jealousy is normal and, interestingly, might in fact hold couples together rather than drive them apart.

Friendships and Adaptation Across the Life Span

Abstract

Friends foster self-esteem and a sense of well-being, socialize one another, and support one another in coping with developmental transitions and life stress. Friends engage in different activities with one another across the life span, but friendship is conceived similarly by children and adults. Friends and friendships, however, are not all alike. The developmental significance of having friends depends on the characteristics of the friends, especially whether the friends are antisocial or socially withdrawn. Outcomes also depend on whether friendships are supportive and intimate or fractious and unstable. Among both children and adults, friendships have clear-cut developmental benefits at times but are mixed blessings at other times.

Keywords

friendships; life-span development; relationships

Willard W. Hartup[1] and Nan Stevens

Institute of Child Development, University of Minnesota, Minneapolis, Minnesota (W.W.H.),
and Department of Psychogerontology, University of Nijmegen, Nijmegen, The Netherlands (N.S.)

Friendships are important to the well-being of both children and adults. Parents worry if their children do not have friends; adolescents are anxious and upset when they lose their friends; and older adults go to considerable lengths to maintain old friendships and establish new ones. People who have friends generally feel better about themselves and others than do people who do not have friends. Recent studies, however, show that over the life span, the dynamics of friendship are complicated. These relationships sometimes contain a "dark side," and in these instances, developmental benefits are mixed.

In this report, we begin by showing that understanding friendships across the life span requires thinking about these relationships from two perspectives: It is necessary to consider, first, what friendships mean to both children and adults and, second, what distinctive patterns of social interaction characterize friendships. We then suggest that, in order to appreciate the significance of friends over the life span, one must take into account (a) whether a person does or does not have friends, (b) characteristics of the person's friends, and (c) the quality of these relationships.

HOW TO THINK ABOUT FRIENDSHIPS IN LIFE-SPAN PERSPECTIVE

The significance of friendship across the life span can be established only by examining what children and adults believe to be the social meaning (essence) of these relationships, as well as the social exchanges they actually have with their friends. When researchers examine what people believe friendships to be, or what elements constitute a friendship, reciprocity is always involved. Friends may or may not share likes and dislikes, but there is always the sense that one supports and sustains one's friends and receives support in return. Most people do not describe the relation between friends narrowly as a *quid pro quo*, but rather describe the relationship broadly as *mutuality*—that is, friendship involves social giving and taking, and returning in kind or degree. Children, adolescents, newlyweds, middle-aged adults, and soon-to-be retirees differ relatively little from one another in their emphasis on these reciprocities when asked to describe an ideal friend (Weiss & Lowenthal, 1975). Older people describe their friendships more elaborately and with greater subtlety than children do, but then older people generally describe other persons in more complex terms than younger persons do. Consequently, we can assert that the meaning structure specifying friendships changes relatively little from the preschool years through old age; social reciprocities are emphasized throughout the life span (Hartup & Stevens, 1997).

The actual exchanges that occur between friends change greatly with age. Social reciprocities between toddlers are reflected in the time they spend together and the connectedness of their interaction; reciprocities between kindergartners are more elaborated but remain basically concrete ("We play"). Among adolescents, friends engage in common activities (mainly socializing) and social disclosure; among young adults, friendships become "fused" or "blended" with work and parenting. Among older persons, friendships are separated from work once again and centered on support and companionship. The behavioral structures associated with friendship thus change greatly across the life span, generally in accordance with the distinctive tasks or challenges that confront persons at different ages.

HAVING FRIENDS

Occurrence

As early as age 3 or 4, children show preferences for interacting with particular children, and the word "friend" enters their vocabularies. About 75% of preschool-aged children are involved in mutual friendships as identified by mothers or nursery school teachers or measured in terms of the time the children spend together. Mutual friends among school-aged children and older persons are usually identified by asking individuals to name their "best friends," "good friends," or "casual friends," categories differentiated in terms of time spent together and intimacy. Among teenagers, 80% to 90% report having mutual friends, usually including one or two best friends and several good friends. The proportion of people who have friends remains high through adulthood, then declines in old age. More older persons, however, have friends than do not. Small numbers of individuals, about 7%, have no friends in adulthood; after age 65, this friendless group increases to 12% for women and 24% for men.

Friendship networks vary in size according to age and sex. During the nursery school years, boys have an average of two friends, whereas girls have one; during the school years, the number of best friends varies from three to five. Girls' networks are usually smaller and more exclusive than boys' during childhood; this situation reverses, however, in adolescence. Number of friends remains fairly constant through adolescence and early adulthood. Newlyweds have the largest numbers of friends, with fewer friendships being maintained during middle age. Friendship networks increase again before retirement, but a decline oc-

curs following retirement, owing primarily to the loss of casual friends. Close friendships, however, are frequently retained into old, old age (Hartup & Stevens, 1997).

The amount of time spent with friends is greatest during middle childhood and adolescence; in fact, teenagers spend almost a third of their waking time in the company of friends. The percentage of time spent with friends declines until middle age, when adults spend less than 10% of their time with friends. A slight increase occurs at retirement, although it is not as great as one might expect (Larson, Zuzanek, & Mannell, 1985).

Behavior With Friends and Nonfriends

More positive engagement (i.e., more talk, smiling, and laughter) is observed among friends than among nonfriends in childhood and adolescence. Friends also have more effective conflict management and a more mutual orientation when working together (Newcomb & Bagwell, 1995). Differences in behavior between friends and mere acquaintances are similar in adulthood: Self-disclosure occurs more frequently and involves more depth of disclosure among friends than nonfriends; friends are more directive and authoritative with one another than nonfriends.

Companionship and talk continue to distinguish interactions between friends in middle and old age. Sharing, exchange of resources, and emotional support remain salient, especially during crises, such as divorce. Problem solving involves more symmetrical interaction between friends than between nonfriends; conflicts are more effectively managed. Adults' conflicts with friends center on differences in values and beliefs, as well as lifestyles. Conflicts between older friends mainly concern expectations related to age and resource inequities.

Developmental Significance

From early childhood through old age, people with friends have a greater sense of well-being than people without friends. Friendlessness is more common among people who seek clinical assistance for emotional and behavioral problems than among better adjusted persons (Rutter & Garmezy, 1983). But these results mean relatively little: They do not clarify

whether friends contribute to well-being or whether people who feel good about themselves have an easier time making friends than those who do not.

Longitudinal studies show that children entering first grade have better school attitudes if they already have friends and are successful both in keeping old ones and making new ones (Ladd, 1990). Similarly, among adolescents, psychological disturbances are fewer when school changes (e.g., from grade to grade or from primary school to middle school) occur in the company of friends than when they do not (Berndt & Keefe, 1992). Once again, the direction of influence is not clear: Does merely having friends support successful coping with these transitions, or are those people who are better able to cope with these transitions also able to make friends more easily?

Despite these difficulties in interpretation, well-controlled longer term studies extending from childhood into adulthood show similar patterns, thereby strengthening the conclusion that friendships are in some way responsible for the outcome. Self-esteem is greater among young adults who had friends while they were children than among those who did not, when differences in childhood self-esteem are controlled for statistically. Social adjustment in adulthood, however, is more closely related to having been generally liked or disliked by classmates than to having had mutual friends (Bagwell, Newcomb, & Bukowski, 1998).

CHARACTERISTICS OF ONE'S FRIENDS

Although friends may support positive developmental outcomes through companionship and social support, these outcomes depend on who one's friends are. Friendships with socially well-adjusted persons are like money in the bank, "social capital" that can be drawn upon to meet challenges and crises arising every day. In contrast, poorly adjusted friends may be a drain on resources, increasing one's risk of poor developmental outcomes.

Children of divorce illustrate these dynamics: Preadolescents, adolescents, and young adults whose parents have divorced are at roughly three times the risk for psychosocial problems as their peers whose parents are not divorced. Preadolescents who have positive relationships with both custodial and noncustodial parents have a significantly reduced risk if the parents are well-adjusted; friends do not provide the same protection. In contrast, resilience among adolescents whose parents are divorced is influenced by friends as well as family. Specifically, adolescent children of divorce are more resilient (better adapted) if they have both family and friends who have few behavior problems and who are socially mature. Friends continue to promote resilience among the offspring of divorce during early adulthood, but again friends provide this benefit only if they are well-adjusted themselves (Hetherington, in press). Two conclusions can be drawn: First, social capital does not reside merely in having friends, but rather resides in having socially competent friends; and second, whether friends are a protective factor in social development depends on one's age.

Research indicates that the role of friendships as a risk factor also depends on one's age. Friendship risks are especially evident among antisocial children and adolescents. First, antisocial children are more likely to have antisocial friends than other children. Second, antisocial behavior increases as a consequence of associating with antisocial friends. Antisocial children have poor social skills and thus are not good models. Relationships between antisocial children are also problematic: Interactions are more contentious and conflict-ridden, more marked by talk about deviance and talk that is deviant in its social context (e.g., swearing), and more lacking in intimacy than exchanges between nonaggressive children (Dishion, Andrews, & Crosby, 1995). Other studies show that behavior problems increase across the transition from childhood to adolescence when children have stable relationships with friends who have behavior problems themselves (Berndt, Hawkins, & Jiao, in press).

FRIENDSHIP QUALITY

Friendships are not all alike. Some are marked by intimacy and social support, others by conflict and contention. Some friends engage in many different activities, others share narrower interests. Some friendships are relatively stable, others are not. These features of friendships differentiate relationships among both children and adolescents,

and define some of the ways that relationships differ from one another among adults.

Friendship quality is related to the psychological well-being of children and adolescents and to the manner in which they manage stressful life events. During the transition from elementary to secondary school, for example, sociability and leadership increase among adolescents who have stable, supportive, and intimate friendships, but decline or do not change among other adolescents. Similarly, social withdrawal increases among students with unstable, poor-quality friendships, but not among students who have supportive and intimate friendships (Berndt et al., in press).

Friendship quality contributes to antisocial behavior and its development. Conflict-ridden and contentious relationships are associated with increases in delinquent behavior during adolescence, especially among young people with histories of troublesome behavior; increases in delinquent behavior are smaller for youngsters who have supportive and intimate friends (Poulin, Dishion, & Haas, in press). Friendship quality is also important to the adaptation of young women from divorced families: Those who have supportive and intimate friendships tend to be resilient, but those who have nonsupportive friendships tend not to be resilient (Hetherington, in press).

Among older adults, support from friends also compensates for missing relationships (e.g., partners). Emotional support and receiving assistance from friends are among the most important protections against loneliness for persons without partners (Dykstra, 1995). There may be two sides to this coin, however: Older widows with "problematic" social ties (e.g., widows with friends who break promises, invade their privacy, and take advantage of them) have lower psychological well-being than widows whose social ties are not problematic (Rook, 1984). In other words, the absence of problematic qualities in these relationships may be as important as the presence of positive qualities.

CONCLUSION

Friendships are developmentally significant across the life span. The meaning assigned to these relationships changes relatively little with age, al-

though the behavioral exchanges between friends reflect the ages of the individuals involved. Whether friendships are developmental assets or liabilities depends on several conditions, especially the characteristics of one's friends and the quality of one's relationships with them.

Recommended Reading

Blieszner, R., & Adams, R. G. (1992). *Adult friendship*. Newbury Park, CA: SAGE.

Bukowski, W. M., Newcomb, A. F., & Hartup, W. W. (Eds.). (1996). *The company they keep: Friendship in childhood and adolescence*. New York: Cambridge University Press.

Hartup, W. W., & Stevens, N. (1997). (See References)

Matthews, S. H. (1986). *Friendships through the life course*. Beverly Hills, CA: SAGE.

Note

1. Address correspondence to Willard W. Hartup, Institute of Child Development, University of Minnesota, 51 E. River Rd., Minneapolis, MN 55455.

References

Bagwell, C. L., Newcomb, A. F., & Bukowski, W. M. (1998). Preadolescent friendship and peer rejection as predictors of adult adjustment. *Child Development*, 69, 140–153.

Berndt, T. J., Hawkins, J. A., & Jiao, Z. (in press). Influences of friends and friendships on adjustment to junior high school. *Merrill-Palmer Quarterly*.

Berndt, T. J., & Keefe, K. (1992). Friends' influence on adolescents' perceptions of themselves in school. In D. H. Schunk & J. L. Meece (Eds.), *Students' perceptions in the classroom* (pp. 51–73). Hillsdale, NJ: Erlbaum.

Dishion, T. J., Andrews, D. W., & Crosby, L. (1995). Anti-social boys and their friends in early adolescence: Relationship characteristics, quality, and interactional process. *Child Development, 66*, 139–151.

Dykstra, P. (1995). Loneliness among the never and formerly married: The importance of supportive friendships and a desire for independence. *Journals of Gerontology: Psychological*

Sciences and Social Sciences, 50B, S321–S329.

Hartup, W. W., & Stevens, N. (1997). Friendships and adaptation in the life course. *Psychological Bulletin, 121,* 355–370.

Hetherington, E. M. (in press). Social capital and the development of youth from nondivorced, divorced, and remarried families. In W. A. Collins & B. Laursen (Eds.), *Minnesota Symposia on Child Psychology: Vol. 30. Relationships as developmental contexts.* Hillsdale, NJ: Erlbaum.

Ladd, G. W. (1990). Having friends, keeping friends, making friends, and being liked by peers in the classroom: Predictors of children's early school

adjustment? *Child Development, 61,* 1081–1100.

Larson, R., Zuzanek, J., & Mannell, R. (1985). Being alone versus being with people: Disengagement in the daily experience of older adults. *Journal of Gerontology, 40,* 375–381.

Newcomb, A. F., & Bagwell, C. (1995). Children's friendship relations: A meta-analytic review. *Psychological Bulletin, 117,* 306–347.

Poulin, F., Dishion, T. J., & Haas, E. (in press). The peer paradox: Relationship quality and deviancy training within male adolescent friendships. *Merrill-Palmer Quarterly.*

Rook, K. S. (1984). The negative side of social interaction: Impact on psycho-

logical well-being. *Journal of Personality and Social Psychology, 46,* 1156–1166.

Rutter, M., & Garmezy, N. (1983). Developmental psychopathology. In P. H. Mussen (Series Ed.) & E. M. Hetherington (Vol. Ed.), *Handbook of child psychology: Vol. 4. Socialization, personality, and social development* (4th ed., pp. 775–911). New York: Wiley.

Weiss, L., & Lowenthal, M. F. (1975). Life-course perspectives on friendship. In M. F. Lowenthal, M. Thurnher, & D. Chiriboga (Eds.), *Four stages of life: A comparative study of women and men facing transitions* (pp. 48–61). San Francisco: Jossey-Bass.

From *Current Directions in Psychological Science,* June 1999, pp. 76–79. © 1999 by the American Psychological Society. Reprinted by permission of Blackwell Publishers.

Emotional Intelligence: What the Research Says

When integrating the concept of emotional intelligence into curriculum practice, educators need to understand the models, rely on solid research, and—as always—tread carefully.

Casey D. Cobb and John D. Mayer

Emotional intelligence was popularized by Daniel Goleman's 1995 best-selling book, *Emotional Intelligence*. The book described emotional intelligence as a mix of skills, such as awareness of emotions; traits, such as persistence and zeal; and good behavior. Goleman (1995) summarized the collection of emotional intelligence qualities as "character."

The public received the idea of emotional intelligence enthusiastically. To some, it de-emphasized the importance of general IQ and promised to level the playing field for those whose cognitive abilities might be wanting. To others, it offered the potential to integrate the reasoning of a person's head and heart. Goleman made strong claims: Emotional intelligence was "as powerful," "at times more powerful," and even "twice as powerful" as IQ (Goleman, 1995, p. 34; Goleman, 1998, p. 94). On its cover, *Time* magazine declared that emotional IQ "may be the best predictor of success in life, redefining what it means to be smart" (Gibbs, 1995). Goleman's book became a *New York Times*—and international—best-seller.

The claims of this science journalism extended easily to the schools. *Emotional Intelligence* concluded that developing students' emotional competencies would result in a "'caring community,' a place where students feel respected, cared about, and bonded to classmates" (Goleman, 1995, p. 280). A leader of the social and emotional learning movement referred to emotional intelligence as "the integrative concept" underlying a curriculum for emotional intelligence (Elias et al., 1997, pp. 27, 29). And the May 1997 issue of *Educational Leadership* extensively covered the topic of emotional intelligence.

Two Models

This popular model of emotional intelligence was based on, and added to, a 1990 academic theory and subsequent publications now referred to as the *ability* approach to emotional intelligence. The logic behind the ability model was that emotions are signals about relationships. For example, sadness signals loss. We must process emotion—perceive, understand, manage, and use it—to benefit from it; thus, emotional processing—or emotional intelligence—has great importance (Mayer & Salovey, 1997; Salovey & Mayer, 1990).

The concept of emotional intelligence legitimates the discussion of emotions in school.

The ability model argued for an emotional intelligence that involves perceiving and reasoning abstractly with information that emerges from feelings. This argument drew on research findings from areas of nonverbal perception, empathy, artificial intelligence, and brain research. Recent empirical demonstrations have further bolstered the case (Mayer, Caruso, & Salovey, 1999; Mayer, DiPaolo, & Salovey, 1993; 1990; Mayer & Salovey, 1993; Salovey & Mayer, 1990).

The ability model made no particular claims about the potential predictive value of emotional intelligence. In fact, even several years after the publication of Goleman's book, psychologists view the popular claims about predicting success as ill-defined, unsupported, and implausible (Davies, Stankov, & Roberts, 1998; Epstein, 1998). Rather, the ability version emphasizes that emotional intelligence exists. If emotional intelligence exists and qualifies as a traditional or standard intelligence (like general IQ), people who are labeled *bleeding hearts* or *hopeless romantics* might be actually engaged in sophisticated information processing. Moreover, the concept of emotional intelligence legitimates the discussion of emotions in schools and other organizations because emotions reflect crucial information about relationships.

Two models of emotional intelligence thus developed. The first, the ability model, defines emotional intelligence as a set of abilities and makes claims about the importance of emotional information and the potential uses of reasoning well with that information. The second, which we will refer to as the mixed model, is more popularly oriented. It mixes emotional intelligence as an ability with social competencies, traits, and behaviors, and makes wondrous claims about the success this intelligence leads to.

Educational leaders have experimented with incorporating emotional learning in schools. For the most part, emotional intelligence is finding its way into schools in small doses, through socioemotional learning and character education programs. But examples of grander plans are evolving, with a few schools organizing their entire curriculums around emotional intelligence. One state even attempted to integrate emotional learning into all its social, health, and education programs (Elias et al., 1997; Rhode Island Emotional Competency Partnership, 1998).

Educational practices involving emotional intelligence should be based on solid research, not on sensationalistic claims.

The problem is that some educators have implemented emotional intelligence programs and policies without much sensitivity to the idea that there is more than one emotional intelligence model. We have expressed concern that school practices and policies on emotional intelligence relied on popularizations that were, in some instances, far ahead of the science on which they were presumably based (Mayer & Cobb, 2000). The early claims of the benefits of emotional intelligence to students, schools, and beyond were made without much empirical justification.

We hope that emotional intelligence is predictive of life success or that it leads to good behavior, but we recognize that it is fairly early in the game. We are also wary of the sometimes faddish nature of school reform and the grave fate of other hastily implemented curricular innovations. Consider the rush by California to

implement self-esteem programs into its schools in the late 1980s (Joachim, 1996). Substantial resources were exhausted for years before that movement was deemed a failure. The construct of emotional intelligence comes at a time when educators are eager to find answers to problems of poor conduct, interpersonal conflict, and violence plaguing schools; however, educational practices involving emotional intelligence should be based on solid research, not on sensationalistic claims. So, what *does* the research say?

Identifying emotions in faces, pictorial designs, music, and stories are typical tasks for assessing the emotional perception area of emotional intelligence.

Measuring Emotional Intelligence

Emotional intelligence, whether academically or popularly conceived, must meet certain criteria before it can be labeled a psychological entity. One criterion for an intelligence is that it can be operationalized as a set of abilities. Ability measures—measures that ask people to solve problems with an eye to whether their answers are right or wrong—are the sine qua non of assessing an intelligence. If you measure intelligence with actual problems (such as, What does the word *season* mean?), you can assess how well a person can think. If you simply ask a student how smart she is (for example, How well do you solve problems?)—a so-called self-report—you cannot be certain that you are getting an authentic or genuine answer. In fact, the correlation between a person's score on an intelligence test and self-reported intelligence is almost negligible. Early evidence suggests that self-reported emotional intelligence is fairly unrelated to actual ability (Mayer, Salovey, & Caruso, 2000).

Ability-based testing of emotional intelligence has centered on the Mayer-Salovey-Caruso Emotional Intelligence Test (MSCEIT) and its precursor, the Multifactor Emotional Intelligence Scale (MEIS). Both tests measure the four areas of emotional intelligence: perception, facilitation of thought, understanding, and management (Mayer, Caruso, & Salovey, 1999). For example, look at the pictures of the faces on this page. Is the person happy? Sad? Are other emotions expressed? Identifying emotions in faces, pictorial designs, music, and stories are typical tasks for assessing the area of emotional intelligence called emotional perception.

Another type of MSCEIT question asks, When you are feeling slow and sour, which of the following emotions does this most closely resemble: (A) frustration, (B) jealousy, (C) happiness, or (D) joy? Most people would probably choose *frustration* because people become frustrated when they move too slowly and are disappointed (or sour) that things aren't going as planned. This kind of question measures the second area of emotional intelligence: emotional facilitation of thought.

A third type of MSCEIT question tests individuals' knowledge about emotions: Contempt is closer to which combination of emotions: *anger and fear* or *disgust and anger?* Such a question assesses emotional understanding.

The final type of MSCEIT questions measures emotional management. These questions describe a hypothetical situation that stirs the emotions (such as the unexpected break-up of a long-term relationship) and then ask how a person should respond to obtain a given outcome (for example, staying calm).

One crucial aspect of assessing emotional intelligence lies in the method by which answers are scored. Scoring a standard IQ test is fairly straightforward, with clear-cut, defensible answers for every item. The responses on a test of emotional intelligence are better thought of as *fuzzy sets*—certain answers are more right or plausible than others, and only some answers are absolutely wrong all the time. To assess the relative correctness of an answer, we can use consensus, expertise or target criteria (or some combination). A correct response by way of the consensus approach is simply the answer most frequently selected by test-takers. Answers can also be deemed correct by such experts as psychologists or other trained professionals. Finally, correct responses can be validated using a target criterion. For instance, the actual emotional reaction of an anonymously depicted spouse facing a difficult decision could serve as the targeted response in a test item that described his or her situation.

The MSCEIT and MEIS are undergoing considerable scrutiny from the scientific community. Although not everyone is convinced yet of their validity, the tests do provide the most dramatic evidence thus far for the existence of an emotional intelligence. Early findings provide strong evidence that emotional intelligence looks and behaves like other intelligences, such as verbal intelligence, but remains distinct enough to stand alone as a separate mental ability. Like other intelligences, emotional intelligence appears to develop with age (Mayer, Caruso, & Salovey, 1999).

Predictive Value

The first emotional intelligence tests were used two years *after* the popular claims of 1995, so the actual findings lag behind the popular perception of a well-established area of research. One important pattern is emerging, however. Preliminary research (primarily from unpublished studies and dissertations) from the MEIS suggests a modest relationship between emotional intelligence and lower levels of "bad" behaviors.

In one study, high scores in emotional intelligence moderately predicted the absence of adult bad behavior,

such as getting into fights and arguments, drinking, smoking, and owning firearms (Mayer, Caruso, Salovey, Formica, & Woolery, 2000). In a dissertation study, the MEIS-A measured the emotional intelligence of fifty-two 7th and 8th graders in an urban school district (Rubin, 1999). Analyses indicated that higher emotional intelligence was inversely related to teacher and peer ratings of aggression among students. In another study, researchers reported that higher MEIS-A scores among 200 high school students were associated with lower admissions of smoking, intentions to smoke, and alcohol consumption (Trinidad & Johnson, 2000). The conclusion suggested by such research is that higher emotional intelligence predicts lower incidences of "bad" behavior. As for the claims about success in life—those studies have yet to be done.

What Can Schools Do?

Educators interested in emotional intelligence of either the ability or mixed type are typically directed to programs in social and emotional learning (Goleman, 1995; Goleman, 1996; Mayer & Salovey, 1997). These programs had been around for years before the introduction of the emotional intelligence concept. Some aspects of the programs overlap with the ability approach to emotional intelligence. This overlap occurs when programs ask early elementary children to "appropriately express and manage" various emotions and "differentiate and label negative and positive emotions in self and others," or call for students to integrate "feeling and thinking with language" and learn "strategies for coping with, communicating about, and managing strong feelings" (Elias et al., 1997, p. 133–134). Other aspects of these programs are specifically more consistent with the mixed (or popular) models than the ability approach in that they include distinct behavioral objectives, such as "becoming assertive, self-calming, cooperative," and "understanding responsible behavior at social events" (p. 135). There is also an emphasis on such values as honesty, consideration, and caring.

What may work better, at least for some students, is helping them develop the capacity to make decisions on their own in their own contexts.

What would a curriculum based on an ability model look like? Basically, it would drop the behavioral objectives and values and focus on emotional reasoning.

Choosing Approaches

The emotional intelligence curriculum (or ability model) and the social and emotional learning curriculum (or mixed model) both overlap and diverge. The emotional ability approach focuses only on teaching emotional reasoning. The social and emotional learning curriculum mixes emotional skills, social values, and behaviors. In the case of these two approaches, less—that is, the pure ability model—may be better. What troubles us about the broader social and emotional learning approach is that the emphasis on students getting along with one another could stifle creativity, healthy skepticism, or spontaneity—all valued outcomes in their own right. Teaching people to be tactful or compassionate as full-time general virtues runs counter to the "smart" part of emotional intelligence, which requires knowing when to be tactful or compassionate and when to be blunt or even cold and hard.

Moreover, a social and emotional approach that emphasizes positive behavior and attitudes can be a real turn-off for a negative thinker—often the very student that the teacher is trying to reach. Research supports this concern: Positive messages appear less believable and less sensible to unhappy people than sad messages do (Forgas, 1995). We suspect that troubled students will be alienated by insistent positivity. There may be nothing wrong with trying such approaches, but they may not work.

Correctly perceiving emotional information is part of the way that children make sense of things.

What may work better at least for some students, is helping them develop the capacity to make decisions on their own in their own contexts. This type of education is knowledge-based and is more aligned with an ability model of emotional intelligence. It involves teaching students emotional knowledge and emotional reasoning, with the hope that this combination would lead children to find their own way toward making good decisions.

Most children will require gentle guidance toward the good. We wonder, however, whether we can achieve this goal better by example and indirect teaching than by the direct, uniform endorsement of selected values in the curriculum.

How Might the Ability Curriculum Work?

The teaching of emotional knowledge has been a facet of some curriculums for years. For example, educators can help children perceive emotions in several ways. Elementary teachers could ask the class to name the feelings that they are aware of and then show what they look or feel like (for example, Show me sad). Similarly, teachers could ask students to identify the emotions depicted by various pictures of faces. Children can also

learn to read more subtle cues, such as the speed and intonation of voice, body posture, and physical gestures.

Correctly perceiving emotional information is one way children make sense of things. The ability to perceive emotions can be further fine-tuned as a student ages. Consider the level of sophistication required for an actor to put on a convincing expression of fear—and for the audience to recognize it as such.

Students can also learn to use emotions to create new ideas. For instance, asking students in English class to write about trees as if they were angry or delighted facilitates a deeper understanding of these emotions.

Understanding emotions should also be a goal of the curriculum. For example, social studies expert Fred Newmann (1987) has suggested that higher-order thinking can be enhanced through empathic teaching. A social studies teacher could show images of the Trail of Tears, the forced exodus of the Cherokee from their homeland, and have students discuss the feelings involved. This could help students vicariously experience what those perilous conditions were like. In literature courses, teachers who point out the feelings of a story character, such as a triumphant figure skater or a despairing widow, can teach a great deal about what emotions tell us about relationships. Because the ability version of emotional intelligence legitimizes discussing emotions by considering them to convey information, it also supports emotionally evocative activities—such as theater, art, and interscholastic events—that help kids understand and learn from personal performance.

Emotional Intelligence in Schools

Educators looking to incorporate emotional intelligence into their schools should be aware that the two different models of emotional intelligence suggest two somewhat different curricular approaches. The model of emotional intelligence that makes its way into schools should be empirically defensible, measurable, and clear enough to serve as a basis for curriculum development. We believe that an ability-based curriculum, which emphasizes emotional knowledge and reasoning, may have advantages because it reaches more students.

References

Davies, M., Stankov, L., & Roberts, R. D. (1998). Emotional intelligence: In search of an elusive construct. *Journal of Personality & Social Psychology, 75,* 989–1015.

Elias, M. J., Zins, J. E., Weissberg, R. P., Frey, K. S., Greenberg, M. T., Haynes, N. M., Kessler, R., Schwab-Stone, M. E., & Schriver, T. P. (1997). *Promoting social and emotional learning: Guidelines for educators.* Alexandria, VA: ASCD.

Epstein, S. (1998). *Constructive thinking: The key to emotional intelligence.* Westport, CT: Praeger.

Forgas, J. P. (1995). Mood and judgement: The affect infusion model (AIM). *Psychological Bulletin, 117*(1), 39–66.

Gibbs, N. (1995, October 2). The EQ factor. *Time, 146*(14), 60–68.

Goleman, D. (1995). *Emotional intelligence*. New York: Bantam.

Goleman, D. (1996). *Emotional intelligence: A new vision for educators* [Videotape]. Port Chester, NY: National Professional Resources.

Goleman, D. (1998, November/December). What makes a leader? *Harvard Business Review, 76*, 93–102.

Joachim, K. (1996). The politics of self-esteem. *American Educational Research Journal, 33*, 3–22.

Mayer, J. D., Caruso, D. R., & Salovey, P. (1999). Emotional intelligence meets standards for a traditional intelligence. *Intelligence, 27*, 267–298.

Mayer, J. D., Caruso, D. R., Salovey, P., Formica, S., & Woolery, A. (2000). Unpublished raw data.

Mayer, J. D., & Cobb, C. D. (2000). Educational policy on emotional intelligence: Does it make sense? *Educational Psychology Review, 12*(2), 163–183.

Mayer, J. D., DiPaolo, M. T., & Salovey, P. (1990). Perceiving affective content in ambiguous visual stimuli: A component of emotional intelligence. *Journal of Personality Assessment, 54*, 772–781.

Mayer, J. D., & Salovey, P. (1993). The intelligence of emotional intelligence. *Intelligence, 17*(4), 433–442.

Mayer, J. D., & Salovey, P. (1997). What is emotional intelligence? In P. Salovey & D. Sluyter (Eds.), *Emotional development and emotional intelligence: Implications for educators* (pp. 3–31). New York: BasicBooks.

Mayer, J. D., Salovey, P., & Caruso, D. R. (2000). Models of emotional intelligence. In R. J. Sternberg (Ed.), *Handbook of Intelligence* (pp. 396–420). Cambridge: Cambridge University Press.

Newmann, F. M. (1987). *Higher order thinking in the teaching of social studies: Connections between theory and practice*. Madison, WI: National Center on Effective Secondary Schools. (ERIC Document Reproduction Service No. 332 880)

Rhode Island Emotional Competency Partnership. (1998). *Update on emotional competency*. Providence, RI: Rhode Island Partners.

Rubin, M. M. (1999). *Emotional intelligence and its role in mitigating aggression: A correlational study of the relationship between emotional intelligence and aggression in urban adolescents*. Unpublished manuscript, Immaculata College, Immaculata, PA.

Salovey, P., & Mayer, J. D. (1990). Emotional intelligence. *Imagination, Cognition, & Personality, 9*(3), 185–211.

Trinidad, D. R., & Johnson, A. (2000). *The association between emotional intelligence and early adolescent tobacco and alcohol use*. Unpublished manuscript, University of Southern California, Los Angeles, CA.

Casey D. Cobb (casey.cobb@unh.edu) is Assistant Professor of Education and **John D. Mayer** is Professor of Psychology at the University of New Hampshire, 62 College Rd., Durham, NH 03824.

From *Educational Leadership,* November 2000, pp. 14-18. © 2000 by the Association for Supervision and Curriculum Development. All rights reserved.

nurturing
empathy

How seeing the world through another's
eyes not only makes a child compassionate
but helps him learn right from wrong

BY JULIA GLASS

On mellow summer evenings, my neighbor Holly Lance and I used to get our 2-year-old sons together outside for "run them bone tired" playdates. One evening, as they were sprinting and cavorting with typical pinball momentum, Holly's son, Stefan, burst into tears. Holding his elbow in obvious pain, he collapsed in his mother's arms. My son approached his inconsolable playmate with a look of alarm. He watched Stefan cry for a few seconds, then walked to a nearby wall, bumped his head against it, and erupted into sobs to rival Stefan's.

I had never seen Alec do anything so peculiar. Was he trying to upstage his friend? It was Holly who said, "What a sweet thing to do!" And then I saw that Alec had clearly been attempting—if somewhat clownishly—to comfort someone he loved. I'd long since begun to encourage Alec's verbal, physical, and musical abilities, but what about his emotional abilities? Should I be nurturing this flair for compassion? I wondered.

"At its simplest, empathy means feeling the same thing another person's feeling; at its most sophisticated, it's understanding his entire life situation," says Martin Hoffman, Ph.D., professor of psychology at New York University and author of *Empathy and Moral Development: Implications for Caring and Justice.*

It's empathy that leads us, as adults, not just to help out friends and family but also to stop for a driver stranded by the side of the road, point a bewildered tourist in the right direction, even water a thirsty tree. Without it, our species would probably be extinct, says Hoffman. It is also a key to moral internalization—our children's increasing ability, as they grow, to make decisions by themselves that weigh others' needs and desires against their own.

The root of empathy is linking what an emotion feels like for you with what it feels like for others.

Given the importance of this attribute, here's how to recognize empathy's earliest signs and encourage it to blossom.

Born to Connect

There you are squeezing melons in the produce aisle, your 1-year-old babbling blissfully away, when a baby over in the snack-foods section starts to wail. All too predictably, so does yours. Experts believe that such copycat grief may be an emotional reflex that helps "train" our nature toward a more genuine form of compassion.

"The root of empathy is being able to recognize a link between what it feels like for you to be in a particular emotional state and what that feels like for another person, and it looks as if we're born with a primitive form of that kind of identification," says Alison Gopnik, Ph.D., a psychology professor at the University of California at Berkeley and coauthor of The Scientist in the Crib. "Even within an hour of birth, babies will try to make the same facial expression they see someone else making." Over the next few months, infants strive to coordinate their gestures and vocalizations as well as their expressions with those of adults around them.

At about 9 months, a baby begins to pay attention to how others feel about things. Confronted with an unfamiliar object—a toy robot or pureed squash—he'll instantly look at Mom to read her take. If she looks apprehensive, he'll hold back; if she looks pleased, he'll probably dive right in. While this reveals a new depth of perception, it also shows that babies have yet to grasp the most fundamental principle of civilized society: Each of us is a separate being with individual proclivities and feelings. You can't comprehend the feelings of another person until you grasp the concept that there is such a thing as another person.

You Are You, I Am I: Discovering Others

"For most of the first year, babies are pretty confused about what's going on around them," says Hoffman. "If they see another baby fall down and need comfort from his mother, they'll cry and need comfort too."

About midway through the second year, most toddlers begin to recognize themselves in a mirror—seeing themselves as unique, distinct objects. They now see other people as separate—but only physically. They have yet to learn that different people have different inner states as well. So when one toddler sees another in distress, her instinct is to fetch her own mother rather than her playmate's, to placate the child with her own favorite toy. She'll recognize the suffering as belonging to someone else but can't imagine any appropriate remedy other than the one that would suit her. This impulse is one of the most common early signs of what we recognize as genuine empathy, and it may continue even after kids gain a greater sense of what makes other people tick.

When 4-year-old Shai Karp's mother was rushed to the hospital for an appendectomy, he went along and sat with her as she was being checked in for surgery. "He'd brought his favorite stuffed animal, Tumby—short for the 'tumble dry low' on its label," says his mother, Judy

Wilner. "As I sat there, feeling miserable, Shai insisted I keep Tumby with me that night."

3 empathy busters

"Empathy is innate, but you can stunt its development," says psychologist Martin Hoffman, Ph.D. Try not to:

Overindulge. Just as an authoritative, "because I said so" style of parenting may prevent children from understanding the whys and wherefores of considerate behavior, so may overly permissive parenting. Kids raised without enough limits may come to feel very entitled—and entitlement, which focuses on the self, is anything but empathic.

Smother. Empathizing with another's strong feelings sometimes requires keeping a respectful distance, especially when a child needs to retreat for a time with a difficult emotion, such as shame or guilt. Resist the urge to try to protect kids from such strong emotions.

Stress competition. "In middle-class America, consideration of others is valued very highly," says Hoffman, "but so is individual achievement." For the first few years of life, those two values rarely collide; mothers may compare kids' developmental milestones, for instance, but such competition takes place mainly between parents. Come the school years, that changes.

"If a kid does excel, it's normal to feel some empathic distress for friends who don't do as well," says Hoffman, but many parents just want their kids to feel good about succeeding and don't acknowledge their empathy. Likewise, students who perform poorly need a more compassionate response than a dose of tutoring and a well-meant "You'll do better next time." The competition won't go away; what's important is to recognize its dark side and discuss how it affects your child's feelings toward peers.

Somewhat ironically, the age at which this type of generosity arises is exactly when, behaviorally speaking, the Tubby custard hits the fan. Because just as toddlers are trying to learn how to make other people feel better, they're also learning how to make other people—most notably, their parents—feel decidedly worse. And it's not just, as I used to think, that Mother Nature throws in these random adorable moments to pacify our rage; the two tendencies are closely intertwined.

The Altruistic Twos?

Toward the end of the second year, children begin to understand that other people have thoughts, feelings, and wants different from their own—often through a process of trial and error. When a toddler trying to comfort his friend sees that his own favorite toy doesn't do the trick, he'll try the friend's favorite toy instead or he'll fetch the friend's mom.

Preschoolers begin to perceive subtler feelings, such as that a classmate may be sad because he misses his parents.

This stage marks a primitive but true form of empathy, says Hoffman, one when children not only start to recognize the different experiences of other people but also, when necessary, reach out to them. "Empathy isn't just a feeling; it's a motive," he stresses. Whether we're throwing a bridal shower or helping a friend cope with a death in the family, empathy spurs us to partake in someone else's experience. We don't always act on the urge, but when we do, it often makes us feel good.

This eventful early age is also a period of intensive experimenting to find out what makes people different from one another. "It's around age two that we begin to see children perform these lovely altruistic acts—and do things precisely because we don't want them to," says Gopnik. "The same impulse that leads a child to think, 'Mom's crying, I'm not; I can comfort her,' also leads to 'Mom doesn't want me to touch that lamp; I can touch that lamp, I'm going to touch it.' If you think about what we want to encourage—understanding how other people feel—the 'terrible twos' is a part of that." (For more on promoting this understanding, see "Encouraging Compassion," at right.)

Toward a More Mature Compassion

From this point on, children refine and enlarge their perspective on other people's inner lives. In the preschool years, says Hoffman, they begin to perceive more subtle, removed feelings—such as that a classmate may be sad because he misses his parents. They also learn that a single event can lead to different reactions from different people. Sometime between ages 5 and 8—having grasped their own gender and ethnic identity—they begin to look at each person around them as having a distinct personal history and to consider its influences on that person's experiences and feelings. "They also start to see how having different personalities makes people react differently, and they begin to take that into account when dealing with people," adds Gopnik.

Children are now on the threshold of what Hoffman says is a highly sophisticated form of empathy—empathy for another's experience beyond the immediate situation, a skill that we work on for the rest of our lives. They can

encouraging compassion

"Showing affection to kids helps them feel secure and loved," says psychologist Hoffman, "and that contributes to their ability to feel consideration for others. Being a model of empathy—actively helping others—is also important." Beyond these fairly obvious gestures, you can encourage compassion if you:

•**Discipline in ways that invoke natural empathy.** By the end of the second year, scoldings constitute some two-thirds of all parent-child interactions, says Hoffman. And much of the offending behavior involves situations in which the child hurts or upsets someone else.

When your child is the transgressor, it's important not just to let him know he was wrong but also to be specific about the consequences of his actions. Saying, "You made me angry when you poured your milk on the table because now I have to mop it up and we don't have any more" or "You hurt his feelings when you grabbed that airplane—how would you feel if he grabbed it from you?" is an essential step toward making a child feel both guilt for the behavior and responsibility for how other people feel. In time, the ability to anticipate that guilt can motivate kids to "do the right thing."

•**Encourage conciliatory gestures.** Ask your child to apologize or give the person he hurt a hug, pat, or kiss.

•**Don't stifle his emotions.** Adults may try too quickly to "fix" a child's bad feelings—to distract him from sadness with treats, negotiate to thwart his anger, or otherwise derail an emotion that may help teach him the less pleasant aspect of human nature. This doesn't mean you have to accept misbehavior in the name of letting your child "feel"; part of learning to be empathic is learning that we can't act on every emotion we have.

•**Make feelings a topic of discussion.** When you see other people in different situations, ask your child to imagine what those people might be feeling. And don't limit yourself to real life. Talk about your child's emotional response to books, TV shows, and videos.

•**Revel in role-playing games.** "They let kids feel what it's like to be somebody else—a daddy, a baby," says psychologist Alison Gopnik, Ph.D. "That's important to empathy. When my son was three, I'd say, 'I'm going to be Alexei, and you be Mommy.' I'd be difficult and carry on, and he'd say things like 'You can't do that! It's going to be a big mess and I'm going to have to clean it up!' It was a great way to work out some of our conflicts."—J.G.

see that some people have generally happy or sad lives, and they can begin to empathize with entire groups of people (the homeless, earthquake victims, firefighters battling an inferno).

Last Thanksgiving a friend's 4-year-old daughter had a poignant moment. "AnnaBess walked into the kitchen when her father was dressing the turkey," recalls her mother, Wendy Greenspun. "She started crying and said, 'Daddy, that turkey doesn't want to be dead! He wants to be alive! He wants to be with his friends.' She was extremely upset for almost an hour." Whether or not AnnaBess was expressing an unusually precocious empathy, this much is clear: She was saddened by another creature's hardship, and her outrage occurred spontaneously—without prompting by anyone else.

For when it comes to raising empathic children, says Hoffman, parents need not fret about following some rule book or missing a narrow window of opportunity. "The beauty of empathy," he says, "is that it comes naturally. It doesn't have to be forced. You need only nourish it."

JULIA GLASS *recently won her third Nelson Algren Fiction Award and a fellowship in writing from the New York Foundation for the Arts.*

From *Parenting* magazine, June/July 2001, p. 72. © 2001 by The Parenting Group. Reprinted by permission.

What's in a face?

Do facial expressions reflect inner feelings?
Or are they social devices for influencing others?

BY BETH AZAR
Monitor staff

After 30 years of renewed interest in facial expression as a key clue to human emotions, frowns are appearing on critics' faces. The face, they say, isn't the mirror to emotions it's been held out to be.

The use of facial expression for measuring people's emotions has dominated psychology since the late 1960s when Paul Ekman, PhD, of the University of California, San Francisco, and Carroll Izard, PhD, of the University of Delaware, reawakened the study of emotion by linking expressions to a group of basic emotions.

Many took that work to imply that facial expressions provided the key to people's feelings. But in recent years the psychology literature has been sprinkled with hotly worded attacks by detractors who claim that there is no one-to-one correspondence between facial expressions and emotions. In fact, they argue, there's no evidence to support a link between what appears on someone's face and how they feel inside.

But this conflict masks some major areas of agreement, says Joseph Campos, PhD, of the University of California at Berkeley. Indeed, he says, "there is profound agreement that the face, along with the voice, body posture and hand gestures, forecast to outside observers what people will do next."

The point of contention remains in whether the face also says something about a person's internal state. Some, such as Izard, say, "Absolutely." Detractors, such as Alan Fridlund, PhD, of the University of California, Santa Barbara, say an adamant "No." And others, including Campos and Ekman, land somewhere in the middle. The face surely can provide important information about emotion, but it is only one of many tools and should never be used as a "gold standard" of emotion as some researchers, particularly those studying children, have tended to do.

"The face is a component [of emotion]," says Campos. "But to make it the center of study of the human being experiencing an emotion is like saying the only thing you need to study in a car is the transmission. Not that the transmission is unimportant, but it's only part of an entire system."

WHERE IT ALL BEGAN

Based on findings that people label photos of prototypical facial expressions with words that represent the same basic emotions—a smile represents joy, a scowl represents anger—Ekman and Izard pioneered the idea that by carefully measuring facial expression, they could evaluate people's true emotions. In fact, since the 1970s, Ekman and his colleague Wallace Friesen, PhD, have dominated the field of emotion research with their theory that when an emotion occurs, a cascade of electrical impulses, emanating from emotion centers in the brain, trigger specific facial expressions and other physiological changes—such as increased or decreased heart rate or heightened blood pressure.

If the emotion comes on slowly, or is rather weak, the theory states, the impulse might not be strong enough to trigger the expression. This would explain in part why there can sometimes be emotion without expression, they argue. In addition, cultural "display rules"—which determine when and whether people of certain cultures display emotional expressions—can derail this otherwise automatic process, the theory states. Facial expressions evolved in humans as signals to others about how they feel, says Ekman.

> **"The face is like a switch on a railroad track. It affects the trajectory of the social interaction the way the switch would affect the path of the train."**
>
> *Alan Fridlund*
> *University of California, Santa Barbara*

"At times it may be uncomfortable or inconvenient for others to know how we feel," he says. "But in the long run, over the course of evolution, it was useful to us as signalers. So, when you see an angry look on my face, you know that I may be preparing to respond in an angry fashion, which means that I may attack or abruptly withdraw."

THE FACE IS LIKE A SWITCH

Although Fridlund strongly disagrees with Ekman in his writings, arguing that expressions carry no inherent meaning, the two basically agree that facial expressions forecast people's future actions. But instead of describing expressions from the point of view of the expresser, as Ekman tends to do, Fridlund thinks more in terms of people who perceive the expressions.

Expressions evolved to elicit behaviors from others, says Fridlund. So, a smile may encourage people to approach while a scowl may impel them to stay clear, and a pout may elicit words of sympathy and reassurance. And, he contends, expressions are inherently social. Even when people are alone they are holding an internal dialogue with another person, or imagining themselves in a social situation.

"The face is like a switch on a railroad track," says Fridlund. "It affects the trajectory of the social interaction the way the switch would affect the path of the train."

Thinking of facial expressions as tools for influencing social interactions provides an opportunity to begin predicting when certain facial expressions will occur and will allow more precise theories about social interactions, says Fridlund. Studies by him and others find that expressions occur most often during pivotal points in social interactions—during greetings, social crisis or times of appeasement, for example.

"At these pivotal points, where there's an approach, or proximity, or more intimacy, the face as well as the gestures form a kind of switching station for the possibilities of social interactions," says Fridlund.

The University of Amsterdam's Nico Frijda, PhD, agrees that expressions are a means to influence others. They also, he believes, occur when people prepare to take some kind of action whether there are others present or not. For example, if you're scared and want to protect yourself, you frown and draw your brows in preparation—what Ekman would call a "fear" expression. But there is no one-to-one correspondence between the face and specific emotions, Frijda contends.

"There is some affinity between certain emotions and certain expressions," he says, "if only because some emotions imply a desire for vigorous action, and some facial expressions manifest just that."

NOT A 'GOLD STANDARD'

Herein lies the major point of contention within the facial expression community, says Berkeley's Campos.

"All sides agree that the face—and voice and posture, for that matter—forecast what a person will do next," he says. "But over and above that, is feeling involved?"

Although much work in the emotion literature relies on a link between facial expression and emotions, there's a paucity of evidence supporting it.

"There's some sense in which faces express emotion, but only in the sense that everything expresses emotion," says psychologist James Russell, PhD, of the University of British Columbia, a long-time critic of the expression-emotion link. "Music does, posture does, words do, tone of voice does, your behavior does. The real question is, 'Is there anything special about faces?' And there we really don't know much."

What's more likely, argues Russell, is that facial expressions tell others something about the overall character of a person's mood—whether it's positive or negative—and context then provides details about specific emotions.

Others, including Ekman and Campos, contend that the face can display information about emotions. But, they admit, it is by no means a "gold standard." The face is only one of many measures researchers can use to infer emotion. And those who only examine faces when trying to study emotion will jump to false conclusions.

"There is a link between facial expression and emotion," explains developmental psychologist Linda Camras, PhD, of DePaul University. "But it's not a one-to-one kind of relationship as many once thought. There are many situations where emotion is experienced, yet no prototypic facial expression is displayed. And there are times when a facial expression appears with no corresponding emotion."

In a classic set of experiments with infants, Camras found that some facial expressions can occur in the absence of the emotions they supposedly represent.

"An emotion has to be plausible [for the situation you're examining]," she says. "You can't do blind coding of facial expression and necessarily be on the right track, even for infants."

But to say, as Fridlund does, that there's no connection between some facial expressions and some emotions is simply wrong, says Ekman. When we look at people's expressions, he says, we don't receive direct information about their heart rate or other physiological changes that accompany emotions. We might even think, "He's going to whack me" rather than "He's angry," says Ekman.

"But these signals—facial expressions and physiological changes associated with internal emotions—can't exist independently," he contends.

FURTHER REFERENCE

Ekman, P., & Rosenberg, E. (1997). *What the Face Reveals*. New York: Oxford University Press.

Fridlund, A. (1994). *Human Facial Expression: An Evolutionary View*. San Diego, CA: Academic Press.

Russell, J., & Fernandez-Dols, J. M. (Eds.) (1997). *The Psychology of Facial Expression*. New York: Cambridge University Press.

From *Monitor on Psychology*, January 2000, pp. 44-45. © 2000 by the American Psychological Association. Reprinted by permission.

How to Spot a Liar

With some careful observation— and a little help from new software—anyone can learn to be a lie detector

By JAMES GEARY/London
With reporting by Eric Silver/Jerusalem

"You can tell a lie but you will give yourself away. Your heart will race. Your skin will sweat… I will know. I am the lie detector." Thus began each episode of Lie Detector, a strange cross between a relationship counseling session and an episode of the Jerry Springer Show that ran on British daytime television last year. Against a backdrop of flashing computer screens and eerie blue light, participants—usually feuding couples but sometimes warring neighbors or aggrieved business partners—sat on a couch and were quizzed by the program's host. A frequent topic of discussion was one guest's suspicion that his or her partner had been unfaithful. The person suspected of infidelity denied it, of course, and the object of the show was to find out—through cross-examination and computer analysis—whether that person was telling the truth.

However much we may abhor it, deception comes naturally to all living things. Birds do it by feigning injury to lead hungry predators away from nesting young. Spider crabs do it by disguise: adorning themselves with strips of kelp and other debris, they pretend to be something they are not—and so escape their enemies. Nature amply rewards successful deceivers by allowing them to survive long enough to mate and reproduce. So it may come as no surprise to learn that human beings—who, according to psychologist Gerald Jellison of the University of South California, are lied to about 200 times a day, roughly one untruth every five minutes—often deceive for exactly the same reasons: to save their own skins or to get something they can't get by other means.

But knowing how to catch deceit can be just as important a survival skill as knowing how to tell a lie and get away with it. A person able to spot falsehood quickly is unlikely to be swindled by an unscrupulous business associate or hoodwinked by a devious spouse. Luckily, nature provides more than enough clues to trap dissemblers in their own tangled webs—if you know where to look. By closely observing facial expressions, body language and tone of voice, practically anyone can recognize the telltale signs of lying. Researchers are even programming computers—like those used on Lie Detector—to get at the truth by analyzing the same physical cues available to the naked eye and ear. "With the proper training, many people can learn to reliably detect lies," says Paul Ekman, professor of psychology at the University of California, San Francisco, who has spent the past 15 years studying the secret art of deception.

In order to know what kind of lies work best, successful liars need to accurately assess other people's emotional states. Ekman's research shows that this same emotional intelligence is essential for good lie detectors, too. The emotional state to watch out for is stress, the conflict most liars feel between the truth and what they actually say and do.

Even high-tech lie detectors don't detect lies as such; they merely detect the physical cues of emotions, which may or may not correspond to what the person being tested is saying. Polygraphs, for instance, measure respiration, heart rate and skin conductivity, which tend to increase when people are nervous—as they usually are when lying. Nervous people typically perspire, and the salts contained in perspiration conduct electricity. That's why a sudden leap in skin conductivity indicates nervousness—about getting caught, perhaps?—which might, in turn, suggest that someone is being economical with the truth. On the other hand, it might also mean that the lights in the television studio are too hot—which is one reason polygraph tests are inadmissible in court. "Good lie detectors don't rely on a single sign," Ekman says, "but interpret clusters of verbal and nonverbal clues that suggest someone might be lying."

Those clues are written all over the face. Because the musculature of the face is directly connected to the areas of the brain that process emotion, the countenance can be a window to the soul. Neurological studies even suggest that genuine emotions travel different pathways through the brain than insincere ones. If a patient paralyzed by stroke on one side of the face, for example, is asked to smile deliberately, only the mobile side of the mouth is raised. But tell that same person a funny joke, and the patient breaks into a full and spontaneous smile. Very few people—most notably, actors and politicians—are able to consciously control all of their facial expressions. Lies can often be caught when the liar's true feelings briefly leak through the mask of deception. "We don't think before we feel," Ekman says. "Expressions tend to show up on the face before we're even conscious of experiencing an emotion."

One of the most difficult facial expressions to fake—or conceal, if it is genuinely felt—is sadness. When someone is truly sad, the forehead wrinkles with grief and the inner corners of the eyebrows are pulled up. Fewer than 15% of the people Ekman tested were able to produce this eyebrow movement voluntarily. By contrast, the lowering of the eyebrows associated with an angry scowl can be replicated at will by almost everybody. "If someone claims they are sad and the inner corners of their eyebrows don't go up," Ekman says, "the sadness is probably false."

The smile, on the other hand, is one of the easiest facial expressions to counterfeit. It takes just two muscles—the zygomaticus major muscles that extend from the cheekbones to the corners of the lips—to produce a grin. But there's a catch. A genuine smile affects not only the corners of the lips but also the orbicularis oculi, the muscle around the eye that produces the distinctive "crow's-feet" associated with people who laugh a lot. A counterfeit grin can be unmasked if the lip corners go up, the eyes crinkle but the inner corners of the eyebrows are not lowered, a movement controlled by the orbicularis oculi that is difficult to fake. The absence of lowered eyebrows is one reason why false smiles look so strained and stiff.

Ekman and his colleagues have classified all the muscle movements—ranging from the thin, taut lips of fury to the arched eyebrows of surprise—that underlie the complete repertoire of human facial expressions. In addition to the nervous tics and jitters that can give liars away, Ekman discovered that fibbers often allow the truth to slip through in brief, unguarded facial expressions. Lasting no more than a quarter of a second, these fleeting glimpses of a person's true emotional state—or "microexpressions," as Ekman calls them—are reliable guides to veracity.

In a series of tests, Ekman interviewed and videotaped a group of male American college students about their opinions regarding capital punishment. Some participants were instructed to tell the truth—whether they were for or against the death penalty—and some were instructed to lie. Liars who successfully fooled the interviewer received $50. Ekman then studied the tapes to map the microexpressions of mendacity.

One student, for example, appeared calm and reasonable as he listed the reasons why the death penalty was wrong. But every time he expressed these opinions, he swiftly, almost imperceptibly, shook his head. But the movement is so subtle and quick many people don't even see it until it's pointed out to them. While his words explained the arguments against capital punishment, the quick, involuntary shudder of his head was saying loud and clear, "No, I don't believe this!" He was, in fact, lying, having been for many years a firm supporter of the death penalty.

THE LYIN' KING

Four signs that may indicate deception

1. AN EMBLEM is a gesture with a specific meaning, like shrugging the shoulders to say, "I don't know." An emblem may be a sign of deceit if only part of the gesture is performed (a one-shoulder shrug, for example) or if it is performed in a concealed manner.

2. MANIPULATORS are repetitive touching motions like scratching the nose, tapping the foot or twisting the hair. They tend to increase when people are nervous, and may be an attempt to conceal incriminating facial expressions.

3. AN ILLUSTRATOR is a movement that emphasizes speech. Illustrators increase with emotion, so too few may indicate false feelings while too many may be an attempt to distract attention from signs of deceit on the face.

4. MICROEXPRESSIONS flash across the face in less than a quarter of a second—a frown, for example, that is quickly covered up by a grin. Though fleeting, they can reveal subtle clues about the true feelings that a person may wish to repress or conceal.

"With proper training, many people can learn to reliably detect lies."

"It would be an impossible world if no one lied."

James Geary/London
With reporting by Eric Silver/Jerusalem.

Another student also said that he was against the death penalty. But during the interview, he spoke very slowly, paused often, and rarely looked the interrogator in the eye, instead fixing his gaze on some vague point on the floor. Speech that is too slow (or too fast), frequent hesitations, lack of direct eye contact: these are all classic symptoms of lying. But this man was telling the truth. He paused and hesitated because he was shy. After all, even honest and normally composed individuals can become flustered if they believe others suspect them of lying. His lack of eye contact could be explained by the fact that he came from Asia, where an averted gaze is often a sign of deference and respect, not deception. This scenario highlights Ekman's admonition that before branding someone a liar, you must first know that person's normal behavior patterns and discount other explanations, such as cultural differences.

Ekman has used this tape to test hundreds of subjects. His conclusion: most people are lousy lie detectors, with few individuals able to spot duplicity more than 50% of the time. But Ekman's most recent study, published last year in Psychological Science, found that four groups of people did significantly better than chance: members of the U.S. Central Intelligence Agency, other U.S. federal law enforcement officers, a handful of Los Angeles County sheriffs and a group of clinical psychologists. Reassuringly, perhaps, the federal officials performed best, accurately detecting liars 73% of the time. What makes these groups so good at lie catching? According to Ekman, it's training, experience and motivation. The jobs—and in some cases, the lives—of everyone in these groups depend on their ability to pick up deceit.

Ekman has used his findings to assist law enforcement agents—including members of the U.S. Secret Service and Federal Bureau of Investigation, Britain's Scotland Yard and the Israeli police force—in criminal investigations and antiterrorist activities. He refuses to work with politicians. "It is unlikely that judging deception from demeanor alone will ever be admissible in court," Ekman says. "But the research shows that it's possible for some people to make highly accurate judgments about lying without any special aids, such as computers."

But for those who still prefer a bit of technological assistance, there's the Verdicator—a device that, according to its 27-year-old inventor Amir Liberman, enables anyone equipped with a personal computer and a phone or microphone to catch a liar. A person's tone of voice can be just as revealing as the expression on his face. A low tone, for example, can suggest a person is lying or is stressed, while a higher pitch can mean excitement. Liberman claims the Verdicator, a $2,500 piece of software produced by Integritek Technologies in Petah Tikvah near Tel Aviv, is between 85% and 95% accurate in determining whether the person on the other end of the line is lying, an accuracy rate better than that for traditional polygraphs. "Our software knows how to size you up," Liberman boasts.

The Verdicator delivers its results by analyzing voice fluctuations that are usually inaudible to the human ear. When a person is under stress, anxiety may cause muscle tension and reduce blood flow to the vocal cords, produc-

ing a distinctive pattern of sound waves. Liberman has catalogued these patterns and programmed the Verdicator to distinguish among tones that indicate excitement, cognitive stress—the difference between what you think and what you say—and outright deceit. Once linked to a communications device and computer, the Verdicator monitors the subtle vocal tremors of your conversational partner and displays an assessment of that person's veracity on the screen. "The system can tell how nervous you are," Liberman explains. "It builds a psychological profile of what you feel and compares it to patterns associated with deception." And the Verdicator has one great advantage over the polygraph: the suspect doesn't need to know he's being tested. To be accurate, though, the Verdicator must pick up changes—which might indicate deceit—in a person's normal voice.

During the Monica Lewinsky scandal, Liberman demonstrated the system on President Clinton's famous disclaimer, "I did not have sexual relations with that woman." After analyzing an audio tape of the statement 100 times, the Verdicator showed that Clinton "was telling the truth," Liberman says, "but he had very high levels of cognitive stress, or 'guilt knowledge.' He didn't have sexual relations, but he did have something else."

Integritek will not name the law enforcement agencies, banks or financial institutions that are using the Verdicator. But company president Naaman Boury says that last year more than 500 Verdicators were sold in North and South America, Australia, Asia and Europe. The Japanese firm Atlus is marketing a consumer version of the Verdicator in Asia. "We get the best results—close to 95% accuracy—in Japan," Liberman reports. "The Japanese feel very uncomfortable when lying. We get the poorest results—nearer 85% accuracy—in Russia, where people seldom seem to say what they really feel."

In moderation, lying is a normal—even necessary—part of life. "It would be an impossible world if no one lied," Ekman says. But by the same token, it would be an intolerable world if we could never tell when someone was lying. For those lies that are morally wrong and potentially harmful, would-be lie detectors can learn a lot from looking and listening very carefully. Cheating partners, snake oil salesmen and scheming politicians, beware! The truth is out there.

James Geary/London
With reporting by Eric Silver/Jerusalem

From *Time Europe*, March 13, 2000, pp. 44–49. © 2000 by Time Inc. Reprinted by permission.

Shyness: The New Solution

The results of a recent survey are shaking up our ideas about shyness and pointing to a surprising new approach for dealing with it.

BY BERNARDO CARDUCCI, PH.D.

At the core of our existence as human beings lies a powerful drive to be with other people. There is much evidence that in the absence of human contact people fall apart physically and mentally; they experience more sickness, stress and suicide than well-connected individuals. For all too many people, however, shyness is the primary barrier to that basic need.

For more than two decades, I have been studying shyness. In 1995, in an article in PSYCHOLOGY TODAY, I, along with shyness pioneer Philip Zimbardo, Ph.D., summed up 20 years of shyness knowledge and research, concluding that rates are rising. At the same time, I ran a small survey that included five open-ended questions asking the shy to tell us about their experiences.

The thousands of responses we received have spawned a whole new generation of research and insight. In addition to the sheer volume of surveys, my colleague and I were surprised at the depth of the comments, often extending to five or 10 handwritten pages. It was as if we had turned on a spigot, allowing people to release a torrent of emotions. They understood that we were willing to listen. For that reason, perhaps, they were not at all shy about answering. This article represents the first analysis of their responses.

The New View

"My ex-wife picked me to marry her, so getting married wasn't a problem. I didn't want to get divorced, even though she was cheating on me, because I would be back out there trying to socialize. [But] I have a computer job now, and one of my strengths is that I work well alone."

Traditionally, shyness is viewed as an intrapersonal problem, arising within certain individuals as a result of characteristics such as excessive self-consciousness, low self-esteem and anticipation of rejection. The survey responses have shown, however, that shyness is also promoted by outside forces at work in our culture, and perhaps around the globe.

In addition, our research has led us to conclude that there is nothing at all wrong with being shy. Certainly shyness can control people and make them ineffective in classroom, social and business situations. Respondents told us that they feel imprisoned by their shyness. It is this feeling that seems to be at the core of their pain. But ironically, we find that the way to break out of the prison of shyness may be to embrace it thoroughly. There are many steps the shy can take to develop satisfying relationships without violating their basic nature.

The Cynically Shy

"My shyness has caused major problems in my personal/social life. I have a strong hate for most people. I also have quite a superiority complex. I see so much stupidity and ignorance in the world that I feel superior to virtually everyone out there. I'm trying [not to], but it's hard."

Of the many voices of shy individuals we "heard" in response to our survey, one in particular emerged very clearly. Among the new patterns our analysis identified was a group I call the cynically shy. These are people who have been rejected by their peers because of their lack of social skills. They do not feel connected to others—and they are angry about it. They feel a sense of alienation. And like the so-called trench coat mafia in

The Eight Habits of Highly Popular People

By Hara Estroff Marano

If you were ever the last person picked for a team or asked to dance at a party, you've probably despaired that popular people are born with complete self-confidence and impeccable social skills. But over the past 20 years, a large body of research in the social sciences has established that what was once thought the province of manna or magic is now solidly our own doing—or undoing. Great relationships, whether friendships or romances, don't fall out of the heavens on a favored few. They depend on a number of very sophisticated but human-scale social skills. These skills are crucial to developing social confidence and acceptance. And it is now clear that everyone can learn them.

And they should. Recent studies illustrate that having social contact and friends, even animal ones, improves physical health. Social ties seem to impact stress hormones directly, which in turn affect almost every part of our body, including the immune system. They also improve mental health. Having large social networks can help lower stress in times of crisis, alleviate depression and provide emotional support.

Luckily, it's never too late to develop the tools of the socially confident. Research from social scientists around the world, including relationship expert John Gottman, Ph.D., and shyness authority Bernardo Carducci, Ph.D., show that the most popular people follow these steps to social success:

1. Schedule Your Social Life

It is impossible to hone your social skills without investing time in them. Practice makes perfect, even for the socially secure. Accordingly, the well-liked surround themselves with others, getting a rich supply of opportunities to observe interactions and to improve upon their own social behaviors.

You need to do the same. Stop turning down party invitations and start inviting people to visit you at home. Plan outings with close friends or acquaintances you'd like to know better.

2. Think Positive

Insecure people tend to approach others anxiously, feeling they have to prove that they're witty or interesting. But self-assured people expect that others will respond positively—despite the fact that one of the most difficult social tasks is to join an activity that is already in progress.

3. Engage in Social Reconnaissance

Like detectives, the socially competent are highly skilled at information gathering, always scanning the scene for important details to guide their actions. They direct their focus outward, observing others and listening actively.

Socially skilled people are tuned in to people's expression of specific emotions, sensitive to signals that convey such information as what people's interests are, whether they want to be left alone or whether there is room in an activity for another person.

To infer correctly what others must be feeling, the socially confident are also able to identify and label their own experience accurately. That is where many people, particularly men, fall short.

Good conversationalists make comments that are connected to what is said to them and to the social situation. The connectedness of their communication is, in fact, one of its most outstanding features. Aggressive people actually make more attempts to join others in conversation but are less successful at it than the socially adept because they call attention to themselves, rather than finding a way to fit into ongoing group activity. They might throw out a statement that disrupts the conversation, or

respond contentiously to a question. They might blurt something about the way they feel, or shift the conversation to something of interest exclusively to themselves.

"You don't have to be interesting. You have to be interested," explains John Gottman, Ph.D., professor of psychology at the University of Washington. "That's how you have conversations."

4. Enter Conversations Gracefully

Timing is everything. After listening and observing on the perimeter of a group they want to join, the socially competent look for an opportunity to step in, knowing it doesn't just happen. It usually appears as a lull in the conversation.

Tuned in to the conversational or activity theme, the deft participant asks a question or elaborates on what someone else has already said. This is not the time to shift the direction of the conversation, unless it comes to a dead halt. Then it might be wise to throw out a question, perhaps something related to events of the day, and, if possible, something tangentially related to the recent discussion. The idea is to use an open-ended question that lets others participate. "Speaking of the election, what does everybody think about so-and-so's decision not to run?"

"People admire the person who is willing to take a risk and throw out a topic for conversation, but you have to make sure it has general appeal," says Bernardo Carducci, Ph.D., director of the Shyness Research Institute at Indiana University Southeast. Then you are in the desirable position of having rescued the group, which confers immediate membership and acceptance. Once the conversation gets moving, it's wise to back off talking and give others a chance. Social bores attempt to dominate a discussion. The socially confident know that the goal is to help the group have a better conversation. *(continued)*

Littleton, Colorado, they adapt a stance of superiority as they drift away from others.

Their isolation discourages them from having a sense of empathy, and this leads them to dehumanize others and take revenge against them. This process is the same one used by the military to train young boys to kill. The difference is, the military is now in your house, on your TV, in your video games.

Inside the Shy Mind

"As we talked, I felt uneasy. I worried about how I looked, what I said, how I said what I said, and so forth. Her compliments made me uncomfortable."

One of the solutions to shyness is a greater understanding of its internal dynamics. It is important to note that a critical feature of shyness is a slowness to warm up. Shy people simply

5. Learn to Handle Failure

It is a fact of life that everyone will sometimes be rejected. Rebuffs happen even to popular people. What distinguishes the socially confident from mere mortals is their reaction to rejection. They don't attribute it to internal causes, such as their own unlikability or inability to make friends. They assume it can result from many factors—incompatibility, someone else's bad mood, a misunderstanding. And some conversations are just private.

Self-assured people become resilient, using the feedback they get to shape another go at acceptance. Studies show that when faced with failure, those who are well-liked turn a negative response into a counterproposal. They say things like, "Well, can we make a date for next week instead?" Or they move onto another group in the expectation that not every conversation is closed. And should they reject others' bids to join with them, they do it in a polite and positive way. They invariably offer a reason or counter with an alternative idea: "I would love to talk with you later."

6. Take Hold of Your Emotions

Social situations are incredibly complex and dynamic. One has to pay attention to all kinds of verbal and nonverbal cues, such as facial expression and voice tone, interpret their meaning accurately, decide on the best response for the scenario, and then carry out that response—all in a matter of microseconds. No one can pay attention to or correctly interpret what is going on, let alone act skillfully, without a reasonable degree of control over their own emotional states, especially negative emotions such as anger, fear, anxiety—the emotions that usually arise in situations of conflict or uncertainty.

Recently, studies have found that people who are the most well-liked also have a firm handle on their emotions. It isn't that they internalize all their negative feelings. Instead, they shift attention away from distressing stimuli toward positive aspects of a situation. In other words, they have excellent coping skills. Otherwise, they become overly reactive to the negative emotions of others and may resort to aggression or withdraw from social contact.

7. Defuse Disagreements

Since conflict is inevitable, coping with confrontations is one of the most critical of social skills. It's not the degree of conflict that sinks relationships, but the ways people resolve it. Disagreements, if handled well, can help people know themselves better, improve language skills, gain valuable information and cement their relationships.

Instead of fighting fire with fire, socially confident people stop conflict from escalating; they apologize, propose a joint activity, make a peace offering of some kind, or negotiate. And sometimes they just change the subject. That doesn't mean that they yield to another's demands. Extreme submissiveness violates the equality basic to healthy relationships—and a sense of self-worth.

As people gain social competence, they try to accommodate the needs of both parties. Managing conflict without aggression requires listening, communicating—arguing, persuading— taking the perspective of others, controlling negative emotions, and problem-solving. Researchers have found that when people explain their point of view in an argument, they are in essence making a conciliatory move. That almost invariably opens the door for a partner to offer a suggestion that ends the standoff.

8. Laugh A Little

Humor is the single most prized social skill, the fast track to being liked—at all ages. Humor works even in threatening situations because it defuses negativity. There's no recipe for creating a sense of humor. But even in your darkest moments, try to see the lighter side of a situation.

If you need more help, call the American Psychological Association at 1-800-964-2000 for a referral to a therapist near you. For further resources check http://www.shyness .com/.

---

require extra time to adjust to novel or stressful situations, including even everyday conversations and social gatherings.

They also need more time to master the developmental hurdles of life. The good news is that shy people eventually achieve everything that everyone else does—they date, marry, have children. The bad news is, it takes them a little longer.

An unfortunate consequence of the shy being on this delayed schedule is that they lack social support through many important life experiences. When they start dating and want to talk about first-date jitters, for example, their peers will be talking about weddings. As a result, the shy may need to take an especially active role in finding others who are in their situation. One way is to build social support by starting groups of like-minded people. Another is to seek out existing groups of shy people, perhaps via the Internet. While technology often works against the shy, it can also lend them an unexpected helping hand.

Our research reveals the fact that the shy tend to make unrealistic social comparisons. In a room full of others, their attention is usually drawn to the most socially outstanding person, the life of the party—against whom they compare themselves, unfavorably, of course. This is just a preemptive strike. Typically, they compound the negative self-appraisal by attributing their own comparatively poor performance to enduring and unchangeable internal characteristics—"I was born shy" or "I don't have the gift of gab." Such attributions only heighten self-consciousness and inhibit performance.

The shy are prone to such errors of attribution because they believe that they are always being evaluated by others. Self-consciously focused on their own shortcomings, they fail to look around and notice that most people are just like them—listeners, not social standouts. Our surveys show that 48% of people are shy. So not only are the shy not alone, they probably have plenty of company at any social function.

The No. 1 problem area for the shy is starting a relationship. Fifty-eight percent told us they have problems with introductions; they go to a party but nothing happens. Forty percent said their problem was social; they had trouble developing friendships. Only seven percent of the shy have a problem with intimacy. If you get into an intimate relationship, shyness no longer seems to be a problem. Unfortunately, it's hard to get there.

The New Cultural Climate

It is no secret that certain technological advances—the Internet, e-mail, cell phones—are changing the conditions of the culture we live in, speeding it up and intensifying its complexity. This phenomenon, dubbed hyperculture, has trickled down to alter the nature of day-to-day interactions, with negative consequences for the shy. In this cultural climate, we lose patience quickly because we've grown accustomed to things happening faster and faster. We lose tolerance for those who need time to warm up. Those who are not quick and intense get passed by. The shy are bellwethers of this change: They are the first to feel its effects. And so it's not surprising that hyperculture is actually exacerbating shyness, in both incidence and degree.

Another effect of hyperculture is what I call identity intensity. Our society is not only getting faster, it is getting louder and brighter. It takes an increasingly powerful personality to be recognized. We see this in the emergence of shock jocks like Howard Stern and outrageous characters like Dennis Rodman. People have to call attention to themselves in ways that are more and more extreme just to be noticed at all. That, of course, puts the shy at a further disadvantage.

We are also undergoing "interpersonal disenfranchisement." Simply put, we are disconnecting from one another. Increasingly, we deal with the hyperculture cacophony by cocooning—commuting home with headphones on while working on our laptops. We go from our cubicle to the car to our gated community, maintaining contact with only a small circle of friends and family. As other people become just e-mail addresses or faceless voices at the other end of electronic transactions, it becomes easier and easier to mistreat and disrespect them. The cost of such disconnection is a day-to-day loss of civility and an increase in rudeness. And, again, the shy pay. They are the first to be excluded, bullied or treated in a hostile manner.

As we approach the limits of our ability to deal with the complexities of our lives, we begin to experience a state of anxiety. We either approach or avoid. And, indeed, we are seeing both phenomena—a polarization of behavior in which we see increases in both aggression, marked by a general loss of manners that has been widely observed, and in withdrawal, one form of which is shyness. Surveys we have conducted reliably show that over the last decade and a half, the incidence of shyness has risen from 40% to 48%.

So it is no accident that the pharmaceutical industry has chosen this cultural moment to introduce the antidepressant Paxil as a treatment for social phobia. Paxil is touted as a cure for being "allergic to people." One of the effects of hyperculture is to make people impatient for anything but a pill that instantly reduces their anxiety level.

The use of Paxil, however, operates against self-awareness. It makes shyness into a medical or psychiatric problem, which it has never been. It essentially labels as pathology what is a personality trait. I think it is a mistake for doctors to hand out a physiological remedy when we know that there are cognitive elements operating within individuals, communication difficulties existing between individuals, and major forces residing outside of individuals that are making it difficult for people to interact.

It is much easier for the shy to take a pill, doctors figure, than for them to take the time to adjust to their cautious tendencies, modify faulty social comparisons or learn to be more civil to others. The promise of Paxil does not include teaching the shy to develop the small talk skills they so desperately need.

Strategies of the Shy

"I have tried to overcome my shyness by being around people as much as possible and getting involved in the conversation; however, after a few seconds, I become quiet. I have a problem keeping conversation flowing."

In our survey, we asked people what they do to cope with their shyness. What we found surprised us. The shy put a lot of effort into overcoming their shyness, but the strategies they use are largely ineffective, sometimes even counterproductive. Occasionally their solutions are potentially dangerous.

> *Once the shy learn to focus more on the lives of other people, shyness no longer controls them.*

Ninety-one percent of shy respondents said they had made at least some effort to overcome their shyness. By far, the top technique they employ is forced extroversion. Sixty-seven percent of them said they make themselves go to parties, bars, dances, the mall—places that will put them in proximity to others. That is good. But unfortunately, they expect the others to do all the work, to approach them and draw them out of their isolation. Simply showing up is not enough. Not only is it ineffective, it cedes control of interactions to others.

But it exemplifies the mistaken expectations the shy often have about social life. Hand in hand with the expectation that others will approach them is their sense of perfectionism. The shy believe that anything they say has to come out perfect, sterling, supremely witty, as if everyday life is some kind of sitcom. They believe that everybody is watching and judging them—a special kind of narcissism.

Their second most popular strategy is self-induced cognitive modification: thinking happy thoughts, or the "Stuart Smalley Effect"—remember the sketch from *Saturday Night Live*? "I'm good enough, I'm smart enough, and, doggone it, people like me." Twenty-two percent of the shy try to talk themselves into not being shy. But just talking to yourself doesn't work. You have to know how to talk to other people. And you have to be around other people. The shy seldom combine extroversion with cognitive modification.

Fifteen percent of the shy turn to self-help books and seminars, which is great. But not enough people do it.

> *Shy people tend either to reveal information about themselves too quickly, or hold back and move too slowly.*

And about 12% of the shy turn to what I call liquid extroversion. They are a distinct population of people, who, often beginning in adolescence, ingest drugs or alcohol to deal with their shyness. They self-medicate as a social lubricant, to give them courage. And while it may remove inhibitions, it doesn't provide them with what they desperately need—actual social skills, knowledge about how to be with others. Further, drinking interferes with their cognitive functioning.

Liquid extroversion poses the great danger of overconsumption of alcohol. Indeed, we have found in separate studies that a significant proportion of problem drinkers in the general population are shy.

SHYNESS SURVEY

- 64% of shy individuals view their shyness as a result of external factors beyond their control, such as early family experiences, overprotective parents or peer victimization.

- 24% attribute shyness to internal factors within their control, such as intrapersonal difficulties, like low self-esteem and high self consciousness, or interpersonal difficulties, like poor social skills and dating difficulties.

- 62% experience feelings of shyness daily.

- 82% report shyness as an undesirable experience.

- **Types of individuals who make the shy feel shy:**

75% strangers
71% persons of the opposite sex, in a group
65% persons of the opposite sex, one-on-one
56% persons of the same sex, in a group
45% relatives, other than immediate family
38% persons of the same sex, one-on-one
22% their parents
20% siblings

- 46% believe their shyness can be overcome.

- 7.2% do not believe their shyness can be overcome.

- 85% are willing to work seriously at overcoming shyness.

But "shy alcoholics" tell us they do not like having to drink to perform better; they feel uneasy and lack confidence in their true selves. They begin to believe that people will like them only if they are outgoing, not the way they really are. Interest-ingly, the largest program for problem drinkers, Alcoholics Anonymous, works squarely against shy people. Whereas the shy are slow to warm up, AA asks people to stand up right away, to be highly visible, to immediately disclose highly personal information. It is my belief that there needs to be an AA for the shy, a program that takes into consideration the nature and dynamics of shyness. A meeting might, for example, begin by having a leader speak for the first 45 minutes while people get comfortable, followed by a break in which the leader is available to answer questions. That then paves the way for a general question-and-answer period.

Cyberbonding

"I can be anyone I want to be on the Internet and yet mostly be myself, because I know I will never meet these people I'm talking with and can close out if I get uncomfortable."

"I think the Internet hinders people in overcoming their shyness. You can talk to someone but you don't have to actually interact with them. You can sit in your room and not REALLY socialize."

Another strategy of the shy is electronic extroversion. The Net is a great social facilitator. It enables people to reach out to many others and join in at their own speed, perhaps observing in a chat room before participating. Still, Internet interaction requires less effort than face-to-face interaction, so it may increase their frustration and cause difficulties in real-life situations where social skills are not only required, but born and learned.

We know that people start out using the Internet for informational purposes, then progress to use that is social in nature, such as entering chat rooms; some then progress to personal use, talking about more intimate topics and disclosing information about themselves. The danger of electronic extroversion is that anonymity makes it easy for the shy to misrepresent themselves and to deceive others, violating the trust that is the foundation of social life.

And talk about disconnecting. The irony of a World Wide Web packed with endless amounts of information is that it can also be isolating. As individuals head to their own favorite bookmarked sites, they cut out all the disagreement of the world and reinforce their own narrow perspective, potentially leading to alienation, disenfranchisement and intolerance for people who are different.

In addition, the shy are more vulnerable to instant intimacy because of their lack of social know-how. Normally, relationships progress by way of a reasonably paced flow of self-disclosure that is reciprocal in nature. A disclosure process that moves too quickly—and computer anonymity removes the stigma of getting sexually explicit—doesn't just destroy courtship; it is a reliable sign of maladjustment. Shy people tend either to reveal information about themselves too quickly, or hold back and move too slowly.

Like most cultural influences, the Internet is neither devil nor angel. It's a social tool that works in different ways, depending on how it's used.

The Solution to Shyness

"I was very shy as a kid. Every situation scared me if it required interacting with others. After high school and into college, I became much less shy. I consciously made each interaction an exercise in overcoming shyness. Just talking to people I didn't know, getting a part-time job, volunteering. I had always been afraid to sing in front of people, but now I sing all the time. That's a big deal to me."

Every shy person believes that shyness is a problem located exclusively within the self. But our work suggests that the solution to shyness lies outside the self. To break free of the prison of shyness, you must stop dwelling on your own insecurities and become more aware of the people around you.

Through our survey, we have identified a group of people we call the successfully shy. Essentially, they recognize that they are shy. They develop an understanding of the nature and dynamics of shyness, its impact on the body, on cognitive processes and on behavior. And they take action based on that self-awareness. The successfully shy overcome their social anxiety by letting go of their self-consciousness, that inward focus of attention on the things they can't do well (like tell a joke). They accept that they aren't great at small talk or that they get so nervous in social situations that they can't draw on what is inside their mind. Or that they are paying so much attention to their feelings that they don't pay full attention to the person they're talking to. In place of self-consciousness, they substitute self-awareness. Rather than becoming anxious about their silence in a conversation, they plan ahead of time to have something to say, or rehearse asking questions. They arrive early at parties to feel comfortable in their new setting. By contrast, less successful shy people arrive late in an effort to blend in.

The fact is, these are the same kinds of strategies that non-shy people employ. Many of them develop a repertoire of opening gambits for conversation. When among others, they engage in social reconnaissance—they wait to gather information about speakers and a discussion before jumping in.

The successfully shy also take steps at the transpersonal level, getting involved in the lives of others. They start small, making sure their day-to-day exchanges involve contact with other people. When they pick up a newspaper, for instance, they don't just put their money on the counter. They focus on the seller, thanking him or her for the service. This creates a social environment favorable to positive interactions. On a larger scale, I encourage volunteering. Once the shy are more outwardly focused on the lives of other people, shyness no longer controls them.

The successfully shy don't change who they are. They change the way they think and the actions they make. There is nothing wrong with being shy. In fact, I have come to believe that what our society needs is not less shyness but a little more.

READ MORE ABOUT IT

Shyness: A Bold New Approach, Bernardo J. Carducci, Ph.D. (HarperCollins, 1999)

The Shy Child, Philip G. Zimbardo, Ph.D., Shirley L. Radl (ISHK Book Service, 1999)

Bernardo Carducci, Ph.D., is the director of the Shyness Research Institute at Indiana University Southeast. His last article for PSYCHOLOGY TODAY, *also on shyness, appeared in the December 1995 issue.*

Reprinted from *Psychology Today*, January/February 2000, pp. 38–45, 78. © 2000 by Bernardo Carducci.

Revealing Personal Secrets

Abstract
Both the health benefits and the potential drawbacks of revealing personal secrets (i.e., those that directly involve the secret keeper) are reviewed. Making the decision to reveal personal secrets to others involves a trade-off. On the one hand, secret keepers can feel better by revealing their secrets and gaining new insights into them. On the other hand, secret keepers can avoid looking bad before important audiences (such as their bosses or therapists) by not revealing their secrets. Making a wise decision to reveal a personal secret hinges on finding an appropriate confidant—someone who is discreet, who is perceived by the secret keeper to be nonjudgmental, and who is able to offer new insights into the secret.

Keywords
revealing secrets; new insights; confidants

Anita E. Kelly[1]
Department of Psychology, University of Notre Dame, Notre Dame, Indiana

Psychologists and lay persons have long believed that keeping personal secrets is stressful and that unburdening oneself of such secrets offers emotional relief and physiological benefits. Supporting this notion is recent experimental research that has demonstrated the health benefits of revealing personal secrets (i.e., ones that directly involve the secret keeper). These findings lead to several key questions: Why do these health benefits occur? When does revealing personal secrets to various confidants backfire? And, finally, when should someone reveal his or her personal secrets?

SECRECY

Secrecy involves actively hiding private information from others. The most painful or traumatic personal experiences are often concealed, and most secrets are likely to involve negative or stigmatizing information that pertains to the secret keepers themselves. For example, people may keep secret the fact that they have AIDS, are alcoholic, or have been raped. Secrecy has also been called self-concealment and active inhibition of disclosure.

HEALTH BENEFITS OF REVEALING SECRETS

The belief that secrecy is problematic is supported by studies showing that, on average, people who tend to conceal personal information have more physical problems, such as headaches, nausea, and back pains, and are more anxious, shy, and depressed than people who do not tend to conceal personal information. Recent research has also shown that gay men who tend to conceal their sexual orientation from others are at a greater risk for cancers and infectious diseases than those who do not conceal their orientation.

Moreover, research has shown that talking or writing about private traumatic experiences is associated with health benefits, such as improved immunological functioning and fewer visits to the doctor. For example, a survey of spouses of suicide and accidental-death victims demonstrated that participants who had talked about the loss of their spouses with family and friends suffered fewer health problems the year after the loss than participants who did not speak with others about their loss (Pennebaker & O'Heeron, 1984). These correlations remained even in an analysis that statistically adjusted for the number of friends these individuals had before and after the loss of the spouse.

Particularly compelling evidence concerning the benefits of revealing secrets has emerged from a series of in-the-field and laboratory experiments. One experiment showed that advanced-breast-cancer patients who were randomly assigned to a group that was designed to encourage them to talk about their emotions survived twice as long as patients assigned to a routine oncological-care group (Spiegel, Bloom, Kraemer, & Gottheil, 1989). In another experiment, medical students were randomly assigned to write about either private traumatic events or control topics for four consecutive days and then were vaccinated against hepatitis B (Petrie, Booth, Pennebaker, Davison, & Thomas, 1995). The group that wrote about traumatic events had significantly higher antibody levels against hepatitis B at the 4- and 6-month follow-ups than did the control group, suggesting that emotional expression of traumatic experiences can lead to improved immune functioning.

WHAT IS IT ABOUT REVEALING SECRETS THAT IS BENEFICIAL?

It is believed that revealing secrets offers these health benefits because the revealer gains new insights into the trauma and no longer has to expend cognitive and emotional resources actively hiding the trauma (Pennebaker, 1997). It has also been suggested that gaining catharsis (i.e., expressing pent-up emotions behaviorally) may play an important role in reducing one's level of emotional arousal surrounding a troubling event (Polivy, 1998), even though some studies have raise the questions of whether catharsis actually purges or provokes emotions (Polivy, 1998).

Because of the controversy surrounding the benefits of catharsis, my colleagues and I recently conducted an experiment that directly compared the effect of gaining catharsis with the effects of gaining new insights into one's troubling secrets (Kelly, Klusas, von Weiss, & Kenny, 1999, Study 2). Undergraduates ($N = 85$) were randomly assigned to one of three groups, which differed as to whether they were asked (a) to try to gain new insights through writing about their secrets, (b) to try to gain catharsis by writing about their secrets, or (c) to write about their previous day. The results revealed that the new-insights group felt significantly better about their secrets after their writing than did the other groups, and thus the findings support the idea that the key to recovery from troubling secrets is gaining new insights. Correlational analyses of the content of the writing showed that participants' coming to terms with their secrets mediated the relation between their gaining new insights and feeling better about their secrets. In other words, it was only through coming to terms with their secrets that participants seemed to benefit from gaining new insights into them. These findings are consistent with the results from a series of writing-about-trauma studies which showed that when participants increased their use of words associated with insightful and causal thinking, they tended to experience improved physical health (Pennebaker, Mayne, & Francis, 1997, Study 1).

The reason why gaining new insights is likely to be curative is that people may be able to find closure on the secrets and avoid what has been termed the Zeigarnik effect, wherein people actively seek to attain a goal when they have failed to attain the goal or failed to disengage from it. Zeigarnik (1927) showed that people continue to think about and remember interrupted tasks more than finished ones, suggesting that they may have a need for completion or resolution of events. Revealing a secret with the explicit intention of gaining a new perspective on it may help people feel a sense of resolution about the secret.

SELF-PRESENTATION AND THE ROLE OF THE CONFIDANT

The findings from the experiments described so far clearly suggest that it is healthy to reveal one's secrets. However, almost all of the experiments conducted to date have involved revealing secrets in an anonymous setting, and the health benefits observed in those experiments may not generalize to circumstances in which people reveal unfavorable or stigmatizing information about themselves to important audiences (e.g., their coworkers or friends) in their everyday interactions. In such circumstances, the revealers may perceive that they are being rejected by and alienated from the listeners.

Supporting this concern are the results from a 9-year longitudinal study of initially healthy, HIV-positive gay men who were sensitive to social rejection. Those who tended to conceal their sexual orientation from others experienced a slower progression of HIV-related symptoms than did those who tended to reveal their sexual orientation to others (Cole, Kemeny, & Taylor, 1997). These results qualify these same researchers' finding, referred to earlier, that gay men who tended to conceal their sexual orientation were at a greater risk for cancers and infectious diseases.

The essence of the problem with revealing personal, undesirable information is that revealers may come to see themselves in undesirable ways if others know their stigmatizing secrets. A number of experiments from the self-presentation literature have demonstrated that describing oneself as having undesirable qualities, such as being depressed or introverted, to various audiences leads to negative shifts in one's self-beliefs and behaviors (e.g., Schlenker, Dlugolecki, & Doherty, 1994; Tice, 1992). Moreover, a recent in-the-field study showed that among a sample of therapy outpatients who had received an average of 11 therapy sessions, the clients (40.5%) who reported that they were keeping a relevant secret from their counselors actually had a greater reduction in their symptomatology than did those who were not keeping a relevant secret (Kelly, 1998). These results were obtained after adjusting for clients' social-desirability scores (i.e., scores indicating their tendency to try to "look good" to other people) and their tendency to keep secrets in general. It is possible that clients hid negative aspects of themselves in an effort to provide desirable views of themselves for their therapists.

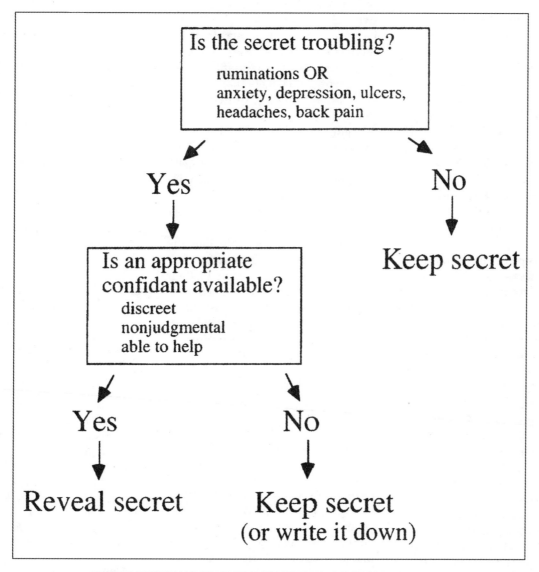

FIGURE 1. DECISION-MAKING MODEL FOR REVEALING SECRETS (FROM KELLY & MCKILLOP, 1996).

Another problem associated with revealing one's secrets is that confidants often cannot be trusted to keep the secrets or to protect one's identity. For example, in a study of college students' self-reports, the students indicated that when someone disclosed an emotional event to them, they in turn revealed the emotional disclosure to other people in 66% to 78% of the cases—despite the fact that these students were intimates of the original revealers in 85% of the cases (Christophe & Rime, 1997). Moreover, original disclo-sures that were of a high emotional intensity were more likely to be shared with others and were told to more people (specifically, to more than two people, on average) than disclosures that were low or moderate in emotional intensity. In addition, another study showed that in 78% of the cases in which the original event was disclosed to others, the name of the original revealer was explicitly mentioned. Christophe and Rime recommended that if people do not want others to learn about their emotional experiences, then they should avoid sharing the experiences with others altogether. It is important to note, however, that these researchers did not specifically ask the confidants if they had been sworn to secrecy.

In sum, two sets of findings qualify the conclusion that revealing secrets leads to health benefits. First, the findings from the self-presentation literature suggest that revealing undesirable personal information to important audiences can have negative implications for one's self-image. Second, studies have shown that confidants often cannot be trusted to keep a secret or to protect the revealer's identity; therefore, revealing secrets may damage one's reputation.

WHEN TO REVEAL SECRETS

The findings just discussed, taken together, call attention to the trade-offs involved in revealing personal secrets. Revealing secrets can help a person feel better if he or she gains new insights into them, and yet not revealing secrets may help a person look good before important audiences (such as one's boss and therapist). A way to avoid the negative side of revealing personal secrets is to carefully select a confidant. There is empirical support for the idea that if a troubled secret keeper has a confidant who can be trusted not to reveal a secret, is perceived by the secret keeper to be nonjudgmental, and is able to offer the secret helper new insights into the secret, then the secret keeper should reveal the secret to that person (see the model in Fig. 1; Kelly & McKillop, 1996). At the same time, however, because there are risks to one's identity associated with revealing secrets to others, people should reveal their personal secrets only if keeping the secrets seems to be troubling. Specifically, if a secret keeper is experiencing the symptoms that have been found to be associated with self-concealment, such as depression, ulcers, and headaches, then he or she should consider the possibility that the symptoms are the result of the secret keeping and should reveal the secret to an appropriate confidant. The rationale for taking such a risk is that even if the secret is not actually causing the symptoms, the secret helper is still unlikely to be harmed as a result of having revealed personal information to a discreet, nonjudgmental, and insightful confidant.

A limitation to the model for when to reveal secrets is the finding (Kelly, 1998), discussed earlier, that even with trained therapists who presumably fit all of the positive qualities of confidants, clients who were keeping a relevant secret experienced greater symptom reduction than those who were not keeping one. The seeming contradiction between this finding and the model can be resolved by the fact that the model emphasizes the revealer's perception of the confidant as non-judgmental. It is likely that, at times, clients may imagine, or even accurately perceive, that their therapists are judgmental, particularly when the clients have committed unusually heinous acts, such as savagely beating their children. In such instances, the clients' decision to avoid revealing some of the details of their secrets to their therapists may not be problematic. It is possible that the clients may instead benefit from either discussing the themes of their secrets (e.g., experiencing uncontrollable anger) with the therapists or, as the model suggests, privately writing about the secrets in an effort to gain new insights into them.

CONCLUSION

Even though there is some exciting experimental evidence that revealing one's secrets leads to health benefits, these findings must be viewed with caution because the experiments have involved anonymous revealing of secrets and the findings may not generalize to everyday interactions with confidants. Researchers have not paid sufficient attention to the role of the confidant, and there is some preliminary evidence pointing to the possibility that revealing secrets, even to one's therapist, might backfire. Future research will need to examine the trade-offs between revealing and not revealing secrets to confidants who offer varying degrees of support. There is also a need for research assessing how a person's perceptions of such support can affect his or her self-images.

Recommended Reading

Derlega, V. J., Metts, S., Petronio, S., & Margulis, S. T. (1993). *Self-disclosure*. Newbury Park, CA: Sage.

Kelly, A. E., & McKillop, K. J. (1996). (See References)

Lane, J. D., & Wegner, D. M. (1995). The cognitive consequences of secrecy. *Journal of Personality and Social Psychology, 69*, 237–253.

Pennebaker, J. W. (1995). *Emotion, disclosure, and health*. Washington, DC: American Psychological Association.

Pennebaker, J. W. (1997). (See References)

Acknowledgments—I thank Thomas V. Merluzzi for his thoughtful feedback on a draft of this article.

Notes

1. Address correspondence to Anita E. Kelly, Department of Psychology, University of Notre Dame, Notre Dame, IN 46556; e-mail: kelly.79@nd.edu.

References

Christophe, V., & Rime, B. (1997). Exposure to the social sharing of emotion: Emotional impact, listener responses and secondary social sharing. *European Journal of Social Psychology, 27*, 37–54.

Cole, S. W., Kemeny, M. E., & Taylor, S. E. (1997). Social identity and physical health: Accelerated HIV progression in rejection-sensitive gay men. *Journal of Personality and Social Psychology, 72*, 320–335.

Kelly, A. E. (1998). Clients' secret keeping in outpatient therapy. *Journal of Counseling Psychology, 45*, 50–57.

Kelly, A. E., Klusas, J., von Weiss, R., & Kenny, C. (1999). *What is it about revealing secrets that leads to health benefits?* Unpublished manuscript, University of Notre Dame, Notre Dame, IN.

Kelly, A. E., & McKillop, K. J. (1996). Consequences of revealing personal secrets. *Psychological Bulletin, 120*, 450–465.

Pennebaker, J. W. (1997). *Opening up: The healing power of expressing emotions*. New York: Guilford Press.

Pennebaker, J. W., Mayne, T. J., & Francis, M. E. (1997). Linguistic predictors of adaptive bereavement. *Journal of Personality and Social Psychology, 72*, 863–871.

Pennebaker, J. W., & O'Heeron, R. C. (1984). Confiding in others and illness rate among spouses of suicide and accidental-death victims. *Journal of Abnormal Psychology, 93*, 473–476.

Petrie, K. J., Booth, R. J., Pennebaker, J. W., Davison, K. P., & Thomas, M. G. (1995). Disclosure of trauma and immune response to a hepatitis B vaccination program. *Journal of Consulting and Clinical Psychology, 63,* 787–792.

Policy, J. (1998). The effects of behavioral inhibition: Integrating internal cues, cognition, behavior, and affect. *Psychological Inquiry, 9,* 181–204.

Schlenker, B. R., Dlugolecki, D. W., & Doherty, K. (1994). The impact of self-presentations on self-appraisals and behavior: The power of public commitment. *Personality and Social Psychology Bulletin, 20,* 20–33.

Spiegel, D., Bloom, J. H., Kraemer, H. C., & Gottheil, E. (1989). Effects of psychosocial treatment of patients with metastatic breast cancer. *Lancet, 2,* 888–891.

Tice, D. M. (1992). Self-concept change and self-presentation: The looking glass self is also a magnifying glass. *Journal of Personality and Social Psychology, 63,* 435–451.

Zeigarnik, B. (1927). Uber das behalten von erledigten und unerledigten handlungen. *Psychologische Forschung, 9,* 1–85.

From *Current Directions in Psychological Science*, August 1999, pp. 105–109. © 1999 by Anita E. Kelly and the American Psychological Society. Reprinted by permission of Blackwell Publishers.

Welcome to the Love Lab

Words can heal an ailing relationship—or seal its negative fate.

By John Gottman, Ph.D. and Sybil Carrere, Ph.D.

The way a couple argues can tell you a lot about the future of their relationship. In fact, just three minutes of fighting can indicate whether the pair will flourish with time or end in ruin.

The 10-year study that led to this discovery was one of many we've conducted over the years. John Gottman began his groundbreaking research on married couples 28 years ago. Since then, his University of Washington laboratory—dubbed the "Love Lab"—has focused on determining exactly what makes marriages thrive or fail. With the help of a remarkable team and hundreds of couples, we can now predict a relationship's outcome with 88% to 94% accuracy.

To do this, we watch couples during spats and analyze partners' communication patterns and physiology, as well as their oral descriptions of their relationship histories. We then follow the pairs over time to see whether their patterns and descriptions lead to happy outcomes or breakups. We have learned that some negative emotions used in arguments are more toxic than others: Criticism, contempt, defensiveness and stonewalling (withdrawing from a discussion, most frequently seen among men) are all particularly corrosive. On the other hand, we have repeatedly found that happy couples use five times more positive behaviors in their arguments than negative behaviors. One way they do this is by using humor to break the tension in an argument. This is a kind of a "repair" effort to mend conflict. We find that happy couples also use expressions of affection for their partner and acknowledge their partner's point of view ("I'm sorry I hurt your feelings") in order to keep quarrels from getting too heated.

We have learned much from our couples over the last 11 years that we try to bring to our own marriages. Two things: One is the importance of building and maintaining a friendship in your marriage so that you give your partner the benefit of the doubt when times are tough. This takes constant work. The second thing is that you have a choice every time you say something to your partner. You can say something that will either nurture the relationship or tear it down. You may win a particular fight with your spouse, but you could lose the marriage in the long run.

In this article, we show just how we diagnose the health of a marriage. Using three examples of dialogue from real couples discussing their problems, we will illustrate how reading between the lines of people's arguments can predict where some marriages have gone wrong—and why others have stayed strong. Welcome to the "Love Lab!"

Susan, 45, and Bob, 47, have been married for 23 years.

Bob: Um, communication. The question is…

Susan: How we disagree.

B: On communication?

S: You don't see a need for it.

B: Oh yeah.

S: You just said you kept to yourself.

B: Well, yeah, I just…. I dunno. Idle chitchat, I guess.

Defensiveness; Tension

S: You what?

B: Idle chitchat, I guess, if that is what you refer to as communication.

S: What do you mean, chitchat?

B: General run-of-the-mill bull.

S: There's nonverbal communication if you're tuned in.

B: (Nods head)

S: Like that man said in that canoeing class, as they went over the rapids, that they were still communicating.

B: That's true. What do you think we need to talk about more then? Huh?

S: Well, I think when there's a problem, or I'm trying to tell you something, sometimes I shouldn't have to say anything. You can know when I'm in a hurry or tired.

B: I just take communication as being, uh, should we sit down and discuss things more fully.

S: We don't sit down and discuss anything unless it's a problem, or if somebody gets mad. You know lots of families have what they call, which is kinda silly, but a weekly meeting or some time when they just sit down and talk about everything that has been going on there all week, what they like and don't like.

B: We used to have those at home.

S: That's a little far-fetched, maybe, but I'm just saying.

B: I know. I just…

S: It makes sense.

B: …you know what major problem we have at work is communication.

S: It's a problem everywhere.

B: Yeah. Yeah.

S: People don't say what they mean.

B: Or assume that people know what they mean or want.

S: Well, how many times have I asked you what's wrong, and you say nothing. And then a month later you say what was wrong and I couldn't have guessed it in a million years.

B: I don't know why that is. Why, you know, you can ask almost anybody at work what's bothering them.

S: But you never ask me what's wrong.

B: Maybe I know.

Expressing Hidden Life Dream: Wants Husband to take Active Interest

S: No, I don't think you do.

B: Maybe I just enjoy the quietness of it. I don't know.

S: Well, seriously, I think that as long as we've been married that you don't know very much about me at all.

B: No, I think it's true, about both of us maybe.

GOTTMAN SAYS: This couple rates quite low in marital satisfaction. They are also emotionally disengaged, with high depression in addition to marital distress. The marriage has generally low conflict, but also low positivity (shared romance, humor, affection)—the best marker of emotional disengagement. Our findings suggest that, in general, emotionally disengaged couples divorce later in life than those who have a "hotter," more explosive pattern of unhappiness, although this couple did not break up.

This couple is also in a state of gridlocked conflict. Susan and Bob keep coming close to resolving their issue, which is that Bob would rather keep to himself than communicate. But they don't—they keep recycling it over and over again. Emotional disengagement is often a later stage of continued gridlock. After a while, a "hot" couple begins polarizing their positions, digging in and becoming more stubborn, vilifying one another, then trying to isolate the problem. Unfortunately, most gridlocked conflict cannot be permanently enclaved, and negotiations to fix a problem reach a stalemate.

The reason gridlocked conflicts don't get resolved is because there is an underlying life dream within each person that isn't being fulfilled. Susan's dream is expressed when she says, "You never ask me what's wrong." Bob responds that "maybe I just enjoy the quietness"—that he prefers emotional distance to fighting—but she sadly replies that he doesn't know her at all. They are lacking in what we call "love maps," which spouses construct by being interested in each other and tracking each other's stresses, hopes, dreams, concerns, etc. Her latent wish for love maps keeps them from agreeing to the weekly meeting plan.

This couple is still married, but unhappily so.

Valerie, 24, and Mark, 25, have a young baby. They have recently moved, and both have new jobs.

Valerie: (Laughter) We don't go that long without talking.

Mark: I know, I just start going stir-crazy.

V: The problem…

M: Huh?

Despite Initial Humor, The Problem Surfaces

V: …is, you told me that when you took the job as manager at Commonwealth that you'd come home in the afternoons and spend some time with us.

M: That's right, but I did not say that it would start in the first week when I'm trying to do two different jobs. I gotta get myself replaced. Right now, I'm not just a manager.

V: It's been three weeks.

M: Well, I just don't go out on the street and say "Hey you. Want to sell insurance?" It's not that easy. There's two people in the program. One of them is probably gonna be hired within the next couple weeks. But in the meantime it's tough. It's just the way it's gotta be.

V: I realize that.

M: Okay.

V: But.

M: At midnight when you get off work and you're all keyed up, I'm all worn out. I haven't been stimulated for two hours.

V: I realize that. That doesn't bother me that much, you going to sleep at night.

M: I'll just be starting to go to sleep and you'll go "Are you listening to me?" I'll be trying to stay awake…

V: I'm laughing about it usually. I'm not upset about it.

M: I don't know by then. I'm half out.

V: But now with me having a car, you'll be able to go to sleep early and get up with Stephanie a little bit. That's one of my big problems. I'm not getting any sleep. I don't get to sleep until two.

M: I've been getting up with her.

V: You've been real good about that.

M: Okay.

V: I guess I just wish that you didn't have to go in early.

M: Yeah, we don't get a whole lot of time together.

V: When I have the car, I can get out and get stuff then. I feel like I'm stuck at home and here you are…

M: I'll be able to meet you for lunch and stuff. I guess that wasn't any big problem.

V: It is a problem. It seems like we talk about it every day.

M: Yeah, we do.

V: That's about the only thing we really complain about.

M: Yeah. The last couple nights I tried to take you out to the lake and look at the stars and stuff, so…

V: I know.

M: We just need to get used to our schedules.

V: That first week I was so, I was real upset cause it seemed like all I did was stay home with Stephanie all morning till three and just work all evening. I wasn't doing anything. It didn't seem like we had family gatherings every weekend. We never had time to go out, just the two of us.

M: I got a little surprise for ya next weekend.

Criticism; Conflict Renewed

V: Yeah, it's always next weekend. It's never this weekend.

M: Eight weekends in a row.

V: I just went from not working at all and being home. We've both been through major job changes and all.

M: And I can't breathe.

V: But we're getting used to it and I feel so much better about going to work at three

(o'clock), three-thirty now than I did that first week.

M: Um.

V: I just wish I had more time to do what I wanted to do. I, it's just being…

M: I'll, I'll be able to stay…

V: …a wife and mother.

M: …to stay at home during the days a little bit more or I'll have to go in early but then I can take a couple of hours off in the afternoons.

Retaliation with Anger

V: Do you have to go in early every day?

M: I'm going to go in early every day.

V: Why?

M: 'Cause there are things I need to do every morning.

V: I think you just like going in to your office.

M: You don't know a thing about it then. Randy was in there early every day, tell me why?

V: Yeah, but he was home at a decent hour too.

M: He stays out late.

V: Eight to eight or eight to nine every day.

M: Every day.

V: Now, then, I don't want you taking that job. You forget it.

M: No.

GOTTMAN SAYS: This couple also has low levels of marital satisfaction. Unlike the previous couple, they have the "hot," corrosive kind of marital conflict characterized by what I call the "Four Horsemen of the Apocalypse": criticism, contempt, defensiveness and stonewalling. This type of conflict tends to lead to early divorce.

However, also unlike the previous couple, there is still a lot of strength in their relationship. Their friendship is intact. There is humor and affection, and they are confident that they can resolve their conflict.

Though the couple begins their discussion very well, by laughing, Valerie soon expresses anger because Mark's new job is demanding so much of his time. She then repairs this with humor and more affection. This shows that there is still quite a bit of strength in this marriage. The respite is only temporary; Valerie raises the family issue again. But Mark agrees affectionately, showing another strength: He makes her problems "their" problems.

They are doing very well discussing the problem until Valerie's angry line about going in early every day. This leads to a pattern of her anger and his defensiveness in response. So there is still a lot of strength in their interaction, but something is keeping him from fully understanding how hard it is for her to have him gone so much. Something is deteriorating in this relationship and it's exemplified by her ultimatums and his resistance.

When we were doing this research, we didn't intervene to help couples, and this one, unfortunately, divorced after seven years of marriage. Now I think we can prevent this type of marital meltdown. The secrets are in keeping fathers involved with their babies so they make the same kind of philosophical transformation in meaning that their wives are probably making; in teaching couples what to expect during this transition to parenthood; and in helping them with the inevitable marital conflict, sleepless irritability and depression that often follow a new baby.

Wilma, 31, and Harris, 35, have been married 11 years.

Wilma: The communication problem. Tell me your feelings. (Both laughing)

Harris: A lot of times I don't know. I've always been quiet.

W: Is it just because you have nothing to talk about, or is it because you don't want to talk about it?

H: A lot of times I don't know.

W: Okay. Example: when we went to Lake Bariessa. I mean, I can understand that you couldn't find your way around and everything, that was fine. But it still doesn't hurt to open your lips, you know?

H: I was kind of burned out that day…

W: Well, you suggested we go…

H: I was trying to take you out somewhere, then I was trying to figure out my money in the bank and I end up coming short…

W: You did all that driving up there…

H: Yeah. And I was trying to figure out my bank account and how I was going to, you know, have the gas money for the week.

W: But, like, when we got there, you didn't want to talk. We got off the truck, we got set up and you ate your sandwich. Your little bologna sandwich. (Both laughing)

H: Yeah. I was starving. (Laughing)

W: I didn't know you were. And then it was like, you still didn't want to talk, so Dominique and me started playing tennis.

H: It was almost time to go then and I had to drive back. I didn't want to check it out.

W: Yeah. I thought it was such a nice drive.

H: I didn't know it was going to be that far.

W: And I really appreciate that.

H: Thank you very much.

Playful Acceptance of Differences

W: You're welcome. I don't mind you talking about bills all the time, but we can only pay what we can pay, so why worry?

H: 'Cause that's how I am.

W: You shouldn't do that.

H: Well, I can't help it. I'm always trying to be preventive.

W: Okay, "Preventive." (Laughter)

H: I can't help it. I have learned from my mistakes. Have you ever heard of people worried about bills?

W: I've heard of those people. I'm one of those people.

H: And I'm one of those people, whether you know it or not.

W: The thing is, I just pay what I can. You can't give everybody money at the same time when you don't have it to give.

H: The only thing I can do is have life insurance for me and you. I paid the kids'. Now I can't pay ours.

W: So you haven't paid the insurance in a month and a half?

H: I paid the kids, but I haven't been able to pay ours.

W: You see, you don't say anything, so I've been thinking that everything is okay.

H: Yeah, I gathered that. (Laughter)

W: (Laughter) Honestly. We need to figure out how we can pay that before it's due. I mean, the same thing with the phone bill.

H: But you haven't been trying to keep that down. Yappity yappity yap!

W: Well, we'll try to figure it out. We'll both of us try to take something out.

H: Right. That's what I'd like.

W: All right. Work with me baby. And now maybe you'll start talking more. See, now you're sitting up here talking about this. And like that day at the park. We could have talked about that. It was a nice relaxing moment to discuss things.

H: I don't know what happened then. When I got there, I was blown out.

W: If you sit and talk with me like this…

H: When do we have a chance to sit down?

W: On weekends.

H: I don't think we have enough time on weekends to sit down.

W: See, that's why I said we need to take a day for ourselves. Momma would keep Dominique for a day. We've got to start focusing on ourselves more.

H: Mmm-hmm.

W: Just every now and then so we can do something for ourselves, even if it isn't anything more than taking in a movie.

H: Yeah.

W: Or go have dinner. When was the last time we had dinner in a restaurant?

H: That would be nice. Or go to a movie. How do you do it? First you go have dinner, then you go to a movie. (Laughter)

W: Or if you go to a movie early enough, you can go have dinner afterwards.

H: Right.

W: Right.

GOTTMAN SAYS: Wilma and Harris have a long-term, stable and happy marriage. They easily discuss two long-standing marital issues: the fact that he doesn't talk very much and she wants him to, and their financial differences. These issues are never going to change fundamentally. Our research has revealed that 69% of couples experience "perpetual problems"—issues with no resolution that couples struggle with for many years. Our data now lead us to believe that whenever you marry someone, your personality differences ensure that you and your partner will grapple with these issues forever. Marriages are only successful to the degree that the problems you have are ones you can cope with.

For most perpetual conflicts in marriages, what matters is not conflict resolution, but the attitudes that surround discussion of the conflict. Wilma and Harris both basically accept that there will always be differences between them, and they essentially accept one another as they are. Still, it is their ability to exchange viewpoints, making each other feel comfortable and supported all the while, that keeps them from getting gridlocked.

This couple, which is typical of our long-term couples, are real pros at being married and at using positive affect—like humor and gentle teasing—to de-escalate conflict. This is likely a sign that they are keeping their arousal levels low. Notice the wide array of strategies used to alleviate potential tension, such as expressing appreciation, softening complaints, responding nondefensively, backing down and using humor. The two of them do this together.

What these middle-aged spouses do is exactly what newlyweds who wind up stable and happy do, and this process moves them toward some semblance of problem-solving. What this master couple has effectively accomplished is to actualize the great marital paradox: that people can only change if they don't feel they have to.

Harris and Wilma make it look easy, just like a high-wire act makes it look easy. They are "athletes" at marriage, and that is one reason we study long-term marriages. There is a marital magic in what they do. The only function of my research is to make this marital magic clear so therapists can teach it to other couples.

READ MORE ABOUT IT

The Seven Principles for Making Marriage Work, John Gottman, Ph.D. (Crown, 1999)
The Marriage Clinic, John Gottman, Ph.D. (W. W. Norton, 1999)

John Gottman, Ph.D., is William Mifflin Professor of Psychology at the University of Washington in Seattle. Sybil Carrere, Ph.D., is a research scientist at the University of Washington in Seattle.

Reprinted with permission from *Psychology Today*, October 2000, pp. 42–47, 87. © 2000 by Sussex Publishers, Inc.

Finding
Real Love

Human beings crave intimacy, to love and be loved.
Why then do people feel isolated in their intimate relationships?
Four researchers and clinicians, Ayala Malach Pines, Shirley Glass,
Lisa Firestone and Joyce Catlett, discuss the alienation that affects
so many people and how to overcome it.

By Cary Barbor

We need to be close to other people as surely as we need food and water. But while it's relatively easy to get ourselves a good meal, it is difficult for many of us to create and maintain intimacy with others, particularly with a romantic partner. There are many variables that affect the quality of our relationships with others; it's difficult to pin it on one thing or another. But in this article, based on a symposium recently held at the annual American Psychological Association convention in Washington, D.C., four mental health professionals discuss their ideas about how we sabotage our intimate relationships—and what we can do to fix them.

> The first decision
> we make about a
> relationship is
> the partner we choose.

Choose to Lose?

Many factors influence the level of intimacy we enjoy in our relationships. The various decisions we make, and our behavior toward one another, are what foster closeness or drive us apart. These decisions are all under our control, although we are influenced by old patterns that we must work to change.

The first decision we make about a relationship is the partner we choose. Whom we fall in love with determines the level of intimacy in our relationships, according to Ayala Malach Pines, Ph.D., who heads the behavioral sciences in management program at Ben-Gurion University in Israel. We often choose partners who remind us of significant people from our childhood—often our parents—and we set out to recreate the patterns of our childhood. Let's look at an example:

Tara met Abe at a party. She was instantly attracted to the tall, lean man with a faraway look in his eyes. Abe, who had been standing alone, was delighted when Tara approached him with her open smile and outstretched hand. She was not only beautiful, but she struck him as warm and nurturing as well. The conversation between them flowed instantly. It felt comfortable and easy. Eventually, they fell in love, and after a year, they were married.

At first things were wonderful. They had the kind of closeness Tara had always dreamed about with her father. Though she was sure he loved her, she never felt she had her father completely to herself. Even when he held her on his lap, he had a faraway look. But with Abe things were different. He was there with her completely.

The intimacy between them also felt terrific to Abe. It was not the kind of suffocating closeness he always dreaded—the kind of intrusive closeness he experienced as a child with his mother, who used to enter his room uninvited and arrange his personal belongings with no regard to his privacy. But Tara was different. She did not intrude.

The View People have conflicting views and beliefs about relationships. Here are a few common ones:

1. Relationships are important and central in affecting a person's life.

2. Relationships are generally unstable. Young people marrying for the first time face a 40% to 50% chance of divorce.

3. There is a good deal of dishonesty in relationships. People are duplicitous in many ways: sexually, emotionally, etc.

4. Relationships are often based on emotional hunger and desperation. People mistake longing and desperation for love.

5. Few long-term relationships are based on high-level choices. Often people "take what they can get."

6. Choices can be made for negative as well as positive reasons. For example, people have a tendency to select mates who are similar to a parent, which can be good or bad.

7. People confuse sex with love. During the early phase of a relationship, attraction and pleasure in sex are often mistaken for love.

8. People feel they are failures unless they succeed in finding mates.

(Source: *Fear of Intimacy,* 1999)

Many factors influence the level of intimacy we enjoy in our relationships. The various decisions we make, and our behavior toward one another, are what foster closeness or drive us apart.

But occasionally, Abe would come home from work tired and annoyed. All he wanted was a drink and to sit with the paper until he could calm down and relax. Seeing him that way, Tara would become concerned. "What is going on?" she would ask anxiously. "Nothing," he would answer. Sure that there was something very wrong, and assuming that it must be something about her or their marriage, Tara would insist that he tell her. She reminded him of his mother, and he responded the way he did with his mother: by withdrawing. To Tara, this felt similar to the way her

father behaved. She responded in the same way she did when her father withdrew: by clinging. The struggle between them continued and became more and more intense over time, with Tara demanding more intimacy and Abe demanding more space.

Recreating the Family

Like Abe and Tara, people choose partners who help them recreate their childhood struggles. Tara fell in love with a man with "a faraway look in his eyes," and subsequently had to struggle for greater intimacy. Abe fell in love with a woman who was "warm and nurturing," then spent a lot of energy struggling for more space.

Tara's unresolved intimacy issues complement Abe's. For example, one partner (often the woman) will fight to break down defenses and create more intimacy while the other (often the man) will withdraw and create distance. So the "dance of intimacy" follows: If the woman gets too

close, the man pulls back. If he moves too far away, she pursues, and so on.

To achieve greater intimacy, the partners must overcome the anxiety that compels them to take their respective parts in that dance. In the example, Tara needs to control her abandonment anxiety and not pursue Abe when he withdraws, and Abe needs to control his engulfment anxiety when Tara pursues him and not withdraw. Working to overcome these anxieties is an opportunity to resolve childhood issues and can be a major healing experience for both partners.

Infidelity: The Road Back

If a couple can't overcome their anxieties and achieve a balance, however, fear and an inability to achieve intimacy will linger. This can create a vulnerability to affairs, says Shirley P. Glass, Ph.D., a clinical psychologist in private practice in Baltimore. Either partner may feel burned out from trying to get his or her emotional intimacy needs met in the relationship. A pursuing woman, who wonders if her needs will ever be met, may withdraw out of hopelessness. Yet her partner may think that the relationship has improved because the complaining has stopped. Meanwhile, she could be supplementing her unmet intimacy needs through an extramarital relationship that could ultimately lead to separation or divorce.

Once an affair has occurred, it only serves to erode intimacy further. Intimacy requires honesty, openness and self-disclosure. The deception that accompanies an affair makes this impossible. In addition, if the affair partner becomes the confidante for problems in the marriage, it can be threatening to the marriage because it creates a bond of friendship between the affair partners that goes beyond sexuality.

For trust to be rebuilt and intimacy reestablished, the walls of deception created by the affair need to be broken down. The spouse needs to be back on the "inside" of the partnership and the extramarital partner on the "outside." The involved spouse must stop all personal exchanges with the affair partner and disclose to the marital partner any unavoidable encounters with the affair partner, without prompting. Unfaithful partners can only regain credibility by being completely honest. People report that they recover from their partner having a sexual relationship with another person before they recover from being deceived.

But if both partners can be totally honest, and if communication in the partnership improves, there is a good chance that the marriage can survive the infidelity and the relationship can become strong again.

Overcoming Fear of Intimacy

It is our fear of intimacy that inspires these ingenious ways of avoiding it. This raises the question: How can we overcome our fear of intimacy? We can start by breaking down our defenses.

We all bring defenses to relationships, and, unfortunately, it is often these defenses that spell trouble. We develop our defenses and negative beliefs in childhood. They are what we utilized to protect ourselves against emotional pain and, later, against anxiety about death.

A core defense that often leads to the downfall of a partnership is "the fantasy bond," according to Lisa Firestone, Ph.D., adjunct faculty at the University of California Santa Barbara Graduate School of

Education, and Joyce Catlett, M.A., co-author of *Fear of Intimacy*, published recently by the American Psychological Association. The fantasy bond is an illusion of a connection to another person. It develops first with the mother or primary parent figure, and people often try to recreate it in their adult relationships.

People use various techniques to reestablish this primary relationship. They may first select a partner who fits their model, someone they can relate to in the way they related to their parent or other family member. They can distort their partner and perceive them as being more like this significant person than they are. Third, if all else fails, they tend to provoke their partner into the behavior they seek. All of these mechanisms curtail their ability to relate and make it less likely that people will be successful in achieving true intimacy in their relationships.

A secondary defense that helps preserve the fantasy bond is, according to Firestone and Catlett, "the voice." All people tend to carry on some form of internal dialogue within themselves as though another person were talking to them: reprimanding them, denouncing them, divulging negative information about others, and so on.

In intimate relationships, both individuals may be listening to the dictates of their respective voices. Unfortunately, these only create more defensiveness. Both partners may use rationalizations promoted by "the voice" to ward off loving responses from the other and justify their distancing behavior.

Speak Up, Therapeutically

A technique developed by Robert Firestone, Ph.D., and used to reverse this process and allow greater intimacy is voice therapy. Voice therapy brings these internalized negative thoughts to consciousness. The goal of voice therapy with couples is to help each individual identify the "voice attacks" that are creating conflict and distance in the relationship. In identifying specific self-criticisms as well as judgmental, hostile thoughts about the other, each partner is able to relate more openly.

Here is an example of someone using voice therapy. Sheryl is in a four-year relationship and was starting to have problems. She and her partner Mark came to therapy for help, and they progressed through these four steps of voice therapy over the course of treatment. Following is a glimpse into Sheryl's process.

Formulate the problem each individual perceives is limiting his or her satisfaction within the relationship.

Sheryl: The feeling I have is that I've always liked Mark, but lately I feel like I can't stand it when he's nice to me. I feel like I have a mean streak.

Therapist: In response to his liking you.

Sheryl: Yes.

Verbalize self-critical thoughts and negative perceptions of the other in the form of the voice, and let go of the feelings associated with them.

Therapist: What are you telling yourself about the relationship?

Sheryl: It's like, 'Don't show him anything, don't show him you like him.' I tell myself, 'Just don't show it, you're such a sucker if you show it.' When he's vulnerable I just want to squash him. And it's for no reason except for he's being sweet.

Develop insight into the origins of the voice and make connections between past experience and present conflicts.

Sheryl: I've seen myself be like my mother millions of times. In previous relationships I've acted so much like her, I didn't even know it. I saw her as being a really critical person, she was very critical of my father. And she would be mean to him. Sometimes I act like that myself.

Alter behaviors and communications in a direction that counteracts the dictates of the voice.

Therapist: So the hope is for you to hang in there and to tolerate the anxiety of giving up these defenses and the fantasized connection you have with your mother. If you do sweat it out then you'll be able to have more in your life. It takes a lot of courage to go through that process but it's really worth it.

Sheryl: I feel like it would make me sad, too, because I would feel a lot. When I have that other point of view, I feel big and mean. And when I just let things be, and don't act in ways to push Mark away, I feel like a soft, sweet person.

After trying voice therapy, Sheryl reported that she felt closer to Mark. She noticed a shift in her feelings, both in accepting his caring about her and genuinely caring about him.

In therapy sessions, both partners reveal negative thoughts and attitudes toward himself or herself and each other. In this way, they share each other's individual psychotherapy. In tracing back the source of their self-attacks and cynical views to early family interactions, they gain perspective on each other's problems and feel more compassion for their mates as well as

The Ideal and Not So Ideal

Interactions in an ideal and healthy relationship:	Interactions in an unhealthy relationship:
1. Nondefensiveness and openness	**1.** Angry and negative reactions to feedback; being closed to new experiences
2. Honesty and integrity	**2.** Deception and duplicity
3. Respect for the other's boundaries, priorities and goals, separate from self	**3.** Overstepping boundaries Other seen only in relation to self
4. Physical affection and responsive sexuality	**4.** Lack of affection, inadequate or impersonal, routine sexuality
5. Understanding—lack of distortion of the other	**5.** Misunderstanding—distortion of the other
6. Noncontrolling, nonmanipulative and nonthreatening behavior	**6.** Manipulations of dominance and submission
(Source: *Fear of Intimacy*, 1999)	(Source: *Fear of Intimacy*, 1999: The Glendon Association)

themselves. Changing old patterns often brings up anxiety, so part of the treatment is to learn to tolerate the anxiety and work through it, so the partners can maintain the behavioral changes and ultimately increase intimacy.

Homework

For couples who are not in therapy, there are many ways to change destructive patterns that prevent intimacy. Partners could become aware of the times when they attack themselves or think negatively about their partner. They could record their self-critical thoughts and hostile attitudes in a journal; they could reveal the contents of their destructive thoughts to a trusted friend or to their mate. They could assess how close to reality these thoughts are (usually not very). Each could set goals for what he or she wants out of the relationship and then keep track of how closely his or her actions match these goals.

Another good idea for couples is to make an active effort to move away from isolated couple interaction and toward an extended circle of family and friends. This often affords a better perspective and provides a potential background for understanding and breaking destructive, habitual patterns of relating. Partners need to admit to themselves and their partner if they have become distant, and that their actions are no longer loving or respectful. By reawakening their feeling for one another, they can achieve a higher level of intimacy.

We always have choices to make about intimacy—from the partners we choose to the way we interact with them each day. Recognizing our patterns, tolerating our anxieties, and working together on our relationships will help us overcome our fear of intimacy. Learning how best to communicate with each other and treat one another will help us enjoy loving, lasting relationships.

READ MORE ABOUT IT

Fear of Intimacy, Robert Firestone and Joyce Catlett (American Psychological Association Books, 1999)

The Trauma of Infidelity: Research and Treatment, Shirley Glass (Norton Professional Books, 2001)

Falling in Love: Why We Choose the Lovers We Choose, Ayala Malach Pines (Routledge, 1999)

Combating Destructive Thought Processes: Voice Therapy and Separation Theory, Robert Firestone (Sage Publications, 1997)

Romantic Jealousy: Causes, Symptoms and Cures, Ayala Malach Pines (Routlege, 1998)

Cary Barbor is a freelance writer based in New York. Her work has appeared on CBS Healthwatch *and in* Walking *and* Women's Sports and Fitness, *among other publications.*

Reprinted with permission from *Psychology Today,* January/February 2001, p. 42. © 2001 by Sussex Publishers, Inc.

PRESCRIPTION FOR PASSION

Jealousy ignites rage, shame, even life-threatening violence.
But it is just as necessary as love. In fact, it preserves and protects that fragile emotion. Consider it a kind of old-fashioned mate insurance, an evolutionary glue that holds modern couples together.

BY DAVID M. BUSS, PH.D.

Every human alive is an evolutionary success story. If any of our ancestors had failed to survive an ice age, drought, predator or plague, the previously inviolate chain of descent would have been irreparably broken, and we would not be alive to tell the tale. Each of us owes our existence to thousands of generations of successful ancestors. As their descendants, we have inherited the passions that led to their success—passions that drive us, often blindly, through a lifelong journey in the struggle for survival, the pursuit of position and the search for relationships.

These passions have many sides. They inspire us to achieve life's goals. They impel us to satisfy our desire for sex, our yearning for prestige and our quest for love. But passions also have a darker, more sinister side. The same passions that inspire us to love can lead to the disastrous choice of a mate, the desperation of unrequited obsession or the terror of stalking. Jealousy can keep a couple committed or drive a man to savagely beat his wife.

Jealousy's Two Faces

Jealousy poses a paradox. Consider that in a sample of 651 university students who were actively dating, more than 33% reported that jealousy posed a significant problem in their current relationship. The problems ranged from loss of self-esteem to verbal abuse, from rage-ridden arguments to the terror of being stalked. But the irony of jealousy, which can shatter the most harmonious relationships, is that it flows from deep and abiding love. The paradox was reflected in O.J. Simpson's statement: "Let's say I committed this crime [the slaying of ex-wife Nicole Brown Simpson]. Even if I did, it would have to have been because I loved her very much, right?"

Consider these findings: 46% of a community sample said jealousy was an inevitable consequence of true love. St. Augustine noted this link when he declared, "He that is not jealous is not in love." Shakespeare's tormented Othello "dotes, yet doubts, suspects, yet strongly loves." Women and men typically interpret a partner's jealousy as a sign of the depth of their love; a partner's absence of jealousy as a lack of love. The psychologist Eugene Mathes of Western Illinois University asked a sample of unmarried but romantically involved men and women to complete a jealousy test. Seven years later, he contacted the participants again and asked them about the current status of their relationship. Roughly 25% had married, while 75% had broken up. The jealousy scores from seven years earlier for those who married averaged 168, whereas the scores for those who broke up registered significantly lower at 142. These results must be interpreted cautiously; it's just one study with a small sample. But it points to the idea that jealousy might be inexorably linked with long-term love. In fact, it may be integral to it.

Evolution of an Alarm

Jealousy is an adaptive emotion, forged over millions of years, symbiotic with long-term love. It evolved as a primary defense against threats of infidelity and abandonment. Coevolution tells us that reciprocal changes occur sequentially in interacting species or between the sexes in one species. As a result, women have become excellent detectors of deception, as indicated by their superiority in decoding nonverbal signals. Men, in turn, can be notoriously skilled at deceiving women.

Jealousy is activated when one perceives signs of defection—a strange scent, a sudden change in sexual behavior, a suspicious absence. It gets triggered when a partner holds eye contact with someone else for a split second too long, or when a rival stands too close to your loved one or is suddenly fascinated by the minutia of his or her life. These signals alert us to the possibility of infidelity, since they have been statistically linked with relationship loss over the long course of human evolutionary history.

Margaret Mead called jealousy 'a festering spot in every personality...'

Obviously, episodes of extreme irrational or pathological jealousy can destroy an otherwise solid marriage. In most instances, however, it's not the experience of jealousy per se that's the problem. Rather, it's the real threat of defection by a partner interested in a real rival. In 1931, Margaret Mead disparaged jealousy as "undesirable, a festering spot in every personality so afflicted, an ineffective negativistic attitude which is more likely to lose than to gain any goal." Her view has been shared by many, from advocates of polyamory, a modern form of open marriage, to religious treatises. But properly used, jealousy can enrich relationships, spark passion and amplify commitment. The total absence of jealousy, rather than its presence, is a more ominous sign for romantic partners, for it portends emotional bankruptcy.

This was certainly true for one wife, who, noting her husband's lack of jealousy, grew to feel unloved and began acting out. She raged at him, harassing him on the telephone at work, causing him great embarrassment. When the husband sought help from a therapist, he was advised to act the part of the jealous husband. Having learned over many years how a jealous person behaves, he was able to perform the role so skillfully and subtly that his wife of 21 years didn't realize he was role-playing. While he had seldom called home in the past, he now called his wife frequently to check on her, to see whether she was home and to ask exactly what she was doing. He made suspicious and critical remarks about any new clothes she wore, and expressed displeasure when she showed the slightest interest in another man. The result was dramatic. The wife, flattered by her husband's attentiveness and newfound interest, stopped her jealous behavior completely. She became pleasant and loving toward her husband and expressed remorse over

her earlier behavior. At an eight-month follow-up, she was still behaving more lovingly toward her husband, but as a precaution he still played the jealous one from time to time.

Evoking Jealousy

Once jealousy evolved in the human repertoire, it became fair game for partners to exploit for their own purposes. Eliciting jealousy intentionally emerged as an assessment device to gauge the strength of a mate's commitment. Both sexes do it, but not equally. In one study, 31% of women, but only 17% of men, reported that they had intentionally elicited jealousy in their romantic partner. Women and men also employ different tactics. In our study of newlyweds, we found that women more than men report flirting with others in front of a partner, showing interest in others, going out with others and talking to another man at a party, all to make their partner jealous or angry.

William Tooke, Ph.D., and his colleagues at the State University of New York at Plattsburgh have found strong sex differences in several clusters of acts designed to induce jealousy. First, women intentionally socialize with other people. One woman said that she purposefully neglected to invite her partner along when she went out with friends. Another said she made a point of talking with members of the opposite sex when she and her boyfriend went out to a bar. A third indicated that she made sure to casually mention to her boyfriend how much fun she had when she was out partying without him.

The second jealousy-inducing strategy centered on intentionally ignoring a partner. One woman reported acting distant and uninterested in her partner to make him think she didn't care about him that much. Another said she deliberately failed to answer her phone when she knew her boyfriend was calling so he would think she was out with someone else. Yet another told her boyfriend she did not have time to see him, even though it was the weekend.

The third mode of strategic jealousy induction was especially effective at pushing men's jealousy buttons—direct flirtation with other men. One woman reported dancing closely and seductively with someone her partner didn't like while he stood on the sidelines. Several reported going out to bars with members of the opposite sex and coming back to the boyfriend a bit intoxicated. Others reported that they

dressed in especially sexy outfits while going out without their boyfriends, a sure method of fanning a man's jealous flames.

A more subtle and ingenious tactic for evoking jealousy involves merely smiling at other men while out with a partner. Antonia Abbey, Ph.D., of Wayne State University, discovered a fascinating difference in how men and women interpret a woman's smiles. When women smile, men often erroneously read into it sexual interest, mistaking friendliness for romantic intent. Martie Haselton, Ph.D., of the University of Texas at Austin, and I have labeled men's sexual inference as "adaptive bias" in mind reading because it's part of men's unconscious strategy of casual sex. By inferring sexual interest from a woman's smile, men are more likely to make sexual overtures.

So when a woman smiles at another man while at a party with her partner, she deftly exploits the evolved psychology of two different men. The smile causes its target to think she's sexually interested in him, so he makes advances. Simultaneously, it evokes her partner's jealousy, so he gets angry both about the rival and about his perception that she's encouraging the other man. The upshot might be a confrontation between the two rivals or a lovers' quarrel. But who can blame a woman just for being friendly? No other method for strategically inducing jealousy is as effective, for it makes two men dance to a woman's tune with merely a well-timed glance.

Who Needs Jealousy?

Why do women walk such a dangerous tightrope, trifling with a mechanism known to unleash male violence? Gregory White, Ph.D., of Southern Oregon University, conducted an in-depth study of 150 heterosexual couples in California to find out. He first asked each of the 300 participants whether they had ever intentionally tried to make their partner jealous and why. Only a few women reported that they induced jealousy to punish their partner. Eight percent reported doing it to bolster their self-esteem. Ten percent admitted doing it to act out feelings of revenge on a partner for a previous wrong. Increasing a partner's commitment, however, was cited by 38% of women. By evoking jealousy, a woman causes her partner to believe that she has attractive alternatives available, so that if he does not display greater commitment she might depart for greener mating pastures. Women who successfully use this tactic are more likely to keep the commitment of their mates. Fully 40% of women, the largest group, reported using jealousy to test the strength of the bond. By evoking jealousy, a woman gains valuable information about the depth and consistency of her partner's commitment.

By evoking jealousy, a woman is telling her partner she could leave for greener mating pastures.

Women reap this benefit most when the need to test the bond is especially strong: Women whose partners have been away for a while, those whose partners experience a sudden surge in status, and women who feel they might be perceived as less desirable than their partner, all need vital appraisals of a man's commitment.

For both sexes, the key to understanding who needs jealousy is determining who has the most to lose. White asked all 300 participants to rate whether they were more, equally or less involved in the relationship than their partner. Relative involvement is a powerful clue as to which partner is more desirable on the mating market, according to the principle of least interest—the less interested partner has the upper hand on the scale of desirability. Although 61% of the couples were well matched in their level of involvement, 39% showed a mismatch. Does this index of relative involvement predict who will deploy the jealousy-induction strategy? The effect for men was modest: 15% of those who were less involved intentionally induced jealousy; 17% of those equally involved did, as did 22% of the men more involved. So there is a slight tendency for the less desirable men to attempt to evoke more jealousy.

The results for women were more dramatic. Whereas only 28% of the women who were less involved reported intentionally inspiring jealousy, fully 50% of the women who were more involved than their partner reported doing so. Since women who fall below their partners in overall desirability confront commitment problems more poignantly than other women, they induce jealousy to correct the imbalance.

Strategically inducing jealousy serves several key functions for women. It can bolster self-esteem because of the attention it attracts from other men. It can increase a partner's commitment by making him realize how desirable she really is. And it can test the strength of the bond: If he reacts to her flirtations with emotional indifference, she knows he lacks commitment; if he gets jealous, she knows he's in love. Evoking jealousy, although it inflicts a cost on the partner, provides valuable information that's difficult to secure otherwise. And it often works.

Jealousy can also spark or rekindle sexual passion

Virgil Sheets, Ph.D., and his colleagues at Indiana State University confirmed that one of the most common reactions in men whose jealousy is aroused is to increase the attention they pay to their partners. After becoming jealous, men report that they are more likely to "try to keep track of what my partner is doing," "do something special for my partner" and "try to show my partner more attention."

Although evoking jealousy can serve a useful function, it must be used with skill and intelligence to avoid unleashing unintended consequences.

Igniting Sexual Passion

Jealousy can also spark or rekindle sexual passion in a relationship. Consider the case of Ben and Stacy, a couple attending an intensive five-day jealousy workshop conducted by the Israeli psychologist Ayala Pines, Ph.D. Ben, 15 years older than Stacy, had been married before, but had been divorced for five years when he first got involved with Stacy.

Although Stacy had had a few romantic relationships, she was still a virgin when they met. Ben was flattered at the attentions of a woman as young and attractive as Stacy, but soon became bored with their sex life, and yearned for sex with other women. This unleashed intense jealousy in Stacy, which brought them into the workshop to solve what Ben described as "her problem." He saw no reason that he should not sleep with other women. During the early days of the workshop, Ben brought up Stacy's insecurity and jealousy, indicated his disapproval and proceeded to flirt with the other women in the group. During one session, Stacy was berated by the group for being so jealous. Tears streamed down her cheeks and others in the group responded with hugs and affection. The most attractive man in the group was especially supportive. He continued to comfort her, even after the session ended and Ben and the others had left the room. Hugging turned to kissing and eventually they had passionate sex right on the floor.

When Ben discovered the infidelity, he was furious, saying, "You hurt me more than any woman has done, and I trusted you to protect my feelings." Over the next two days the therapy group focused on Ben's jealousy. But when asked by the therapist whether any good had come of the event, he replied, "When we made love afterward, it was the most passionate sex we had ever had. It was unbelievably intense and exciting." Stacy agreed.

Ben's jealousy revived the sexual passion in their relationship. Why? Astute readers already have clues to the most probable explanations: The other man's attention reaffirmed Stacy's attractiveness in Ben's eyes. When it penetrates men's minds that other desirable men are interested in their partner, they perceive their partner as more sexually radiant.

There is also an evolutionary reason that Ben's jealousy reignited his passion for Stacy. A man whose partner has just been inseminated by another man is most at risk for genetic cuckoldry. By having sex with Stacy immediately following her infidelity, he reduced the odds that she would become pregnant with another man's child, although he obviously didn't think about it in those terms. The passionate nature of the sex implies that she had an orgasm, which causes the woman to retain more sperm. Increased sperm retention, in ancestral times, would have meant an increased likelihood of conception. Ben was merely a modern player in an ancient ritual in which men competed with one another in the battle for successful fertilization.

Emotional Wisdom

In my studies, I have discovered that some signs of jealousy are accurately interpreted as acts of love. When a man drops by unexpectedly to see what his partner is doing, this mode of jealous vigilance functions to preserve the safe haven of exclusivity while simultaneously communicating love. When a woman loses sleep thinking about her partner and wondering whether he's with someone else, it indicates simultaneously the depth of her love and the intensity of her jealousy. When a man tells his friends he is madly in love with a woman, it serves the dual purpose of conveying love and warning potential rivals to keep their hands off.

It is unlikely that love, with its tremendous psychological investment, could have evolved without a defense to shield it from the constant threat of rivals and the possibility of betrayal from a partner.

Jealousy evolved to fill that void, motivating vigilance as the first line of defense, and violence as the last. In its extreme forms, this vital shield has been called delusional, morbid and pathological, a symptom of neurosis and a syndrome of psychosis. Therapists try to expunge it from patients and individuals try to suppress it in themselves.

The experience of jealousy can be psychologically painful. But it alerts us to real threats from real rivals. It tells us when a partner's sexual indifference might not merely mean he or she is distracted by work. It causes us to remember subtle signals that, when properly assembled, portend a real defection.

Evolution has equipped all of us with a rich menu of emotions, including jealousy, envy, fear, rage, joy, humiliation, passion and love. The knowledge that comes with a deeper understanding of our dangerous passions will not eliminate conflicts between lovers, between rivals or between lovers who become rivals. But it may, in some small measure, give us the emotional wisdom to deal with them.

READ MORE ABOUT IT

The Red Queen: Sex and the Evolution of Human Nature, Matt Ridley (Penguin, 1995)

Romantic Jealousy: Causes, Symptoms, Cures, Ayala M. Pines, Ph.D. (Routledge, 1998)

This article is from Dangerous Passion *by David Buss, Ph.D. (Free Press, 2000). He is a professor of psychology at the University of Texas at Austin.*

Reprinted from *Psychology Today*, May/June 2000, pp. 54–61. Excerpted from *Dangerous Passion: Why Jealousy Is as Necessary as Love and Sex*, by David M. Buss. © 2000 by David M. Buss, by permission of The Free Press, a division of Simon & Schuster, Inc.

UNIT 5

Dynamics of Personal Adjustment: The Individual and Society

Unit Selections

37. **The Teening of Childhood**, Kay S. Hymowitz
38. **The Betrayal of the American Man**, Susan Faludi
39. **Coping With Crowding**, Frans B. M. de Waal, Filippo Aureli, and Peter G. Judge
40. **Nobody Left to Hate**, Elliot Aronson
41. **Speak No Evil**, Dennie Hughes
42. **Work, Work, Work, Work!** Mark Hunter
43. **Don't Face Stress Alone**, Benedict Carey

Key Points to Consider

- Is America becoming a teen-centered society? If you believe the answer is yes, why do you think this is happening? What role does the media play? Do you think this social change is a positive or negative one?

- Susan Faludi maintains that the American man has been betrayed. What does she mean by this? What are your personal feelings about this betrayal? If you believe there has been betrayal, what caused it? Do you think someone of the opposite sex would agree with you? Can anything be done to clarify the role of men and of masculinity in our society? Explain.

- What is crowding? How does crowding differ from other concepts such as density? Is crowding more negative than positive? Why might early research be incorrect about the effects of crowding?

- What is the definition of prejudice? Do you, yourself, hold any biases? From where does prejudice originate? What is it that perpetuates the "isms" (racism, sexism, ageism, and other prejudices)?

- Why do families fight? Why is it important to reduce family conflict? How can we reduce family conflict?

- Do Americans work more today than ever before? If you answered yes, why are Americans working harder? Why are boundaries blurring between free time and work? Do you think work should take precedence over family and leisure time?

- What is workaholism? Why does it cause stress? What is the Type A personality? Can friends and family members really help us cope better with stress? When friends do provide us with moral and emotional support, what is this called?

 **Links: www.dushkin.com/online/**
These sites are annotated in the World Wide Web pages.

AFF Cult Group Information
  http://www.csj.org/index.html
Explanations of Criminal Behavior
  http://www.uaa.alaska.edu/just/just110/crime2.html
National Clearinghouse for Alcohol and Drug Information
  http://www.health.org
Schools Health Education Unit (SHEU)
  http://www.sheu.org.uk/sheu.htm

The passing of each decade brings changes to society. Some historians have suggested that changes are occurring more rapidly than in the past. In other words, history appears to take less time to occur. How has American society changed historically? The inventory is long. Technological advances can be found everywhere. Not long ago, few people knew what "user-friendly" and zip drive signified. Today these terms are readily identified with the rapidly changing computer industry. Twenty-five years ago, Americans felt fortunate to own a 13-inch television that received three local stations. Now people feel deprived if they cannot select from 250 different worldwide channels on their big, rear-screen sets. Today we can e-mail a message to the other side of the world faster than we can propel a missile to the same place.

In the Middle Ages, Londoners worried about the bubonic plague. Before vaccines were available, people feared polio and other diseases. Today much concern is focused on the transmission and cure of AIDS, the discovery of more carcinogenic substances, and the greenhouse effect. In terms of mental health, psychologists see few hysterics, the type of patient seen by Sigmund Freud in the 1800s. Psychosomatic ulcers, alcohol, and drug addiction are more common today. In other words, lifestyle, more than disease, is killing Americans. Similarly, issues concerning the changing American family continue to grab headlines.

Nearly every popular magazine carries a story or two bemoaning the passing of the traditional, nuclear family and the decline in "family values." And as if these spontaneous or unplanned changes are not enough to cope with, some individuals are intentionally trying to change the world. Witness the continuing dramatic changes in Eastern Europe and the Middle East, for example.

This list of societal transformations, while not exhaustive, reflects society's continual demand for adaptation by each of its members. However, it is not just society at large that places stress on us. Smaller units within society, such as our work group, demand constant adaptation by individuals. Work groups expand and contract with every economic fluctuation. Even when group size remains stable, new members come and go as turnover takes place; hence, changes in the dynamics of the group occur in response to the new personalities. Each of these changes, welcome or not, probably places less strain on society as a whole and more stress on the individual, who then needs to adjust or cope with the change.

This unit addresses the interplay between the individual and society (or culture) in producing the problems each creates for the other.

The first few essays feature ideas about general societal issues such as the "teening" of American childhood, fuzzy gender roles, and racism. In the unit's first article, "The Teening of Childhood," Kay Hymowitz expresses her opinion that children are growing up too fast. In other words, 8-year-olds often look and act more like 15-year-olds, or at least aspire to being an adolescent before their time. Hymowitz clearly blames the media for this social change.

The feminist movement has also created continuing changes in American society. In the second article, noted author Susan Faludi, who first wrote about the feminist movement, offers excerpts from her new book on masculinity. Faludi contends that American men have no idea today of what their role should be and how the ideal man should behave.

The next article, "Coping With Crowding," discusses early as well as recent research on the effects of crowding. Crowding is an important issue because the world population continues to grow. The early research, which showed that crowding was probably detrimental, is criticized. Newer research suggests that we are much better at coping with environmental changes (such as an increase in number of people present) than believed earlier.

In the next article, "Nobody Left to Hate," another common social issue is discussed—prejudice. Social psychologists believe that prejudice is learned and can be overcome by new ways of thinking. In this article, Elliott Aronson shares with the reader the technique, known as the jigsaw classroom, for overcoming racial and ethnic bigotry in schools. Aronson also claims that this technique can alter the whole school climate and make schools more harmonious.

We next move from society at large to smaller groups: The group of interest in the first article in this unit is the family. Families can be congenial or families can experience turmoil and dysfunction. In "Speak No Evil," Dennie Hughes examines the touchy and closeted world of family conflict. Much family conflict is blamed on miscommunication. Hughes suggests ways that families can fight fair and reduce conflict through improving communication.

The tendency to be all work and no play places each of us under immense stress. In "Work, Work, Work, Work!" Mark Hunter discusses how the boundaries between work and home and work and leisure have blurred. We seem to be working all the time, a tendency that Hunter says is unhealthy. Fortunately, Hunter also shares tips for coping with this increased pressure to work endless hours.

As just noted, individuals who work, work, work often face much stress. Stress is a modern American plague that affects our physical and psychological states. Benedict Carey suggests, in "Don't Face Stress Alone," that social support (help from and talking with friends) is highly effective in managing stress. In so doing, Carey also furnishes the reader with helpful information about the Type A, or workaholic, personality.

THE TEENING OF CHILDHOOD

BY KAY S. HYMOWITZ

A KID'S GOTTA do what a kid's gotta do!" raps a cocksure tyke on a 1998 television ad for the cable children's network Nickelodeon. She is surrounded by a large group of hip-hop-dancing young children in baggy pants who appear to be between the ages of three and eight. In another 1998 ad, this one appearing in magazines for the Gap, a boy of about eight in a T-shirt and hooded sweatshirt, his meticulously disheveled hair falling into his eyes and spilling onto his shoulders, winks ostentatiously at us. Is he neglected (he certainly hasn't had a haircut recently) or is he just street-smart? His mannered wink assures us it's the latter. Like the kids in the Nickelodeon ad, he is hip, aware, and edgy, more the way we used to think of teenagers. Forget about what Freud called latency, a period of sexual quiescence and naïveté; forget about what every parent encounters on a daily basis—artlessness, shyness, giggling jokes, cluelessness. These media kids have it all figured out, and they know how to project the look that says they do.

The media's darling is a child who barely needs childhood. In the movies, in magazines, and most of all on television, children see image upon irresistible image of themselves as competent sophisticates wise to the ways of the world. And maybe that's a good thing too, since their parents and teachers appear as weaklings, narcissists, and dolts. That winking 8-year-old in the Gap ad tells the story of his generation. A gesture once reserved for adults to signal to gullible children that a joke was on its way now belongs to the child. This child gets it; it's the adults who don't.

There are plenty of signs that the media's deconstruction of childhood has been a rousing success. The enthusiastic celebration of hipness and attitude has helped to socialize a tough, "sophisticated" consumer child who can assert himself in opposition to the tastes and conservatism of his parents. The market aimed at children has skyrocketed in recent years, and many new products, particularly those targeting the 8- to 12-year-olds whom marketers call tweens, appeal to their sense of teen fashion and image consciousness. Moreover, kids have gained influence at home. In part, this is undoubtedly because of demographic changes that have "liberated" children from parental supervision. But let's give the media their due. James McNeal, who has studied childhood consumerism for many decades, proclaims the United States a "filiarchy," a bountiful kingdom ruled by children.

Lacking a protected childhood, today's media children come immediately into the noisy presence of the media carnival barkers. Doubtless, they learn a lot from them, but their sophistication is misleading. It has no relation to a genuine worldliness, and understanding of human hypocrisy or life's illusions. It is built on an untimely ability to read the glossy surfaces of our material world, its symbols of hipness, its image-driven brands and production values. Deprived of the concealed space in which to nurture a full and independent individuality, the media child unthinkingly embraces the dominant cultural gestures of ironic detachment and emotional coolness. This is a new kind of sophistication, one that speaks of a child's diminished expectations and conformity rather than worldliness and self-knowledge.

Nowadays when people mourn the media's harmful impact on children, they often compare the current state of affairs to the Brigadoon of the 1950s. Even those who condemn the patriarchal complacency of shows like *Father Knows Best* or *Ozzie and Harriet* would probably concede that in the fifties parents did not have to fret over rock lyrics like *Come on bitch... lick up the dick* or T-shirts saying KILL YOUR PARENTS. These were the days when everyone, including those in the media, seemed to revere the protected and long-lived childhood that had been the middle-class ideal since the early 19th century.

But the reality of fifties media was actually more ambiguous than the conventional wisdom suggests. The fifties saw the rise of television, a medium that quickly opened advertisers' and manufacturers' eyes to the possibility of promoting in children fantasies of pleasure-filled freedom from parental control, which in turn fertilized the fields for liberationist ideas that came along in the next decade. American parents had long struggled to find a balance between their children's personal drives and self-expression and the demands of common life, but television had something else in mind. It was fifties television that launched the media's two-pronged attack on the preconditions of traditional childhood, one aimed directly at empowering children, the other aimed at undermining the parents who were trying to civilize them. By the end of the decade, the blueprint for today's media approach to children was in place.

The first prong of attack was directed specifically at parents—or, more precisely, at Dad. Despite the assertions of those who see in *Father Knows Best* and *Ozzie and*

Harriet evidence that the fifties were a patriarchal stronghold, these shows represent not the triumph of the old-fashioned family but its feeble swan song.[1] Dad, with his stodgy ways and stern commandments, had been having a hard time of it since he first stumbled onto television. An episode of *The Goldbergs*, the first television sitcom and a remake of a popular radio show featuring a Jewish immigrant family, illustrates his problem: Rosalie, the Goldbergs' 14-year-old daughter, threatens to cut her hair and wear lipstick. The accent-laden Mr. Goldberg tires to stop her, but he is reduced to impotent blustering: "I am the father in the home, or am I? If I am, I want to know!" It is the wise wife who knows best in this house; she acts as an intermediary between this old-world patriarch and the young country he seems unable to understand. "The world is different now," she soothes.[2] If this episode dramatizes the transgenerational tension inevitable in a rapidly changing immigrant country, it also demonstrates how television tended to resolve that tension at Dad's blushing expense. The man of the fifties television house was more likely to resemble the cartoon character Dagwood Bumstead ("a joke which his children thoroughly understand" according to one critic)[3] than Robert Young of *Father Knows Best*. During the early 1950s, articles began to appear decrying TV's "male boob" with titles like "What Is TV Doing to MEN?" and "Who Remembers Papa?" (an allusion to another early series called *I Remember Mama*).[4] Even *Ozzie and Harriet* was not *Ozzie and Harriet*. Ozzie, or Pop, as he was called by his children, was the Americanized and suburbanized papa who had been left behind in city tenements. Smiling blandly as he, apparently jobless, wandered around in his cardigan sweater, Ozzie was the dizzy male, a portrait of grinning ineffectuality. It is now coincidence that *Ozzie and Harriet* was the first sitcom to showcase the talents of a child character, when Ricky Nelson began his career as a teen idol. With parents like these, kids are bound to take over.

Still, the assumption that the first years of television were happy days for the traditional family has some truth to it. During the early fifties, television was widely touted as about the best thing that had ever happened to the family—surely one of the more interesting ironies of recent social history. Ads for the strange new appliance displayed a beaming mom and dad and their big-eyed kids gathered together around the glowing screen. It was dubbed the "electronic hearth." Even intellectuals were on board; early sociological studies supported the notion that television was family-friendly. Only teenagers resisted its lure. They continued to go to the movies with their friends, just as they had since the 1920s; TV-watching, they said, was family stuff, not an especially strong recommendation in their eyes.

In ORDER to turn television into the children's oxygen machine that it has become, television manufacturers and broadcasters during the late forties and early fifties had to be careful to ingratiate themselves with the adults who actually had to purchase the strange new contraption. Families never had more than one television in the house, and it was nearly always in the living room, where everyone could watch it. Insofar as the networks sought to entice children to watch their shows, they had to do so by convincing Mom that television was good for them. It was probably for these reasons that for a few short years children's television was more varied and of higher quality than it would be for a long time afterward. There was little to offend, but that doesn't mean it was bland. In an effort to find the best formula to attract parents, broadcasters not only showed the familiar cowboy and superhero adventure series but also experimented with circus and science programs, variety shows, dramas, and other relatively highbrow fare, for example, Leonard Bernstein's *Young People's Concerts*. Ads were sparse. Since the networks had designed the earliest children's shows as a lure to sell televisions to parents, they were not thinking of TV as a means of selling candy and toys to kids; almost half of those shows had no advertising at all and were subsidized by the networks. At any rate, in those days neither parents nor manufacturers really thought of children as having a significant role in influencing the purchase of anything beyond, perhaps, cereal, an occasional cupcake, or maybe a holiday gift.

This is not to say that no one had ever thought of advertising to children before. Ads targeting youngsters had long appeared in magazines and comic strips. Thirties radio shows like *Little Orphan Annie* and *Buck Rogers in the Twenty-Fifth Century* gave cereal manufacturers and the producers of the ever-popular Ovaltine a direct line to millions of children. But as advertisers and network people were gradually figuring out, when it came to transporting messages directly to children, radio was a horse and buggy compared to the supersonic jet known as television, and this fact changed everything. By 1957, American children were watching TV an average of an hour and a half each day. And as television became a bigger part of children's lives, its role as family hearth faded. By the mid-fifties, as television was becoming a domestic necessity, manufacturers began to promise specialized entertainment. Want to avoid those family fights over whether to watch the football game or Disneyland? the ads queried. You need a *second* TV set. This meant that children became a segregated audience in front of the second screen, and advertisers were now faced with the irresistible opportunity to sell things to them. Before television, advertisers had no choice but to tread lightly around children and to view parents as judgmental guardians over the child's buying and spending. Their limited appeals to kids had to be more than balanced by promises to parents, however spurious, of health and happiness for their children.

That balance changed once television had a firm foothold in American homes and advertisers could begin their second prong of attack on childhood. With glued-to-the-tube children now segregated from adults, broadcasters soon went about pleasing kids without thinking too much about parents. The first industry outside of the tried-and-true snacks and cereals to capitalize on this opportunity was, predictably, toys.[5] By the mid-fifties, forward-looking toy manufacturers couldn't help but notice that Walt Disney was making a small fortune selling Mickey Mouse ears and Davy Crockett coonskin hats to the viewers of his *Disneyland* and *The Mickey Mouse Club*. Ruth and Eliot Handler, the legendary owner-founders of Mattel Toys, were the first to follow up. They risked their company's entire net worth on television ads during *The Mickey Mouse Club* for a toy called "the burp gun"; with 90 percent of the nation's kids watching, the gamble paid off bigger than anyone could have ever dreamed.

It's important to realize, in these days of stadium-sized toy warehouses, that until the advent of television, toys were nobody's idea of big business. There simply was not that big a market out there. Parents themselves purchased toys only as holiday or birthday presents, and they chose them simply by going to a specialty or department store and asking advice from a salesperson. Depression-traumatized grandparents, if they were still alive, were unlikely to arrive for Sunday dinner bearing Baby Alive dolls or Nerf baseball bats and balls. And except for their friends, children had no access to information about new products. At any rate, they didn't expect to own all that many toys. It's no wonder toy manufacturers had never shown much interest in advertising; in 1955 the "toy king" Lous Marx had sold fifty million dollars' worth of toys and had spent the grand total of $312 on advertising.

The burp gun ad signaled the beginning of a new era, a turning point in American childhood and a decisive battle in the filiarchal revolution. Toy sales almost tripled between 1950 and 1970. Mattel was now a boom company with sales rising from $6 million in 1955 to $49 million in 1961.[6] Other toy manufacturers who followed Mattel onto television also watched their profits climb.

But the burp gun ad was also a watershed moment, because it laid the groundwork for today's giant business of what Nickelodeon calls "kid kulture," a phenomenon that has helped to alter the dynamic between adults and children. Television transformed toys from a modest holiday gift enterprise mediated by parents into an ever-present, big-stakes entertainment industry enjoyed by kids. Wholesalers became less interested in marketing particular toys to adults than in the manufacturer's plans for promotional campaigns to seduce children. In short, the toy salesman had pushed open the front door, had crept into the den while Mom and Dad weren't looking, and had whispered to Dick and Jane, without asking their parents' permission, of all the happiness and pleasure they could have in exchange for several dollars of the family's hard-earned money.

That the burp gun had advanced more power to children became more apparent by 1959, when Mattel began to advertise a doll named Barbie. Barbie gave a hint as to just how far business was ready to take the filiarchal revolution that had been set in motion by the wonders of television. Regardless of the promotional revolution it had unleashed, the burp gun was a familiar sort of toy, a quirky accessory to the battlefield games always enjoyed by boys. But Barbie was something new. Unlike the baby dolls that encouraged little girls to imitate Mommy, Barbie was a swinger, a kind of Playboy for little girls. She had her own Playboy Mansion, called Barbie's Dream House, and she had lots of sexy clothes, a car, and a boyfriend. The original doll had pouty lips—she was redesigned for a more open California look in the sixties—and she was sold in a leopard skin bathing suit and sunglasses, an accessory whose glamour continues to have iconic status in the children's market. In fact, though it isn't widely known, Barbie was copied from a German doll named Lili, who was in turn modeled on a cartoon prostitute. Sold in bars and tobacco shops, Lili was a favorite of German men, who were suckers for her tight (removable) sweater and short (removable) miniskirt.

Barbie has become so familiar that she is seen as just another citizen of the toy chest, but it's not exaggeration to say that she is one of the heroes in the media's second prong of attack on childhood. She proved not only that toy manufacturers were willing to sell directly to children, bypassing parents entirely, but that they were willing to do so by undermining the forced and difficult-to-sustain latency of American childhood. According to marketing research, mothers without exception *hated* Barbie. They believed she was too grown-up for their 4-to-12-year-old daughters, the toy's target market. The complaint heard commonly today—that by introducing the cult of the perfect body Barbie promotes obsessive body consciousness in girls, often resulting in eating disorders—is actually only a small part of a much larger picture. Barbie symbolized the moment when the media and the businesses it promoted dropped all pretense of concern about maintaining childhood. They announced, first, that they were going to flaunt for children the very freedom, consumer pleasure, and sex that parents had long been trying to delay in their lives. And, second, they were going to do this by initiating youngsters into the cult of the teenager. If this formula sounds familiar, it's because it remains dominant today. Barbie began the media's teening of childhood; today's media images and stories are simply commentary.

ADS TARGETING children make perfect companion pieces to stories of family rot and children savvy enough to roll their eyes amusingly through all the misery. In ads today, the child's image frequently appears in extreme close-up—the child as giant. Appealing to children's fantasies of omnipotent, materialistic freedom, advertisers portray an anarchic world of misrule in which the pleasure-seeking child reigns supreme.[7] Spot, the red dot on the logo of containers of 7 Up, comes to life, escapes from the refrigerator, and tears through the house causing riotous havoc.[8] A Pepsi ad shows screaming teens and preteens gorging themselves with cake, pouring Pepsi over their heads, and jumping on the bed with an electric guitar. "Be young, have fun, drink Pepsi," says the voice-over.[9] Adult characters—even adult voice-overs and on-camera spokespeople—have been banished in favor of adolescent voices in the surfer-dude mode.[10] Any old folks left standing should prepare to be mocked. Perceived as carping, droning old-timers who would deny the insiders their pleasure or fun, adults are the butts of the child-world joke. They are, as the *New York Times'* Charles McGrath noted after surveying Saturday morning cartoons, "either idiots, like the crazed geek who does comic spots in 'Disney's 1 Saturday Morning,' or meanies, like the crochety, incompetent teachers and principals on the cartoons 'Recess' and 'Pepper Ann.'"[11] Teachers are, of course, citizens of the adult geekville as well: In one typical snack food ad, kids break out of the halls of their school or behind the back of dimwitted teachers droning on at the chalkboard.[12]

The misleading notion that children are autonomous figures free from adult influence is on striking display in ads like these. Children liberated from parents and teachers are only released into new forms of control. "Children will not be liberated," wrote one sage professor. "They will be dominated."[13] Nineteenth-century moralists saw in the home a haven from the increasingly harsh and inhuman marketplace. The advantage of hindsight allows us to see how this arrangement benefited children. The private home and its parental guardians could exercise their influence on children relatively unchallenged by commercial forces. Our own children, on the other hand, are creatures—one is tempted to say slaves—of the marketplace almost immediately.

The same advertisers who celebrate children's independence from the stodgy adult world and all its rules set out to educate children in its own strict regulations. They instruct children in the difference between what's in and what's out, what's hip and what's nerdy—or, to quote the inimitable Beavis and Butthead, "what's cool and what sucks." Giving new meaning to the phrase *hard sell*, today's ads demonstrate for children the tough posture of the sophisticated child who is savvy to the current styles and fashions. In a contest held by Polaroid for its Cool Cam promotion, the winning entry, from a Manassas, Virginia, girl, depicted a fish looking out a fishbowl at the kids in the house and sneering, "The only thing cool about these nerds is that they have a Cool Cam." Polaroid marketed the camera with a pair of sunglasses, the perennial childhood signifier of sophistication.

It should be clear by now that the pose the media has in mind for children—cool, tough, and sophisticated independence—is that of the teenager. The media's efforts to encourage children to identify with the independent and impulsive consumer teen—efforts that began tentatively, as we say, with Barbie—have now gone into over-

drive. Teenagers are everywhere in children's media today. Superheroes like Mighty Morphin Power Rangers and Teenage Mutant Ninja Turtles are teenagers. Dolls based on the TV character Blossom; her suggestively named friend, Six; and her brother, Joey, portray teenagers, as do the dolls based on the TV series *Beverly Hills, 90210*, not to mention the ever-popular Barbie herself. Even the young children dressed in baggy pants who sing *A kid's gotta do what a kid's gotta do* for Nickelodeon are, for all intents and purposes, teenagers.

By populating kid's imaginative world with teenagers, the media simultaneously flatters children's fantasies of sophistication and teaches them what form those fantasies should take. Thus, the media's "liberation" of children from adults also has the mischievous effect of binding them more closely to the peer group. In turn, the peer group polices its members' dress and behavior according to the rules set by this unrecognized authority. In no time at all, children intuit that teens epitomize the freedom, sexiness, and discretionary income—not to mention independence—valued in our society. Teens do not need their mommies to tell them what to wear or eat or how to spend their money, nor do they have sober responsibilities to restrain them from impulse buying.

These days, the invitation to become one of the teen in-crowd arrives so early that its recipients are still sucking their thumbs and stroking their blankies. During the preschool lineup on Nickelodeon one morning, there was a special Nickelodeon video for a song entitled "I Need Mo' Allowance." In this video the camera focuses on a mock heavy metal rock band consisting of three teenaged boys in baggy pants and buzz cuts who rasp a chorus that includes lines like *Mo' allowance to buy CDs!* A dollar sign flashes repeatedly on the screen. This video was followed by an ad for a videotape of *George of the Jungle*. "This George rides around in a limo, baby and looks great in Armani," jeers the dude announcer. "It's not your parents' *George of the Jungle!*" Change the channel to *Sesame Street*, and although the only ads you'll get are for the letter *H* or the number 3, you may still see an imitation MTV video with a group of longhaired, bopping, stomping muppets singing *I'm so cool, cool, cool!* That few 3-year-olds know the first thing about Armani, limos, or even cool is irrelevant; it's time they learned.

Many companies today have "coolhunters" or "street teams," that is, itinerant researchers who hang out in clubs, malls, and parks and look for trends in adolescent styles in clothes, music, and slang to be used in educating younger consumer trainees. Advertisers can then broadcast for children an aesthetic to emblazon their peer group identity. Even ads for the most naive, childlike products are packed with the symbols of contemporary cool. The Ken doll, introduced in 1993, has hair tinted with blond streaks and wears an earring and a thick gold chain around his neck. The rock and roll which accompanies many of these ads is the pulsing call to generational independence now played for even the youngest tot. The

Honey Comb Bear (in sunglasses) raps the virtues of his eponymous cereal. The 1998 Rugrats movie is accompanied by musicians like Elvis Costello and Patti Smith. With a name like Kool-Aid, how could the drink manufacturer continue its traditional appeal to parents and capture today's child sophisticate as well? The new Mr. Kool Aid raps his name onto children's brains.

As math or geography students, American children may be mediocre, but as consumers they are world-class. They learn at prodigiously young ages to obey the detailed sumptuary laws of the teen material world, a world in which status emanates out of the cut of a pair of jeans or the stitching of a sneaker. M/E Marketing Research found that kids make brand decisions by the age of four.[14] *Marketing to and Through Kids* recounts numerous stories of kids under 10 unwilling to wear jeans or sneakers without a status label. One executive at Converse claims that dealers inform him that children as young as two are "telling their parents what they want on their feet." Another marketing executive at Nike notes, "The big shift we've been seeing is away from unbranded to more sophisticated branded athletic shoes at younger and younger ages." At Nike the percentage of profit attributable to young children grew from nothing to 14 percent by the early nineties.[15]

Nowhere has the success of media education been more dramatically apparent than among 8-to-12-year-old "tweens." The rise of the tween has been sudden and intense. In 1987 James McNeal, perhaps the best-known scholar of the children's market, reported that children in this age group had an income of $4.7 billion. In 1992 in an article in *American Demographics* he revised that figure up to $9 billion, *an increase of almost 100 percent in five years*.[16] While children spent almost all their money on candy in the 1960s, they now spend two-thirds of their cash on toys, clothes, movies, and games they buy themselves.[17]

The teening of those we used to call preadolescents shows up in almost everything kids wear and do. In 1989 the Girl Scouts of America introduced a new MTV-style ad with rap music in order to, in the words of the organization's media specialist, "get away from the uniformed, goody-goody image and show that the Girl Scouts are a fun, mature, cool place to be."[18] Danny Goldberg, the chief executive officer of Mercury Records, concedes that teenagers have been vital to the music industry since the early days of Sinatra. "But now the teenage years seem to start at eight or nine in terms of entertainment tastes," he says. "The emotions are kicking in earlier."[19] A prime example is Hanson, a rock-and-roll group whose three members achieved stardom when they were between the ages of 11 and 17. Movie producers and directors are finding it increasingly difficult to interest children this age in the usual children's fare. Tweens go to *Scream*, a horror film about a serial killer, or *Object of My Affection*, a film about a young woman who falls in love with a homosexual man.[20] After the girl-driven success of *Titanic*, Buffy Shutt, president of marketing at Universal Pictures, marveled, "They're amazing consumers."[21] Mattel surely agrees, as evidenced by their Barbie ad. "You, girls, can do anything." Clothing retailers are scrambling for part of the tween action. All over the country companies like Limited Too, Gap Kids, Abercrombie and Fitch, and Gymboree have opened stores for 6-to-12-year-olds and are selling the tween look—which at this moment means bell bottoms, ankle-length skirts or miniskirts, platform shoes, and tank tops.[22] Advertisers know that kids can spot their generational signature in a nanosecond—the hard rock and roll, the surfer-dude voices, the baggy pants and bare midriffs shot by tilted cameras in vibrant hues and extreme close-ups—and they oblige by offering these images on TV, the Internet, in store displays, and in the growing number of kid magazines.[23]

The seduction of children with dreams of teen sophistication and tough independence, which began with Barbie and intensified markedly in the last decade, appears to have had the desired effect: It has undermined childhood by turning children into teen consumers. This new breed of children won't go to children's movies and they won't play with toys. One of the stranger ironies of the rise of the tween is that toy manufacturers, who with the introduction of Barbie began the direct hard sell to children and were the first to push the teening of American childhood, have been hoist with their own petard. The 1998–99 Toy Industry Factbook of the Toy Manufacturer's Association says that the industry used to think of kids between birth and 14 as their demographic audience, but with the emergence of tweens they have had to shrink that audience to birth to 10.[24] Even seven- and eight-year-olds are scorning Barbie.[25]

Who needs a doll when you can live the life of the teen vamp yourself? Cosmetic companies are finding a bonanza among this age group. Lines aimed at tweens include nail polish, hair mascara, lotions, and lip products like lipstick, lip gloss, "lip lix." Sweet Georgia Brown is a cosmetic line for tweens that includes body paints and scented body oils with come-hither names like Vanilla Vibe or Follow Me Boy. The Cincinnati design firm Libby Peszyk Kattiman has introduced a line of bikini underwear for girls. There are even fitness clubs and personal trainers for tweens in Los Angeles and New York.[26]

Marketers point at broad demographic trends to explain these changes in the child market, and they are at least partially correct. Changes in the family have given children more power over shopping decisions. For the simple reason that fewer adults are around most of the time, children in single-parent homes tend to take more responsibility for obtaining food and clothes. Market researchers have found that these kids become independent consumers earlier than those in two-parent homes.[27] Children of working mothers also tend to do more of the family shopping when at around age eight or nine they can begin to get to the store by themselves. Though candy, toy, and cereal manufacturers had long been well aware of the money potential of tween cravings, by the mid-eighties, even though their absolute numbers were falling, tweens began to catch the eye of a new range of businesses, and ads and marketing magazines started to tout the potential of this new niche. The reason was simple: Market research revealed that more and more children in this age group were shopping for their own clothes, shoes, accessories, and drug-store items—indeed, they were even shopping for the family groceries. Just as marketers had once targeted housewives, now they were aiming at kids.[28] Jeans manufacturer Jordache was one of the first companies to spot the trend. "My customers are kids who can walk into a store with either their own money or their mothers'," the company's director of advertising explained at the time. "The dependent days of tugging on Mom or Dad's sleeve are over." Now as the number of children is rising again, their appeal is even more irresistible. Packaged Facts, a division of the worldwide research firm Find/SVP, has said that the potential purchasing power of today's kids "is the greatest of any age or demographic group in our nation's history."[29]

And there is another reason for the increasing power of children as consumers: By the time they are tweens, American children have simply learned to expect a lot of stuff.[30] Many of them have been born to older mothers; the number of first babies born to women over 30 has quadrupled since 1970, and the number born to women over 40 doubled in the six years between 1984 and 1990. Older mothers are more likely to have established careers and to be in the kind of financial position that allows them to shower their kids with toys and expensive clothes.[31] Also, grandparents are living longer and more comfortably, and they often arrive with an armload of toys, sports equipment, and fancy dresses. (The products of the children's clothes company Osh Kosh B'Gosh are known in the trade as "granny bait.") Divorce has also helped to inflate the child market: Many American children divide their time between parents, multiplying by two the number of soccer balls and Big Bird toothbrushes they must own. But as we have seen before, impersonal social forces have found support in human decisions. Important as they are, demographics by themselves can't explain 10-year-olds who have given up dolls for mascara and body oil. The teening of childhood has been a consummation the media devoutly wished—and planned. The media has given tweens a group identity with its own language, music, and fashion. It has done this by flattering their sense of being hip and aware almost-teens rather than out-of-it little kids dependent on their parents. On discovering the rising number of child customers, Jordache Jeans did not simply run ads for kids; they ran ads showing kids saying things like "Have you ever seen your parents naked?" and "I hate my mother. She's prettier than me." When Bonne Bell cosmetics discovered the rising sales potential of younger shoppers, they did not merely introduce a tween line, which some parents might think bad enough; they introduced it with the kind of in-your-face language that used to send children to bed without dinner: "We know how to be cool. We have our own

ideas. And make our own decisions. Watch out for us." Sassaby's "Watch your mouth, young lady" is a smirking allusion to old-fashioned childhood that is meant to sell a line of lip "huggers" and "gloss overs."

There is little reason to think that children have found the freedom and individuality that liberationists assumed they would find now that they have been liberated from old-fashioned childhood and its adult guards. The rise of the child consumer and the child market itself is compelling evidence that children will always seek out some authority for rules about how to dress, talk, and act. Today's school-age children, freed from adult guidance, turn to their friends, who in turn rely on a glamorous and flattering media for the relevant cultural messages. Recent studies have found that children are forming cliques at younger ages than in previous years and that those cliques have strict rules about dress, behavior, and leisure. By the fifth or sixth grade, according to *Peer Power: Preadolescent Culture and Identity*, girls are gaining status "from their success at grooming, clothes, and other appearance-related variables."[32] Teachers and principals also see an increasing number of 10- and 11-year-olds who have given up toys for hair mousse and name-brand jeans and who heckle those who do not. What matters to this new breed of child is, according to Bruce Friend, vice president of worldwide research and planning at Nickelodeon, "being part of the in-crowd" and "being the first to know what's cool."[33] These "free" children "are extremely fad conscious"; moreover, according to *American Demographics*, tweens' attraction to fads has "no saturation points."[34] Look for the tween consumer to become even more powerful.

A diminished home life and an ever more powerful media constitute a double blow against the conditions under which individuality flourishes. Whereas in the past eccentric or bookish children might have had the privacy of their home to escape the pressures of their media-crazed peers, today such refuge has gone the way of after-school milk and cookies. And if you think that at least such children have been freed of the pressure of yesterday's domineering fathers and frustrated mothers, you might want to reconsider. As Hannah Arendt once noted, "The authority of a group, even a child group, is always considerably stronger and more tyrannical than the severest authority of an individual person can ever be." The opportunity for an individual to rebel when bound to a group is "practically nil"; few adults can do it.[35] The truth is, yesterday's parent-controlled childhood protected children not only from sex, from work, and from adult decisions but also from the dominance of peers and from the market, with all its pressures to achieve, its push for status, its false lures, its passing fads.

But in the anticultural filiarchy which is replacing traditional childhood, adults no longer see their job as protecting children from the market. In fact, it is not that the child's hurried entrance into the market means that parents are increasingly failing to socialize children. It's the other way around. Children are viewed by manufacturers as the "opinion leaders in the household," according to a vice president at Keebler.[36] Manufacturers believe that children are exercising influence over family purchases never before remotely associated with the young. Holiday Inn and Delta Airlines have established marketing programs aimed at children, and *Sport Illustrated for Kids* publishes ads from American Airlines, IBM, and car manufacturers.[37]

While simply turning off the TV would help, at this point television is only one part of the picture. Kids learn of their sophisticated independence from retail displays and promotions, from magazines and direct mailings. With their captive audience, schools, too, have become an advertiser's promised land: Kids see ads in classrooms, on book order forms, on Channel One, on the Internet, on school buses, and now even in textbooks. Book order forms distributed in schools throughout the country from the putatively educational firm Scholastic look like cartoons and provide children with the opportunity to order stickers, autograph books, fan biographies, and books based on popular movies and television shows. Practically every Fortune 500 company has a school project, according to the *New York Times*, and many administrators expect that in the near future we will be seeing signs like CHEERLEADERS BROUGHT TO YOU BY REEBOK in school gyms.[38] "It isn't enough just to advertise on television," Carol Herman, a senior vice president of Grey Advertising, explains. "You've got to reach the kids throughout their day—in school, as they're shopping at the mall ....r at the movies. You've got to become part of the fabric of their lives."[39]

The scorched earth policy in the name of the filiarchy requires that ever younger children be treated as potential customers, once again in the guise of education. When *Sesame Street* arrived on the airwaves in 1969, no one imagined that preschoolers could be a significant market segment. In fact, the improbability of preschool purchasing power was the reason *Sesame Street* had to appear on public television in the first place; no one wanted to put a lot of money into creating and broadcasting a program for kids who had no purchasing power. How short-sighted that was! By 1994 Children's Television Workshop was bringing in $120 million a year largely on the strength of its over 5,000 licensed products. The list includes not just educational items like books and audio-tapes but bubble bath, pajamas, underwear, and Chef Boyardee Sesame Street pasta. Toy manufacturers gradually caught on to the power of the littlest people, especially where their education was concerned. The number of preschool toys exploded in the decades after *Sesame Street* was introduced, and many of them were stamped with a seal of approval from some expert or other—or with the image of Ernie or Big Bird, which in the minds of many amounted to the same thing.

And now *Teletubbies* has arrived to help carve out the *pre*-preschool market and to give power to the littlest peo-

ple. *Teletubbies* was designed for one- and two-year-olds, and though no one has ever explained how it could possibly be educational for babies to watch television, it is clear that when toddlers see pictures of the four vividly hued plush and easily identified characters (with television screens on their stomachs) on bottles or bibs, they will cry for them and PBS will rake it in. In anticipation of opening up this new market segment, the media went into overdrive. Pictures of the characters appeared in ads in trade and consumer magazines and were plastered on buses in New York City and on a giant billboard in Times Square. The show was a topic on *Letterman, Today*, and *Nightline*. "If this isn't the most important toy at Christmas this year, then something desperately wrong will have happened," gloated Kenn Viselman, whose Itsy Bitsy Entertainment Company has the rights to *Teletubbies* products. "This show had more advance press than *Titanic*." Wondered one critic, "Where does it end: A TV in the amniotic sac?" But marketers were thrilled; according to the president of another licensing company, before now "the one-to-two-year-old niche hasn't been filled very well."[40] The one-to-two-year-old niche? McNeal has said that children become aware of the market as early as two months of age.[41] There is no more unmistakable sign of the end of childhood as Americans have known it.

REFERENCES

1. The history presented in this article is take from Lynn Spigel, *Make Room for TV: Television and the Family Ideal in Post-war America* (Chicago: University of Chicago Press, 1992); Gerard Jones, *Honey, I'm Home: Sitcoms: Selling the American Dream* (New York: Grove Weidenfeld, 1992); William Melody, *Children's Television: The Economics of Exploitation* (New Haven, Conn.: Yale University Press, 1973); Cy Schneider, *Children's Television: The Art, the Business and How It Works* (Chicago: NTC Business Books, 1987). Mark Crispin Miller, "Deride and Conquer," in *Watching Television*, ed. Todd Gitlin (New York: Pantheon Books, 1986), traces the "long decline of Dad" (pp. 196ff.) and the triumph of the ironic tone.
2. Quoted in Jones, p. 42.
3. Arthur Asa Berger, *The Comic-Stripped American: What Dick Tracy, Blondie, Daddy Warbucks and Charlie Brown Tell Us About Ourselves* (New York: Walker, 1973), p. 103.
4. Spigel, p. 60.
5. The history of toy advertising and Barbie comes from Schneider, pp. 18–26; G. Wayne Miller, *Toy Wars: The Epic Struggle Between G.I. Joe, Barbie, and the Companies That Make Them* (New York: Random House, 1998), p. 67; Gary Cross, *Kids' Stuff: Toys and the Changing World of American Childhood* (Cambridge: Harvard University Press, 1997), chap. 6.
6. Cross, pp. 165–166.
7. Ellen Seiter, *Sold Separately: Parents and Children in the Consumer Culture* (New Brunswick, N.J.: Rutgers University Press, 1993), notes this same theme (in chap. 4), and several of my examples come from there. Seiter, like other academics today writing in the Ariès tradition, believes Kid Kulture can "express a resistance to the middle-class culture of parenting... that may be very healthy indeed," (p. 232). In other words, she finds ads genuinely subversive.

8. Example from Selina S. Guber and Jon Berry, *Marketing to and Through Kids* (New York: McGraw-Hill, 1993), p. 133.

9. Patricia Winters, "Pepsi Harkens Back to Youth," *Advertising Age*, January 25, 1993. p. 3.

10. Seiter (p. 130) quotes research, comparing boys' toy ads from the fifties and those of today which finds that the adult male voice-over or on-camera spokesman has almost entirely disappeared.

11. Charles McGrath, "Giving Saturday Morning Some Slack," *New York Times Magazine*, November 9, 1997, p. 54.

12. Seiter, p. 121.

13. John E. Coons, "Intellectual Liberty and the Schools," *Notre Dame Journal of Law, Ethics, and Public Policy*, vol. 1, 1985, p. 503.

14. "News/Trends—Kidpower," *Fortune*, March 30, 1987, pp. 9–10.

15. Guber and Berry, pp. 27, 78.

16. James McNeal, "Growing Up in the Market, *American Demographics*, October 1992, p. 47.

17. Figure cited in Lisa Bannon, "As Children Become More Sophisticated, Marketers Think Older," *Wall Street Journal*, October 13, 1998, p. A1. McNeal says that aggregate spending on or for children between ages four and twelve doubled every decade in the 1960s, 1970s, and 1980s. In the 1990s the children's market picked up more steam: between 1990 and 1997, it had already tripled.

18. Jane Weaver, "Girl Scout Campaign: Shedding Old Image for Media Cool," *Adweek*, September 11, 1989, p. 11.

19. Quoted in Bernard Weinraub, "Who's Lining Up at Box Office? Lots and Lots of Girls," *New York Times*, Arts Section, February 23, 1998, p. 1.

20. Bannon, p. A8; Michele Willens, "Young and in a Niche That Movies Neglect," *New York Times*, Arts and Leisure Section, June 14, 1998, pp. 13–14.

21. Quoted in Weinraub, p. 4.

22. Bannon, pp. A1, 8.

23. The number of magazines for children almost doubled between 1986 and 1991. S.K. List, "The Right Place to Find Children," *American Demographics*, February 1992, pp. 44–47.

24. Toy Industry Factbook at www.toy-tma.com/PUBLICATIONS/factbook98/economics.html.

25. Bannon, p. A1.

26. Laura Klepacki, "Courting the 'Tweenie' Boppers," *WWD*, February 27, 1998, p. 10; Becky Ebenkamp, "Packaging: Sara Lee Repackages Youthful Underwear to Better Draw Juniors," *Brandweek*, January 5, 1998, p. 36.

27. James McNeal and Chyon-Hwa Yeh, "Born to Shop," *American Demographics*, June 1993, p. 37.

28. Carrier Telegardin, "Growing Up Southern: The Kids Take Over," *Atlanta Journal-Constitution*, June 7, 1993, p. E1. According to Telegardin, "America's new housewife [is] the housekid."

29. Quoted in Toy Industry Factbook. See also "Generation Y," *Business Week*, February 15, 1999, pp. 80–88, for how this generation is changing the marketplace.

30. The psychologist Marilyn Bradford found that preschoolers ask for an average of 3.4 toys for Christmas and receive 11.6. Cited in Gary Cross, "Too Many Toys," *New York Times*, November 24, 1995, p. 35.

31. Lisa Gubernick and Marla Matzer, "Babies as Dolls," *Forbes*, February 27, 1995, p. 78.

32. Patricia A. Adler and Peter Adler, *Peer Power: Preadolescent Culture and Identity* (New Brunswick, N.J.: Rutgers University Press, 1998), p. 55. Tellingly, by 1991 shoes and clothing were the fastest-growing categories among children up to age twelve and accounted for 13 percent of their spending, up from an unmeasurably small amount in 1988, according to Susan Antilla, "'I Want' Now Gets," *New York Times*, Education Life, April 4 1993, p. 17. See also Carol Pogash, "The Clothing Boom in the Land of the Little People," *Los Angeles Times*, August 29, 1995, p. 22.

33. Interview by the author, July 1998.

34. Judith Waldrop, "The Tween Scene," *American Demographics*, September 1992, p. 4.

35. Hannah Arendt, "Crisis in Education," *Partisan Review*, Fall 1958, p. 500.

36. Quoted in Guber and Berry, p. 84. See also Claire Collins, "Fighting the Holiday Advertising Blitz," *New York Times*, December 1, 1994, p. C4; Matt Murray, "Hey Kids! Marketers Want Your Help!" *Wall Street Journal*, May 6, 1997, pp. B1, 8; Antilla, p. 17; Steven A. Holmes, "Shoppers! Deciding? Just Ask Your Child," *New York Times*, Week in Review, January 8, 1995, p. 4; Becky Ebenkamp, Mike Beirne, and Christine Bittar, "Products for the Sophisticated Little Nipper," *Brandweek*, February 22, 1999. pp. 1, 53.

37. See Don Oldenberg, "Consummate Consumer: Children's Business: America's 90 Billion Plus Youth Market," *Washington Post*, July 6, 1995, p. C5.

38. Deborah Stead, "Classrooms and Commercialism," *New York Times*, Education Life, January 5, 1997, p. 30.

39. Quoted in Michael F. Jacobson and Laurie Ann Mazur, *Marketing Madness: A Survival Guide for a Consumer Society* (New York: Westview Press, 1995), p. 21. See also Carrie Goerne, "Marketers Try to Get More Creative at Reaching Teens," *Marketing News*, August 5, 1991, pp. 2, 6; Judann Dagnoli, "Consumer's Union Hits Kids Advertising," *Advertising Age*, July 23, 1990, p. 4.

40. Quoted in Lawrie Mifflin, "Critics Assail PBS over Plan for Toys Aimed at Toddlers," *New York Times*, April 20, 1998, p. A17.

41. Quoted in Oldenberg, p. C5. Mary Ellen Podmolik, "Kids' Clothing Boom," *Chicago Sun Times*, Financial Section, August 21, 1994, p. 1, quotes McNeal to the effect that 10 percent of a two-year-old's vocabulary is made up of brand names.

Kay S. Hymowitz is a senior fellow at the Manhattan Institute, a contributing editor at City Journal, *and an affiliate scholar at the Institute for American Values. This article is adapted from her recent book,* Ready or Not. *Copyright © 1999 by Kay S. Hymowitz. Reprinted by permission of The Free Press, an imprint of Simon & Schuster, Inc.*

From *American Educator*, Spring 2000, pp. 20–25. Reprinted with permission of the author and *American Educator*, the quarterly journal of the American Federation of Teachers.

The Betrayal Of The American Man

BOOK EXCERPT: **Her groundbreaking 'Backlash' looked at the 'undeclared war on women.' Now in 'Stiffed,' the author explores the unseen war on men—the pressure to be masculine in a culture that no longer honors traditional codes of manhood**.

By Susan Faludi

When I listen to the sons born after World War II, born to the fathers who won that war, I sometimes find myself in a reverie. I imagine a boy, in bed pretending to sleep, waiting for his father. The door opens, and the hall light streams in, casting a cutout shadow man across the bedroom floor. A minute later, the boy, wearing his coonskin cap and clutching his flashlight, races after his father along the shadowy upper hallway, down the stairs and out the screen door. The man and the boy kneel on the scratchy wool of the father's old navy peacoat, and the father snaps off the boy's flashlight. The father directs the boy's vision to a faraway glimmer. Its name is Echo. The boy looks up, knowing that the satellite his father is pointing out is more than just an object; it is a paternal gift rocketing him into his future, a miraculous inheritance encased in the transit of an artificial star, infinitesimally tiny, impossibly bright.

I knew this boy. Like everyone else who grew up in the late 1950s and early 1960s, I knew dozens of him. He was Bobby on the corner, who roamed the neighborhood with his cap gun and holster, terrorizing girls and household pets. He was Frankie, who blew off part of his pinkie while trying to ignite a miniature rocket in the schoolyard. Even if he wasn't brought out into the backyard and shown a satellite glinting in the sky, he was introduced to the same promise and the same vision, and by such a father. Many of these fathers were veterans of World War II or Korea, but their bloody paths to virility were not ones they sought to pass on, or usually even discuss. This was to be the era of manhood after victory, when the pilgrimage to masculinity would be guided not by the god of war Mars, but by the dream of a pioneering trip to the planet Mars. The satellite; here was a visible patrimony, a visual marker of vaulting technological power and progress to be claimed in the future by every baby-boom boy. The men of the fathers' generation had "won" the world and now they were giving it to their sons.

Four decades later, as the nation wobbled toward the millennium, its pulse-takers all seemed to agree that a domestic apocalypse was underway: American manhood was under siege. Newspaper editors, legislators, preachers, marketers, no matter where they perched on the political spectrum, had a contribution to make to the chronicles of the "masculinity crisis." Right-wing talk-radio hosts and left-wing men's-movement spokesmen found themselves uncomfortably on common ground. MEN ON TRIAL, the headlines cried, THE TROUBLE WITH BOYS. Journalists—myself included—raced to report on one young-male hot spot after another: Tailhook, the Citadel, the Spur Posse, South Central gangsters, militiamen blowing up federal buildings and abortion clinics, schoolyard shooters across the country.

CLOSING OF THE AMERICAN JOB

In the new economy, work moved from vital production and job security to paper pushing and massive layoffs

The Broken Promise

On the surface, said Richard Foster, who came to McDonnell Douglas in the late '60s to work in the NASA space lab, life as an aerospace man seemed to offer the ultimate in masculine freedom. "It was idyllic," he told me. "All these little green lawns and houses all in a row. You could drive the freeways and plan your life out." But as time went on, he came to feel that it had all been planned without him, that he was expected to take the initiative in a game in which he was not even a player. "You began to feel so isolated," he said. Like the rest of the managers, he "belonged" to the company in only the most tenuous way. In the end, he would become a casualty of various corporate "cost-reduction" programs five times, his salary plunging from $80,000 to $28,000 to zero. Which was why he was sitting in a vinyl banquette in a chain restaurant in the shadow of McDonnell Douglas's blueglass tower in the middle of the afternoon, talking to me. "The next thing you know," he said, "you're standing outside, looking in. And you begin to ask, as a man, what is my role? What is it, really, that I do?"

About 11 miles up the road, a starkly different kind of leave-taking was unfolding at the Long Beach Naval Shipyard, one of the military bases slated for closure in 1995. If McDonnell Douglas had been the emblematic postwar corporation—full of functionaries whose jobs were unclear, even to themselves—the shipyard represented a particular vintage of American masculinity, monumental in its pooled effort, indefatigable in its industry and built on a sense of useful productivity. Ike Burr, one of the first black men to break into upper management, was a shipfitter who climbed steadily to project superintendent. "Everything you ever dreamed of is here," Burr said. Unlike the McDonnell Douglas men, he wasn't referring to his dream house in the suburbs. He was talking about the work itself. "The shipyard is like a world within itself. Most items are one-of-a-type items, done once and not to be repeated. There's satisfaction in it, because you start and complete something. You *see* what you've created. The world of custom-made is finished—except here." After the shipyard's closing was announced, Burr postponed his official signing-out. He had found a temporary job at another military installation and was always "too busy" to get back to Long Beach to turn in his badge. But one morning he arrived to pay his last respects. He dressed sharply for the occasion: double-breasted gray suit, paisley tie and matching pocket hankie, even a hint of cologne. The morning management meeting was underway and he had been asked to stop by. He offered a few pointers, and then the shipyard commander gave an impromptu speech—about how Burr was the kind of guy "you could rely on to get the job done." Then he handed Burr a homemade plaque with a lengthy inscription.

Burr tucked it under his arm, embarrassed by the attention. "I better go get the signing-out business over," he said, his voice bumping over choppy seas. He headed out to make the rounds and get his termination physical. By late afternoon, Ike Burr had arrived at a small office, to sign a form surrendering the code word that gave him access to the yard. Though he burst out laughing as he signed, his words belied the laughter. "I have nothing in my possession," he said. "I have lost everything."

S.F.

In the meantime, the media's softer lifestyle outlets happily turned their attention to male-crisis lite: the retreat to cigar clubs and lap-dancing emporiums, the boom in male cosmetic surgery and the abuse of steroids, the brisk sales of Viagra. Social scientists pontificated on "endangered" young black men in the inner cities, Ritalin-addicted white "bad boys" in the suburbs, "deadbeat dads" everywhere and, less frequently, the anguish of downsized male workers. Social psychologists issued reports on a troubling rise in male-distress signals—from depressive disorders to suicides to certain criminal behaviors.

Pollsters investigated the electoral habits of a new voting bloc they called "the Angry White Male." Marketers hastened to turn the crisis into entertainment and profits from TV shows like "The Man Show" to T shirts that proclaimed DESTROY ALL GIRLS or WIFE BEATER. And by the hundreds of thousands, men without portfolio confirmed the male-crisis diagnosis, convening in

Washington for both the black Nation of Islam-led Million Man March and a largely white, evangelical-led Promise Keepers rally entitled, hopefully, "Stand in the Gap."

If so many concurred in the existence of a male crisis, consensus collapsed as soon as anyone asked the question Why. Everyone proposed a favorite whipping boy or, more often, whipping girl, and blame-seekers on all sides went after their selected culprits with righteous and bitter relish. Feminist mothers, indulgent liberals, videogame makers or testosterone itself all came under attack.

At Ground Zero of the Masculinity Crisis

THE SEARCH FOR AN ANSWER TO that question took me on a six-year odyssey, with stops along the way at a shuttered shipyard in Long Beach, a suburban living room where a Promise Keepers

group met, a Cleveland football stadium where fans grieved the loss of their team, a Florida horse farm where a Vietnam vet finally found peace, a grassy field in Waco where militiamen searched for an enemy and a slick magazine office where young male editors contended with a commodified manhood. But I began investigating this crisis where you might expect a feminist journalist to begin: at the weekly meetings of a domestic-violence group. Wednesday evenings in a beige stucco building a few blocks from the freeway in Long Beach, Calif., I attended a gathering of men under court order to repent the commission of an act that stands as the emblematic masculine sin of our age. What did I expect to divine about the broader male condition by monitoring a weekly counseling session for batterers? That men are by nature brutes? Or, more optimistically, that the efforts of such a group might point to methods of "curing" such beastliness?

GHETTO STAR

In a South-Central gang, Kody Scott finally felt useful as a man. But the biggest part of the 'work' was promoting the gangster image.

Glamour in the 'Hood

My father's generation was the last responsible generation," said Sanyika Shakur (now Kody Scott's legally adopted name) as he welcomed me in August 1997 to his girlfriend's two-bedroom house in California's San Fernando Valley. Four years had passed since the publication of Shakur's best-selling memoir, "Monster: The Autobiography of an L.A. Gang Member," written while he was serving a four-year sentence for robbery at Pelican Bay State Prison. The book's cover photo of the pumped-up, bare-chested author clutching a semiautomatic MAC-10, combined with the much-advertised news of his six-figure advance, turned the former member of the Eight-Tray Gangsters (a Crips set in South-Central L.A.) into what he rightly called a "ghetto star."

Shakur had just been released from jail three days earlier, after a year's sentence for a parole violation, his second such since the publication of what was supposed to be his transformational autobiography. He had fled after his first violation, and the police eventually found him on a neighborhood porch, receiving a long line of autograph seekers. The dictates of a celebrity culture demanded a manhood forged by being glamorous, not responsible.

Getting a rep:
'If the media knows about you, damn, that's the top,' says Scott

---

As a young man, he had still hoped that he could demonstrate a workmanlike "usefulness" within his gang set. "You put in work and you feel needed in a gang. People would call on me because they needed me. You feel useful, and you're useful in your capacity as a man. You know, 'Don't send me no boys. Send me a man!'" But he

was beginning to see his former life in a different light. What he once perceived as "work" now seemed more like PR. "What the work was," he said, "was anything you did in *promotion* for the gang." He found it amusing how the media viewed gangs as clannish and occult. "We're not a secret society. Our whole thing is writing on walls, tattoos on necks, maintaining visibility. Getting media coverage is the s—t! If the media knows about you, damn, that's the top. We don't recognize ourselves unless we're recognized on the news."

Kody Scott's image-enhancement strategies were not homegrown. "I got all these ideas from watching movies and watching television. I was really just out there acting from what I saw on TV." And he wasn't referring to "Superfly" or "Shaft." "Growing up, I didn't see one blaxploitation movie. Not one." His inspiration came from shows like "Mission: Impossible" and "Rat Patrol" and films like "The Godfather." "I would study the guys in those movies," he recalled, "how they moved, how they stood, the way they dressed, that whole winning way of dressing. Their tactics became my tactics. I went from watching "Rat Patrol" to being in it. His prime model was Arthur Penn's 1967 movie "Bonnie and Clyde." "I watched how in 'Bonnie and Clyde' they'd walk in and say their whole names. They were getting their reps. I took that and applied it to my situation." Cinematic gangsterism was his objective, and it didn't seem like much of a reach. "It's like there's a thin line in this country now between criminality and celebrity. Someone has to be the star of the 'hood. Someone has to do the advertising for the 'hood. And it's like agencies that pick a good-looking guy model. So it became, 'Monster Kody! Let's push him out there!'" He grinned as he said this, an aw-shucks smile that was, doubtless, part of his "campaign."

S.F.

Either way, I can see now that I was operating from an assumption both underexamined and dubious: that the male crisis in America was caused by something men were doing unrelated to something being done to them. I had my own favorite whipping boy, suspecting that the crisis of masculinity was caused by masculinity on the rampage. If male violence was the quintessential expression of masculinity run amok, then a domestic-violence therapy group must be at the very heart of this particular darkness.

I wasn't alone in such circular reasoning. I was besieged with suggestions along similar lines from journalists, feminists, antifeminists and other willing advisers. Women's rights advocates mailed me news clips about male office stalkers and computer harassers. That I was not ensconced in the courtroom for O. J. Simp-

son's murder trial struck many of my volunteer helpers as an appalling lapse of judgment. "The perfect case study of an American man who thinks he's entitled to just control everything and everybody," one of them suggested.

But then, I had already been attending the domestic-violence group for several months—the very group O. J. Simpson was, by coincidence, supposed to have attended but avoided with the promise that he would speak by phone to a psychiatrist—and it was already apparent to me that these men's crises did not stem from a preening sense of entitlement and control. Each new member in the group, called Alternatives to Violence, would be asked to describe what he had done to a woman, a request that was met invariably with the disclaimer "I was out of control." The counselors would then expend much en-

ergy showing him how he had, in fact, been in control the entire time. He had chosen his fists, not a knife; he had hit her in the stomach, not the face. No doubt the moment of physical contact for these men had grown out of a desire for supreme control fueled by a need to dominate. I cannot conceive of a circumstance that would exonerate such violence. By making the abusive spouse take responsibility for his actions, the counselors were pursuing a worthy goal. But the logic behind the violence still remained elusive.

A serviceman who had turned to nightclub-bouncer jobs and pastry catering after his military base shut down seemed to confirm the counselors' position one evening shortly before his "graduation" from the group. "I denied it before," he said of the night he pummeled his girlfriend. "I thought I'd blacked out. But looking back at that night, I didn't black out. I was feeling good. I was in power, I was strong, I was in control. I felt like a man." But what struck me most strongly was what he said next: that moment of control had been the only one in his recent life. "That feeling of power," he said, "didn't last long. Only until they put the cuffs on. Then I was feeling again like I was no man at all."

He was typical in this regard. The men I got to know in the group had, without exception, lost their compass in the world. They had lost or were losing jobs, homes, cars, families. They had been labeled outlaws but felt like castoffs. There was something almost absurd about these men struggling, week after week, to recognize themselves as dominators when they were so clearly dominated, done in by the world.

Underlying all the disagreement over what is confusing and unnerving to men runs a constant line of thinking that blinds us—whatever our political beliefs—to the nature of the male predicament. Ask feminists to diagnose men's problems and you will often get a very clear explanation: men are in crisis because women are properly challenging male dominance. Ask antifeminists and you will get a diagnosis that is, in one respect, similar. Men are troubled, many conservative pundits say, because women have gone far beyond their demands for equal treatment and now are trying to take power away from men.

The veterans of World War II were eager to embrace a manly ideal that revolved around providing rather than dominating. Ultimately, society double-crossed them.

Both the feminist and antifeminist views are rooted in a peculiarly modern American perception that to be a man means you are at the controls at all times. The popular feminist joke that men are to blame for everything is the flip side of the "family values" reactionary expectation that men should be in charge of everything.

The man controlling his environment is today the prevailing American image of masculinity. He is to be in the driver's seat, the king of the road, forever charging down the open highway, along that masculine Möbius strip that cycles endlessly through a numbing stream of movies, TV shows, novels, advertisements and pop tunes. He's a man because he won't be stopped. He'll fight attempts to tamp him down; if he has to, he'll use his gun. But we forget the true Daniel Boone frontiersmanship was only incidentally violent, and was based on creating, out of wilderness, a communal context to which a man could moor himself through work and family.

Modern debates about how men are exercising or abusing their control and power neglect to raise whether a lack of mooring, a lack of context, is causing men's anguish. If men are the masters of their fate, what do they do about the unspoken sense that they are being mastered, in the marketplace and at home, by forces that seem to be sweeping away the soil beneath their feet? If men are mythologized as the ones who make things happen, then how can they begin to analyze what is happening to them?

More than a quarter century ago, women began to free themselves from the box in which they were trapped by feeling their way along its contours, figuring out how it was shaped and how it shaped them. Women were able to take action, paradoxically, by understanding how they were acted upon. Men feel the contours of a box, too, but they are told that box is of their own manufacture, designed to their specifications. Who are they to complain? For men to say they feel boxed in is regarded not as laudable political protest but as childish whining. How dare the kings complain about their castles?

What happened to so disturb the sons of the World War II GIs? The prevailing narrative that the sons inherited—fashioned from the battlefronts of Europe and the Pacific, laid out in countless newspapers, newsreels and movies—was a tale of successful fatherhood and masculine transformation: boys whose Depression-era fathers could neither provide for them nor guide them into manhood were placed under the benevolent wing of a vast male-run orphanage called the army and sent into battle. There, firm but kindly senior officers acting as surrogate fathers watched over them as they were tempered into men in the heat of a heroic struggle against malevolent enemies. The boys, molded into men, would return to find wives, form their families and take their places as adults in the community of a nation taking its place as a grown-up power in the world.

This was the story America told itself in dozens of war movies in which tough but tenderhearted commanding officers prepared their appreciative "boys" to assume their responsibilities in male society. It was the theme behind the 1949 film "Sands of Iwo Jima," with John Wayne as Sergeant Stryker, a stern papa molding his wet-behind-the-ears charges into a capable fraternity. "Before I'm through with you, you're gonna move like one man and think like one man," he tells them. "If I can't teach you one way, I'll teach you another, but I'm gonna get the job done." And he gets the job done, fathering a whole squad of youngsters into communal adulthood.

The veterans of World War II were eager to embrace a masculine ideal that revolved around providing rather than dominating. Their most important experiences had centered on the support they had given one another in the war, and it was this that they wished to replicate. As artilleryman Win Stracke told oral historian Studs Terkel in "The Good War," he came home bearing this most cherished memory: "You had 15 guys who for the first time in their lives could help each other without cutting each other's throat or trying to put down somebody else through a boss or whatever. I had realized it was the absence of competition and all those phony standards that created the thing I loved about the army."

The fathers who would sire the baby-boom generation would try to pass that experience of manhood on intact to their sons. The grunts who went overseas and liberated the world came home to the expectation that they would liberate the country by quiet industry and caretaking. The vets threw themselves into their federally funded educations, and later their defense-funded corporate and production-line jobs, and their domestic lives in Veterans Administration-financed tract homes. They hoped their dedication would be in the service of a higher national aim.

For their children, the period of soaring expectations that followed the war was truly the era of the boy. It was the culture of "Father Knows Best" and "Leave It to Beaver," of Pop Warner rituals and Westinghouse science scholarships, of BB guns and rocket clubs, of football practice and lettered jackets, of magazine ads where "Dad" seemed always to be beaming down at his scampy, cowboy-suited younger son or proudly handing his older son the keys to a brand-new convertible. It was a world where, regardless of the truth that lay behind each garden gate, popular culture led us to believe that fathers were spending every leisure moment in roughhouse play and model-air-plane construction with their beloved boys.

GONE TO SOLDIERS EVERY ONE

Michael Bernhardt went to Vietnam to honor his sense of justice. But the war destroyed his idea of manhood.

The Dogs of War

As far back as Michael Bernhardt could remember watching World War II movies, he could remember wanting to serve. The summers of his boyhood in the backyards of Long Island were one long idyll of war play on an imagined European front. "We had leaders," he said. "We attacked things with dirt bombs. We thought war was where we'd all go in together like D-Day and be part of this big coordinated army that would *do* something. And then you'd come back and have war stories to tell."

At his father's urging, Bernhardt headed off to college. But his mind was still on a military career. He joined not only Army ROTC but a special elite unit run by the Green Berets. Then in 1967, in the middle of his sophomore year, he dropped out and enlisted in the Army. He had only the haziest sense of what was going on in Vietnam: "It appeared to be about a small country that was having communism shoved down its throat, while we were trying, at least *ostensibly*, to give people a chance to do what they wanted to do. If I didn't go, somebody'd have to go in my place, which went against everything I'd grown up with."

Bernhardt ended up in Vietnam with Charlie Company, on the ground as a horrified witness to the My Lai massacre. He was the first soldier to break the silence and talk in public about what had happened in the face of the Army's cover-up. That decision caused great tension with the father he loved. "He believed that dissent and opposition to the government were uncalled for," said Bernhardt. "He never doubted authority. Nor did I. Up until Vietnam, it never occurred to me that I'd be opposed to the authorities, not in a million years."

After Bernhardt left the Army, he found himself sinking into another quagmire, the collapsing American economy of the 1970s. He bounced around Florida, working on a land surveyor's crew, then at a sign shop that made billboards for Sheraton and Kmart. He lived in a trailer, parked in a vacationer's lot on the Gulf of Mexico. But it wasn't really the recession that threw his peacetime life into disarray. Vietnam had changed forever his idea of a code of masculinity. "For years, I had been asking myself, did I do the right stuff? And I had thought that you just added it all up and you could say, This is my manliness score. You get points for going through the service, and bonus points for extra military stuff, and points for a job and a marriage and kids. But it didn't add up. There were all these people walking around with a high score who weren't much of a man in my estimation." Finally, he stopped keeping score, went back to college and got a degree in biology. He married and bought 10 acres of land in the Florida panhandle where he and his wife keep horses and a dozen stray dogs and cats. "In Charlie Company, cowardice and courage was all turned around. If you showed any sign of caring, it was seen as a sign of weakness. If you were the least bit concerned about the civilians, you were considered pathetic, definitely not a man." Now he's turned that experience around once more. "If you can define your manhood in terms of caring," he said, "then maybe we can come back from all that."

S.F.

In the aspiring middle-class suburb where I came of age, there was no mistaking the belief in the boy's pre-eminence; it was evident in the solicitous attentions of parents and schoolteachers, in the centrality of Cub Scouts and Little League, in the community life that revolved around boys' championships and boys' scores—as if these outposts of tract-home America had been built mainly as exhibition rings for junior-male achievement, which perhaps they had.

The "New Frontier" of space turned out to be a void no man could conquer, let alone colonize. The astronaut was no Daniel Boone, just a flattened image for TV viewers to watch.

The speech that inaugurated the shiny new era of the 1960s was the youthful John F. Kennedy's address to the Democratic National Convention, a month before the launch of Echo. The words would become, along with his Inaugural oration, a haunting refrain in adolescent male consciousness. What Kennedy implicitly presented was a new rite of passage for an untested male generation. "The New Frontier of which I speak is not a set of promises," he told them. "It is a set of challenges." Kennedy understood that it was not enough for the fathers to win the world for their sons; the sons had to feel they had won it for themselves. If the fathers had their Nazis and "Nips," then Kennedy would see to it that the sons had an enemy, too. He promised as much on Inauguration Day in 1961, when he spoke vaguely but unremittingly of communism's threat, of a country that would be defined by its readiness to "pay any price" and "oppose any foe." The fight was the thing, the only thing, if America was to retain its masculinity.

The drumrolls promised a dawning era of superpower manhood to the boy born on the New Frontier, a masculine honor and pride in exchange for his loyalty. Ultimately, the boy was double-crossed. The fix was in from the start: corporate and cold-war America's promise to continue the World War II GI's wartime experience of belonging, of meaningful engagement in a mission, was never authentic. "The New Frontier" of space turned out to be a void that no man could conquer, let along colonize. The astronaut was no Daniel Boone; he was just a flattened image for TV viewers to watch—and eventually, to be bored by. Instead of sending its sons to Normandy, the government dispatched them to Vietnam, where the enemy was unclear and the mission remained a tragic mystery. The massive managerial bureaucracies of postwar "white collar" employment, especially the defense contractors fat on government largesse, produced "organization men" who often didn't even know what they were managing—and who suspected they weren't really needed at all. What these corporations offered was a secure job, not a vital role—and not even that secure. The postwar fathers' submission to the national-security state would, after a prosperous period of historically brief duration, be rewarded with pink slips, with massive downsizing, union-breaking and outsourcing. The boy who had been told he was going to be the master of the universe and all that was in it found himself master of nothing.

As early as 1957, the boy's diminished future was foreshadowed in a classic sci-fi film. In "The Incredible Shrinking Man," Scott Carey has a good job, a suburban home, a pleasure boat, a pretty wife. And yet, after he passes through a mist of atomic radiation while on a boating vacation in the Pacific, something happens. As he tells his wife in horror, "I'm getting smaller, Lou, every day."

As Carey quite literally shrinks, the promises made to him are broken one by one. The employer who was to give him lifetime economic security fires him. He is left with only feminine defenses, to hide in a doll house, to fight a giant spider with a sewing pin. And it turns out that the very source of his diminishment is implicitly an atomic test by his own government. His only hope is to turn himself into a celebrated freak and sell his story to the media. "I'm a big man!" Carey says with bitter sarcasm. "I'm famous! One more joke for the world to laugh at."

The more Carey shrinks, the more he strikes out at those around him. "Every day I became more tyrannical," he comments, "more monstrous in my domination of my wife." It's a line that would ring a bell for any visitor to the Alternatives to Violence group and for any observer of the current male scene. As the male role has diminished amid a sea of betrayed promises, many men have been driven to more domineering and some even "monstrous" displays in their frantic quest for a meaningful showdown.

The Ornamental Culture

IF FEW MEN WOULD DO WHAT Shawn Nelson did one evening in the spring of 1995, many could relate. A former serviceman whose career in an army tank unit had gone nowhere, a plumber who had lost his job, a former husband whose wife had left him, the 35-year-old Nelson broke into the National Guard armory, commandeered an M-60 army tank and drove it through the streets of San Diego, flattening fire hy-

drants, crushing 40 cars, downing enough utility poles to cut off electricity to 5,000 people. He was at war with the domestic world that he once thought he was meant to build and defend. He was going to drive that tank he had been meant to command if it killed him. And it did. The police shot Shawn Nelson to death through the turret hatch.

If a man could not get the infrastructure to work for him, he could at least tear it down. If the nation would not provide an enemy to fight, he could go to war at home. If there was to be no brotherhood, he would take his stand alone. A handful of men would attempt to gun down enemies they imagined they saw in family court, employee parking lots, McDonald's restaurants, a Colorado schoolhouse and, most notoriously, a federal office building in Oklahoma. A far greater number would move their destruction of the elusive enemy to the fantasy realm to a clear-cut and controllable world of action movies and video combat, televised athletic tournaments and pay-per-view ultimate-fighting bouts.

But none of it would satisfy, because the world and the fight had changed.

What is left out of the nostalgia of baby-boom men for their heroic World War II fathers is how devastatingly unfathered and unprepared for manhood some of those sons were

---

A few glamorous men understood intuitively that in the coming media and entertainment age the team of men at work would be replaced by the individual man on display. Elevated onto the new pedestal of mass media and entertainment, they were unreachable. Like the astronauts who were their forebears, the new celebrated men—media stars, moussed models, telegenic baby moguls—existed in a realm from which all lines to their brothers had been cut. Where we once lived in a society in which men participated by being useful in public life, we now are surrounded by a culture that encourages people to play almost no functional public roles, only decorative or consumer ones.

Ornamental culture has proved the ultimate expression of the century, sweeping away institutions in which men felt some

sense of belonging and replacing them with visual spectacles that they can only watch and that benefit global commercial forces they cannot fathom. Celebrity culture's effects on men go far beyond the obvious showcasing of action heroes and rock musicians. The ordinary man is no fool: he knows he can't be Arnold Schwarzenegger. Nonetheless, the culture re-shapes his most basic sense of manhood by telling him that masculinity is something to drape over the body, not draw from inner resources; that it is personal, not societal; that manhood is displayed, not demonstrated. The internal qualities once said to embody manhood—surefootedness, inner strength, confidence of purpose—are merchandised to men to enhance their manliness. What passes for the essence of masculinity is being extracted and bottled and sold back to men. Literally, in the case of Viagra.

The culture that '90s men are stranded in was birthed by their fathers' generation—by men who, weary of Depression and wartime deprivation, embraced the new commercialized American dream. What gets left out of the contemporary nostalgia of baby-boom men for their World War II fathers—evidenced in the huge appetite for the film "Saving Private Ryan" and books like Tom Brokaw's "The Greatest Generation"—is what those fathers did after the war. When "Dateline NBC" produced a documentary based on Brokaw's book, celebrating the World War II "tougher than tough" heroes, especially relative to their pampered sons, the troubling subtext was how devastatingly unfathered those sons were, how inadequately they'd been prepared for manhood by their "heroic" fathers.

The men I came to know in the course of researching this book talked about their father's failures in the most private and personal terms, pointing inevitably to the small daily letdowns: "My father didn't teach me how to throw a ball" or "My father was always at work." That their fathers had emotionally or even literally abandoned the family circle was painful enough. But these men suspected, in some way hard to grasp, that their fathers had deserted them in the public realm, too. "My father never taught me how to be a man" was the refrain I heard over and over again. Down the generations, the father wasn't simply a good sport who bought his son a car for graduation. He was a human bridge connecting the boy to an adult life of public engagement and responsibility.

WHAT'S TROUBLING TROUBLED BOYS

As old measures of masculinity faded, the swaggering boys of the Spur Posse made a game of sexual conquest

Who's Keeping Score

The Spur Posse burst out of the orderly suburb of Lakewood, Calif., as America's dreaded nightmare—teenage boys run amok, a microcosm of a misogynistic and violent male culture. In March 1993 police arrested nine Spurs, ages 15 to 19, on suspicion of nearly 20 counts of sexual crimes. In the end, prosecutors concluded that the sex was consensual and all but one count were dropped. But for a time that spring, it was difficult to flip the channels without running into one Spur or another, strutting and bragging their way through the TV talk shows. "You gotta get your image out there," explained Billy Shehan, then 19, a Spur who was not among those arrested but who, despite honor grades and a promising future, felt compelled to hit the media circuit. "It all about building that image on a worldwide basis." Tirelessly, the Spurs repeated the details of their sex-for-points intramural contest, in which each time you had sex with a girl you racked up a point. And for four years running, the winner was Billy Shehan—with a final score of 67.

The media-paid trip that Billy took to New York City with two fellow Spurs started out with many promises. "First they said to us, 'New York! For free!'" Billy recalled. "'We'll give you $1,000, and you'll have limos every day, and elegant meals, and elegant this and elegant that.'" On the ride from the airport to the hotel, Billy felt like a long-exiled prince come to claim his kingdom. "Here I was in this limo in this giant-ass city, and it was like I owned the taxis and the cars, I owned the buildings and all the girls in the windows in the buildings. I felt like I could do whatever I wanted. I had instant exposure."

For the next week and a half, the shows vied for the Spurs' attention. "For 11 days, these guys were our best friends," Billy said of the TV producers. "They showered admiration on us." One night, Billy said, a senior staffer from "Night Talk With Jane Whitney" took them in a limo to a strip bar, a club in Queens called Goldfingers. "The Maury Povich Show" wooed the boys by sending them our for the evening with four young women from the program's staff. Afterward, the Spurs took a cab to Times Square. "Everything was a fantasy," Billy recalled, "like I was in Mauryland. Like the whole city was a talk show." Billy had his tape recorder out, and he was talking into it as he walked. Suddenly, two hands reached out from the darkness and yanked him between two buildings. "He was holding something against me that felt like a gun," Billy said. The man ripped the tape recorder out of his hands, extracted his wallet and fled. Billy lay in his hotel room all night listening to his heart pound. The next morning he phoned the staff of "The Maury Povich Show" and demanded that they reimburse him for the robbery. When they declined, he refused to go on the program. "I felt they owed me something."

Billy did, however, make an appearance on "Night Talk With Jane Whitney," where he would be much vilified for his boast about scoring his 67th point that week with a girl he lured back to his hotel room. And then he'd return home, poorer and without taped memories. "For a while when I got back," Billy said, "everybody recognized me because of the shows. But now…" His voice trailed off. "Uh, you know something sort of funny?" he said. "I didn't get that [final sex] point. The producer said, 'Act like you got a point on the show.' So I did." He gave a short, bitter laugh. "I even wrote a song about it later. 'Everyone thought I was a 67, when I was just a 66.'"

S.F.

The guiding standards of the fathers, the approving paternal eye, has nearly vanished in this barren new landscape, to be replaced by the market-share standards of a commercial culture, the ogling, ever-restless eye of the camera. By the end of the century, every outlet of the consumer world—magazines, ads, movies, sports, music videos—would deliver the message that manhood had become a performance game to be won in the marketplace, not the workplace, and that male anger was now part of the show. An ornamental culture encouraged young men to see surliness, hostility and violence as expressions of glamour. Whether in Maxim magazine or in Brut's new "Neanderthal" ads, boorishness became a way for men to showcase themselves without being feminized before a potentially girlish mirror. But if celebrity masculinity enshrined the pose of the "bad boy," his rebellion was largely cosmetic. There was nowhere for him to take a grievance because there was no society to take it to. In a celebrity culture, earnestness about social and political change was replaced by a pose of "irony" that was really just a sullen and helpless paralysis.

In a culture of ornament, manhood is defined by appearance, by youth and attractiveness, by money and aggression, by posture and swagger and "props," by the curled lip and flexed biceps, by the glamour of the cover boy and by the market-bartered "individuality" that sets one astronaut or athlete or gangster above another. These are the same traits that have long been designated as the essence of feminine vanity—the objectification and mirror-gazing that women have denounced as trivializing and humiliating qualities imposed on them by a misogynist culture. No wonder men are in such agony. At the close of the century, men find themselves in an unfamiliar world where male worth is measured only by participation in a celebrity-driven consumer culture and awarded by lady luck.

The more I consider what men have lost—a useful role in public life, a way of earning a decent living, respectful treatment in the culture—the more it seems that men are falling into a status oddly similar to that of women at midcentury. The '50s housewife, stripped of her connections to a wider world and invited to fill the void with shopping and the ornamental display of her ultrafemininity, could be said to have morphed into the '90s man, stripped of his connections to a wider world and invited to fill the void with consumption and a gym-bred display of his ultramasculinity. The empty compensations of a "feminine mystique" are transforming into the empty compensations of a masculine mystique, with a gentlemen's cigar club no more satisfying than a ladies' bake-off.

But women have rebelled against this mystique. Of all the bedeviling questions my travels and research raised, none struck me more than this: why don't contemporary men rise up in protest against their betrayal? If they have experienced so many of the same injuries as women, the same humiliations, why don't they challenge the culture as women did? Why can't men seem to act?

The stock answers don't suffice. Men aren't simply refusing to "give up the reins of power," as some feminists have argued. The reins have already slipped from most of their hands. Nor are men merely chary of expressing pain and neediness, particularly in an era where emoting is the coin of the commercial realm. While the pressures on men to imagine themselves in control of their emotions are impediments to male revolt, a more fundamental obstacle overshadows them. If men have feared to tread where women have rushed in, then maybe women have had it easier in one very simple regard: women could frame their struggle as a battle against men.

For the many women who embraced feminism in one way or another in the 1970s, that consumer culture was not some intangible force; they saw it as a cudgel wielded by men against women. The mass culture's portfolio of sexist images was propaganda to prop up the myth of male superiority, the argument went. Men, not the marketplace, many women believed, were the root problem and so, as one feminist activist put it in 1969, "the task of the women's liberation movement is to collectively combat male domination in the home, in bed, on the job." And indeed, there were virulent, sexist attitudes to confront. But the 1970s model of confrontation could get feminism only halfway to its goal.

The women who engaged in the feminist campaigns of the '70s were able to take advantage of a ready-made model for revolt. Ironically, it was a male strategy. Feminists had a clearly defined oppressive enemy: the "patriarchy." They had a real frontier to conquer: all those patriarchal institutions, both the old ones that still rebuffed women, like the U.S. Congress or U.S. Steel, and the new ones that tried to remold women, like Madison Avenue or the glamour and media-pimp kingdoms of Bert Parks and Hugh Hefner. Feminists also had their own army of "brothers": sisterhood. Each GI Jane who participated in this struggle felt useful. Whether she was

working in a women's-health clinic or tossing her bottles of Clairol in a "freedom trash can," she was part of a greater glory, the advancement of her entire sex. Many women whose lives were touched by feminism felt in some way that they had reclaimed an essential usefulness; together, they had charged the barricades that kept each of them from a fruitful, thriving life.

The male paradigm of confrontation, in which an enemy could be identified, contested and defeated, proved useful to activists in the civil-rights movement, the antiwar movement, the gay-rights movement. It was, in fact, the fundamental organizing principle of virtually every concerted countercultural campaign of the last half century. Yet it could launch no "men's movement." Herein lies the critical paradox, and the source of male inaction: the model women have used to revolt is the exact one men not only can't use but are trapped in.

Men have no clearly defined enemy who is oppressing them. How can men be oppressed when the culture has already identified them as the oppressors, and when even they see themselves that way? As one man wrote plaintively to Promise Keepers, "I'm like a kite with a broken string, but I'm also holding the tail." Men have invented antagonists to make their problems visible, but with the passage of time, these culprits—scheming feminists, affirmative-action proponents, job-grabbing illegal aliens—have come to seem increasingly unconvincing as explanations for their situation. Nor do men have a clear frontier on which to challenge their intangible enemies. What new realms should they be gaining—the media, entertainment and image-making institutions of corporate America? But these are institutions already run by men; how can men invade their own territory? Is technological progress the frontier? Why then does it seem to be pushing men into obsolescence, socially and occupationally? And if the American man crushes the machine, whose machine has he vanquished?

The male paradigm of confrontation has proved worthless to men. Yet maybe that's not so unfortunate. The usefulness of that model has reached a point of exhaustion anyway. The women's movement and the other social movements have discovered its limits. Their most obvious enemies have been sent into retreat, yet the problems persist. While women are still outnumbered in the executive suites, many have risen in the ranks and some have

achieved authoritative positions often only to perpetuate the same transgressions as their male predecessors. Women in power in the media, advertising and Hollywood have for the most part continued to generate the same sorts of demeaning images as their male counterparts. Blaming a cabal of men has taken feminism about as far as it can go. That's why women have a great deal at stake in the liberation of the one population uniquely poised to discover and employ a new paradigm—men.

Beyond the Politics of Confrontation

THERE ARE SIGNS THAT MEN ARE seeking such a breakthrough. When the Million Man March and Promise Keepers attracted record numbers of men, pundits scratched their heads—why would so many men want to attend events that offered no battle plan, no culprit to confront? No wonder critics who were having trouble placing the gatherings in the usual frame of political conflict found it easier to focus their attentions on the reactionary and hate-mongering attitudes of the "leaders" of these movements, concluding that the real "agenda" must be the anti-Semitism of the Nation of Islam's Louis Farrakhan or the homophobia and sexism of Promise Keepers founder Bill McCartney. But maybe the men who attended these mass gatherings weren't looking for answers that involved an enemy. As Farrakhan's speech, chock-full of conspiracy theories and numerological codes, dragged on, men in droves hastened for the exits. "What was really fantastic about the day was just being together with all these men, and thinking about what I might do differently," George Henderson, a 48-year-old social worker, told me as he headed out early. The amassing of huge numbers of men was a summoning of courage for the unmapped journey ahead.

American men have generally responded well as caretakers in times of crisis, whether that be in wars, depressions or natural disasters. The pre-eminent contemporary example of such a male mobilization also comes on the heels of a crisis: gay men's response to AIDS. Virtually overnight, just as the Depression-era Civilian Conservation Corps built dams and parks and salvaged farmland, so have gay men built a network of clinics, legal and psychological services, fund-raising and political-action brigades, meals on wheels, even laundry assistance. The courage of these caregivers has generated, even in this homophobic nation, a wellspring of admiration and respect. They had a job to do and they did it.

Social responsibility is not the special province of masculinity; it's the lifelong work of all citizens in a community where people are knit together by meaningful and mutual concerns. But if husbanding a society is not the exclusive calling of "husbands," all the better for men's future. Because as men struggle to free them-selves from their crisis, their task is not, in the end, to figure out how to be mascu-line—rather, their masculinity lies in figur-ing out how to be human. The men who worked at the Long Beach Naval Shipyard, where I spent many months, didn't go there and learn their crafts as riggers, weld-ers and boilermakers to be masculine; they were seeking something worthwhile to do. Their sense of their own manhood flowed out of their utility in a society, not the other way around.

And so with the mystery of men's non-rebellion comes the glimmer of an open-ing, a chance for men to forge a rebellion commensurate with women's and, in the course of it, to create a new paradigm for human progress that will open doors for both sexes. That was, and continues to be, feminism's dream, to create a freer, more humane world. It will remain a dream without the strength and courage of men who are today faced with a historic oppor-tunity: to learn to wage a battle against no enemy, to own a frontier of human liberty, to act in the service of a brotherhood that includes us all.

Reprinted from *Newsweek*, September 13, 1999, pp. 48-58. Excerpted from *Stiffed: The Betrayal of the American Man*, © 1999 by Susan Faludi. Reprinted by permission of William Morrow/HarperCollins Publishers, Inc.

Coping with CROWDING

A persistent and popular view holds that high population density inevitably leads to violence. This myth, which is based on rat research, applies neither to us nor to other primates

by Frans B. M. de Waal, Filippo Aureli and Peter G. Judge

In 1962 this magazine published a seminal paper by experimental psychologist John B. Calhoun entitled "Population Density and Social Pathology." The article opened dramatically with an observation by the late 18th-century English demographer Thomas Malthus that human population growth is automatically followed by increased vice and misery. Calhoun went on to note that although we know overpopulation causes disease and food shortage, we understand virtually nothing about its behavioral impact.

This reflection had inspired Calhoun to conduct a nightmarish experiment. He placed an expanding rat population in a crammed room and observed that the rats soon set about killing, sexually assaulting and, eventually, cannibalizing one another. Much of this activity happened among the occupants of a central feeding section. Despite the presence of food elsewhere in the room, the rats were irresistibly drawn to the social stimulation—even though many of them could not reach the central food dispensers. This pathological togetherness, as Calhoun described it, as well as the attendant chaos and behavioral deviancy, led him to coin the phrase "behavioral sink."

In no time, popularizers were comparing politically motivated street riots to rat packs, inner cities to behavioral sinks and urban areas to zoos. Warning that society was heading for either anarchy or dictatorship, Robert Ardrey, an American science journalist, remarked in 1970 on the voluntary nature of human crowding: "Just as Calhoun's rats freely

chose to eat in the middle pens, we freely enter the city." Calhoun's views soon became a central tenet of the voluminous literature on aggression.

In extrapolating from rodents to people, however, these thinkers and writers were making a gigantic leap of faith. A look at human populations suggests why such a simple extrapolation is so problematic. Compare, for instance, per capita murder rates with the number of people per square kilometer in different nations—as we did, using data from the United Nations' *1996 Demographic Yearbook*. If things were straightforward, the two ought to vary in tandem. Instead there is no statistically meaningful relation.

But, one could argue, perhaps such a relation is obscured by variation in national income level, political organization or some other variable. Apparently not, at least for income. We divided the nations into three categories—free-market, former East Block and Third World—and did the analysis again. This time we did find one significant correlation, but it was in the other direction: it showed more violent crime in the least crowded countries of the former East Block. A similar trend existed for free-market nations, among which the U.S. had by far the highest homicide rate despite its low overall population density. The Netherlands had a population density 13 times as high, but its homicide rate was eight times lower.

Knowing that crime is generally more common in urban areas than it is in the

countryside, we factored in the proportion of each nation's population that lives in large cities and controlled for it. But this correction did nothing to bring about a positive correlation between population density and homicide. Perhaps because of the overriding effects of history and culture, the link between available space and human aggression—if it exists at all—is decidedly not clear-cut.

Even if we look at small-scale human experiments, we find no supporting evidence. Crowding of children and college students, for instance, sometimes produced irritation and mild aggression, but in general, people seemed adept at avoiding conflict. Andrew S. Baum and his co-workers in the psychiatry department at the Uniformed Services University found that dormitory residents who shared facilities with many people spent less time socializing and kept the doors to their rooms closed more often than did students who had more space. Baum concluded that the effects of crowding are not nearly as overwhelming as originally presumed. Published in the 1980s, these and other findings began to undermine, at least in the scientific community, the idea that people and rats react in the same ways to being packed together. In modern society, people commonly assemble in large masses—during their daily commute to work or during holiday-season shopping expeditions—and most of the time they control their behavior extraordinarily well.

RHESUS MONKEYS from three different settings show different rates of grooming—that is, of calming one another. The monkeys seem to adapt to crowded conditions by grooming more frequently. Among the males, grooming of each other and of females was more common when they lived in crowded conditions than when they lived in more spacious quarters. Among female non-kin, aggression was common and increased further with crowding but was accompanied by increased grooming, which served to reduce conflicts.

Calhoun's model, we must conclude, does not generally apply to human behavior. Is this because our culture and intelligence makes us unique, or is the management of crowding part of an older heritage? To answer this question, we turn to the primates.

PRIMATES ARE NOT RATS

Primate research initially appeared to support the harrowing scenario that had been presented for rats. In the 1960s scientists reported that city-dwelling monkeys in India were more aggressive than were those living in forests. Others claimed that monkeys in zoos were excessively violent. Those monkeys were apparently ruled by terrifying bullies who dominated a social hierarchy that was considered an artifact of captivity—in other words, in the wild, peace and egalitarianism prevailed. Borrowing from the hyperbole of popularizers, one study of crowding in small captive groups of baboons even went so far as to report a "ghetto riot."

As research progressed, however, conflicting evidence accumulated. Higher population density seemed to increase aggression occasionally—but the opposite was also true. One report, for instance, described intense fighting and killing when a group of macaques were released into a corral 73 times *larger* than their previous quarters had been. Then, after two and a half years in the corral, a similar increase in aggression occurred when the monkeys were crowded back into a small pen.

Whereas the macaque study manipulated population density through environmental change, other early research did so by adding new monkeys to existing groups. Given the xenophobic nature of monkeys, these tests mainly measured their hostile attitude toward strangers, which is quite different from the effect of density. The better controlled the studies became, the less clear-cut the picture turned out to be. Increased population density led to increased aggression in only 11 of the 17 best-designed studies of the past few decades.

In the meantime, the view of wild primates was changing. They were no longer the purely peaceful, egalitarian creatures people had presumed them to be. In the 1970s field-workers began reporting sporadic but lethal violence in a wide range of species—from macaques to chimpanzees—as well as strict and well-defined hierarchies that remained stable for decades. This view of an often anxiety-filled existence was confirmed when researchers found high levels of the stress hormone cortisol in the blood of wild monkeys [see "Stress in the Wild," by Robert M. Sapolsky; SCIENTIFIC AMERICAN, JANUARY 1990].

As the view of primates became more complex, and as the rat scenario was weakened by counterexamples, researchers began to wonder whether primates had developed a means to reduce conflict in crowded situations. We saw the first hint of this possibility in a study of the world's largest zoo colony of chimpanzees in Arnhem, the Netherlands. The apes lived on a spacious, forested island in the summer but were packed together in a heated building during the winter. Despite a 20-fold reduction in space, aggression increased only slightly. In fact, the effect of crowding was not entirely negative: friendly grooming and greetings, such as kissing and submissive bowing, increased as well.

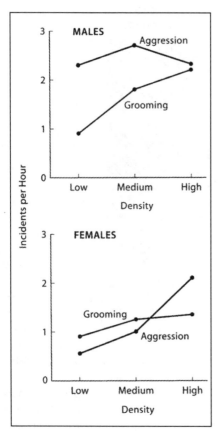

SOURCE: Peter G. Judge and Frans B.M. de Waal

BRYAN CHRISTIE

We wondered if this conciliatory behavior mitigated tension and proposed a way to test this possibility. Without ignoring the fact that crowding increases the potential for conflict, we predicted that primates employ counterstrategies—including avoiding potential aggressors and offering appeasement or reassuring body contact. Because some of the skills involved are probably acquired, the most effective coping responses would be expected in animals who have experienced high density for a long time. Perhaps they develop a different "social culture" in the same way that people in different places have varying standards of privacy and interpersonal comfort zones. For example, studies show that white North Americans and the British keep greater distances from others during conversations than Latin Americans and Arabs do.

FRANS B. M. DE WAAL

CHIMPANZEES IN THE WILD have hostile territorial relations with other groups, and in captivity they are bothered by the presence of noisy neighboring chimps. By examining apes under three conditions—those living in a crowded space and able to hear their neighbors, those living in a crowded space without such worrisome sounds, and those living in isolated large compounds (photograph right)—we were able to measure the association between aggression, space and stress. Aggression (photograph above) remained the same, but stress varied with neighbors' noise. Chimpanzees in small spaces exposed to vocalizations from other groups showed the highest levels of the stress hormone cortisol.

COPING CULTURE

We set about finding several populations of monkeys that were of the same species but that had been living in different conditions to see if their behavior varied in discernible ways. We collected detailed data on 122 individual rhesus monkeys at three different sites in the U.S.: in relatively cramped outdoor pens at the Wisconsin primate center in Madison, in large open corrals at the Yerkes primate center in Atlanta and on Morgan Island off the coast of South Carolina. These last monkeys had approximately 2,000 times more space per individual than the highest-density groups. All three groups had lived together for many years, often for generations, and included individuals of both sexes. All the groups had also been in human care, receiving food and veterinary treatment, making them comparable in that regard as well.

Rhesus society typically consists of a number of subgroups, known as matrilines, of related females and their offspring. Females remain together for life, whereas males leave their natal group at puberty. Rhesus monkeys make a sharp distinction between kin and non-kin: by far the most friendly contact, such as groom-

FRANS B.M. DE WAAL

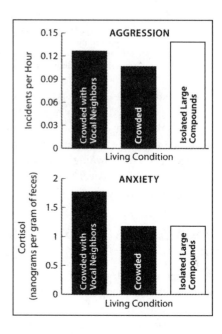

BRYAN CHRISTIE

ing, takes place within the matrilines. Females of one matriline also fiercely support one another in fights against other matrilines. Because of their strict hierarchy and pugnacious temperament, rhesus seemed to be ideal subjects. We figured that if this aggressive primate showed coping responses, our hypothesis would have withstood its most rigorous test.

Our first finding was, surprisingly, that density did not affect male aggressiveness. Adult males increasingly engaged in friendly contact under crowded conditions. They groomed females more, and likewise the females groomed the males more frequently. (Grooming is a calming behavior. In another study, we demonstrated that a monkey's heart rate slows down when it is being groomed.) Females also bared their teeth more often to the males—the rhesus way of communicating low status and appeasing potentially aggressive dominant monkeys.

Females showed a different response with other females, however. Within their own matrilines they fought more but did not change the already high level of friendly interaction. In their dealings with other matrilines, they also showed more aggression—but here it was coupled with more grooming and submissive grinning.

These findings make sense in light of the differences between kin and non-kin relationships. Related females—such as sisters and mothers and daughters—are so strongly bonded that their relationships are unlikely to be disrupted by antagonism. Rhesus monkeys are used to managing intrafamilial conflict, cycling through fights and reconciliations, followed by comforting contact. Crowding does little to change this, except that they may have to repair frayed family ties more often. Between matrilines, on the other hand, crowding poses a serious challenge. Normally, friendly contact between matrilines is rare and antagonism common. But reduced escape opportunities make the risk of escalated conflict greater in a confined space. And our data indicated that female rhesus monkeys make a concerted effort at improving these potentially volatile relationships.

EMOTIONS IN CHECK

In a second project, we turned our attention to chimpanzees. As our closest animal relatives, chimpanzees resemble us in appearance, psychology and cognition. Their social organization is also humanlike, with well-developed male bonding—which is rare in nature—reciprocal exchange and a long dependency of offspring on the mother. In the wild, male chimpanzees are extremely territorial, sometimes invading neighboring territories and killing enemy males. In captivity such encounters are, of course, prevented.

We collected data on more than 100 chimpanzees in various groups at the Yerkes primate center. Although some groups had only a tenth the space of others, cramped quarters had no measurable impact on aggression. In contrast to the monkeys, chimpanzees maintained their grooming and appeasement behavior—no matter the situation. If crowding did induce social tensions, our chimpanzees seemed to control them directly.

We usually do not think of animals as holding in their emotions, but chimpanzees may be different. These apes are known for deceptive behavior—for instance, they will hide hostile intentions behind a friendly face until an adversary has come within reach. In our study, emotional control was reflected in the way chimpanzees responded to the vocalizations of neighboring groups. Such noises commonly provoke hooting and charging displays, which in wild chimpanzees serve to ward off territorial intrusion.

In a confined space, however, excited reactions trigger turmoil within the group. We found that chimpanzees in the most crowded situations had a three times *lower* tendency to react to neighbors' vocalizations than chimpanzees with more space did. Chimpanzees may be smart enough to suppress responses to external stimuli if those tend to get them into trouble. Indeed, field-workers report that chimpanzee males on territorial patrol suppress all noise if being detected by their neighbors is to their disadvantage.

The inhibition of natural responses is not without cost. We know that continuous stress has the potential to suppress the immune system and therefore has important implications for health and longevity. We developed two noninvasive techniques to measure stress in our chimpanzees. One was to record the rate of self-scratching. Just as with college students who scratch their heads when faced with a tough exam question, self-scratching indicates anxiety in other primates. Our second technique was to collect fecal samples and analyze them for cortisol.

Both measures showed that groups of chimpanzees who had little space and heard neighbors' vocalizations experienced more stress. Space by itself was not a negative factor, because in the absence of noisy neighbors, chimpanzees in small spaces showed the same stress level as those with a good deal of space.

So even though chimpanzees fail to show a rise in aggression when crowded, this does not necessarily mean that they are happy and relaxed. They may be working hard to maintain the peace. Given a choice, they would prefer more room. Every spring, when the chimpanzees at the Arnhem zoo hear the door to their outdoor island being opened for the first time, they fill the building with a chorus of ecstasy. They then rush outside to engage in a pandemonium in which all of the apes, young and old, embrace and kiss and thump one another excitedly on the back.

The picture is even more complex if we also consider short periods of acute crowding. This is a daily experience in human society, whether we find ourselves on a city bus or in a movie theater. During acute crowding, rhesus monkeys show a rise in mild aggression, such as threats, but not violence. Threats serve to keep others at a distance, forestalling unwanted contact. The monkeys also avoid one another and limit active social engagement, as if they are trying to stay out of trouble by lying low.

Chimpanzees take this withdrawal tactic one step further: they are actually less aggressive when briefly crowded. Again, this reflects greater emotional restraint. Their reaction is reminiscent of people on an elevator, who reduce frictions by minimizing large body movements, eye contact and loud verbalizations. We speak of the elevator effect, therefore, as a way in which both people and other primates handle the risks of temporary closeness.

Our research leads us to conclude that we come from a long lineage of social animals capable of flexibly adjusting to all kinds of conditions, including unnatural ones such as crowded pens and city streets. The adjustment may not be without cost, but it is certainly preferable to the frightening alternative predicted on the basis of rodent studies.

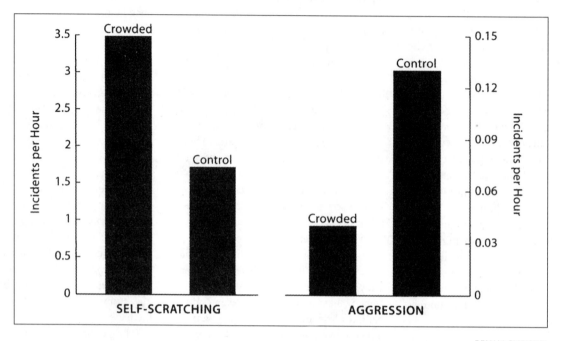

BRYAN CHRISTIE

During brief periods of crowding, people often limit social interaction—a way of avoiding any conflict. Chimpanzees do the same, reducing their aggressive interactions. This doesn't mean that crowded situations do not induce anxiety. Chimpanzees packed together tend to scratch themselves more often—a sign of stress.

We should add, though, that even the behavioral sink of Calhoun's rats may not have been entirely the product of crowding. Food competition seemed to play a role as well. This possibility contains a serious warning for our own species in an ever more populous world: the doomsayers who predict that crowding will inevitably rip the social fabric may have the wrong variable in mind. We have a natural, underappreciated talent to deal with crowding, but crowding combined with scarcity of resources is something else.

FURTHER INFORMATION

THE HIDDEN DIMENSION. E. T. Hall. Doubleday, 1966.

CROWDING. A. Baum in *Handbook of Environmental Psychology*, Vol. 1. Edited by D. Stokols and I. Altman. Wiley, 1987.

THE MYTH OF A SIMPLE RELATION BETWEEN SPACE AND AGGRESSION IN CAPTIVE PRIMATES. F. B. M. de Waal in *Zoo Biology* supplement, Vol. 1, pages 141–148; 1989.

INHIBITION OF SOCIAL BEHAVIOR IN CHIMPANZEES UNDER HIGH-DENSITY CONDITIONS. F. Aureli and F. B. M. de Waal in *American Journal of Primatology*, Vol. 41, No. 3, pages 213–228; March 1997.

RHESUS MONKEY BEHAVIOUR UNDER DIVERSE POPULATION DENSITIES: COPING WITH LONG-TERM CROWDING. P. G. Judge and F. B. M. de Waal in *Animal Behaviour*, Vol. 54, no. 3, pages 643–662; September 1997.

FRANS B. M. DE WAAL, FILIPPO AURELI and PETER G. JUDGE share a research interest in the social relationships and behavioral strategies of nonhuman primates. Their work on aspects of this topic will appear in Natural Conflict Resolution, *to be published by the University of California Press. De Waal, author of* Chimpanzee Politics *and* Good Natured, *worked for many years at the Arnhem zoo in the Netherlands before coming to the U.S., where he is now director of the Living Links Center at the Yerkes Regional Primate Research Center in Atlanta and professor of psychology at Emory University. Aureli is a senior lecturer in biological and earth sciences at Liverpool John Moores University in England. Judge is an assistant professor at Bloomsburg University in Pennsylvania and a research associate at Yerkes.*

From *Scientific American*, May 2000, pp. 76–81. © 2000 by Scientific American, Inc. Reproduced with permission. All rights reserved.

Nobody Left to Hate

by Elliot Aronson

In 1971 a highly explosive situation had developed in Austin, Texas—one that has played out in many cities across the United States. Austin's public schools had recently been desegregated and, because the city had always been residentially segregated, white youngsters, African American youngsters, and Mexican-American youngsters found themselves sharing the same classroom for the first time in their lives. Within a few weeks, long-standing suspicion, fear, distrust, and antipathy among the groups produced an atmosphere of turmoil and hostility, exploding into interethnic fistfights in corridors and schoolyards across the city.

The school superintendent called me in to see if I could do anything to help students learn to get along with one another. After observing what was going on in classrooms for a few days, my graduate students and I concluded that intergroup hostility was being exacerbated by the competitive environment of the classroom.

Let me explain. In every classroom we observed, the students worked individually and competed against one another for grades. Here is a description of a typical fifth-grade classroom we observed:

The teacher stands in front of the class, asks a question, and waits for the children to indicate that they know the answer. Most frequently, six to ten youngsters raise their hands. But they do not simply raise their hands, they lift themselves a few inches off their chairs and stretch their arms as high as they can in an attempt to attract the teacher's attention. To say they are eager to be called on is an incredible understatement. Several other students sit quietly with their eyes averted, as if trying to make themselves invisible. These are the ones who don't know the answer. Understandably, they are trying to avoid eye contact with the teacher because they do not want to be called on.

When the teacher calls on one of the eager students, there are looks of disappointment, dismay, and unhappiness on the faces of the other students who were avidly raising their hands but were not called on. If the selected student comes up with the right answer, the teacher smiles, nods approvingly, and goes on to the next question. This is a great reward for the child who happens to be called on. At the same time that the fortunate student is coming up with the right answer and being smiled upon by the teacher, an audible groan can be heard coming from the children who were striving to be called on but were ignored. It is obvious they are disappointed because they missed an opportunity to show the teacher how smart and quick they are. Perhaps they will get a chance next time. In the meantime, the students who didn't know the answer breathe a sigh of relief. They have escaped being humiliated this time.

The teacher may have started the school year with a determination to treat every student equally and encourage all of them to do their best, but the students quickly sorted themselves into different groups. The "winners" were the bright, eager, highly competitive students who fervently raised their hands, participated in discussions, and did well on tests. Understandably, the teacher felt gratified that these students responded to her teaching. She praised and encouraged them, continued to call on them, and depended on them to keep the class going at a high level and at a reasonable pace.

Then there were the "losers." At the beginning, the teacher called on them occasionally, but they almost invariably didn't know the answer, were too shy to speak, or couldn't speak English well. They seemed embarrassed to be in the spotlight; some of the other students made snide comments—sometimes under their breath, occasionally out loud. Because the schools in the poorer section of town were substandard, the African American and Mexican-American youngsters had received a poorer education prior to desegregation. Consequently, in Austin it was frequently these students who were among the "losers." This tended unfairly to confirm the unflattering stereotypes that the white kids had about minorities. The "losers" were considered stupid or lazy.

The minority students also had preconceived notions about the white kids: they considered them pushy show-offs and teachers' pets. These stereotypes were seemingly confirmed by the way most of the white students behaved in the competitive classroom.

After a while, the typical classroom teacher stopped trying to engage the students who weren't doing well. She or he felt it was kinder not to call on them and expose them to ridicule by the other students. In effect, a silent pact was made with the losers: to leave them alone as long as they weren't disruptive. Without really meaning to, the teacher gave up on these students—and so did the rest of the class. Without really meaning to, the teacher contributed to the difficulty the students were experiencing. After a while, these students tended to give up on themselves as well—perhaps believing that they *were* stupid—because they sure weren't getting it.

The jigsaw classroom facilitates interaction among all students in the class, leading them to value one another as contributors to their common task.

It required only a few days of intensive observation and interviews for us to have a pretty good idea of what was going on in these classrooms. We realized we needed to do something drastic to shift the emphasis from a relentlessly competitive atmosphere to a more cooperative one. It was in this context that we invented the *jigsaw strategy*.

THE JIGSAW CLASSROOM

Jigsaw is a specific type of group learning experience that requires everyone's cooperative effort to produce the final product. Just as in a jigsaw puzzle, each piece—each student's part—is essential for the production and full understanding of the final product. If each student's part is essential, then each student is essential. That is precisely what makes this strategy so effective.

Here's how it works. The students in a history class, for example, are divided into small groups of five or six students each. Suppose their task is to learn about World War II. In one jigsaw group, let us say that Sara is responsible for researching Hitler's rise to power in prewar Germany. Another member of the group, Steven, is assigned to cover concentration camps; Pedro is assigned Britain's role in the war; Lin is to research the contribution of the Soviet Union; Babu will handle Japan's entry into the war; and Monique will read about the development of the atom bomb. Eventually each student will come back to her or his jigsaw group and will try to present a vivid, interesting, well-organized report to the group. The situation is specifically structured so that the only access any member has to the other five assignments is by listening intently to the report of the person reciting. Thus, if Babu doesn't like Pedro or he thinks Sara is a nerd, if he heckles them or tunes out while they are reporting, he cannot possibly do well on the test that follows.

To increase the probability that each report will be factual and accurate, the students doing the research do not immediately take it back to their jigsaw group. After completing their research, they must first meet with the students from each of the jigsaw groups who had the identical assignment. For example, those students assigned to the atom bomb topic meet together to work as a team of specialists, gathering information, discussing ideas, becoming experts on their topic, and rehearsing their presentations. This is called the "expert" group. It is particularly useful for those students who might have initial difficulty learning or organizing their part of the assignment for it allows them to benefit from listening to and rehearsing with other "experts," to pick up strategies of presentation, and generally to bring themselves up to speed.

After this meeting, when each presenter is up to speed, the jigsaw groups reconvene in their initial heterogeneous configuration. The atom bomb expert in each group teaches the other group members what she or he has learned about the development of the atom bomb. Each student in each group educates the whole group about her or his specialty. Students are then tested on what they have learned from their fellow group members about World War II.

What is the benefit of the jigsaw classroom? First and foremost it is a remarkably efficient way to learn the material. But even more important, the jigsaw process encourages listening, engagement, and empathy by giving each member of the group an essential part to play in the academic activity. Group members must work together as a team to accomplish a common goal—each person depends on all the others. No student can achieve her or his individual goal (learning the material, getting a good grade) unless everyone works together as a team. Group goals and individual goals complement and bolster each other. This "cooperation by design" facilitates interaction among all students in the class, leading them to value one another as contributors to their common task.

Our first intervention was with fifth graders. First we helped several fifth-grade teachers devise a cooperative jigsaw structure for the students to learn about the life of Eleanor Roosevelt. We divided the students into small groups—diversified in terms of race, ethnicity, and gender—and made each student responsible for a certain portion of Roosevelt's biography. Needless to say, at least one or two of the students in each group were already viewed as losers by their classmates.

Carlos was one such student. Carlos was very shy and felt insecure in his new surroundings. English was his second language. He spoke it quite well but with a slight accent. Try to imagine his experience: After attending an inadequately funded, substandard neighborhood school consisting entirely of Mexican-American students like himself, he was suddenly bussed across town to the middle-class area of the city and catapulted into a class with Anglo students who spoke English fluently and seemed to know much more than he did about all the subjects taught in the school—and were not reluctant to let him know it.

When we restructured the classroom so that students were now working together in small groups, this was terrifying to Carlos at first. He could no longer slink down in his chair and hide in the back of the room. The jigsaw structure made it necessary for him to speak up when it was his turn to recite. Carlos gained a little confidence by rehearsing with the others who were also studying Roosevelt's work with the United Nations, but he was understandably reticent when it was his turn to teach the students in his jigsaw group. He blushed, stammered, and had difficulty articulating the material he had learned. Skilled in the ways of the competitive classroom, the other students were quick to pounce on Carlos' weakness and began to ridicule him.

One of my research assistants was observing that group and heard some of its members make comments such as, "Aw, you don't know it, you're dumb, you're stupid. You don't know what you're doing. You can't even speak English." Instead of admonishing them to "be nice" or "try to cooperate," she made one simple but powerful statement. It went something like this: "Talking like that to Carlos might be fun for you to do, but it's not going to help you learn anything about what Eleanor Roosevelt accomplished at the United Nations—and the exam will be given in about fifteen minutes." What my assistant was doing was reminding the students that the situation had changed. The same behavior that might have seemed useful to them in the past, when they were competing against each other, was now going to cost them something very important: the chance to do well on the upcoming exam.

Old, dysfunctional habits do not die easily, but they do die. Within a few days of working with jigsaw, Carlos' groupmates gradually realized that they needed to change their tactics. It was no longer in their own best interest to rattle Carlos; he wasn't the enemy—he was on their team. They needed him to perform well in order to do well themselves. Instead of taunting him and putting him down, they started to gently ask him questions. The other students began to put themselves in Carlos' shoes so they could ask questions that didn't threaten him and would help him recite what he knew in a clear and understandable manner.

After a week or two, most of Carlos' groupmates had developed into skillful interviewers, asking him relevant questions to elicit the vital information from him. They became more patient, figured out the most effective way to work with him, helped him out, and encouraged him. The more they encouraged Carlos, the more he was able to relax; the more he was able to relax, the quicker and more articulate he became. Carlos' groupmates began to see him in a new light. He became transformed in their minds from a "know-nothing loser who can't even speak English" to someone they could work with, someone they could appreciate, maybe even someone they could like.

Moreover, Carlos began to see himself in a new light: as a competent, contributing member of the class who could work with others from different ethnic groups. His self-esteem grew, and as it grew his performance improved even more; and as his performance continued to improve, his groupmates continued to view him in a more and more favorable light.

Within a few weeks, the success of the jigsaw was obvious to the classroom teachers. They spontaneously told us of their great satisfaction over the way the atmosphere of their classrooms had been transformed. Adjunct visitors (such as music teachers and the like) were little short of amazed at the dramatically changed atmosphere in the classrooms. Needless to say, this was exciting to my graduate students and me. But, as scientists, we were not totally satisfied; we were seeking firmer, more objective evidence—and we got it.

Jigsaw students from poorer neighborhoods showed enormous academic improvement; they scored significantly higher on objective exams than the poorer students in traditional classes.

Because we had randomly introduced the jigsaw intervention into some classrooms and not others, we were able to compare the progress of the jigsaw students with that of the students in traditional classrooms in a precise, scientific manner. After only eight weeks there were clear differences, even though students spent only a small portion of their classtime in jigsaw groups. When tested objectively, jigsaw students expressed significantly less prejudice and negative stereotyping, showed more self-confidence, and reported that they liked school better than children in traditional classrooms.

Moreover, this self-report was bolstered by hard behavioral data. For example, the students in jigsaw classrooms were absent less often than those in traditional classrooms. In addition, the jigsaw students from poorer neighborhoods showed enormous academic improvement over the course of eight weeks; they scored significantly higher on objective exams than the poorer students in traditional classes, while those students who were already doing well continued to do well—as well as their counterparts in traditional classes.

JIGSAW AND BASKETBALL

You might have noticed a rough similarity between the kind of cooperation that goes on in a jigsaw group and the kind of cooperation that is necessary for the smooth functioning of an athletic team. Take a basketball team, for example. If the team is to be successful, each player must play her or his role in a cooperative manner. If each player is hellbent on being the highest scorer on the team, then each will shoot whenever the opportunity arises.

In contrast, on a cooperative team, the idea is to pass the ball crisply until one player manages to break clear for a relatively easy shot. If I pass the ball to Sam, and Sam whips a pass to Jameel, and Jameel passes to Tony, who breaks free for an easy lay-up, I'm elated even though I didn't receive credit for either a field goal or an assist. This is true cooperation.

As a result of this cooperation, athletic teams frequently build a cohesiveness that extends to their relationship off the court. They become friends because they have learned to count on one another. There is one difference between the outcome of a typical jigsaw group and that of a typical high-school basketball team, however, and it is a crucial difference. In high school, athletes tend to hang out with each other and frequently exclude nonathletes from their circle of close friends. In short, the internal cohesiveness of an athletic team often goes along with the exclusion of everyone else.

In the jigsaw classroom, we circumvented this problem by the simple device of shuffling groups every eight weeks. Once a group of students was functioning well together—once the barriers had been broken down and the students showed a great deal of liking and empathy for one another—we would re-form the groupings. At first the students would resist this re-forming of groups. Picture the scene: Debbie, Carlos, Tim, Patty, and Jacob have just gotten to know and appreciate one another and they are doing incredibly good work as a team. Why should they want to leave this warm, efficient, and cozy group to join a group of relative strangers?

Why, indeed? After spending a few weeks in the new group, the students invariably discover that the new people are just about as interesting, friendly, and wonderful as their former group. The new group is working well together and new friendships form. Then the students move on to their third group, and the same thing begins to happen. As they near the end of their time in the third group, it begins to dawn on most students that they didn't just luck out and land in groups with four or five terrific people. Rather, they realize that just about *everyone* they work with is a good human being. All they need to do is pay attention to each person, to try to understand

her or him, and good things will emerge. That is a lesson well worth learning.

ENCOURAGING GENERAL EMPATHY

Students in the jigsaw classroom become adept at empathy. When we watch a movie, empathy is what brings tears or joy in us when sad or happy things happen to a character. But why should we care about a character in a movie? We care because we have learned to feel and experience what that character experiences—as if it were happening to us. Most of us don't experience empathy for our sworn enemies. So most moviegoers watching *Star Wars*, for example, will cheer wildly when the Evil Empire's spaceships are blown to smithereens. Who cares what happens to Darth Vader's followers.

Is empathy a trait we are born with or is it something we learn? I believe we are born with the capacity to feel for others. It is part of what makes us human. I also believe that empathy is a skill that can be enhanced with practice. It I am correct, then it should follow that working in jigsaw groups would lead to a sharpening of a youngster's general empathic ability, because to do well in the group the child needs to practice feeling what her or his groupmates feel.

To test this notion, one of my graduate students, Diane Bridgeman, conducted a clever experiment in which she showed a series of cartoons to ten-year-old children. Half of the children had spent two months participating in jigsaw classes; the others had spent that time in traditional classrooms. In one series of cartoons, a little boy is looking sad as he waves goodbye to his father at the airport. In the next frame, a letter carrier delivers a package to the boy. When the boy opens the package and finds a toy airplane inside, he bursts into tears. Diane asked the children why they thought the little boy burst into tears at the sight of the airplane. Nearly all of the children could answer correctly: because the toy airplane reminded him of how much he missed his father.

Then Diane asked the crucial question: "What did the letter carrier think when he saw the boy open the package and start to cry?" Most children of this age make a consistent error: they assume that everyone knows what they know. Thus, the youngsters in the control group thought the letter carrier would know the boy was sad because the gift reminded him of his father leaving.

But the children who had participated in the jigsaw classroom responded differently. They were better able to take the perspective of the letter carrier—to put themselves in his shoes. They realized that he would be confused at seeing the boy cry over receiving a nice present because the letter carrier hadn't witnessed the farewell scene at the airport. Offhand, this might not seem very important. After all, who cares whether kids have the ability to figure out what is in the letter carrier's mind? In point of fact, we should all care—a great deal.

Here's why: the extent to which children can develop the ability to see the world from the perspective of another human being has profound implications for empathy, prejudice, aggression, and interpersonal relations in general. When you can feel another person's pain, when you can develop the ability to understand what that person is going through, it increases the probability that your heart will open to that person. Once your heart opens to another person, it becomes virtually impossible to bully that other person, to taunt that other person, to humiliate that other person—and certainly to kill that other person. If you develop the general ability to empathize, then your desire to bully or taunt anyone will decrease. Such is the power of empathy.

This isn't a new idea. We see it, for example, in William Wharton's provocative novel *Birdy*. One of the protagonists, Alphonso, a sergeant in the army, takes an immediate dislike for an overweight enlisted man, a clerk typist named Ronsky. There are a great many things that Alphonso dislikes about Ronsky. At the top of his list is Ronsky's annoying habit of continually spitting—he spits all over his desk, his typewriter, and anyone who happens to be in the vicinity. Alphonso cannot stand the guy and has fantasies of punching him out. Several weeks after meeting him, Alphonso learns that Ronsky had earlier taken part in the Normandy invasion and had watched in horror as several of his buddies were cut down before they even had a chance to hit the beach. It seems that his constant spitting was a concrete manifestation of his attempt to get the bad taste out of his mouth. Upon learning this, Alphonso sees his former enemy in an entirely different light. He sighs with regret and says to himself, "Before you know it, if you're not careful, you can get to feeling for everybody and there's nobody left to hate."

WHO CAN BENEFIT?

We now have almost thirty years of scientific research demonstrating that carefully structured cooperative learning strategies are effective. Students learn material as well as, or better than, students in traditional classrooms. The data also show that through cooperative learning the classroom becomes a positive social atmosphere where students learn to like and respect one another and where taunting and bullying are sharply reduced. Students involved in jigsaw tell us that they enjoy school more and show us that they do by attending class more regularly.

It goes without saying that the scientific results are important. But on a personal level, what is perhaps even more gratifying is to witness, firsthand, youngsters actually going through the transformation. Tormentors evolve into supportive helpers and anxious "losers" begin to enjoy learning and feel accepted for who they are.

The jigsaw classroom has shown us the way to encourage children to become more compassionate and empathic toward one another. Accordingly, it stands to reason that this technique could provide a simple, inexpensive, yet ideal solution to the recent epidemic of school shootings that is plaguing the United States.

However, it can be misleading to suggest that jigsaw sessions always go smoothly. There are always problems, but most can be prevented or minimized. And I don't mean to imply that competition, in and of itself, is evil; it isn't. But, at any age, a general atmosphere of exclusion that is ruthless and relentless is unpleasant at best and dangerous at worst.

The poet W. H. Auden wrote, "We must love one another or die." It is a powerful statement, but perhaps too powerful. Ideally, it's best to bring people together in cooperative situations before animosities develop. In my judgment, however, although loving one another is very nice, it isn't essential. What is essential is that we learn to *respect* one another and to feel empathy and compassion for one another—even those who seem very different from us in race, ethnicity, interests, appearance, and so on.

In Austin our goal was to reduce the bigotry, suspicion, and negative racial stereotyping that was rampant among the city's public school students. We didn't try to persuade students with rational or moral arguments, nor did we declare National Brotherhood Week. Such direct strategies have proven notoriously ineffective when it comes to changing deep-seated emotional attitudes of any kind.

Rather, we engaged the scientifically proven mechanism of self-persuasion: we placed students in a situation where the only way they could hope to survive was to work with and appreciate the qualities of others who were previously disliked. Self-interest may not be the prettiest of motives for changing behavior, but it is an opening—and an open door is better than one that is bolted shut.

Elliot Aronson is a distinguished social psychologist and fellow of the American Academy of Arts and Sciences. He has received a variety of national and international awards for his teaching, scientific research, and writing, including the American Psychological Association's highest award in 1999 for a lifetime of scientific contributions. This article is adapted from his new book, Nobody Left to Hate: Teaching Compassion After Columbine (*W. H. Freeman and Company, April 2000*).

From *The Humanist*, May/June 2000, pp. 17-21. © 2000 by The Humanist. Reprinted by permission.

SPEAK *NO* EVIL

Like the happy ending in Alice and Brad's story, you can also find techniques to fight fair. Here, we consult with one of America's foremost experts on how to keep your home life happy with the thoughtful turn of a phrase.

BY DENNIE HUGHES

What is it about families and fighting? Like love and marriage, it seems you really can't have one without the other: No matter how happy and healthy a relationship with a loved one is, arguing, disagreeing, misunderstanding, locking horns, knock-down-drag-outs—fighting by any name—is a fact of family life.

Hot-button topics like money, raising kids and trust are as pertinent today as they were a century ago. But now those conflicts are being played out in a society that seems more than ever prone to violence and less willing to take responsibility for its actions.

While most families are not as volatile as, let's say, Tony Soprano's (HBO's beleaguered mob under-boss who struggles with two "families;" see story, page 10), I have yet to meet one that is conflict-free.

Fighting with family is especially wrenching—and seemingly inevitable. Within the family is where we are the most needy, and the most vulnerable. What wife doesn't know how to bring out the worst in her "better half?" Which child hasn't brawled with a sibling, or with a parent he or she deemed "embarrassing" or "out of touch?" What in-law is meddle-free? When it comes to family feuding, most of us can agree that the very people we turn to for comfort can be our biggest source of frustration.

Why do we fight with the people we are supposed to care about the most? Is there a way to avoid fighting or at least minimize the damage?

This is the subject I recently sat down to discuss with Deborah Tannen, the internationally acclaimed expert on communication. I was looking forward to hearing her research on how what we say can make or break family relationships, which she explores in her latest book, appropriately titled, *I Only Say This Because I Love You* (how many times have we heard *that* preceding a particularly painful putdown from a loved one?). A linguist by training, Tannen is famous for her work on the powerful dynamics of language, especially between men and women.

But my respect for Tannen is based on something more personal than a book. A good friend of mine, a no-nonsense, fearless female who is finishing radiation treatments in her battle with breast cancer, told me that Tannen's 1990 best seller, *You Just Don't Understand: Women and Men in Conversation*, saved her then-20-year-marriage. "The book helped my husband and me learn how to communicate and ultimately keep our marriage together," she said. "And now, eight years later, I cannot imagine how I would've gotten through chemo and radiation if we hadn't stayed together."

Armed with this proof that sometimes words do speak louder than actions, I sat down to dinner with Deborah in New York recently to explore how communication affects conflict within today's families.

Since Tannen studies the influence of speech on behavior, I asked her about the language of family fighting. So much of it— "sibling rivalry," "teenage rebellion" and the ongoing "battle of the sexes"—is expressed in war terms. Is it possible that these fightin' words influence our behavior?

Tannen believes they do, noting that within Western culture, we approach everything as a battle or war. Whether it's outrageous daytime talk shows like Jerry Springer's that encourage audience members to taunt guests, or Chris Matthews-style news "analysis" with assorted guests duking it out over politics, the same rules apply: He who is loudest and most aggressive gets the most air time—and comes off the winner. Ours is a nation of fighters, not listeners, unable to resolve a disagreement, determined to win.

Apply this culture of confrontation, which glamorizes fighting and makes it look fun, to family relationships, and Tannen finds an emotional pressure cooker. Family represents a safe haven and a sense of belonging. It's a place where you can be yourself and be loved for who you are. But this sense of acceptance can also be a license to criticize—or worse. A parent doesn't think twice about telling an adult child how to raise the grandchildren; the working wife has no problem thanking the stay-at-home dad for making dinner—and interjecting that it wasn't quite healthy enough. From the caring comes its nasty cousin: criticism.

"When family members say 'I only say this because I love you,' and follow up with a critical statement, the only message you hear is often the criticism," said Tannen. In short, if members of your own family find you lacking, how could anyone else find you acceptable? Perhaps that's where the term "killing with kindness" really comes from: Meaning well doesn't always end well.

Another critical factor fueling family fights is nature—that is, what Tannen sees as the natural differences in the way men and women communicate. While there are exceptions to every rule, the research is clear: For women, talk is the ultimate intimacy. Men, however, don't feel comfortable talking about their feelings and tend to speak like a report card ("How was my day? B+"). Men's friendships are created by doing things together: Women create bonds by sharing secrets and talking about the most personal aspects of their lives. Tannen says that women's "rapport" talk vs. men's "report" talk promotes the miscommunications that so often prompt arguments between them.

Men—focused on getting to the point of a conversation—are also power-oriented when it comes to fighting. Once engaged, they want to win. This means not admitting any wrongdoing, and by no means apologizing. Women, on the other hand, want to be listened to and understood. They also want a fight to end with an apology. I know I cannot get past a disagreement without one, whether it's from me or the other person.

Research shows that the apology is a huge point of contention between the sexes. Tannen agrees it is a good tool to end a fight. But insisting on it can also make things worse. "Women feel the apology sends the message 'I am remorseful,' and therefore gives them a reason to think this apologizer won't repeat the behavior," she said. "Men, however, don't think an apology is necessary, and often view the mere request as a humiliation tactic or power play." She adds that it's related to the way we grow up: Girls say "I'm sorry" as a courtesy; boys equate it with having to "say uncle," where giving in is a public humiliation.

That doesn't mean men can't change. I grew up in a household where my mom ex-pected an apology, and my dad, king of the castle, always complied.

Women, Tannen says, can also learn to look for other verbal or even physical cues from the man or boy who indicates remorse.

Men and women may generally communicate in two different dimensions, but once kids enter the picture, an entirely new dynamic must come into play. Parents have to put aside their different, even opposing styles and present a united front in a disagreement with their child.

Parents should also keep in mind that, just as natural gender instincts wreak havoc on communication styles, it can also be a factor in conflict with their kids. Don't expect boys to be as open as girls about why they are angry or hurt. Tannen says you should try to get boys to discuss their anger in the way men communicate with their friends: by sharing an activity that takes the concentration off the conversation. "Going for a drive or cleaning the car together allows the non-communicative child to feel more comfortable talking."

In the tension-filled teen years, parents can avoid a lot of fights by listening more and criticizing less. Even if the end result is still "no," Tannen notes that teenagers who feel their parents have tried to understand their point of view instead of immediately telling them that their ideas are wrong are less combative.

So what's the secret to keeping the peace or at the least from going to pieces when it comes to fighting with family members? Not surprisingly, "There are no simple answers," said Tannen. There are, however, a few key elements to keep in mind to work things out without totally working each other over:

- **Be careful how you give suggestions or criticisms.** Very often, advice or a suggestion can make the person at the receiving end feel inadequate. Tannen suggests that before you criticize, ask yourself *why* you need to and whether you have the type of history where you are both open to it.
- **Fight fairly.** That means avoid sarcasm, insults, exaggeration or name-

calling, all guaranteed to escalate the fight. Be direct about what the problem is, stick to the topic and avoid dredging up past troubles. State your case, allow the other person to talk without interruption (there's nothing more infuriating than having someone talk over you), and force yourself to listen to the other side. Finally, if you can avoid it, try not to fight when you're hungry, tired or on your way out the door. Whereas women can talk about any topic, any time, in free-floating conversation style, according to Tannen, men are uncomfortable randomly discussing touchy topics.

- **Discuss fighting when you aren't fighting.** Sounds like a downer, but put it into perspective: We discuss death and burial options while we're alive, so why not other difficult subjects before emotions kick in? Talk to each other about individual needs, and what you and your loved ones should try *not* to do.
- **Use humor.** My boyfriend and I have worked out a code phrase we use to cut through the anger during a fight. When things get heated, one of us looks at our little 10-pound Chihuahua mix dog and says, "You know, we're upsetting the dog." If my boyfriend, a 6-foot-4, 275-pounder, really wants out of the doghouse with me, he picks her up and pleads, "Candy, protect me! Mommy is being mean to me." Silly, but cracks me up every time.

Is there such a thing as a good, healthy fight? Is it ever acceptable to release some of that anger and frustration and pick a fight? I asked Tannen, the guru of get-along. "Sometimes fighting is healthy if it forces people to confront issues that they otherwise would sweep under the rug," she said thoughtfully. Then, ever the linguist, she added, "However, I'd call it 'risking' a fight instead of 'picking' one." Great spin. Now if only I can convince the recipient of my risk he's not actually being picked on....

Contributing Editor DENNIE HUGHES *writes the magazine's RelationTips column on family issues.*

From *USA Weekend*, May 4-6, 2001, pp. 8-10. © 2001 by Dennie Hughes. Reprinted by permission.

Work Work Work **Work!**

It's taking over our lives—invading our homes, haunting our holidays, showing up for dinner. **Should we care?**

by Mark Hunter

YOU'VE HEARD THE JOKE BY NOW, BUT IT RINGS so true that it bears retelling: A guy reads a headline saying "Clinton creates 8 million jobs", and he cracks wearily, "Yeah, and I got three of 'em."

That gag may be the epitaph of the 1990s. In a very real sense, all of us—not just the 13 percent of us working two or three part-time jobs to survive—have three jobs. There's the work we do for a living, the work we do for ourselves (in many cases, to make sure we still can make a living tomorrow), plus the combination of housework and caregiving. Researchers differ on how much time we put into each of these categories, but most agree on one crucial point: The total keeps growing. As my brother Richard, a vice president of the Gartner Group, a high-tech advisory company, puts it: "It's like trying to fit a size 12 into a size eight shoe."

By far the biggest chunk of our time still goes to the work we do for a living. A survey of some 3,000 employees nationwide by the Families and Work Institute (FWI), a New York nonprofit organization that addresses work and family issues, discovered that over the past two decades, the average time spent at a full-time job has risen from 43.6 to 47.1 hours per week. Over a year, that comes to about four extra weeks—the same figure that Juliet B. Schor arrived at in her controversial 1991 study, *The Overworked American*, one of the first books to document what she called "the decline of leisure."

This fact hit home for me when I returned to the U.S. in 1996 after a decade abroad. I began to notice that not one of the other seven people in my office left their desks at lunchtime, the way folks used to. Throw in that traditional half-hour lunch break, and that's another two-and-a-half hours every week that many people give to work—or about three more weeks per year. Likewise, the Bureau of Labor Statistics reports that since 1985 paid vacation time has declined, and so has the average time that workers take off sick. Not surprisingly, more than one third of

the people in the FWI survey said that they "often or very often feel used up at the end of the workday." It's true that some researchers, like John Robinson, a sociology professor at the University of Maryland, argue that it's mainly the well-off among us who are working more, as a matter of choice, and that on average our leisure time has increased. But that's not what I see all around me.

Simultaneously, the old line between work life and private life is vanishing. In trying to understand why employees often refused to take advantage of maternity leave and flex-time, sociologist Arlie Hochschild, author of *The Time Bind*, discovered, to her amazement, that work has become a form of 'home' and home has become 'work.' "She reports that many people now see their jobs as a more appreciative, personal sort of social world" compared with their homes, where in the age of divorce and double careers, "the emotional demands have become more baffling and complex." When I interviewed 40 men about their work-life tradeoffs, every one of them said that it was easier to be a success on the job than in his personal relationships. Is it just a coincidence that hit TV shows like *Taxi* or *Murphy Brown* substituted the workplace "family" for the domestic setting of *The Brady Bunch*?

Work has penetrated the home in another potent way, notes market researcher Judith Langer, who has interviewed several hundred people on this subject over the past ten years: "People feel that what they're required to do at work has spilled over into the rest of their lives—reading, keeping up with trends in their fields, keeping up with e-mail and voice mail. We had a guy come into a focus group carrying all the publications that had hit his desk that day and complain, 'Monday weighs 20 pounds.'"

Personal technology has turned what once were hobbies into jobs: When my brother goes home from the office, he fires up his PC and checks the online orders for his self-produced harmonica records. And when the one third of Americans with managerial or professional jobs leave home, work follows them on a cell phone, pager, or modem. This past winter I received numerous business-related e-mail messages from an executive who was on a hiking trip deep in the mountains of Utah. (Emergency rescue crews have reported finding stranded hikers in the wilderness who had filled their backpacks with a portable computer, but forgotten to bring enough food and water.) The next time a cell phone rings in a restaurant at dinner-time, notice how many people automatically reach for theirs, because it might be a business call. In the 1960s and 1970s, stress experts called this kind of thing multiphasic behavior, otherwise known as doing several tasks at once. Nowadays we call it efficiency.

The distinction between work and leisure no longer exists

Ironically, the Baby Boomers, who came of age shouting their contempt for the man in the gray flannel suit, have done more than any other generation to erase the line between work and private life. Among the first to spot this paradox was Alvin Toffler in his 1980 futurist manifesto, *The Third Wave*. While most observers took those in the hippie movement for a bunch of unwashed, lazy bums, Toffler realized that they were really the prototype of a new kind of worker, the "prosumer"—people who, like frontier farmers, produce a share of what they consume, from home medicine to clothing (my fiancee creates a wardrobe every two years) to home-baked bread, instead of buying it all in the marketplace. "Once we recognize that much of our so-called leisure time is in fact spent producing goods and services for our own use," he noted, "then the old distinction between work and leisure falls apart."

Just as they turned the home into a workplace, Boomers redefined the ideal workplace as a playground. At the end of the 1970s, pollster Daniel Yankelovich found that this "New Breed" of Americans believed that work should be first and foremost a means to self-fulfillment—unlike their parents, who were taught by the Depression that any job that pays a secure wage was worth keeping. When Catalyst, a New York nonprofit organization that seeks to advance women in business, surveyed more than 800 members of two-career couples about what mattered most to them on the job, at the top of the list were emotional benefits such as supportive management, being able to work on their own, and having control over their product.

Our careers now start earlier and end later, reversing a trend that reached its peak after World War II, when child labor virtually disappeared and retirement became a right. These days, so many teenagers have jobs—and as a result are cutting back on sleep, meals, and homework—

that the National Research Council has called for strict new limits on the hours they're allowed to work. At the same time, the number of people 55 and older who still are in the labor force has increased by 6 million since 1950, and most of that increase is women. The Department of Labor projects that this number is going to grow by another 6 million by the year 2006.

None of this was supposed to happen. Only a generation ago, the conventional wisdom among economists was that America was turning into an "affluent society", in which ever more efficient technology would produce an abundance of wealth that we could enjoy with less and less labor. Science-fiction novelists like Kurt Vonnegut imagined a society in which a tiny elite ran the show, while everyone else sat around bored. In their vision, work would no longer be a burden, but a privilege for the happy few.

There are a lot of reasons why things didn't turn out quite that way. One is the Vietnam War, which heated the American economy to the boiling point just as the oil shocks of the 1970s arrived—a combination that led to double-digit inflation and sapped the value of wages. Then successive waves of recession, mergers, and downsizing crashed through the American economy during the '80s. With few exceptions, one of the surest ways to raise a company's stock price—and along with it the value of its executives' stock options—was to fire a piece of its workforce. (Fortunately, downsizing appears to be losing steam, as Wall Street begins to suspect it as a desperate attempt to make a company's bottom line look good in the short term.) Gradually, overtime pay replaced wage increases as the main way to stay ahead of the bills.

The Baby Boom played a role here, too. With so many Boomers competing for jobs, they became cheap for employers: "For the first time in recent American history," marvels Landon Y. Jones in *Great Expectations: America and the Baby Boom Generation*, "the relative earnings of college graduates *declined*." In order to maintain or, in many cases to surpass, the lifestyles of their parents—more Baby Boomers now own homes and, on average, bigger homes than Americans did in the 1950s—they have gone deeply into debt. About one fourth of the average family's income now goes to pay various creditors, more than in any previous generation.

Just as the feminist revolution was urging women to do something with their lives besides raise kids and clean house, it became difficult for the average family to make ends meet without two incomes. Today, in nearly four out of five couples—compared with one out of five in 1950—both partners are in the labor force, with women working nearly as many hours for pay as men. One positive result is that since the late 1970s men have taken over a steadily growing (though still smaller) share of the childcare and household chores—nearly two hours' worth per day that used to be considered women's work.

Yet even visionary feminists like Dorothy Dinnerstein, who predicted this shift in her landmark 1976 book, *The Mermaid and the Minotaur*, did not foresee that it would also have a negative impact on our intimate lives. The Internet site BabyCenter recently polled roughly 2,000 of its new-mother visitors on whether they did or would return to work after their child was born. Two out of three survey participants said that they would go back to work within six months, but only one out of six said that she found the move "satisfying"; twice as many called it "wrenching." Men are also feeling the pinch." I have absolutely no time for myself or my friends," a married male executive and father complained to a Catalyst researcher. "Not enough time for us as a couple, and even the extended family say they don't see us enough."

> # Work is focusing us to constantly learn new ways of working

In previous decades, surveys showed that the biggest source of problems for married couples was money; now, when both partners are asked what is the biggest challenge they face, the majority of two-career couples answer "too little time." Not surprisingly, a growing number of leading-edge companies now offer working couples flexible schedules, expanded parental leave, and other benefits that allow their employees to reconcile their jobs with their personal lives.

Paradoxically, the same technology that was supposed to make us all wealthy loafers has contributed to the work-life squeeze. Computers and the changes they wrought have eliminated entire categories of jobs—when was the last time, for example, you talked to a human operator, instead of an automated phone tree, when you called a big company? In his book *The End of Work*, Jeremy Rifkin warned that this trend would end by puffing nearly all of us out of a job—a neat Doomsday inversion of the old "affluent society" prophecy. But many economists argue that new jobs will be created by new technology, just as they always have been. Perhaps, but the pressures to adapt to these rapid technological changes are greater than ever.

Computers have even changed the rhythm of our work, giving us more of a say in how the job is done because technology-savvy frontline personnel become responsible for decisions that managers used to make, as they constantly feed information up and down the line. The same applies to managers, whose desktop PCs, equipped with software that does everything from keeping appointments to formatting business letters and writing contracts, have largely replaced personal secretaries. We get more control—which happens to be one of the key measures of job satisfaction—but in return we end up giving more of ourselves to the job.

Beyond requiring us to put in longer hours for fear of losing our jobs, work is changing us in positive ways. In particular, it is literally forcing us to expand beyond the limits of what we previously thought we could accomplish, to constantly learn new ways of working. A lifelong career now means lifelong retraining. As the Radcliffe Public Policy Institute in Cambridge, Massachusetts, reports, "The qualities that once nearly guaranteed lifelong employment—hard work, reliability, loyalty, mastery of a discrete set of skills—are often no longer enough." That message has come through loud and clear. About one out of 12 Americans moonlights from his or her principal job in order to learn new skills or weave a "safety net" in case that job is lost. And American universities, starved for students only a few years ago as the Baby Boom grew up and out of the classrooms, have found a burgeoning new market in older workers. Census data show that by 1996 an incredible 468,000 college students were age 50 and older—an increase of 43 percent since 1990.

I don't have to look far to see that trend at work. My brother's wife earned her degree as a geriatric nurse in her late 40s, and it's now her part-time career. My mother, who runs her own public-relations agency, is working toward a degree as an English-language teacher, which will become her post-"retirement" career. And I'm riding that same train. This year I began teaching myself to write code for the Internet, just like my friend Randy, a former magazine editor who spent years of evenings learning to make Web pages in order to support his family. Why? Because by the year 2006 there will be fewer jobs for journalists, according to the Department of Labor. Like everyone else, I've got a choice between moving up—or out.

And there's real excitement in acquiring fresh skills—including the joy of proving wrong the adage that old dogs can't learn new tricks. But many older workers are not getting a chance to share in that excitement: They are being shunted aside from the retraining they will need to stay in the labor market at a moment when they are the fastest-growing share of the labor force. And the point at which a worker on the rise becomes a worker who's consigned to history is coming earlier in people's careers, usually around age 44, according to the Bureau of Labor Statistics. This situation persists at a time when a 77-year-old astronaut named John Glenn just went back into space—and while the minimum age for receiving Social Security benefits is rising.

Perhaps more managers should look at the hard science on this question. In a survey of the available research, Paula Rayman, director of the Radcliffe Public Policy Institute notes that there are "at least 20 studies showing that vocabulary, general information, and judgment either rise or never fall before age 60." Despite these results, they found that managers "consistently made different hiring, promotion, training, and discipline decisions based *solely* [my emphasis] on the age of the workers."

A recent survey of 405 human-resources professionals found that only 29 percent of them make an active effort to attract and/or retain older workers. Among those em-

six survival tips

THE RULES OF THE GAME MAY HAVE CHANGED, BUT midcareer and older workers still hold a number of aces—among them experience, wisdom, and adaptability. Here's some expert advice on how to play your cards and strengthen your hand for the future, gleaned from John Thompson, head of IMCOR, an interim executive placement firm in Stamford, Connecticut; Peter Cappelli, professor of management at The Wharton School in Philadelphia and author of *The New Deal at Work* (Harvard Business School Press 1999); and management gurus N. Fredric Crandall and Marc J. Wallace, authors of *Work and Rewards in the Virtual Workplace* (AMACOM, 1998)

LEARN WHILE YOU EARN If your company will pay for you to attend college-level courses to up-grade your skills, great. If not, take them anyway. Anything computer-related is a good bet. Microsoft offers training programs via organizations such as AARP.

FLEX YOUR MUSCLES By offering to work hours that younger workers may shun because of family and other commitments, you set yourself apart, especially in the eyes of employers in service industries who need 24-hour or seven-a-day week staffing. Employers such as the Home Shopping Network now rely on mature workers to fill a variety of positions.

CAST A WIDE NET The World Wide Web has radically changed the employment scene. A growing selection of jobs are being posted there, and so are résumés. Take a look at the Working Options section on AARP's Web site at www.aarp.org/working_options/home.html for career guidance and links to resources, including America's Job Bank.

BECOME AN MVP Do something to make yourself invaluable. For example, consider becoming a mentor to a young, up-and-coming manager who may need just the kind of guidance an experienced hand can offer. Another option: Seek out projects that matter to your boss and allow you to showcase your talents.

TEST THE WATERS Temporary workers are the fastest-growing segment of the labor force, for good reason. Companies faced with budget-cutting pressures are loathe to add full-time, permanent workers who drive up salary and benefit costs. It gives you an opportunity to try out an alternate career to see if it really fits. And temporary work often is the pathway to a permanent gig.

BE A COMEBACK KID Even if you're planning to retire or cut back from full-time work, don't forget job possibilities with your current employer. GE's information unit in Rockville, Maryland, offers a Golden Opportunity program that lets retirees work up to 1,000 hours a year, and many firms in Southern California use retirees to help with special engineering projects.

—*Tim Smart*

ployers who have made such efforts, establishing opportunities for advancement, skills training, and part-time work arrangements are the most common. Overall, older employees are rated highly for loyalty and dedication, commitment to doing quality work, reliability in a crisis, solid work performance, and experience. This has given rise to a new phenomenon, in which downsized older workers are coming back to the workplace as consultants, temps. or contingent workers hired to work on specific projects.

Many who possess skills that are high in demand, like computer experts or financial advisers are finding fresh opportunities: Brokerage firms, for example, have discovered that their clients enjoy having investment counselors whose life experience is written on their faces.

Other countries are grappling with this issue as well. The Danish government, for example now offers salaried one-year training programs to unemployed workers over age 50. The German government has made it more costly for companies to downsize. And the French government is experimenting with ways to reduce the hours people spend on the job, to spread the work around. For Americans, however, the likely solution will depend on the ability of older workers to take control of their careers as never before, to think of themselves as independent contractors—units of one, so to speak—and, to do whatever they can to enhance their value. At a time when work has become, all-encompassing for many of us, it remains an eminently desirable endeavor. And although much is uncertain about the future, one thing is clear: Work will be part of it.

Mark Hunter is the author of five books, including The Passions of Men: Work and Love in the Age of Stress *(Putnam, 1988). He lives in Paris.*

From *Modern Maturity*, May/June 1999, pp. 35-41. © 1999 by Mark Hunter. Reprinted by permission.

DON'T FACE STRESS ALONE

It's no news that stress can make you sick. but recent
research says the solution isn't working less or
playing more. It's having someone to confide in.

By Benedict Carey

THE CURE FOR EXCESSIVE STRESS SHOULD be excessive cash. A fat pile of Microsoft common that provides for limo service and trips to the Seychelles and nannies and someone to vacuum those tumbleweed pet hairs that breed in every corner of the house. Better still, a house that cleans itself. That way we'd have time to read Emerson, learn to play some baroque stringed instrument, and sample Eastern gurus like finger food, accumulating vast reserves of inner peace and healing energy....

We're fooling ourselves. Even stinking rich, most of us would often feel rushed, harassed, afraid that the maid's boyfriend had designs on our Swedish stereo components. We'd lose sleep, lose our tempers, and continue to wonder whether stress was killing us. Not because money doesn't buy tranquility; it buys plenty. But because what we call stress is more than the sum of our chores and responsibilities and financial troubles. It's also a state of mind, a way of interpreting the world, a pattern of behavior.

Think of the people you know. There are those who are so consumed with work that they practically sleep with their cell phones, who go wild when they just have to wait in line at the checkout. And then there are those who breeze through the day as pleased as park rangers—despite having deadlines and kids and a broken-down car and charity work and scowling Aunt Agnes living in the spare bedroom. Back in the 1960s cardiologists Ray Rosenman and Meyer Friedman labeled these polar opposites Type A and Type B. They described

Type As as "joyless strivers," people who go through life feeling harried, hostile, and combative. Type Bs, by contrast, are unhurried, even tempered, emotionally secure. In person Type As may be twitchy, prone to interrupt, resentful of conversational diversions. Type Bs are as placid as giraffes, well mannered, affectionately patient. In a landmark 1971 study Rosenman and Friedman found that Type As were about twice as likely to develop coronary artery disease as Type Bs. This was the first evidence of a phenomenon that we now take for granted: People consumed by stress often live short lives.

Almost half of Americans say they'd rather be alone when they're stressed. Only 18 percent would call a friend.

Often. But not always. Some Type As live long and prosper. Some Type Bs succumb to heart attacks before they turn 50. Rosenman and Friedman's theory represented a giant step in tracing a link between disease and personality. But it only partly explained why stress sometimes damages the heart. So the search has been under way to discover a more specific connection between personality and illness. In the past decade findings in fields as seemingly unrelated as sociology and immunology have begun to converge on a surprising answer. Of course it matters if

your life is a high-wire act of clamoring demands and pressing deadlines. And yes, it does make a difference whether you're angry or retiring, effusive or shy, belligerent or thoughtful. But what really matters appears to be something much simpler: whether you have someone in your life who's emotionally on call, who's willing to sit up late and hear your complaints.

HUMAN EMOTIONS ARE A MESSY AFFAIR, fleeting, contradictory, and as hard to define as human beings themselves. So it's no wonder researchers have found themselves groping around the dim and convoluted catacombs of personality, trying to locate the core of the trouble with Type As. Some suspect the real villain may be a specific trait such as hostility, cynicism, or self-centeredness. And indeed, all of these characteristics are prevalent in many people who develop coronary disease. But none has proved terribly useful for predicting who will get sick. The search has been a little like being fitted for glasses: Lens two looks clearer than lens one at first, but then you're not so sure. Still, something's there, all right, and several studies conducted in the late eighties and early nineties have finally brought its ghostly shape into focus.

"If you look across all of these studies for a pattern," says psychologist Margaret Chesney, who has spent the past 20 years doing precisely that, "you see that the hostility questionnaires and the Type A interview and all the other measures—they're all picking up the same thing. It's this person who's often suspicious; who sees people as being in their way; who, when they meet someone new, asks, 'What do you do? Where did you go to school?'—not to make a connection but to assess the competition."

More details emerged in 1989 when psychologists Jerry Suls and Choi Wan of the State University of New York at Albany reviewed the Type A research to look for a common thread. They concentrated on studies whose authors had performed general psychological profiles as well as Type A assessments. As a rule, general psych profiles ask directly about fears, insecurities, childhood traumas, and so on, while the Type A diagnosis focuses on how pressured a person feels and how pleasantly he or she answers aggressive questions.

Suls and Wan had suspected that Type A behavior would be associated with emotional distress. But they found something strange. The Type As did show strains of insecurity and emotional isolation—but none of the anxiety and fear associated with the garden-variety neurotic. These are the sort of people who need counseling but consider therapists overpriced palm-readers. "The picture we're getting is of someone who has deep problems but doesn't admit them," says Suls. "So there are a couple of possibilities here. Either they're in denial. Or they really don't have rich inner lives. They never really think about these things."

They aren't Oprah Winfrey fans, in short. They're happy enough talking about work, fashion, sports—anything but the mushy personal stuff. "If you confront them with that," says Suls, "they get angry. They blow up." As one researcher puts it, "They never let their guard down. If you come close, they wonder, What is this person after?" Spare me the advice, Sigmund, can't you see I'm busy?

This evidence, admittedly raw, is still the subject of much debate, but it has even the most authoritative, skeptical, hard-line figures in the field talking like late-night radio shrinks. Just listen to founding father Rosenman, who has guarded the Type A franchise like a hawk, staring down dozens of psychologists whose work he deemed soft or flawed. "After 40 years of observing and treating thousands of patients, and doing all of the studies, I believe that what's underneath the inappropriate competitiveness of Type As is a deep-seated insecurity. I never would have said that before, but I keep coming back to it. It's different from anxiety in the usual sense,

because Type As are not people who retreat. They constantly compete because it helps them suppress the insecurity they're afraid others will sense.

The people most vulnerable to stress are those who are emotionally isolated. They might have the biggest Rolodex, but they're alone.

"If I felt this way, how would I cover it up? I'd distract myself, go faster and faster, and win over everybody else. I'd look at everyone as a threat, because they might expose me."

Avoiding exposure inevitably means avoiding close relationships. The person Rosenman is describing has friends, sure, but no genuine confidants, no one who's allowed so much as a whiff of frailty. That's why many researchers now believe that the symptom most common among those vulnerable to stress is emotional isolation. As Chesney puts it, "These people might have the biggest Rolodex, but they're alone. They're busy looking for more connections, charming more people. When they feel isolated they get busy. It's a defense mechanism."

According to Jonathan Schedler, a research psychologist affiliated with Harvard University, the tests researchers use to identify hostile personalities essentially measure something he calls interpersonal warmth. "It has to do with whether you see the people in your life as benevolent or malevolent, whether they offer nourishment or frustration," he says. "The fact is, humans are emotionally frail. We need real support from other people, and those who don't acknowledge it are going to feel besieged."

These notions could easily collapse into sentimentality. Yet scientific evidence for the physical benefits of social support is coming in from all sides. At Ohio State University, for example, immunologist Ron Glaser and psychologist Janice Kiecolt-Glaser have found that the biggest slump in immunity during exam periods occurs in medical students who report being lonely. Analyzing data from the Tecumseh Community Health Study, sociologist James House calculated that social isolation was as big a risk factor for illness and death as smoking was. And these were just the warm-up acts. In 1989 David Spiegel of Stanford Medical School measured

the effect of weekly group therapy on women being treated for breast cancer. As expected, those who met in groups experienced less pain than those who didn't. But that wasn't all. The women in counseling survived an average of 37 months—nearly twice as long as those without the group support. Other researchers, including Friedman, have also lengthened some heart patients' lives through group therapy.

The reason remains anyone's guess. Perhaps, as Spiegel has suggested, being in a group makes patients more likely to take their medications, perform prescribed exercise, and so on. Patients may also benefit from advice offered in therapy, which can range from the commonsensical to the cornball: from "slow down, spend more time with your family, and don't sweat the little things" to "control your anger, read more poetry, and verbalize affection." Hardly the sort of wisdom that transforms lives.

If these interventions have anything in common, though, it is the presence of other people. This makes sense if you think of stress the way most doctors do, as a hormonal response to pressure. The body perceives a threat, mental or physical, and releases hormones that hike blood pressure and suppress immune response. According to the theory, some of us (the hostile, the troubled, the Type As) have a higher risk of heart disease or cancer because we secrete more of these hormones more frequently than the average joe. This stress response isn't easy to moderate, but one of the few things that seems to help is contact with a supportive person. In several lab experiments, for instance, psychologists have shown that having a friend in the room calms the cardiovascular response to distressing tasks such as public speaking. It's the secret of group therapy: We relax around our own. The simple grace of company can keep us healthy.

Humans are, after all, social by nature. So perhaps it makes sense that the healthiest among us might be the ones who find solace in companionship, who can defuse building pressure by opening up our hearts to someone else. As the late biologist and writer Lewis Thomas observed, human beings have survived by being useful to one another. We are as indispensable to each other as hummingbirds are to hibiscus.

And by finding ways to help each other out, the latest research hints, we forge the emotional connections that could very well sustain us. Thomas understood this. In a *New York Times* interview in 1993, just

They Touched a Nation

THANKS TO PUBLIC FIGURES WHO SPOKE OUT ABOUT THEIR illnesses, we have all grown more comfortable in the past decade confronting health problems that were long shrouded in lonely silence.

—*Rita Rubin*

MUHAMMAD ALI

It was the most arresting moment of the 1996 Olympics in Atlanta: the former boxer, arm trembling, face frozen, raising the torch to light the ceremonial flame. Calls flooded the National Parkinson's Foundation, which adopted a torch as its symbol.

ANNETTE FUNICELLO

In 1992, when the onetime Mickey Mouse Club girl publicly revealed her diagnosis, we all suddenly knew at least one person with MS: Annette. "She is everyone's extended family member," says Arney Rosenblat of the National Multiple Sclerosis Society.

LINDA ELLERBEE

Months after the journalist underwent a double mastectomy, she produced an emotionally charged special on breast cancer. "I can be fair and honest," she says of the disease. "But objective I cannot be."

RONALD REAGAN

Ever-folksy, the former president announced he had Alzheimer's disease in a handwritten letter addressed to "my fellow Americans" in 1994. He called his gesture "an opening of our hearts."

WILLIAM STYRON

The novelist told of his depression in the New York Times and later in *Darkness Visible: A Memoir of Madness*. "The overwhelming reaction made me feel that inadvertently I had helped unlock a closet from which many souls were eager to come out."

CHRISTOPHER REEVE

"You only have two choices," says the actor whose 1995 fall from a horse left him permanently paralyzed and who has raised millions for spinal injury research. "Either you vegetate and look out the window or activate and try to effect change."

GREG LOUGANIS

Mortified that he'd hid his HIV-positive status when his head wound bloodied the Olympic pool in 1988, the diver finally told his story during an interview with Barbara Walters in 1995.

two weeks before his death, the reporter asked him, "Is there an art to dying?"

"There's an art to living," Thomas replied. "One of the very important things that has to be learned around the time dying becomes a real prospect is to recognize those occasions when we have been useful in the world. With the same sharp insight that we all have for acknowledging our failures, we ought to recognize when we have been useful, and sometimes uniquely useful. All of us have had such times in our lives, but we don't pay much attention to them. Yet the thing we're really good at as a species is usefulness. If we paid more attention to this biological attribute, we'd get a satisfaction that cannot be attained from goods or knowledge."

Benedict Carey has been a staff writer at the magazine since 1988.

From *Health*, April 1997, pp. 74–76, 78. © 1997 by Time Publishing Ventures, Inc. Reprinted by permission.

UNIT 6

Enhancing Human Adjustment: Learning to Cope Effectively

Unit Selections

44. **Self-Help: Shattering the Myths**, Annie Murphy Paul
45. **Think Like a Shrink**, Emanuel H. Rosen
46. **Bad Choices: Why We Make Them, How to Stop**, Mary Ann Chapman
47. **Chronic Anxiety: How to Stop Living on the Edge**, *Harvard Health Letter*
48. **Up From Depression**, Jeff Kelsey
49. **Secrets of Happiness**, Stephen Reiss

Key Points to Consider

- According to the article on self-help books, what are some of the pieces of advice that such books provide? Is the advice good advice? Why or why not? What should guide us in our efforts to promote self-change—science or anecdote? How could you evaluate a self-help book that you found at a bookstore or library?

- Can most individuals successfully cope with everyday difficulties? When do you believe professional intervention is necessary? Can most of us effectively change on our own, so that professional help is not necessary?

- What types of therapy are available? Does one form seem better than another? Which type of therapy might suit you best and why? What ingredients do you think make therapy effective? Do you think therapy is more art than science? Why?

- How can you think like a shrink? What guidelines do therapists use to assess and monitor the mental health of their clients? How might these guidelines be equally useful for you? What is educational psychotherapy?

- What is anxiety? What is an anxiety disorder? Why are some people chronically anxious? What are the symptoms of anxiety disorder? With what other disorders does anxiety coexist? How can we recognize and treat these disorders?

- What is depression? Why do psychologists consider depression and other mood disorders to be detrimental?

 **Links: www.dushkin.com/online/**
These sites are annotated in the World Wide Web pages.

John Suler's Teaching Clinical Psychology Site
http://www.rider.edu/users/suler/tcp.html

Health Information Resources
http://www.health.gov/nhic/Pubs/tollfree.htm

Knowledge Exchange Network (KEN)
http://www.mentalhealth.org

Mental Health Net
http://www.mentalhealth.net

Mind Tools
http://www.psychwww.com/mtsite/

NetPsychology
http://netpsych.com/index.htm

On each college and university campus a handful of students experience overwhelming stress and life-shattering crises. One student learns that her mother, living in a distant city, has terminal cancer. Another receives the sad news that his parents are divorcing. A sorority blackballs a young woman who was determined to become a "sister"; she commits suicide. The sorority members now experience immense guilt.

Fortunately, almost every campus houses a counseling center for students; some universities also offer assistance to employees. At the counseling service, trained professionals are able to offer aid and therapy to troubled members of the campus community.

Many individuals are able to adapt to life's vagaries, even to life's disasters. Others flounder. They simply do not know how to adjust to change. These individuals sometimes seek temporary professional assistance from a therapist or counselor. For these professionals, the difficulty may be how and when to intervene. Very few individuals, fortunately, require long-term care.

There are as many definitions of maladjustment as there are mental health professionals. Some practitioners define mental illness as "whatever society cannot tolerate." Others define it in terms of statistics: "If a majority do not behave that way, then the behavior signals maladjustment." Some professionals suggest that an inadequate self-concept is the cause of maladjustment while others cite a lack of contact with reality. A few psychologists claim that to call one individual ill suggests that the rest are healthy by contrast, when, in fact, there may be few real distinctions among people.

Maladjustment is difficult to define and to treat. For each definition, a theorist develops a treatment strategy. Psychoanalysts press clients to recall their dreams, their childhood, and their intrapsychic conflicts in order to analyze the contents of the unconscious. Humanists encourage clients to explore all of the facets of their lives in order to become less defensive. Behaviorists are usually concerned with observable and therefore treatable symptoms or behaviors. For behaviorists, no underlying causes are postulated to be the roots of adjustment problems. Other therapists, particularly psychiatrists, who are physicians by training, may utilize these therapies and add drugs and psychosurgery.

This brief list of interventions raises further questions. For instance, is one form of therapy more effective, less expensive, or longer lasting than another? Is one diagnosis better treated by a particular form of therapy? Who should make the diagnosis? If two experts disagree on the diagnosis and treatment, how do we decide which one is correct? Should psychologists be allowed to prescribe psychoactive drugs? These questions continue to be debated.

Some psychologists question whether professional intervention is necessary at all. In one well-publicized but highly criticized study, researcher Hans Eysenck was able to show that sponta-neous remission rates were as high as therapeutic "cure" rates. You, yourself, may be wondering whether professional help is always necessary. Can people be their own healers? Is support from friends as productive as professional treatment?

The first two readings offer general information to individuals who are having difficulty adjusting and coping. Specifically, the articles pertain to the process of change as suggested by self-help books or by psychotherapists. In the first article in this unit, "Self-Help: Shattering the Myths," Annie Murphy Paul cross-examines advice provided in psychology books for laypersons. She denounces the advice because it is contrary to scientific evidence. Several different myths perpetuated by self-help books are destroyed when held up to scientific scrutiny.

In a related article, "Think Like A Shrink," Emanuel Rosen, writing for *Psychology Today*, reveals how psychotherapists assess and help individuals cope with problems of daily life. The guidelines Rosen lays out can help even nonprofessionals bring about better mental health for themselves and others. Those truly desiring to help themselves might be better served by reading Rosen's advice than by turning to self-help books.

We next begin a review of situations in which people find themselves and that have the potential of causing coping problems. In the next article, "Bad Choices: Why We Make Them, How to Stop," Ann Chapman asserts that our own destructive behaviors are regulated by the immediate rewards we think we will receive rather than by the long-term destructive consequences. Once we learn how to manage the short-term effects, we can overcome self-destructiveness.

We next look at anxiety—a common consequence of modern life. In the article on anxiety, "Chronic Anxiety: How to Stop Living on the Edge," the issue of long-term anxiety is discussed. Anxiety disorders in general are then described. These disorders often coexist with depression. Methods for treating anxiety are also revealed.

Another very troubling but common disorder is depression. We all feel depressed at times, but for some individuals depression becomes overwhelming and chronic. The next article emphasizes the latter, known as clinical depression. In "Up From Depression," Jeff Kelsey writes that most mood disorders are highly treatable. A combination or psychotherapy and medication can change a very depressed person into a much better functioning individual. Kelsey also provides some guidelines to help people determine just how depressed they might be.

In order to end this anthology on a positive note, we look at happiness in "The Secrets of Happiness." Steven Reiss tells us what happiness is, why we sometimes are unhappy, and how we can reach higher levels of happiness. Happiness is not related to monetary wealth or to meeting physical needs such as the requirement for nourishment. Rather happiness is created when basic and important human values are satisfied.

Self-Help:
Shattering the Myths

BOOKSTORES AND THE INTERNET ARE SPILLING OVER WITH ADVICE FROM THE LATEST SELF-HELP GURUS. PT FINDS OUT WHETHER ANY OF IT MAKES SENSE.

IT'S NO SURPRISE THAT AMERICA—LAND OF SECOND CHANCES, FABLED site of self-invention—also harbors an endless appetite for self-help. From Poor Richard to Dale Carnegie to Tony Robbins, we love the idea that we can fix what's broken by ourselves, without the expensive ministrations of doctor or shrink. The limits of HMOs, and the limitlessness of the Internet, have lately made self-help even more appealing: Americans spent $563 million on self-help books last year, and surfed more than 12,000 Web sites devoted to mental health. An estimated 40% of all health-related Internet inquiries are on mental health topics, and depression is the number-one most researched illness on the Web.

By Annie Murphy Paul

In the spirit of pioneers, we're concocting our own remedies and salving our own wounds. But is it good medicine? Once the preserve of charlatans and psychobabblers, self-help has undergone its own reinvention, emerging as a source of useful information presented by acknowledged authorities. That's not to say snake oil isn't still for sale. Often, the messages of self-help books tend to be vast oversimplifications, misrepresenting a part of the truth for the whole, as the following list of popular misconceptions and distortions demonstrates.

The antidote—the "good" kind of self-help, grounded in research—is also available to those who help themselves. Just keep in mind that even the best self-help may be too simplistic to manage complex problems, and that research, with its emphasis on straight science, may not always offer a clear course of action.

Does venting anger make you more angry?

DISTORTION 1
VENT YOUR ANGER, AND IT'LL GO AWAY.

SELF-HELP BOOKS SAY: "Punch a pillow or punching bag. And while you do it, yell and curse and moan and holler," advises *Facing the Fire: Expressing and Experiencing Anger Appropriately* (Bantam Doubleday Dell, 1995). "Punch with all the frenzy you can. If you are angry at a particular person, imagine his or her face on the pillow or punching bag, and vent your rage physically and verbally."

RESEARCHERS SAY: Pillow punching, like other forms of vigorous exercise, might be helpful for stress management, but recent studies suggest that venting anger may be counterproductive. "Venting anger just keeps it alive," says Brad Bushman, Ph.D., a psychologist at Iowa State University. "People think it's going to work, and when it doesn't, they become even more angry and frustrated."

In addition, several studies show that the outward expression of anger leads to dangerously elevated cardiovascular activity, which may contribute to the development of cardiovascular disease.

THE BEST SELF-HELP BOOKS

GENERAL RESOURCES
The Authoritative Guide to Self-Help Resources in Mental Health By John C. Norcross, Linda Frye Campbell and Thomas P. Smith (Guilford, 2000)

THE BEST SELF-HELP AND SELF-AWARENESS BOOKS
A Topic-by-Topic Guide to Quality Information By Stephen B. Fried and G. Ann Schultis (American Library Association, 1995)
Caring for the Mind: The Comprehensive Guide to Mental Health By Dianne and Robert Hales (Bantam, 1995)

RESOURCES ON ANXIETY
An End to Panic: Breakthrough Techniques for Overcoming Panic Disorder By Elke Zuercher-White (New Harbinger Publications, 1998)
Anxiety & Depression: The Best Resources to Help You Cope Edited By Rich Wemhoff (Resource Pathways, 1998)

RESOURCES ON DEPRESSION
Feeling Good:The New Mood Therapy By David D. Burns (Avon, 1992)
Understanding Depression: A Complete Guide to Its Diagnosis and Treatment By Donald F. Klein, M.D., and Paul H. Wender, M.D. (Oxford University Press, 1993)

SELF-HELP RESOURCES ON OBSESSIVE-COMPULSIVE DISORDER
Getting Control: Overcoming Your Obsessions and Compulsions By Lee Baier (Plume, 1992)
The OCD Workbook: Your Guide to Breaking Free from Obsessive-Compulsive Disorder By Bruce M. Hyman and Cherry Pedrick (New Harbinger Publications, 1999)

RESOURCES FOR TRAUMA AND PTSD
Coping with Post-Traumatic Stress Disorder By Carolyn Simpson and Dwain Simpson (Rosen Publishing Group, 1997)
Coping with Trauma: A Guide to Self-Understanding By Jon G. Allen (American Psychiatric Press, 1995)

THE BEST SELF-HELP WEB SITES

GOVERNMENT-SPONSORED WEB SITES:
Knowledge Exchange Network (operated by the U.S. Dept. of Health and Human Services, Substance Abuse and Mental Health Services Administration, and the Center for Mental Health Services) www.mentalhealth.org
•National Center for PTSD (operated by the U.S. Department of Veterans Affairs) www. dartmouth.edu/dms/ptsd
•National Institute of Mental Health www.nimh.nih.gov

NON-PROFIT SITES
•American Psychiatric Association www.psych.org
•Anxiety Disorders Association of America www.adaa.org
•The Help Center of the American Psychological Association www.helping.apa.org
•The International Society for Mental Health Online www. ismho.org
•National Alliance for the Mentally Ill www.nami.org
•National Depressive and Manic-Depressive Association www.ndmda.org

COMMERCIAL WEB SITES
•Online Psych www.onlinepsych.com
•Basic Information www.realpsychology.com
•Self-Help and Psychology Magazine www.shpm.com

Bushman recently put the so-called "catharsis hypothesis" to the test, deliberately inducing anger in a group of college students by marking nasty comments on essays they had written. Those who slammed a punching bag afterward were more, not less, aggressive to people they subsequently encountered.

"It may be better to do things incompatible with anger like watching a funny movie or listening to music"

WHAT TO DO INSTEAD: A better tack, says Bushman, is to do "anything that's incompatible with anger and aggression." That includes watching a funny movie, reading an absorbing novel, sharing a laugh with a friend, or listening to music. Given time, your anger will dissipate, and then you'll be able to deal with the situation in a more constructive way.

Though Bushman has found that exercise can actually heighten physical arousal and keep anger alive, other studies have concluded that sustained strenuous activity might indeed release anger and improve mood. And nontraditional exercise programs like tai chi, yoga and stretching may not only dissipate negative feelings such as anger but make people more conscious of their mood states, paving the way for them to do something constructive about them.

DISTORTION 2
WHEN YOU'RE DOWN IN THE DUMPS, THINK YOURSELF HAPPY BY FOCUSING ON THE POSITIVE.

SELF-HELP BOOKS SAY: "Close your mental doors behind you on unpleasant circumstances or failures you have experienced," commands Napoleon Hill's *Keys to Positive Thinking* (Plume, 1998). "Use your brain for controlled, optimistic thinking. Take possession of your mind and direct it to images of your choosing. Do not let circumstances or people dictate negative visual images."

RESEARCHERS SAY: Research shows that when we're anxious or stressed—in other words, exactly when we need a mood boost—our minds become unable to provide one.

That's because we're so preoccupied with our troubles that we don't have enough brainpower left over to suppress negative thoughts. And when we try to distract ourselves, pessimistic notions are the only ones that come to mind. "If you're really under stress, putting yourself in a good mood by thinking positive thoughts becomes not only difficult—in fact it backfires, and you get the opposite of what you want," says Daniel Wegner, Ph.D., a psychologist at the University of Virginia.

Feeling down? Go to the mall and lift your spirits

In an experiment, Wegner asked a group of people to put themselves in a good mood—which they did, fairly easily. But when they were also told to keep a nine-digit number in mind, they actually felt worse. The energy they had available to control their mood was reduced by the effort of remembering the number.

If you're upset or anxious, make a list of positive things

WHAT TO DO INSTEAD: "You have to enlist the help of other people," Wegner says. "Talk to friends or relatives or clergy or a therapist, or anyone else who might be able to help you think about other things." Or go to a place where people are enjoying themselves, like a party or the park or the mall, and you'll soon feel your spirits lift. Finally, if you know in advance that you're going to be upset or anxious about something, make a list of positive things that you can refer to when you need it most: your five favorite memories, say, or three occasions to look forward to.

DISTORTION 3
VISUALIZE YOUR GOAL, AND YOU'LL HELP MAKE IT COME TRUE.

SELF-HELP BOOKS SAY: "Hold the image of yourself succeeding, visualize it so vividly, that when the desired success comes, it seems to be merely echoing a reality that has already existed in your mind," suggests *Positive Imaging: The Powerful Way to Change Your Life* (Fawcett Book Group, 1996).

RESEARCHERS SAY: Sports psychologists have shown the power that visualization has on improving performance, but simply imagining that you've achieved your goal won't bring it any closer—and might even put it further out of reach.

Shelley Taylor, Ph.D., a psychologist at UCLA, has reservations about visualizing your goals. "First of all, it separates the goal from what you need to do to get it. And second, it enables you to enjoy the feeling of being successful without actually having achieved anything. That takes away the power of the goal"—and can even make you complacent, unwilling to work hard or take risks to get what you already have in your daydreams.

WHAT TO DO INSTEAD: In addition to picturing your goal as a fait accompli, "you should figure out what the steps to get there are, and then mentally rehearse them," says Taylor.

In an experiment, Taylor asked some students preparing for an exam to imagine their happiness at having received an 'A' on the test, and others to picture themselves sitting in the library, studying their textbooks and going over lecture notes. Those in the second group performed better on the test, and experienced less stress and worry.

For short-term goals, Taylor recommends running through the steps you've laid out once a day; for bigger dreams, you can revisit your plan every time you make some progress, and see if it needs adjusting.

DISTORTION 4
SELF-AFFIRMATIONS WILL HELP YOU RAISE LOW SELF-ESTEEM.

SELF-HELP BOOKS SAY: "Write affirmations on paper and put them in places you will see them—on the bathroom mirror, next to your bed, on the car dashboard," recommends *Life 101: Everything We Wish We Had Learned About Life In School—But Didn't* (Prelude Press, 1991). "You can also record them on endless-loop cassette tapes and play them in the background all day (and night)."

RESEARCHERS SAY: Psychologists say this technique may not be very helpful. Changing how we feel about ourselves is a lot more complicated, explains William Swann, Ph.D., of the University of Texas-Austin. "Self-esteem is based on two components: first, our sense of how likable and lovable we are, and second, our sense of how competent we are" at our jobs and at other activities that demand talent and skill. On those scores, we've been hearing from other people—parents, teachers, bosses, siblings, friends, romantic partners—all our lives, and their opinions of us continue to reinforce our notions of ourselves, good or bad. Self-affirmations, even when endlessly repeated, don't make much of a dent—and when they fail to work, they may leave us even more demoralized.

"The more specific the problem-solving strategies, the more useful. All the strategies presented should be based squarely on science or professional science."

What's more, people with low self-esteem may be especially unpersuaded by self-affirmations. Preliminary research by Swann's colleague at UT, Robert Josephs, Ph.D., indicates that those with poor self-images

SIFTING SCIENCE FROM SNAKE OIL:
How to Find Top Psychology in Pop Psychology

By Stephen B. Fried, Ph.D

AMERICANS TURN RELENTLESSLY TO BOOKS, MAGA-zines, radio, TV and the Internet in the hopes of finding their way to a better, less problem-filled life. But there's a catch. Some of this popular psychology is based on solid psychological science and practice, and some is not. How to distinguish which is which?

• Consider the source of the information. Does it come from a mental health professional? Beware of materials written by fellow sufferers who are laypersons. Experiencing a problem doesn't automatically confer the ability to help others. And what works for one may not work for all.

• The problem that's addressed has to be one that is amenable to change. Psychological states that are genetic, like manic-depressive disorder, are extraordinarily difficult to change. So are those that are at the core of what we think or do, such as sexual orientation. Depression is more responsive to deliberate efforts at change, and panic disorder and issues of sexual performance more susceptible still.

• The material must provide both facts about and specific strategies for dealing with the psychological concern. It's important that the information review the symptoms of any condition, and ideally a self-diagnosis questionnaire should be provided.

• Quality information also takes into account individual differences among readers. Most helpful is an array of techniques for tackling the problem. The more specific the problem-solving strategies, the more useful. And all of the strategies presented should be based squarely on science or professional practice.

• The material should refer the reader to authoritative sources, such as professional organizations. Does it contain a bibliography? A resource guide? These are important for possible follow-ups.

Along with G. Ann Schultis, I have analyzed self-help books and offer these additional guidelines in choosing good ones. The book's title should reflect its contents. The purpose of the book should be stated in the preface or the first chapter.

• Some radio and TV stations air entire programs devoted to psychological matters, often hosted by a "mental health professional." Highly dependent on the skills and knowledge of the host, these programs may play on the voyeuristic interests of listeners who may be titillated tuning into the intimate details of an anonymous caller's life. On the other hand, such programs may reach millions and motivate some to seek professional help because of what they heard.

• TV talk shows may feature "victims" of a particular problem—but they often encourage the very behaviors they are purporting to fix. For instance, a couple with poor interpersonal skills is goaded into fighting before the studio audience. Then a guest therapist (typically the author of a topical self-help book) suggests a quick fix to the problem. In this way, the program reinforces both the antisocial behavior and the idea of overly simple solutions to far more complex matters.

• Psychologically related sites have virtually exploded on the web. Look for those hosted by a reputable organization and that present in-depth coverage of issues. The best Web sites offer bibliographies of relevant articles and books; they also offer a listing of professional organizations.

No matter where you turn for information, you can't abandon your critical thinking skills.

Until he succumbed to a long-term illness last May, Dr. Fried was professor and chairman of psychology at Park University in Missouri.

---

simply don't believe the statements, because they don't value their own opinions very highly. In Josephs' experiment, high self-esteem people were able to pat themselves on the back for solving a set of problems, while "lows" had to hear praise from someone else before they would credit it.

WHAT TO DO INSTEAD: The only way to change the final product—your self-esteem—is to change what goes into making it—feedback from other people. "If you find yourself in bad relationships where your negative self-view is getting reinforced, then either change the way

those people treat you by being more assertive, or change who you interact with," says Swann. "If you're in a job where you're getting denigrated, insist that you be treated more appropriately, or change jobs. Try to do your job better than you've done it before."

IN OTHER WORDS: Stand up for yourself. Surround yourself with people who think you're great, and tell you so. Do your best to live up to their high opinions. And be patient. Self-esteem is the sum of your interactions with others over a lifetime, and it's not going to change overnight.

DISTORTION 5
"ACTIVE LISTENING" CAN HELP YOU COMMUNICATE BETTER WITH YOUR PARTNER.

SELF-HELP BOOKS SAY: "The technique of 'active listening' ensures that you not only hear, but really understand what your partner is trying to tell you," reads *Going the Distance: Finding and Keeping Life-long Love* (Plume, 1993). You do it by "paraphrasing your partner's words, then repeating in your own words what you believe your partner is trying to communicate to you."

RESEARCHERS SAY: There's only one problem with active listening: hardly anyone does it. Although the technique has been promoted by therapists for over three decades, research shows that actual couples—including the long-lasting, lovey-dovey ones—completely ignore it when they argue. "It just doesn't happen," says Sybil Carrere, Ph.D., a psychologist at the University of Washington who's been leading a six-year study of how newlyweds interact. "Intuitively it does make sense, but the fact is that when you look at happy couples, they're not doing it. They're being affectionate, they're using humor to break up tension, they're indicating interest in what their partner has to say—they're doing a lot of positive things. But they're not doing active listening." In fact, one of the few studies that has been conducted on the effects of active listening shows that it does nothing to help couples in distress.

WHAT TO DO INSTEAD: According to Carrere, couples should focus their efforts on three other areas. First, women should try to present their complaints in a calm way: Research shows that men are more likely to listen if their partners tone down hostility and avoid contemptuousness. Second, men need to really listen to their partners, taking their feelings and opinions into account. And third, both sides should do what they can to keep the male half cool and collected. "Men have a tendency when they get into conflict to get physiologically aroused, and then they tend to withdraw from the conflict in order to soothe themselves, which only makes the woman more angry," says Carrere. If the two of you can work together to head his anger off at the pass—by throwing in a joke, maybe, or offering a hug—you'll both be better off.

The five distortions presented here are only a few of the misconceptions you may encounter. To protect yourself against others, be sure to take self-help prescriptions with a measure of skepticism and a healthy dose of common sense.

Reprinted with permission from *Psychology Today*, March/April 2001, pp. 60-68. © 2001 by Sussex Publishers, Inc.

THINK LIKE A SHRINK

Yes, you too can see through the defenses people hide behind. To guide you, just consult the handy primer below. Put together by psychiatrist Emanuel H. Rosen, it distills years of Freudian analytical training into a few simple principles that make sense of our psyches.

Ihave always thought it horribly unfortunate that there is such a tremendous gap between psychiatry and popular culture. Psychiatrists are regularly vilified in entertainment, media, and common thought, and our patients are regularly stigmatized. Indeed, I've yet to see a single movie that accurately portrays what we do. From *Silence of the Lambs* to *The Prince of Tides*, we shrinks have a reputation as crazy unbalanced people who can read people's minds. Even the hit comedy *The Santa Clause* made us out to be bimbos.

To some degree, we've gotten just what we deserve. We've allowed ourselves to become, in the public mind at least, mere pill-pushers and to have our uncommon sense dismissed as having zero significance when, in fact, it applies to every moment of every person's life. It is our failure to educate our patients and the general public about the deeper principles of human functioning that have left us so isolated from our communities.

Most patients come to psychiatrists because they recognize that, to some degree, their perceptions contain some distortions. These are usually defensive. For example, a 40-year-old woman may begin her first session with a psychiatrist complaining of a "biological depression" and demanding Prozac. By the end of the hour, however, she may acknowledge that her husband's 10-year refusal to have sex may have as much to do with her unhappy mood.

In my practice, I've engaged in a kind of educational psychotherapy, explaining simply to patients what they are doing and why they are doing it. The result has been not only remarkably effective but catalytic in speeding up the process of psychotherapy The same approach can help the general public delve beneath social images and better understand the deeper struggles of the people around them, and of themselves as well.

We all play to a hidden audience—Mom and Dad—inside our heads. Especially to Mom, whose nurturing is vital to our self-esteem—though it's not politically correct to say so.

Ideas and principles can be introduced directly without the jargon psychiatrists normally hide behind in professional discussions. Doing this in a compassionate and empathic way could lead to a broadening of the vocabulary of the general public and bring about a wider acceptance of certain basic psychological truths.

The core of what we do as psychotherapists is strip away people's protective strategies. If you understand these defensive strategies and the core issues people tend to defend themselves against, you can see through people and, to a lesser extent, yourself.

Here, then, are some general principles to help you think like a shrink. Master

them and you will—in some cases dramatically—increase your understanding of the world around you. You *can* see through people. *You* can read their minds.

1.

If you want to know how emotionally healthy someone is, look only at their intimate relationships.

Good-looking, athletic, charismatic, confident, rich, or intelligent people are not always emotionally healthy. For example, chronologically they may be adults, but emotionally, they may be two-year-olds. You will not really be able to make any kind of accurate, in-depth assessment of people until you learn to distinguish their superficial physical qualities from meaningful emotional ones. There are at least three key things you want to know:

•Most importantly how long-lived and committed are their current intimate relationships?

•Secondly, how much negative conflict do they experience in their work environments and how long have they held their current jobs?

•Finally what was their childhood experience like in their family of origin? Or, in plain English, did they get along with their family?

2.

How you feel about yourself (your self-esteem) is significantly determined by how nurturing your mother, father, and siblings were to you when you were growing

up—especially your mother, though it is not politically correct to say so.

It is not that mothers are to blame for all of a patient's problems. It is simply that stable healthy mothering is a strong buffer against a tremendous amount of pathology.

3.

How you relate to intimate people is always based on how you related to your family when you were growing up.

Basically, we all keep our families with us forever. We keep them in our heads. For the rest of our lives, we will have tendencies to either take on the roles of our childhood selves or those of our parents. Examine carefully your relationships with your family. It will tell you a lot about who you are.

Men have much more penis envy than women. They're all very preoccupied with their penis—how big it is, how long, how thick, and how deep it goes.

4.

We all play to a hidden audience—Mom and Dad—inside our heads.

You often see people do strange things in their interpersonal interactions. "Where did *that* come from," you often ask. It came from a hidden screenplay that was written in that person's head.

Ostensibly he's reacting to you, but in his head, he's reacting to his mother. In fact, the less he remembers of his childhood, the more he is going to act out with you. This leads nicely to....

5.

People who say they "don't remember" their childhood are usually emotionally troubled.

Physically healthy individuals who can't recall their youth have frequently endured some painful experiences that their minds are blocking out. As a result, they really don't know who they are. They have what we psychiatrists call a diminished sense of identity.

6.

Victims like to be aggressors sometimes, and aggressors are often reconstituted victims.

People actually may become more actively aggressive when they feel forced into a passive position.

7.

Yes, Virginia, there is an "unconscious" or "non-conscious" mind, and it basically determines your life, everything from what job you choose to whom you marry.

All the feelings that you had about yourself, your parents, and family are buried in this "unconscious mind." Also buried here are some very deep fears which will be touched on below

The more aware you are of your unconscious mind, the more freedom you will have.

8.

Sex is critical, no matter what anyone says.

Sex has become passé as an important explanatory factor of human behavior. Nowadays, it is more politically correct to emphasize the role of feelings, thoughts, and emotions than the role of sex. Nonetheless, sexual functioning and sexual history *do* tell you a tremendous amount about what people are really like.

9.

Whenever you have two men, or two women, in a room, you have homosexual tension.

It is a core truth that all people have both heterosexual and homosexual drives. What varies is how you deal with those drives. Just because you have a homosexual impulse or idea has absolutely nothing to do with your sexual orientation. You are defined by your sexual *behavior*, not your sexual *impulses*.

The people in our society who are most against homosexuality are the people who are most uncomfortable with their own homosexual impulses. These impulses are banished from their conscious awareness.

10.

Yes, children do want to be sexual with the opposite sex parent at some point in their young lives, often between the ages of four and six.

Just about everyone is grossed out at the thought of their parents having sex. This is because there is a significant resistance against one's own memory of sexual feelings towards one's parents.

It does not mean, however, that you have to remember your sexual impulses towards a parent to be emotionally healthy. In fact, one of the most common issues an

adult has to deal with is the incomplete repression of this core conflict.

11.

There is indeed such a thing as castration anxiety.

In fact, it's the most frightening core fear that people have. It's probably not only evolutionary adaptive, but emotionally important.

12.

Women do not have nearly as much penis envy as men do.

Men are all deep down very preoccupied with their penis. Concerns usually revolve around how big it is, how long, how thick, and how deep it goes.

This is an important issue that will likely never be researched because it makes everyone way too uncomfortable to talk about. There is more mythology on this subject than the Greeks ever wrote.

13.

The Oedipus complex is what keeps psychiatrists in business.

Though lay people tend to think only of the complex's sexual aspects, it really boils down to competition. It's commonly about being bigger, richer, more powerful, a winner or a loser. The feelings surrounding it are universal—and intense.

Getting through the various stages of psychological development—oral, anal, and Oedipal—can be summarized as teaching you three key things:

•To feel stable and secure, to depend on people reasonably

•To feel in control

•To feel able to compete successfully and to feel like a man or a woman.

Our best defense is a good offense. When people act in an egotistical fashion, their underlying feeling is that they are "dick-less" or impotent.

14.

People are basically the same underneath it all; that is, they all want to satisfy similar deeper needs and quell identical underlying fears.

In general, people all seem to want money, power, and admiration. They want sexual gratification. They want to, as the Bible notes of Judah and Israel, "sit under their vine and fig tree and have none make them afraid." They want to feel secure. They want to feel loved.

Related to this principle: money and intelligence do not protect you. It is only emotional health that keeps you on an even keel; your feelings about yourself and your intimate stable relationships are the only ballast that matters in life.

15.

People often act exactly the opposite of the way they feel, especially when they are unhealthy.

Or: the best defense is a good offense. When people act egotistical, their underlying feeling is that they are "dick-less" or impotent.

16.

More on defenses...

Here is human nature in a nutshell. My favorite line from the movie *The Big Chill* is voiced by the character played by Jeff Goldblum. "Where would you be, where would any of us be, without a good rationalization? Try to live without a rationalization; I bet you couldn't do it."

We distort reality both outside and in our minds in order to survive. Distortions of our inner world are common. *Regression*, one of the most intriguing defenses, can be particularly illuminating to acknowledge; it means acting like a kid to avoid the real world.

"Outside" distortions can get us in very serious trouble.

Denial can be fatal whether it involves alcohol abuse or a herd of charging elephants.

Devaluing, or, in simple terms, throwing the baby out with the bath water, comes in handy when we want to insult somebody. But it can be detrimental—for example, causing us to miss a lecturer's important points because we consider the teacher to be a "total jerk."

Idealizing, or putting people on a pedestal, can be hurtful—say when you realize your ex-Navy Seal stockbroker has been churning your brokerage account.

Projecting feelings onto others is a common defensive distortion. Guilt is a painful feeling, so sometimes we may see other people as angry at us rather than feel guilty ourselves. "I know that you are angry that I forgot your birthday" you say. "Don't deny it."

Strangers who blurt out their entire life story at a first meeting, even if it's with a psychiatrist, are likely to be troubled. They have no "boundary"—and they should.

Finally *splitting* our view of the world into good guys and bad guys is a distortion, even if it makes for a great western.

17.

To be successful in the highly competitive American business marketplace requires a personality ethos that will destroy your intimate relationships.

At this point, you are probably experiencing some confusion. After all, I've been saying that it is unhealthy to be striving continuously to compensate for feelings of inferiority or impotency Yet most people know that it is in fact the strivers who achieve enormous power and success in the world around them.

In order to be emotionally healthy, however, it is necessary for these "winners" to leave their work personalities at the door of their homes and become their natural selves once they cross the threshold. It is absolutely essential that the driven, rushed, acquisitive capitalist ethos not enter into the realm of intimate relationships.

CEOs of corporations and doctors are particularly at risk for this type of contamination of their family life. People who have the best of both worlds—career and relationships—are those who realize that success in the workplace does not make up for lack of success at home.

18.

How well people deal with death is usually identical to how well they have dealt with life.

19.

How people relate to you in everyday life can tell you a lot about their deeper issues, even in a very short time.

You can tell a tremendous amount about somebody's emotional stability and character by the way they say goodbye to you. People who cling or drag out good-

---

byes often have deep-seated issues with separation. Of course, we all have issues with separation; it's a matter of degree. Those of us from loving stable backgrounds carry around a warm fuzzy teddy bear of sorts that helps us cope with saying good-bye and being alone. Without this security blanket of loving memories, being alone or saying good-bye can be hell.

A stranger who tells you his entire life's story on the first interview even if you are a psychiatrist, is also probably emotionally unhealthy because there is no boundary between that person and you—and there should be. After all, you are a stranger to that person.

20.

Listen with your third ear.

One of my mentors at Duke University Medical Center once defined the "third ear" as follows: "While you're listening to what a patient is saying, with your third ear listen to why they are saying it." Psychiatrists listen in a unique way. A family practitioner examines your ears with an otoscope. A psychiatrist examines your feelings with himself as the tool.

When you are interacting with another person, if you notice yourself feeling a certain way the odds are that your companion is somehow intending you to feel that way. You have to be emotionally stable to accurately use yourself as the examining tool.

When you become adept at identifying what you are feeling, the next step is to determine why. There are usually two reasons. Number one, it may be because you are resonating with what the person is feeling. A second possibility is that you are being subtly provoked to play a complementary emotional role in a scene that has an often hidden script.

The process of using one's own heart as a "scope" is hard work. The fancy term for this process is "counter-transference."

21.

Behind every fear, there is a wish.

Wishes that are often consciously unacceptable can be expressed more easily as "fears." Related to this principle is the maxim: "Beware unsolicited denials." A common example is the seemingly spontaneous statement, "I don't really care at all about money!" Hold on to your wallet.

Reprinted from *Psychology Today*, September/October 1998, pp. 54–59. © 1998 by Emanuel H. Rosen. Reprinted by permission.

BAD
Choices

WHY WE MAKE THEM
HOW TO STOP

If cigarettes, gambling, those last 10 pounds, that credit card habit and the one drink too many are standing in between you and your goals, this new formula may finally make the difference. And the good news is, it's all in your hands.

By Mary Ann Chapman, Ph.D.

As the police car pealed out behind Lynn with its lights blinking in her rearview mirror, she remembered with dread that second glass of wine she drank just before leaving the party. Her heart raced as she considered the implications of getting a DWI ticket. She had been preparing to leave the party and knew she had to drive home, so why did she indulge?

Most of the bad choices we make in our lives involve an immediate reward—in Lynn's case, the taste and feel of the extra glass of wine. Like Lynn, we often choose to live now even though we're likely to end up paying the price later. This carpe-diem philosophy becomes even more powerful when the punishment is not a sure thing. In Lynn's case, the probability of her being pulled over by the police was not very high. If she had expected them to stop her, she might have reached for a ginger ale.

Our day-to-day bad choices have alarming results. For example, one-third of Americans are overweight, costing the U.S. government $100 billion each year in treatment of related illnesses.

We're also steeped in debt:

The Consumer Federation of America calculates that 60 million households carry an average credit card balance of $7,000, for a total national credit card debt topping $455 billion. Our failure to make sacrifices now for rewards later is particularly devastating when it comes to following prescribed medical regimens. Studies have found that only half of us take antidepressants, antihypertensives, asthma medications and tuberculosis drugs as prescribed. Such lack of compliance is the major cause of hospital admissions in people who have previously had heart failure, and it's entirely preventable.

Our desire to take the path of least resistance is so strong that we continue our sometimes destructive behavior even though we know, as in the cases of smoking and overeating, it literally may kill us. But we don't need to be slaves to instant gratification. Consider the ways we already suffer in the present for reward in the future: We get tetanus shots to protect against lockjaw and use condoms to reduce the risk of sexually transmitted diseases; we have money taken out of our paychecks for retirement, and parents routinely make sacrifices for

their children's future. The key to breaking a bad habit and adopting a good one is making changes in our daily life that will minimize the influence of the now and remind us of the later. It sounds difficult, but new tricks make it possible.

A look at the animal kingdom reveals clues as to how this is done. Working in a laboratory with pigeons, Howard Rachlin, Ph.D., of the State University of New York at Stony Brook, found that when birds were given a simple choice between immediate and delayed reward, they chose the immediate reward 95% of the time. This was true even though the delayed reward (food) was twice the size of the immediate one.

Then researchers made the task more complicated, giving birds the chance to choose between 1) the same immediate and delayed options as in the first part of the study, or 2) a no-option condition in which they were only allowed access to the delayed reward. This situation is analogous to the choice between going to a gym where you have the option of relaxing in the sauna or hopping on the stationary bicycle, and going to a gym that has only

PT's Good-Choice Guide

	BEHAVIOR	NOW	LATER	STRATEGIES FOR CHANGE
BAD CHOICES	Overeating	Food tastes good, is comforting	You get fat, unhealthy; suffer lowered self-esteem	Only snack when sitting at the table—never in front of the TV; keep inspiring picture or story on the fridge or cupboard; calculate how long it would take to burn off the calories of what you're about to eat
	Eating fast food	Quick; easy; tastes good	Too much fat; not nutritious; not healthful	Identify health-food places close to home; locate low fat/calorie menu items
	Anger	Temporary relief	Problems interacting with others	Apologize immediately for getting angry; reward yourself for situations in which you avoid anger
	Constant complaining	Sympathy from others	Viewed negatively; social repercussions	Tell friends to change topics when you start complaining
	Smoking	Pleasure from cigarette	Lung cancer; possible death	Confine smoking to one designated area (preferably one you don't like); keep a day calendar in your cigarette cupboard and rip off a day for every cigarette pack you open to symbolize days off your life
	Gambling	Occasionally win money	Lose money over the long term	Donate all winnings (preferably to a cause you dislike); keep track of losses, place them prominently; consider ways you could have spent the money you lost
GOOD CHOICES	Healthful eating	Extra effort; taste not as good	Good health; reduced chance of many diseases	Reduce effort by buying preprepared healthful foods or by preparing them over the weekend; dine with a friend who shares an interest in healthy eating
	Saving money	Less money to spend now	Avoid interest charges on loans or credit cards; can afford larger or more meaningful items	Have automatic deductions taken out of your paycheck
	Using condoms	Some say less pleasurable sex	Prevent AIDS, sexually transmitted diseases, pregnancy	Always keep condoms handy; use other techniques to enhance sex; donate money to AIDS causes
	Going to the dentist	Painful, scary	Avoid further pain of root canals, existing cavities	Find a friendly dentist; schedule appointments at the same time as a friend; give yourself a small reward each time you go
	Exercising	Extra effort; give up relaxation time	Improved circulation; reduced risk of disease; weight loss; increased energy; greater self-esteem	Move near a gym; buy weights or a bike; after a workout, write down how good you feel and read it next time you are in a slump
	Overcoming shyness	Disruption of "safe" pattern of behavior	More friends and social activities	Start by prolonging a conversation someone starts with you and make it a habit

exercise equipment—giving you no option but to exercise once you get there.

As the researchers increased the amount of time birds had to wait after selecting between the two alternatives, the birds increasingly chose the second option, to have only the delayed reward available. In this way, the researchers effectively altered the birds' environment to minimize the value of the immediate choice.

BREAKING A BAD HABIT

We can apply the same logic to help us break our bad habits: We need to 1) minimize or avoid the immediate reward, and

2) make the long-term negative consequence seem more immediate.

My friend John, for example, relies too much on his credit card. When the lunch bill comes, he charges the total tab and pockets his colleagues' cash. You may not know John, but I bet you know that he doesn't rush to the bank and deposit that money.

John needs to avoid the immediate positive effect of using his credit card. The most logical step would be to leave it at home—except that he might need it for travel or emergencies. John's best bet would be to do a little preplanning: He could stop by the bank after work to make sure he had enough money for the next day's lunch. Or he could locate an ATM near the restaurant to make it more convenient—and therefore more likely—for him to withdraw cash.

As a reminder of that big scary negative at the end of the month, John could paste his latest credit card bill near his computer, on the refrigerator or someplace he will see it every day. He might also tape the amount he owes to the face of the credit card. These nearly effortless gestures will make it hard for John to readily ignore his problem and help him bridge the gap between now and later.

STARTING A GOOD HABIT

You might be eager to start eating healthy meals, getting regular exercise or making new friends. Most likely, the going will be tough at first, but the potential long-term benefits are well worth it. Once again, the idea is to minimize the immediate—a negative this time—and bridge the distance to the future, the good stuff.

For the past couple of months, I have been trying to get myself to drink a small glass of soy milk every day. Each week I buy a carton of soy milk and after two weeks, I dump it down the drain. I have convinced myself that I need to drink soy milk for the protein and the long-term health benefits. But somehow, the immediate negative of drinking the milk (and even thinking about drinking the milk!) has been seemingly impossible to overcome.

What would help lessen the yuck of soy milk? I tried drinking it in my favorite special cup. That helped a little, but not enough. My new strategy is to mix half a cup of soy milk with regular milk. Every day I drink the soy milk I put an X on my calendar for that day, which makes me feel accomplished and helps me associate drinking the soy milk with a positive consequence. And to make the long-term benefits more immediately apparent, I tore out magazine articles that tout the health benefits of soy and taped them to my refrigerator.

WHEN OLD HABITS DIE HARD

It's never very easy to change, but for some people, it is exceptionally difficult. Twenty-two-year-old Jimmy is a good example. Jimmy's arms are bruised and scarred from his heroin habit. For him, the immense immediate pleasure of heroin far outweighs the long-term consequences of his habit: tuberculosis, lack of money and the inability to hold down a job.

You might not think you have anything in common with Jimmy—or a compulsive gambler or a kleptomaniac. But researchers are beginning to recognize that all of these behavioral patterns involve, to varying extents, maximizing immediate consequences despite huge negative long-term ones.

To find out if some people are more prone to favor the here and now than others, the University of Missouri's Alan Strathman, Ph.D., and his colleagues conducted surveys in Missouri and California. They asked survey participants how much they agreed with statements such as "I consider how things might be in the future and try to influence those things with my day-to-day behavior," and "Convenience is a big factor in the decisions I make or the actions I take." Strathman found that individuals did indeed have varying degrees of what he calls "future orientation"—preference for delayed consequences—and that this orientation remains stable over time. The individual differences were reflected in general health concerns and in environmentally friendly behaviors such as recycling.

The good news is that the behavioral change strategies can work just as well for people who tend to favor the here and now. They don't require special genes or exceptional chemistry. They are very simple and that's their beauty. Time and again, they have been used successfully to help people overcome problems from obesity to sulking to failing grades. These simple strategies are effective because behaviors are mostly learned and, therefore, can be unlearned. They can take us off autopilot and introduce ideas (namely, long-term consequences) that we normally wouldn't consider. Even if we have focused on the short-term all our lives, these strategies can help us maximize our chances of success.

FURTHER READING

Self-Help Without the Hype, R. Epstein (Performance Management Publications, 1997)

Self-Directed Behavior: Self-Modification for Personal Adjustment (seventh edition), D.L. Watson and R.G. Tharp (Books/Cole, 1996)

Managing Everyday Problems, T. A. Brigham (Guilford Press, 1988)

Mary Ann Chapman earned her Ph.D. in experimental psychology from Washington State University in 1994. She is a scientific communications writer in southern California.

Reprinted with permission from *Psychology Today,* September/October 1999, pp. 36–39, 71. © 1999 by Sussex Publishers, Inc.

Chronic Anxiety:

How to Stop Living on the Edge

Feeling nervous is a normal response to stressful situations. Sweaty palms, a racing heart, and butterflies in the stomach are felt by everyone from seasoned performers stepping into the spotlight to the person addressing a group for the first time. These sensations are caused by a rush of stress hormones, such as norepinephrine and cortisol, which prepare the body and mind to rise to a challenge.

Chronic anxiety, however, is very different from the healthy feelings of nervousness that make a speaker effective or enable a sprinter to win a race. Indeed, anxiety disorders are, by definition, psychiatric illnesses that are not useful for normal functioning. Instead of calling a person to action, chronic anxiety can damage relationships, reduce productivity, and make someone terrified of everyday experiences.

> Although anxiety disorders are common, many people do not seek help because they don't realize that treatments are available.

Anxiety illnesses are among the most common disorders, affecting more than 23 million Americans (about 1 in 9). Fortunately, sufferers often get substantial relief from various forms of talk therapy, medication, or both. But the majority of people with anxiety disorders do not seek help because they may not recognize their symptoms as a psychiatric problem or may fear being stigmatized with a "mental illness."

There is strong evidence that anxiety conditions run in families. And recent findings suggest that a genetic predisposition to anxiety, when triggered by certain life experiences (such as early losses or trauma), may alter a person's brain chemistry, causing an illness to surface.

The most common of these conditions and, surprisingly, the least understood is *generalized anxiety disorder* (GAD). Believed to affect about 10 million Americans, it is characterized by unrelenting, exaggerated worry and tension; it can keep people from socializing, traveling, getting a better job, or pursuing a sport or avocation. GAD affects people of both sexes and all ages but is diagnosed more often in adult women, possibly because of hormonal differences or because women seek mental health treatment more frequently than men, whose rate of anxiety may be underestimated. Some mental health experts believe that men manifest anxiety (as well as depression) differently from women: they drink more alcohol, smoke more, and are more prone to aggressive behavior.

The psychiatric diagnosis of GAD is chronic, exaggerated worry and tension that has lasted for more than 6 months, although most people with the disorder can trace it back to childhood or adolescence. They may worry excessively about health, money, family, or work, even when there is no sign of difficulty. And they have trouble relaxing and often have insomnia. Many live from day to day with distressing physical symptoms such as trembling, sweating, muscle tension, or headaches, which tend to worsen when they face even mild stress.

GAD frequently coexists with depression, and certain antidepressants seem to work quite well for people with GAD. Many of these medications regulate levels of brain chemicals such as serotonin and norepinephrine, but scientists do not have a complete understanding of the biology of anxiety or depression or why they often go hand in hand.

A March 1998 symposium in Boston, cosponsored by the National Institute of Mental Health and the Anxiety Disorders Association of America, was among the first dedicated to the interplay between fear and anxiety and the workings of the brain. Some scientists are focusing on a brain structure called the *amygdala*, which regulates fear, memory, and emotion. When a person is exposed to a fearful event, the amygdala coordinates the brain's physical responses, such as increased heart rate and blood pressure. And preliminary research suggests that the release of the stress hormones norepinephrine and cortisol may act in a way that greatly increases memory of the fearful or traumatic event, allowing it to remain vivid for years. (For more on stress hormones, see *Harvard Health Letter*, April 1998.)

Because basic research has uncovered chemical and hormonal differences in how males and females respond to fear and anxiety, investigators are studying the role that estrogen and cyclical hormonal changes may play in women with anxiety disorders.

Late-life anxiety

Although studies indicate that the prevalence of major depression and certain anxiety disorders declines in the over-65 population, depression affects about 1 in 7 in this group. But there are no hard data on how many of them are troubled by chronic anxiety. Researchers, however, believe that GAD is the most common form of anxiety in older people. They estimate that up to two thirds of older individuals with depression have GAD, and the same amount with GAD have depression. (For more on late-life depression, see *Harvard Health Letter*, March 1995.)

Doctors may have difficulty diagnosing anxiety disorders in older people because some of the characteristics of anxiety, such as blood pressure elevations or a racing heart, may be attributable to a physical illness. Indeed, anxiety may be overlooked when a potentially serious medical condition captures a doctor's attention.

Getting well

There are two main roads to treating GAD: talk therapy and medication. Some mental health professionals place great value on *cognitive-behavioral therapy* (CBT); instead of focusing on deep-seated childhood feelings, the therapist helps the patient look realistically at the exaggerated or pessimistic beliefs that flood the mind. Eventually, the person learns to think rationally about his or her fears, and anxiety is reduced.

However, other mental health experts say that although CBT may have an excellent short-term effect, it is not necessarily a lifetime one. Many psychotherapists believe that the only way to help someone reduce chronic anxiety for good is to work with the patient over time so he or she can talk about and process traumatic or fearful events, which may have occurred years earlier. Indeed, many people experience a substantial reduction in anxious thoughts when they explore childhood fears or secrets with a supportive and knowledgeable psychiatrist, psychologist, or social worker.

Finding Help

The following national organizations can provide referrals for mental health professionals and/or support groups in your area.

American Psychiatric Association

Phone: (202) 682-6220
Internet: http://www.psych.org

American Psychological Association

Phone: (202) 336-5800
Internet: http://www.helping.apa.org

Anxiety Disorders Association of America

Phone: (301) 231-9350
Internet: http://www.adaa.org

National Alliance for the Mentally Ill

Phone: (800) 950-NAMI
Internet: http://www.nami.org

Useful medications

Some types of drugs, such as *benzodiazepines* (mild tranquilizers) are taken every day or on an as-needed basis when stress or worry becomes overwhelming; others, such as antidepressants, must be taken daily, sometimes indefinitely. It is best to combine some form of talk therapy with medication, but many people do not feel the need or they lack the financial resources to do both.

Historically, anxiety has been treated with benzodiazepines. These include diazepam (Valium), alprazolam (Xanax), and lorazepam (Ativan). Although many people who consider taking one of these medications or who are currently on one worry that they are addictive, this is usually not the case, particularly if the person has never abused drugs or alcohol in the past. Some individuals may develop a physical dependence on them, which means that they should reduce their dose slowly when going off the medication. Doctors rarely prescribe benzodiazepines for people with addictive tendencies.

Although the medications are generally well tolerated by people who do not abuse them, they can be a problem in older people, because early side effects include drowsiness, impaired reflexes and motor skills, and confusion. Older individuals are more prone to falls and car accidents during the first few weeks of taking a benzodiazepine.

Antidepressants are being used more frequently to treat GAD. They do not generally have the side effects of benzodiazepines and are considered safer and more effective for long-term use. Numerous investigations have shown that the *selective-serotonin reuptake inhibitors (SSRIs)*, sold as Prozac, Paxil, and Zoloft, newer antidepressants such as nefazodone (Serzone), and the older tricyclic antidepressants (imipramine, for example) can significantly reduce symptoms of GAD. A drug called buspirone (BuSpar), which is not an antidepressant but is designed specifically for anxiety, is useful for some people.

The first step in getting help is to see your primary care physician, who can refer you to a mental health professional if you want to explore talk therapy. Another way to find a good counselor is to ask friends or family who have worked with one they liked.

Either your primary care doctor or a psychiatrist can prescribe medication. However, primary care physicians generally do not have time to engage in lengthy or ongoing discussions, so you may prefer to see a mental health professional. Whether you've lived with chronic anxiety for 6 months or 60 years, GAD can be treated. You can get the help you need by asking for it.

Excerpted from *The Harvard Health Letter*, July 1998, pp. 1–3. © 1998 by the President and Fellows of Harvard College. Reprinted by permission.

Up from Depression

Depression is perhaps the most treatable of all mood disorders.

MAJOR DEPRESSION, ALSO KNOWN AS CLINICAL DEPRESSION, IS MORE than an ordinary case of the blues. The disorder drags on for at least two weeks, draining all the color and meaning out of life. Activities that once brought pleasure become tedious chores. Negative thoughts—guilt, worthlessness, hopelessness—crowd out all others.

JEFF KELSEY, M.D.

• About one in every six of us will suffer an episode of depression. But less than half will be accurately diagnosed—and fewer than 15 percent who are diagnosed will get adequate treatment. Yet depression is perhaps the most treatable of all mood disorders: medication, psychotherapy, or both can relieve suffering and restore wellness in 80 to 90 percent of patients, often in a matter of weeks. • The causes of depression are murky. Just as no single factor is to blame for most heart attacks—family history, chronic illness, and unhealthy behaviors usually share responsibility—no single factor appears to cause depression. • Depression likely results from a convergence of multiple biological, psychological, and social factors, from hormones to hard times. Risk factors for major depression include female gender; lower socioeconomic status; separation or divorce; early childhood trauma or parental loss; and other significant negative life events, including major illness or disability. • Heredity may play a role as well. Studies of twins raised apart have demonstrated that depression is genetic. It seems likely that a vulnerability to depression can be inherited. • Some of the most exciting research in depression centers on neurotransmitters, chemical messengers in the brain that carry signals from one neuron to another. Neurotransmitters involved in depression include serotonin, norepinephrine, corticotrophin-releasing factor, dopamine, and substance P. People with depression have alterations in these neurotransmitters.

Treating Depression

MILD TO MODERATE DEPRESSION APPEARS TO RESPOND equally well to psychotherapy (talking therapy) or pharmacotherapy (antidepressant medication). several types of psychotherapy are available for the brief treatment of depression. the effectiveness of two of these types, cognitive-behavioral therapy and interpersonal therapy, has been particularly well-documented. both focus on the present and take a practical, problem-solving approach to treatment.

Psychotherapy: Cognitive-behavioral therapy helps a depressed patient recognize, challenge, and change negative thought patterns and distorted perspectives, producing positive changes in outlook and mood. A depressed individual cannot simply will himself or herself to feel better. It's a common misconception that depression reflects a weakness of character and that depressed people simply need to "try harder." Before change can occur, negative and distorted thought patterns must be identified.

Interpersonal therapy is based on the theory that interpersonal problems can trigger or aggravate depression. Current interpersonal relationships are explored, and specific problem areas are identified as targets of treatment.

Pharmacotherapy: For more-severe depression, antidepressants should be considered—either alone or in combination with psychotherapy. Many people begin to see an improvement within one to three weeks of starting an antidepressant medication. In contrast, untreated major depression typically lasts from six months to two years.

The more episodes of depression a person has had, the longer treatment should last. Eight to 14 months of antidepressant therapy is appropriate for a first episode. For patients who have suffered three or more episodes of depression—especially if the episodes were severe—long-term treatment is suggested.

Selective serotonin reuptake inhibitors (SSRIs) were introduced more than a decade ago. These agents—including fluoxetine (Prozac); sertraline (Zoloft); paroxetine (Paxil); fluvoxamine (Luvox); and citalopram (Celexa)—are safer and have far fewer side effects than the older antidepressants.

Do You Have Depression?

You may have depression if you have suffered from a depressed mood or loss of interest or pleasure in most activities more days than not for at least two weeks; if at least five of the following symptoms have also been present more days than not, for at least two weeks; and if the symptoms are causing difficulties in your life.

- significant weight loss or gain
- change in sleeping patterns (either more or less)
- being noticeably more agitated or slowed down
- fatigue or loss of energy
- feelings of worthlessness or excessive guilt
- difficulty concentrating or making decisions
- recurrent thoughts of death or suicide

It's important to remember that many of these symptoms can be caused by conditions other than depression, such as thyroid deficiency and anemia. In addition, medications prescribed for other illnesses may cause side effects that resemble depression. Anyone who is experiencing symptoms of depression should see a knowledgeable health care provider for an accurate diagnosis.

SSRIs are thought to relieve depression by inhibiting the "reuptake" of serotonin by neurons in the brain. Neurotransmitters like serotonin communicate only two messages: "on" and "off." To signal "on," a neurotransmitter binds, or attaches, to a receptor cell. To signal "off," the neurotransmitter detaches from the receptor. Cells that manufacture norepinephrine, serotonin, or dopamine often will sweep up unbound neurotransmitters, repackage them, and release them again. This recycling is referred to as reuptake. SSRIs slow down the reuptake of serotonin, so that neurons in the brain must manufacture more new serotonin molecules each time an "on" signal needs to be sent. As a result, circulating levels of serotonin in the brain increase.

While the SSRIs are much better tolerated than older antidepressant agents, side effects remain. Common side effects include nausea, insomnia, sedation, headaches, sweating, reduced sexual desire, and difficulty reaching orgasm. The side effects may go away after the first few weeks, as the body adjusts to a new medication. Starting at a low dose and gradually increasing to the desired dose may minimize side effects. Taking the medication after meals may reduce nausea. Even when side effects persist, however, many people are happy to trade depression for these relatively minor complaints.

SNRIs: The New Generation of Antidepressants

A NEW GENERATION OF ANTIDEPRESSANTS, SEROTONIN norepinephrine reuptake inhibitors (SNRIs), has revolu-

tionized the treatment of depression. Serotonin and norepinephrine are neurotransmitters that are believed to be involved in the treatment of major depression. SNRIs include antidepressants such as venlafaxine XR (Effexor XR). Studies have shown that venlafaxine XR may be a more effective antidepressant than fluoxetine (Prozac). The studies demonstrate that a significantly greater number of patients receiving venlafaxine XR, compared with fluoxetine, achieve full remission, which means that patients taking venlafaxine XR were able to reduce their symptoms more completely than those taking fluoxetine.

These efficacy data have raised the bar in treating depression. Physicians are now looking for their treatments to provide not only symptomatic improvement, but also the fullest possible recovery for their patients. It is no longer enough for patients to get better; they need to get well.

Other newer antidepressants also are useful for large numbers of patients. Bupropion (Wellbutrin SR) is thought to act through the norepinephrine system and, perhaps, the dopamine system to treat depression. Two other agents, nefazodone (Serzone) and mirtazapine (Remeron), exert their antidepressant effects not by inhibiting reuptake but by preventing neurotransmitters from binding to receptors. Nefazodone blocks the serotonin type-2 receptor, and mirtazapine blocks the serotonin type-2 and type-3 receptors, along with the norepinephrine alpha-2 receptor.

In general, if an antidepressant has not improved symptoms of depression within four to six weeks, it's time to consider another approach to treatment. The American Psychiatric Association (APA) recommends three broad strategies in such cases. One choice is to switch to an antidepressant with a biochemical profile that is different from the first one. If switching is not desirable, the APA suggests adding thyroid hormone or lithium to the original antidepressant. A third choice is to add a second antidepressant to the first.

The monoamine oxidase inhibitors (MAOIs) and tricyclic antidepressants are older-generation antidepressants that represent valuable alternatives for patients who don't respond to any of the newer-generation agents. Developed in the 1950s, the MAOIs and tricyclic antidepressants were the mainstay of depression treatment for three decades before the SSRIs reached the market.

The MAOIs, including phenelzine (Nardil) and tranylcypromine (Parnate), are presumed to work by inhibiting an enzyme, monoamine oxidase, that is responsible for the metabolism of norepinephrine, serotonin, and dopamine. The MAOIs are highly effective at treating depression, but they are generally harder for patients to tolerate than the SSRIs. Not only do the MAOIs cause more troublesome side effects, but patients on MAOIs also must avoid aged or fermented foods and beverages. Another concern is that the MAOIs can be fatal when taken with certain other prescription medications.

The tricyclic antidepressants include imipramine (Tofranil and others); nortriptyline (Pamelor); desipramine (Norpramin); and amitriptyline (Elavil). Although tricyclic antidepressants are less expensive than newer-generation agents, their side-effect profile and safety concerns are worrisome. Common side effects include dry mouth, constipation, weight gain, dizziness, and rapid heart rate. In addition, an overdose of a tricyclic antidepressant can cause serious heart damage.

Other Therapy: For an unfortunate minority of patients, no combination of drugs seems to control depression. Two nondrug treatments, electroconvulsive therapy (ECT) and transcranial magnetic therapy, can be life-saving for these individuals. ECT is perhaps the most effective treatment for depression that cannot be controlled with drugs or psychotherapy, and it is very safe as currently performed. ECT is generally reserved for patients who have failed other treatments or have a life-threatening depression, due either to suicidal intentions or failure to eat or drink fluids.

Depression and Anxiety

WHILE DEPRESSION AND ANXIETY ARE CONSIDERED SEPARATE clinical conditions, they often are closely intertwined. Epidemiological studies show that of patients who are treated for anxiety, more than one-third also suffer from depression, and nearly two-thirds are diagnosed with another mood or anxiety disorder. Conversely, up to 90 percent of patients being treated for depression exhibit one or more symptoms of anxiety. A better understanding of the relationship between depression and anxiety may have important clinical implications for the management of patients who suffer from these conditions.

Most people experience anxiety at one time or another due to stressful life situations, such as bereavement or illness. But unlike everyday anxiety, clinical anxiety is a chronic, pathological condition. Clinical anxiety may appear in a wide array of forms, including generalized anxiety disorder (GAD), obsessive-compulsive disorder, panic, phobias (fears), or eating disorders.

A person who experiences both anxiety and depression simultaneously may find that the symptoms of one disorder exacerbate the other. For example, the presence of GAD may predict a worse outcome for people with another psychiatric diagnosis, such as depression. In addition, depressed patients with a high level of anxiety are at an increased risk of committing suicide. While treatments for anxiety do exist, venlafaxine XR has been shown to be the first antidepressant that may treat both depression and anxiety.

Major depression is a source of significant suffering and disability for many people—not only the patients themselves, but also their families, friends, and loved ones. Sadly, depression too often goes untreated, despite the availability of many safe and effective therapies, both biological and psychological.

The goal of treatment is to restore the depressed patient to a state of wellness and vitality, without any depressive symptoms at all. Merely lessening symptoms is not enough. With so many treatment options available, no one needs to accept depression as a way of life.

Dr. Kelsey is Assistant Professor and Director of the Mood and Anxiety Disorders Clinical Trials Program in the Department of Psychiatry and Behavioral Sciences at Emory University School of Medicine.

From *Healthline*, January 1999, pp. 6–11. © 1999 by *Healthline*. Reprinted by permission.

Secrets of Happiness

**After psychologist Steven Reiss survived a life-threatening illness,
he took a new look at the meaning of life. Now, based on a survey of more than 6,000 people,
Reiss offers new insights about what it really takes to be happy.**

By Steven Reiss, Ph.D.

Sometimes we are so consumed with our daily lives that we forget to look at the larger picture of who we are and what we need to be happy. We work, raise our children, and manage our chores, but it takes an extraordinary event such as a life-threatening illness, or the death of a loved one, to focus our attention on the meaning of our lives.

I faced death for the first time when I was told I needed a liver transplant a few years ago. I thought about the meaning in my life and why I lived the way I did. I started to question the Pleasure Principle, which says that we are motivated to maximize pleasure and minimize pain. When I was ill, I discovered exactly why I wanted to get better and continue living, and it had little to do with pleasure or pain.

Pleasure theory has been around since the days of ancient Greece and is well-represented in modern-day society and academic psychology. Socrates pondered the idea that pleasure is the basis of morality; he wondered if pleasure indicates moral good and pain indicates evil. Epicurus, the greatest of all pleasures theorists, believed that the key to a happy life was to minimize stomach distress, or anxiety, by changing one's attitudes and beliefs. His rational-emotive philosophy was popular for 700 years in ancient Greece and Rome.

More recently, *Playboy* founder Hugh Hefner used pleasure theory to justify the sexual revolution of the 1960s. Psychologist N. M. Bradburn said that the quality of a person's life can be measured by the excess of positive over negative feelings. So is maximizing pleasure and minimizing

pain the ultimate key to human happiness? No. When I was in the hospital analyzing what made my life satisfying, I didn't focus on the parties. In fact, pleasure and pain were not even considerations.

If pleasure is not what drives us, what does? What desires must we fulfill to live a happy life? To find out what *really* drives human behavior, my graduate students and I asked more than 6,000 people from many stations in life which values are most significant in motivating their behavior and in contributing to their sense of happiness. We analyzed the results to learn how different motives are related and what is behind their root meanings.

The results of our research showed that nearly everything we experience as meaningful can be traced to one of 16 basic desires or to some combination of these desires. We developed a standardized psychological test, called the Reiss Profile, to measure the 16 desires. (See box "The 16 Keys to Happiness.")

Happiness defined

Harvard social psychologist William McDougall wrote that people can be happy while in pain and unhappy while experiencing pleasure. To understand this, two kinds of happiness must be distinguished: feel-good and value-based. Feel-good happiness is sensation-based pleasure. When we joke around or have sex, we experience feel-good happiness. Since feel-good happiness is ruled by the law of diminishing returns, the kicks get harder to come by.

This type of happiness rarely lasts longer than a few hours at a time.

Value-based happiness is a sense that our lives have meaning and fulfill some larger purpose. It represents a spiritual source of satisfaction, stemming from our deeper purpose and values. We experience value-based happiness when we satisfy any of the 16 basic desires—the more desires we satisfy, the more value-based happiness we experience. Since this form of happiness is not ruled by the law of diminishing returns, there is no limit to how meaningful our lives can be.

Malcolm X's life is a good example of both feel-good and value-based happiness. When racial discrimination denied him the opportunity to pursue his childhood ambition of becoming a lawyer, he turned to a life of partying, drugs and sex. Yet this pleasure seeking produced little happiness—by the age of 21, he was addicted to cocaine and sent to jail for burglary. He had experienced a lot of pleasure, yet he was unhappy because his life was inconsistent with his own nature and deeper values. He had known feel-good happiness but not value-based happiness.

After reaching rock bottom, he embraced the teachings of the Nation of Islam and committed himself to his most fundamental values. He led his followers toward greater social justice, married, had a family of his own and found happiness. Although he experienced less pleasure and more anxiety as a leader, he was much happier because he lived his life in accordance with his values.

The 16 basic desires make us individuals. Although everybody embraces these desires, individuals prioritize them differently. Al Gore, for example, has a very strong desire for power. This desire makes him happy when he is in a leadership role, when he gives advice to others, or when he shows how competent and smart he is. George W. Bush has a strong desire for social contact. This desire makes him happy when he socializes and unhappy when he spends a lot of time alone. The two politicians place very different values on the basic desires of power and social contact, which is reflected in their personalities— Gore tends to be overbearing and overeager to get ahead, and Bush tends to be a good ol' boy.

Although everybody wants to attain a certain status, individuals differ in how motivated they are to obtain it. Jackie Kennedy Onassis, for example, had a passion for status—she needed to be wealthy to be truly happy. By obtaining wealth, she thought that she could satisfy her deep desire for respect from her upper-class peers. She spent much of her life pursuing wealth by marrying two multimillionaires. In contrast, Howard Hughes did not care much about status—he didn't care about what people thought of him and spent little time trying to earn their respect. While Jackie Kennedy Onassis placed high value on gaining status and the respect of her social peers, Howard Hughes had both but neither made him happy.

Revenge is another goal that motivates people differently. Now that Regis Philbin has hit the big time with his show "Who Wants To Be A Millionaire," why does he keep reminding us of the times he had been passed over earlier in his career? By embarrassing those who lacked faith in him, Philbin is gaining a measure of revenge. In comparison, John F. Kennedy Jr. did not go after people who criticized him or his family. Revenge can be fun, but it is more motivating for some than for others.

The 16 basic desires

You cannot find enduring happiness by aiming to have more fun or by seeking pleasure. What you need to do, as the 19th-century philosopher J. S. Mill observed, is to satisfy your basic desires and take happiness in passing. First, use the quiz to figure out who you are (see quiz, "The 16 keys to happiness"). Find out which of the 16 desires provide the most meaning in your life. How strongly are you motivated

to obtain a successful marriage, career or family? Do you love a good meal and dining out? Must you be physically fit to be happy? Fortunately, you do not have to satisfy all 16 desires, only the five or six most important to you.

After you identify your most important desires, you need to find effective ways to satisfy them. There is a catch, however. Shortly after you satisfy a desire, it reasserts itself, motivating you to satisfy the desire all over again. After a career success, for example, you feel competent, but only for a period of time. Therefore, you need to satisfy your desires repeatedly.

How can we repeatedly satisfy our most important basic desires and find value-based happiness? Most people turn to relationships, careers, family, leisure and spirituality to satisfy their most important desires.

Since we have the potential to satisfy our basic desires through relationships, we can find greater happiness by finding new relationships or by improving the ones we already have. After looking at the 16 basic desires and estimating the five or six most important to you, do the same for your partner, or have your partner take the quiz. Compare the two lists—the strengths of your relationship are indicated by similar desires, and the weaknesses are indicated by disparate desires.

Shelly and Sam are a good case in point. Before they married, both placed value on romance, fitness and socializing, but they differed on whether or not they should have children. Shelly secretly thought she could change Sam's mind. When Sam still did not want children after a few years of marriage, Shelly did not take her birth control pills one night and ended up having a baby boy. Sam loved his boy, but he didn't enjoy raising him.

What can Shelly and Sam do to improve their relationship and regain happiness? Counseling is worth a try, but even with the best counselor it will be difficult for them to resolve their differences. Their problem is that they prioritize the basic desire for family differently—one enjoys raising children, the other doesn't. The desire for family, which is not easily changed, has pulled them in different directions, turning a happy marriage into an unhappy one. Their best bet to improve their relationship may be to set aside time for activities that satisfy the desires that bind them. If they set aside time to put the romance back in their lives, maybe the strong points in the relationship will outweigh the weak ones. Ultimately, that is

the judgment we all must make, because few relationships are perfect.

Our basic desires can also be satisfied through work. Steven Spielberg, for example, honored his Jewish heritage when he made the movie *Schindler's List,* the Academy award-winning film about the Holocaust. When Spielberg thinks about his accomplishment, he feels a sense of loyalty to his Jewish heritage, an intrinsically valued feeling that satisfies the desire for honor.

Rocky Graziano also found value-based happiness through his career. Graziano was a fighter—that was who he was and who he wanted to be. He was an unhappy juvenile delinquent who got himself into fistfights. But when he became a boxer—rising to the rank of middleweight champion—he finally found work that provided a socially acceptable means for him to satisfy his passion for vengeance. Fighting had gone from a source of displeasure to a source of happiness in his life.

One way to become happier is to find a job or career that is more fulfilling than the one you have now. To do this, you need to analyze how you can use work to better satisfy your five or six most important basic desires. If you have a high desire for acceptance, for example, you need work that exposes you to little evaluation and potential criticism. If you have a high desire for order, you need work that involves minimal ambiguity and exposes you to few changes. If you are a curious person, you need a job that makes you think.

Our basic desires can also be satisfied through leisure activities. Watching sports, for example, provides us with opportunities to repeatedly experience the intrinsically valued feelings of competition, loyalty, power and revenge. When Brandi Chastain kicked the winning field goal and the United States won the 1999 World Cup in women's soccer, a surge of power went through the nation like a bolt of lightning—the crowd roared and people thrust their fists powerfully into the air. Sports produces more or less the same range of intrinsically valued feelings in fans as they do in players, which is why so many people watch.

One of the deepest ways to satisfy our desires is through spirituality. We can satisfy the desire for honor by embracing the religious denomination of our parents. A psychologically important attribute of religion is the emphasis given to the desire for unity, or to open one's heart to God. At least for some, faith is a path toward greater value-based happiness.

the 16 keys to happiness

To increase your value-based happiness, first read the following statements and mark whether they describe you strongly (+), somewhat (0), or very little (-). The ones that describe you strongly show the keys to your happiness--you should aim to satisfy these to increase your happiness. Some tips to help you do this can be found in the main article, and more can be found in the author's book, *Who Am I: The 16 Basic Desires That Motivate Our Happiness and Define Our Personalities.*

DESIRE	STATEMENT	SELF-RATING
CURIOSITY	I have a thirst for knowledge.	_____
ACCEPTANCE	I have a hard time coping with criticism.	_____
ORDER	It upsets me when things are out of place.	_____
PHYSICAL ACTIVITY	Physical fitness is very important to me.	_____
HONOR	I am a highly principled and loyal person.	_____
POWER	I often seek leadership roles.	_____
INDEPENDENCE	Self-reliance is essential to my happiness.	_____
SOCIAL CONTACT	I am known as a fun-loving person.	_____
FAMILY	My children come first.	_____
STATUS	I am impressed by people who own expensive things.	_____
IDEALISM	Compared with most people, I am very concerned with social causes.	_____
VENGEANCE	It is very important to me to get even with those who insult or offend me.	_____
ROMANCE	Compared with my peers, I spend much more time pursuing or having sex.	_____
EATING	I love to eat and often fantasize about food.	_____
SAVING	I hate throwing things away.	_____
TRANQUILITY	It scares me when my heart beats rapidly.	_____

Value-based happiness is the great equalizer in life. You can find value-based happiness if you are rich or poor, smart or mentally challenged, athletic or clumsy, popular or socially awkward. Wealthy people are not necessarily happy, and poor people are not necessarily unhappy. Values, not pleasure, are what bring true happiness, and everybody has the potential to live in accordance with their values.

READ MORE ABOUT IT

Who Am I: The 16 Basic Desires That Motivate Our Happiness and Define Our Personalities, Steven Reiss, Ph.D. (Tarcher/Putnam, 2000)

The Art of Happiness: A Handbook for Living, His Holiness the Dalai Lama and Howard C. Cutler, M. D. (Riverhead Books, 1998)

Steven Reiss, Ph.D., is a professor of psychology and psychiatry at Ohio State University, where he directs the university's Nisonger Center.

Reprinted with permission from *Psychology Today*, January/February 2001, pp. 50-56. © 2001 by Sussex Publishers, Inc.

Glossary

This glossary of psychology terms is included to provide you with a convenient and ready reference as you encounter general terms in your study of psychology and personal growth and behavior that are unfamiliar or require a review. It is not intended to be comprehensive, but taken together with the many definitions included in the articles themselves, it should prove to be quite useful.

abnormal behavior Behavior that contributes to maladaptiveness, is considered deviant by the culture, or that leads to personal psychological distress.

absolute threshold The minimum amount of physical energy required to produce a sensation.

accommodation Process in cognitive development; involves altering or reorganizing the mental picture to make room for a new experience or idea.

acculturation The process of becoming part of a new cultural environment.

acetylcholine A neurotransmitter involved in memory.

achievement drive The need to attain self-esteem, success, or status. Society's expectations strongly influence the achievement motive.

achievement style The way people behave in achievement situations; achievement styles include the direct, instrumental, and relational styles.

acquired immune deficiency syndrome (AIDS) A fatal disease of the immune system.

acquisition In conditioning, forming associations in first learning a task.

actor-observer bias Tendency to attribute the behavior of other people to internal causes and our own behavior to external causes.

acupuncture Oriental practice involving the insertion of needles into the body to control pain.

adaptation The process of responding to changes in the environment by altering responses to keep a person's behavior appropriate to environmental demands.

adjustment How we react to stress; some change that we make in response to the demands placed upon us.

adrenal glands Endocrine glands involved in stress and energy regulation.

adrenaline A hormone produced by the adrenal glands that is involved in physiological arousal; adrenaline is also called epinephrine.

aggression Behavior intended to harm a member of the same or another species.

agoraphobia Anxiety disorder in which an individual is excessively afraid of places or situations from which it would be difficult or embarrassing to escape.

alarm reaction The first stage of Hans Selye's general adaptation syndrome. The alarm reaction is the immediate response to stress; adrenaline is released and digestion slows. The alarm reaction prepares the body for an emergency.

all-or-none law The principle that states that a neuron only fires when a stimulus is above a certain minimum strength (threshold), and when it fires, it does so at full strength.

alogia Individuals with schizophrenia that show a reduction in speech.

alpha Brain-wave activity that indicates that a person is relaxed and resting quietly; 8–12 Hz.

altered state of consciousness (ASC) A state of consciousness in which there is a redirection of attention, a change in the aspects of the world that occupy a person's thoughts, and a change in the stimuli to which a person responds.

ambivalent attachment Type of infant-parent attachment in which the infant seeks contact but resists once the contact is made.

amphetamine A strong stimulant; increases arousal of the central nervous system.

amygdala A part of the limbic system involved in fear, aggression, and other social behaviors.

anal stage Psychosexual stage during which, according to Sigmund Freud, the child experiences the first restrictions on his or her impulses.

anorexia nervosa Eating disorder in which an individual becomes severely underweight because of self-imposed restrictions on eating.

antidepressants Drugs used to elevate the mood of depressed individuals, presumably by increasing the availability of the neurotransmitters norepinephrine and/or serotonin.

antisocial personality disorder Personality disorder in which individuals who engage in antisocial behavior experience no guilt or anxiety about their actions; sometimes called sociopathy or psychopathy.

anxiety disorder Fairly long-lasting disruption of a person's ability to deal with stress; often accompanied by feelings of fear and apprehension.

applied psychology The area of psychology that is most immediately concerned with helping to solve practical problems; includes clinical and counseling psychology as well as industrial, environmental, and legal psychology.

aptitude test Any test designed to predict what a person with the proper training can accomplish in the future.

archetypes In Carl Jung's personality theory, unconscious universal ideas shared by all humans.

arousal theory Theory that focuses on the energy (arousal) aspect of motivation; it states that we are motivated to initiate behaviors that help to regulate overall arousal level.

asocial phase Phase in attachment development in which the neonate does not distinguish people from objects.

assertiveness training Training that helps individuals stand up for their rights while not denying rights of other people.

assimilation Process in cognitive development; occurs when something new is taken into the child's mental picture.

attachment Process in which the individual shows behaviors that promote proximity with a specific object or person.

attention Process of focusing on particular stimuli in the environment.

attention deficit disorder Hyperactivity; inability to concentrate.

attitude Learned disposition that actively guides us toward specific behaviors; attitudes consist of feelings, beliefs, and behavioral tendencies.

attribution The cognitive process of determining the motives of someone's behavior, and whether they are internal or external.

autism A personality disorder in which a child does not respond socially to people.

autonomic nervous system The part of the peripheral nervous system that carries messages from the central nervous system to the endocrine glands, the smooth muscles controlling the heart, and the primarily involuntary muscles controlling internal processes; includes the sympathetic and parasympathetic nervous systems.

aversion therapy A counterconditioning therapy in which unwanted responses are paired with unpleasant consequences.

avoidance conditioning Learning situation in which a subject avoids a stimulus by learning to respond appropriately before the stimulus begins.

avolition Individuals with schizophrenia who lack motivation to follow through on an activity.

Glossary

backward conditioning A procedure in classical conditioning in which the US is presented and terminated before the termination of the CS; very ineffective procedure.

basal ganglia An area of the forebrain that is important to smooth muscle movement and actions. This area works in conjunction with the midbrain to help us avoid moving in choppy, fragmented ways.

behavior Anything you do or think, including various bodily reactions. Behavior includes physical and mental responses.

behavior genetics How genes influence behavior.

behavior modification Another term for behavior therapy; the modification of behavior through psychological techniques; often the application of conditioning principles to alter behavior.

behaviorism The school of thought founded by John Watson; it studied only observable behavior.

belongingness and love needs Third level of motives in Maslow's hierarchy; includes love and affection, friends, and social contact.

biological motives Motives that have a definite physiological basis and are biologically necessary for individual or species survival.

biological response system Systems of the body that are important in behavioral responding; includes the senses, muscles, endocrine system, and the nervous system.

biological therapy Treatment of behavior problems through biological techniques; major biological therapies include drug therapy, psychosurgery, and electroconvulsive therapy.

bipolar disorder Mood disorder characterized by extreme mood swings from sad depression to joyful mania; sometimes called manic depression.

blinding technique In an experiment, a control for bias in which the assignment of a subject to the experimental or control group is unknown to the subject or experimenter or both (a double-blind experiment).

body dysmorphic disorder Somatoform disorder characterized by a preoccupation with an imaginary defect in the physical appearance of a physically healthy person.

body language Communication through position and movement of the body.

bottom-up processing The psychoanalytic process of understanding communication by listening to words, then interpreting phrases, and finally understanding ideas.

brief psychodynamic therapy A therapy developed for individuals with strong egos to resolve a core conflict.

bulimia nervosa Eating disorder in which an individual eats large amounts of calorie-rich food in a short time and then purges the food by vomiting or using laxatives.

California Psychological Inventory (CPI) An objective personality test used to study normal populations.

Cannon-Bard theory of emotion Theory of emotion that states that the emotional feeling and the physiological arousal occur at the same time.

cardinal traits In Gordon Allport's personality theory, the traits of an individual that are so dominant that they are expressed in everything the person does; few people possess cardinal traits.

catatonic schizophrenia A type of schizophrenia that is characterized by periods of complete immobility and the apparent absence of will to move or speak.

causal attribution Process of determining whether a person's behavior is due to internal or external motives.

central nervous system The part of the human nervous system that interprets and stores messages from the sense organs, decides what behavior to exhibit, and sends appropriate messages to the muscles and glands; includes the brain and spinal cord.

central tendency In statistics, measures of central tendency give a number that represents the entire group or sample.

central traits In Gordon Allport's personality theory, the traits of an individual that form the core of the personality; they are developed through experience.

cerebellum The part of the hindbrain that is involved in balance and muscle coordination.

cerebral cortex The outermost layer of the cerebrum of the brain where higher mental functions occur. The cerebral cortex is divided into sections, or lobes, which control various activities.

cerebrum (cerebral hemisphere) Largest part of the forebrain involved in cognitive functions; the cerebrum consists of two hemispheres connected by the corpus callosum.

chromosome Bodies in the cell nucleus that contain the genes.

chunking Process of combining stimuli in order to increase memory capacity.

classical conditioning The form of learning in which a stimulus is associated with another stimulus that causes a particular response. Sometimes called Pavlovian conditioning or respondent conditioning.

clinical psychology Subfield in which psychologists assess psychological problems and treat people with behavior problems using psychological techniques (called psychotherapy).

cognition Mental processes, such as perception, attention, memory, language, thinking, and problem solving; cognition involves the acquisition, storage, retrieval, and utilization of knowledge.

cognitive behavior therapy A form of behavior therapy that identifies self-defeating attitudes and thoughts in a subject, and then helps the subject to replace these with positive, supportive thoughts.

cognitive development Changes over time in mental processes such as thinking, memory, language, and problem solving.

cognitive dissonance Leon Festinger's theory of attitude change that states that, when people hold two psychologically inconsistent ideas, they experience tension that forces them to reconcile the conflicting ideas.

cognitive expectancy The condition in which an individual learns that certain behaviors lead to particular goals; cognitive expectancy motivates the individual to exhibit goal-directed behaviors.

cognitive learning Type of learning that theorizes that the learner utilizes cognitive structures in memory to make decisions about behaviors.

cognitive psychology The area of psychology that includes the study of mental activities involved in perception, memory, language, thought, and problem solving.

cognitive restructuring The modification of the client's thoughts and perceptions that are contributing to his or her maladjustments.

cognitive therapy Therapy developed by Aaron Beck in which an individual's negative, self-defeating thoughts are restructured in a positive way.

cognitive-motivational-relational theory of emotion A theory of emotion proposed by Richard Lazarus that includes cognitive appraisal, motivational goals, and relationships between an individual and the environment.

collective unconscious Carl Jung's representation of the thoughts shared by all humans.

collectivistic cultures Cultures in which the greatest emphasis is on the loyalty of each individual to the group.

comparative psychology Subfield in which experimental psychologists study and compare the behavior of different species of animals.

compulsions Rituals performed excessively such as checking doors or washing hands to reduce anxiety.

concept formation (concept learning) The development of the ability to respond to common features of categories of objects or events.

concrete operations period Stage in cognitive development, from 7 to 11 years, in which the child's ability to solve problems with reasoning greatly increases.

conditioned response (CR) The response or behavior that occurs when the conditioned stimulus is presented (after the CS has been associated with the US).

conditioned stimulus (CS) An originally neutral stimulus that is associated with an unconditioned stimulus and takes on the latter's capability of eliciting a particular reaction.

conditioned taste aversion (CTA) An aversion to particular tastes associated with stomach distress; usually considered a unique form of classical conditioning because of the extremely long interstimulus intervals involved.

conditioning A term applied to two types of learning (classical and operant). Conditioning refers to the scientific aspect of the type of learning.

conflict Situation that occurs when we experience incompatible demands or desires; the outcome when one individual or group perceives that another individual or group has caused or will cause harm.

conformity Type of social influence in which an individual changes his or her behavior to fit social norms or expectations.

connectionism Recent approach to problem solving; the development of neural connections allows us to think and solve problems.

conscientiousness The dimension in the five-factor personality theory that includes traits such as practical, cautious, serious, reliable, careful, and ambitious; also called dependability.

conscious Being aware of experiencing sensations, thoughts, and feelings at any given point in time.

conscious mind In Sigmund Freud's psychoanalytic theory of personality, the part of personality that we are aware of in everyday life.

consciousness The processing of information at various levels of awareness; state in which a person is aware of sensations, thoughts, and feelings.

consensus In causal attribution, the extent to which other people react as the subject does in a particular situation.

conservation The ability to recognize that something stays the same even if it takes on a different form; Piaget tested conservation of mass, number, length, and volume.

consistency In causal attribution, the extent to which the subject always behaves in the same way in a situation.

consolidation The biological neural process of making memories permanent; possibly short-term memory is electrically coded and long-term memory is chemically coded.

contingency model A theory that specific types of situations need particular types of leaders.

continuum of preparedness Martin Seligman's proposal that animals are biologically prepared to learn certain responses more readily than they are prepared to learn others.

control group Subjects in an experiment who do not receive the independent variable; the control group determines the effectiveness of the independent variable.

conventional morality Level II in Lawrence Kohlberg's theory, in which moral reasoning is based on conformity and social standards.

conversion disorder Somatoform disorder in which a person displays obvious disturbance in the nervous system without a physical basis for the problem.

correlation Statistical technique to determine the degree of relationship that exists between two variables.

counterconditioning A behavior therapy in which an unwanted response is replaced by conditioning a new response that is incompatible with it.

creativity A process of coming up with new or unusual responses to familiar circumstances.

critical period hypothesis Period of time during development in which particular learning or experiences normally occur; if learning does not occur, the individual has a difficult time learning it later.

culture-bound The idea that a test's usefulness is limited to the culture in which it was written and utilized.

cumulative response curve Graphed curve that results when responses for a subject are added to one another over time; if subjects respond once every 5 minutes, they will have a cumulative response curve value of 12 after an hour.

curiosity motive Motive that causes the individual to seek out a certain amount of novelty.

cyclothymia disorder A moderately severe problem with numerous periods of hypomanic episodes and depressive symptoms.

death instinct (also called Thanatos) Freud's term for an instinct that is destructive to the individual or species; aggression is a major expression of death instinct.

decay Theory of forgetting in which sensory impressions leave memory traces that fade away with time.

defense mechanisms Psychological techniques to help protect ourselves from stress and anxiety, to resolve conflicts, and to preserve our self-esteem.

delayed conditioning A procedure in classical conditioning in which the presentation of the CS precedes the onset of the US and the termination of the CS is delayed until the US is presented; most effective procedure.

delusion The holding of obviously false beliefs; for example, imagining someone is trying to kill you.

dendrites The branch-like structures of neurons that extend from the cell body (soma). The dendrites are the receivers of neural impulses (electrical and chemical signals) from the axons of other neurons. Although there are some areas of the body that contain dendrites that can act like axon terminals, releasing neurotransmitters in response to impulses and local voltage changes, most dendrites are the receiving branches of the neuron.

dependent variable In psychology, the behavior or response that is measured; it is dependent on the independent variable.

depersonalization disorder Dissociative disorder in which the individual escapes from his or her own personality by believing that he or she does not exist or that his or her environment is not real.

depolarization Any change in which the internal electrical charge becomes more positive.

depression A temporary emotional state that normal individuals experience or a persistent state that may be considered a psychological disorder. Characterized by sadness and low self-esteem.

descriptive statistics Techniques that help summarize large amounts of data information.

developmental psychology Study of physical and mental growth and behavioral changes in individuals from conception to death.

Diagnostic and Statistical Manual of Mental Disorders (DSM) Published by the American Psychiatric Association in 1952, and revised in 1968, 1980, 1987, and 1994, this manual was provided to develop a set of diagnoses of abnormal behavior patterns.

diffusion of responsibility Finding that groups tend to inhibit helping behavior; responsibility is shared equally by members of the group so that no one individual feels a strong commitment.

disorganized schizophrenia A type of schizophrenia that is characterized by a severe personality disintegration; the individual often displays bizarre behavior.

displacement Defense mechanism by which the individual directs his or her aggression or hostility toward a person or object other than the one it should be directed toward; in Freud's dream theory, the process of reassigning emotional feelings from one object to another one.

dissociative disorder Psychological disorder that involves a disturbance in the memory, consciousness, or identity of an individual; types include multiple personality disorder, depersonalization disorder, psychogenic amnesia, and psychogenic fugue.

dissociative fugue Individuals who have lost their memory, relocated to a new geographical area, and started a new life as someone else.

dissociative identity disorder (multiple personality disorder) Dissociative disorder in which several personalities are present in the same individual.

distinctiveness In causal attribution, the extent to which the subject reacts the same way in other situations.

Down syndrome Form of mental retardation caused by having three number 21 chromosomes (trisomy 21).

Glossary

dream analysis Psychoanalytic technique in which a patient's dreams are reviewed and analyzed to discover true feelings.

drive Motivational concept used to describe the internal forces that push an organism toward a goal; sometimes identified as psychological arousal arising from a physiological need.

dyssomnia Sleep disorder in which the chief symptom is a disturbance in the amount and quality of sleep; they include insomnia and hypersomnia.

dysthymic disorder Mood disorder in which the person suffers moderate depression much of the time for at least two years.

ego Sigmund Freud's term for an individual's sense of reality.

egocentric Seeing the world only from your perspective.

eidetic imagery Photographic memory; ability to recall great detail accurately after briefly viewing something.

Electra complex The Freudian idea that the young girl feels inferior to boys because she lacks a penis.

electroconvulsive therapy (ECT) A type of biological therapy in which electricity is applied to the brain in order to relieve severe depression.

emotion A response to a stimulus that involves physiological arousal, subjective feeling, cognitive interpretation, and overt behavior.

empiricism The view that behavior is learned through experience.

encoding The process of putting information into the memory system.

encounter group As in a sensitivity training group, a therapy where people become aware of themselves in meeting others.

endorphins Several neuropeptides that function as neurotransmitters. The opiate-like endorphins are involved in pain, reinforcement, and memory.

engram The physical memory trace or neural circuit that holds memory; also called memory trace.

episodic memory Highest memory system; includes information about personal experiences.

Eros Sigmund Freud's term for an instinct that helps the individual or species survive; also called life instinct.

esteem needs Fourth level of motives in Abraham Maslow's hierarchy; includes high evaluation of oneself, self-respect, self-esteem, and respect of others.

eustress Stress that results from pleasant and satisfying experiences; earning a high grade or achieving success produces eustress.

excitement phase First phase in the human sexual response cycle; the beginning of sexual arousal.

experimental group Subjects in an experiment who receive the independent variable.

experimental psychology Subfield in which psychologists research the fundamental causes of behavior. Many experimental psychologists conduct experiments in basic research.

experimenter bias Source of potential error in an experiment from the action or expectancy of the experimenter; might influence the experimental results in ways that mask the true outcome.

external locus of control In Julian Rotter's personality theory, the perception that reinforcement is independent of a person's behavior.

extraversion The dimension in the five-factor personality theory that includes traits such as sociability, talkativeness, boldness, fun-lovingness, adventurousness, and assertiveness; also called surgency. The personality concept of Carl Jung in which the personal energy of the individual is directed externally.

factor analysis A statistical procedure used to determine the relationship among variables.

false memories Memories believed to be real, but the events never occurred.

fast mapping A process by which children can utilize a word after a single exposure.

fetal alcohol syndrome (FAS) Condition in which defects in the newborn child are caused by the mother's excessive alcohol intake.

five-factor model of personality tracts A trait theory of personality that includes the factors of extraversion, agreeableness, conscientiousness, emotional stability, and openness.

fixed action pattern (FAP) Unlearned, inherited, stereotyped behaviors that are shown by all members of a species; term used in ethology.

fixed interval (FI) schedule Schedule of reinforcement where the subject receives reinforcement for a correct response given after a specified time interval.

fixed ratio (FR) schedule Schedule of reinforcement in which the subject is reinforced after a certain number of responses.

flashbulb memory Memory of an event that is so important that significant details are vividly remembered for life.

forgetting In memory, not being able to retrieve the original learning. The part of the original learning that cannot be retrieved is said to be forgotten.

formal operations period Period in cognitive development; at 11 years, the adolescent begins abstract thinking and reasoning. This period continues throughout the rest of life.

free association Psychoanalytic technique in which the patient says everything that comes to mind.

free recall A verbal learning procedure in which the order of presentation of the stimuli is varied and the subject can learn the items in any order.

frequency theory of hearing Theory of hearing that states that the frequency of vibrations at the basilar membrane determines the frequency of firing of neurons carrying impulses to the brain.

frustration A cause of stress that results from the blocking of a person's goal-oriented behavior.

frustration-drive theory of aggression Theory of aggression that states that it is caused by frustration.

functionalism School of thought that studied the functional value of consciousness and behavior.

fundamental attribution error Attribution bias in which people overestimate the role of internal disposition and underestimate the role of external situation.

gate-control theory of pain Theory of pain that proposes that there is a gate that allows pain impulses to travel from the spinal cord to the brain.

gender-identity disorder (GID) Incongruence between assigned sex and gender identity.

gender-identity/role Term that incorporates gender identity (the private perception of one's sex) and gender role (the public expression of one's gender identity).

gene The basic unit of heredity; the gene is composed of deoxyribonucleic acid (DNA).

general adaptation syndrome (GAS) Hans Selye's theory of how the body responds to stress over time. GAS includes alarm reaction, resistance, and exhaustion.

generalized anxiety disorder Anxiety disorder in which the individual lives in a state of constant severe tension, continuous fear, and apprehension.

genetics The study of heredity; genetics is the science of discovering how traits are passed along generations.

genotype The complete set of genes inherited by an individual from his or her parents.

Gestalt therapy Insight therapy designed to help people become more aware of themselves in the here and now and to take responsibility for their own actions.

grandiose delusion Distortion of reality; one's belief that he or she is extremely important or powerful.

group therapy Treatment of several patients at the same time.

groupthink When group members are so committed to, and optimistic about, the group that they feel it is invulnerable; they become so concerned with maintaining consensus that criticism is muted.

GSR (galvanic skin response) A measure of autonomic nervous system activity; a slight electric current is passed over the skin, and the more nervous a subject is, the easier the current will flow.

hallucinations A sensory impression reported when no external stimulus exists to justify the report; often hallucinations are a symptom of mental illness.

hallucinogens Psychedelic drugs that result in hallucinations at high doses, and other effects on behavior and perception in mild doses.

halo effect The finding that once we form a general impression of someone, we tend to interpret additional information about the person in a consistent manner.

Hawthorne effect The finding that behavior can be influenced just by participation in a research study.

health psychology Field of psychology that studies psychological influences on people's health, including how they stay healthy, why they become ill, and how their behavior relates to their state of health.

heuristic Problem-solving strategy; a person tests solutions most likely to be correct.

hierarchy of needs Abraham Maslow's list of motives in humans, arranged from the biological to the uniquely human.

hippocampus Brain structure in the limbic system that is important in learning and memory.

homeostasis The state of equilibrium that maintains a balance in the internal body environment.

hormones Chemicals produced by the endocrine glands that regulate activity of certain bodily processes.

humanistic psychology Psychological school of thought that believes that people are unique beings who cannot be broken down into parts.

hyperphagia Disorder in which the individual continues to eat until he or she is obese; can be caused by damage to ventromedial hypothalamus.

hypersomnia Sleep disorder in which an individual falls asleep at inappropriate times; narcolepsy is a form of hypersomnia.

hypnosis Altered state of consciousness characterized by heightened suggestibility.

hypochondriasis Somatoform disorder in which the individual is obsessed with fears of having a serious medical disease.

hypothalamus Part of the brain's limbic system; involved in motivational behaviors, including eating, drinking, and sex.

hypothesis In the scientific method, an educated guess or prediction about future observable events.

iconic memory Visual information that is encoded into the sensory memory store.

id Sigmund Freud's representation of the basic instinctual drives; the id always seeks pleasure.

identification The process in which children adopt the attitudes, values, and behaviors of their parents.

identity diffusion In Marcia's adolescent identity theory, the status of individuals who have failed to make a commitment to values and roles.

illusion An incorrect perception that occurs when sensation is distorted.

imitation The copying of another's behavior; learned through the process of observation.

impression formation Developing an evaluation of another person from your perceptions; first, or initial, impressions are often very important.

imprinting A form of early learning in which birds follow a moving stimulus (often the mother); may be similar to attachment in mammals.

independent variable The condition in an experiment that is controlled and manipulated by the experimenter; it is a stimulus that will cause a response.

indiscriminate attachment phase Stage of attachment in which babies prefer humans to nonhumans, but do not discriminate among individual people.

individuation Carl Jung's concept of the process leading to the unification of all parts of the personality.

inferential statistics Techniques that help researchers make generalizations about a finding based on a limited number of subjects.

inferiority complex Adler's personality concept that states that because children are dependent on adults and cannot meet the standards set for themselves they feel inferior.

inhibition Restraint of an impulse, desire, activity, or drive.

insight A sudden grasping of the means necessary to achieve a goal; important in the Gestalt approach to problem solving.

insight therapy Therapy based on the assumption that behavior is abnormal because people do not adequately understand the motivation causing their behavior.

instinct Highly stereotyped behavior common to all members of a species that often appears in virtually complete form in the absence of any obvious opportunities to learn it.

instrumental conditioning Operant conditioning.

intelligence Capacity to learn and behave adaptively.

intelligence quotient (IQ) An index of a person's performance on an intelligence test relative to others in the culture; ratio of a person's mental age to chronological age.

interference Theory of forgetting in which information that was learned before (proactive interference) or after (retroactive interference) causes the learner to be unable to remember the material of interest.

internal locus of control In Rotter's personality theory, the perception that reinforcement is contingent upon behavior.

interstimulus interval Time interval between two stimuli; in classical conditioning, it is the elapsed time between the CS and the US.

intrinsic motivation Motivation inside the individual; we do something because we receive satisfaction from it.

introspection Method in which a subject gives a self report of his or her immediate experience.

introversion The personality concept of Carl Jung in which the personal energy of the individual is directed inward; characterized by introspection, seriousness, inhibition, and restraint.

James-Lange theory of emotion Theory of emotion that states that the physiological arousal and behavior come before the subjective experience of an emotion.

kinesthesis The sense of bodily movement.

labeling of arousal Experiments suggest that an individual experiencing physical arousal that cannot be explained will interpret those feelings in terms of the situation she or he is in and will use environmental and contextual cues.

language acquisition device (LAD) Hypothesized biological structure that accounts for the relative ease of acquiring language, according to Noam Chomsky.

latent dream content In Sigmund Freud's dream theory, the true thoughts in the unconsciousness; the true meaning of the dream.

latent learning Learning that occurs when an individual acquires knowledge of something but does not show it until motivated to do so.

law of effect Edward Thorndike's law that if a response produces satisfaction it will be repeated; reinforcement.

learned helplessness Condition in which a person learns that his or her behavior has no effect on his or her environment; when an individual gives up and stops trying.

learned social motives Social motives that are learned; include achievement and affiliation.

learning The relatively permanent change in behavior or behavioral ability of an individual that occurs as a result of experience.

Glossary

learning styles The preferences students have for learning; theories of learning styles include personality differences, styles of information processing, and instructional preferences.

life instinct (also called Eros) Sigmund Freud's term for an instinct that helps the individual or species survive; sex is the major expression of life instinct.

life structure In Daniel Levinson's theory of adult personality development, the underlying pattern of an individual's life at any particular time; seasonal cycles include preadulthood, early adulthood, middle adulthood, and late adulthood.

linguistic relativity hypothesis Proposal that the perception of reality differs according to the language of the observer.

locus of control Julian Rotter's theory in which a person's beliefs about reinforcement are classified as internal or external.

long-term memory The permanent memory where rehearsed information is stored.

love An emotion characterized by knowing, liking, and becoming intimate with someone.

low-ball procedure The compliance technique of presenting an attractive proposal to someone and then switching it to a more unattractive proposal.

magic number 7 The finding that most people can remember about seven items of information for a short time (in short-term memory).

magnetic resonance imaging (MRI) A method of studying brain activity using magnetic field imaging.

major depressive disorder Severe mood disorder in which a person experiences one or more major depressive episodes; sometimes referred to simply as depression.

maladjustment Condition that occurs when a person utilizes inappropriate abilities to respond to demands placed upon him or her.

manic depressive reaction A form of mental illness marked by alternations of extreme phases of elation (manic phase) and depression.

manifest dream content In Sigmund Freud's dream theory, what is remembered about a dream upon waking; a disguised representation of the unconscious wishes.

maturation The genetically controlled process of growth that results in orderly changes in behavior.

mean The arithmetic average, in which the sum of scores is divided by the number of scores.

median The middle score in a group of scores that are arranged from lowest to highest.

meditation The practice of some form of relaxed concentration while ignoring other sensory stimuli.

memory The process of storing information so that it can be retrieved and used later.

memory attributes The critical features of an event that are used when the experience is encoded or retrieved.

mental age The age level on which a person is capable of performing; used in determining intelligence.

mental set Condition in which a person's thinking becomes so standardized that he or she approaches new problems in fixed ways.

microexpressions Facial expressions that last a fraction of a second. Since microexpressions do not last long, they go undetected in our everyday lives. Microexpressions are a type of nonverbal communication.

Minnesota Multiphasic Personality Inventory (MMPI-2) An objective personality test that was originally devised to identify personality disorders.

mnemonic technique Method of improving memory by combining and relating chunks of information.

modeling A process of learning by imitation in a therapeutic situation.

mood disorder Psychological disorder in which a person experiences a severe disruption in mood or emotional balance.

moral development Development of individuals as they adopt their society's standards of right and wrong; development of awareness of ethical behavior.

motivated forgetting (repression) Theory that suggests that people want to forget unpleasant events.

motivation The forces that initiate and direct behavior, and the variables that determine the intensity and persistence of the behavior.

motivator needs In Frederick Herzberg's theory, the factors that lead to job satisfaction; they include responsibility, the nature of the work, advancement, and recognition.

motive Anything that arouses the individual and directs his or her behavior toward some goal. Three categories of motives include biological, stimulus, and learned social.

Müller-Lyer illusion A well-known illusion, in which two horizontal lines have end lines either going in or out; the line with the end lines going in appears longer.

multiple approach-avoidance conflict Conflict that occurs when an individual has two or more goals, both of which have positive and negative aspects.

multiple attachment phase Later attachment stage in which the baby begins to form attachments to people other than the primary caretaker.

multiple intelligences Howard Gardner's theory that there exists several different kinds of intelligence.

Myers-Briggs Type Indicator (MBTI) Objective personality test based on Carl Jung's type theory.

narcotic analgesics Drugs that have an effect on the body similar to morphine; these relieve pain and suppress coughing.

naturalistic observation Research method in which behavior of people or animals in their normal environment is accurately recorded.

Necker cube A visual illusion. The Necker cube is a drawing of a cube designed so that it is difficult to determine which side is toward you.

negative reinforcement Removing something unpleasant to increase the probability that the preceding behavior will be repeated.

NEO Personality Inventory (NEO-PI) An objective personality test developed by Paul Costa Jr. and Robert McCrae to measure the five major factors in personality; consists of 181 questions.

neodissociation theory Idea that consciousness can be split into several streams of thought that are partially independent of each other.

neuron A specialized cell that functions to conduct messages throughout the body.

neurosis A Freudian term that was used to describe abnormal behavior caused by anxiety; it has been eliminated from *DSM-IV*.

neutral stimulus A stimulus that does not cause the response of interest; the individual may show some response to the stimulus but not the associated behavior.

norm A sample of scores representative of a population.

normal curve When scores of a large number of random cases are plotted on a graph, they often fall into a bell-shaped curve; as many cases on the curve are above the mean as below it.

observational learning In social learning theory, learning by observing someone else behave; people observe and imitate in learning socialization.

obsessions Fears that involve the inability to control impulses.

obsessive compulsive disorder Anxiety disorder in which the individual has repetitive thoughts (obsessions) that lead to constant urges (compulsions) to engage in meaningless rituals.

object permanence The ability to realize that objects continue to exist even if we can no longer see them.

Oedipus complex The Freudian idea that the young boy has sexual feelings for his mother and is jealous of his father and must identify with his father to resolve the conflict.

olfaction The smell sense.

openness The dimension in the five-factor personality theory that includes traits such as imagination, creativity, perception, knowledge, artistic ability, curiosity, and analytical ability; also called intellect.

operant conditioning Form of learning in which behavior followed by reinforcement (satisfaction) increases in frequency.

opponent-process theory Theory that when one emotion is experienced, the other is suppressed.

optimum level of arousal Motivation theory that states that the individual will seek a level of arousal that is comfortable.

organic mental disorders Psychological disorders that involve physical damage to the nervous system; can be caused by disease or by an accident.

organizational psychology Area of industrial psychology that focuses on worker attitudes and motivation; derived primarily from personality and social psychology.

orgasm The climax of intense sexual excitement; release from building sexual tension, usually accompanied by ejaculation in men.

paired-associate learning A verbal learning procedure in which the subject is presented with a series of pairs of items to be remembered.

panic disorder Anxiety disorder characterized by the occurrence of specific periods of intense fear.

paranoid schizophrenia A type of schizophrenia in which the individual often has delusions of grandeur and persecution, thinking that someone is out to get him or her.

partial reinforcement Any schedule of reinforcement in which reinforcement follows only some of the correct responses.

partial reinforcement effect The finding that partial reinforcement produces a response that takes longer to extinguish than continuous reinforcement.

pattern recognition Memory process in which information attended to is compared with information already permanently stored in memory.

Pavlovian conditioning A bond or association between a neutral stimulus and a response; this type of learning is called classical conditioning.

perception The active process in which the sensory information that is carried through the nervous system to the brain is organized and interpreted; the interpretation of sensation.

persecutory delusion A delusion in which the individual has a distortion of reality; the belief that other people are out to get him or her.

person perception The process of using the information we gather in forming impressions of people to make evaluations of others.

personal unconscious Carl Jung's representation of the individual's repressed thoughts and memories.

personality disorder Psychological disorder in which there are problems in the basic personality structure of the individual.

phantom-limb pain Phenomenon in which people who have lost an arm or leg feel pain in the missing limb.

phobias Acute excessive fears of specific situations or objects that have no convincing basis in reality.

physiological needs First level of motives in Abraham Maslow's hierarchy; includes the biological needs of hunger, thirst, sex, exercise, and rest.

placebo An inert or inactive substance given to control subjects to test for bias effects.

plateau phase Second phase in the human sexual response cycle, during which the physiological arousal becomes more intense.

pleasure principle In Freudian theory, the idea that the instinctual drives of the id unconsciously and impulsively seek immediate pleasure.

positive reinforcement Presenting a subject something pleasant to increase the probability that the preceding behavior will be repeated.

Positron Emission Tomography (PET) Similar to the MRI, this method enables psychologists and doctors to study the brain (or any other living tissue) without surgery. PET uses radioactive glucose (instead of a strong magnetic field) to help study activity and locate structures in the body.

postconventional morality Level III in Lawrence Kohlberg's theory, in which moral reasoning is based on personal standards and beliefs; highest level of moral thinking.

posttraumatic stress disorder (PTSD) Condition that can occur when a person experiences a severely distressing event; characterized by constant memories of the event, avoidance of anything associated with it, and general arousal.

Prägnanz (law of) Gestalt psychology law that states that people have a tendency to group stimuli according to rules, and that people do this whenever possible.

preconscious mind In Sigmund Freud's psychoanalytic theory of personality, the part of personality that contains information that we have learned but that we are not thinking about at the present time.

preconventional morality Level I of Lawrence Kohlberg's theory, in which moral reasoning is largely due to the expectation of rewards and punishments.

prejudice An unjustified fixed, usually negative, way of thinking about a person or object.

Premack principle Principle that states that, of any two responses, the one that is more likely to occur can be used to reinforce the response that is less likely to occur.

preoperational thought period Period in cognitive development; from two to seven years, the period during which the child learns to represent the environment with objects and symbols.

primary appraisal Activity of determining whether a new stimulus event is positive, neutral, or negative; first step in appraisal of stress.

primary narcissism A Freudian term that refers to the oral phase before the ego has developed; the individual constantly seeks pleasure.

primary reinforcement Reinforcement that is effective without having been associated with other reinforcers; sometimes called unconditioned reinforcement.

probability (p) In inferential statistics, the likelihood that the difference between the experimental and control groups is due to the independent variable.

procedural memory The most basic type of long-term memory; involves the formation of associations between stimuli and responses.

projection Defense mechanism in which a person attributes his or her unacceptable characteristics or motives to others rather than himself or herself.

projective personality test A personality test that presents ambiguous stimuli to which subjects are expected to respond with projections of their own personality.

proximity Closeness in time and space. In perception, it is the Gestalt perceptual principle in which stimuli next to one another are included together.

psyche According to Carl Jung, the thoughts and feelings (conscious and unconscious) of an individual.

psychoactive drug A drug that produces changes in behavior and cognition through modification of conscious awareness.

psychoanalysis The school of thought founded by Sigmund Freud that stressed unconscious motivation. In therapy, a patient's unconscious motivation is intensively explored in order to bring repressed conflicts up to consciousness; psychoanalysis usually takes a long time to accomplish.

psychobiology (also called biological psychology or physiological psychology) The subfield of experimental psychology concerned with the influence of heredity and the biological response systems on behavior.

psychogenic amnesia A dissociative disorder in which an individual loses his or her sense of identity.

psychogenic fugue A dissociative disorder in which an individual loses his or her sense of identity and goes to a new geographic location, forgetting all of the unpleasant emotions connected with the old life.

Glossary

psychographics A technique used in consumer psychology to identify the attitudes of buyers and their preferences for particular products.

psycholinguistics The psychological study of how people convert the sounds of a language into meaningful symbols that can be used to communicate with others.

psychological dependence Situation in which a person craves a drug even though it is not biologically needed by the body.

psychological disorder A diagnosis of abnormal behavior; syndrome of abnormal adjustment, classified in *DSM*.

psychological types Carl Jung's term for different personality profiles; Jung combined two attitudes and four functions to produce eight psychological types.

psychopharmacology Study of effects of psychoactive drugs on behavior.

psychophysics An area of psychology in which researchers compare the physical energy of a stimulus with the sensation reported.

psychosexual stages Sigmund Freud's theoretical stages in personality development.

psychosomatic disorders A variety of body reactions that are closely related to psychological events.

psychotherapy Treatment of behavioral disorders through psychological techniques; major psychotherapies include insight therapy, behavior therapy, and group therapy.

psychotic disorders The more severe categories of abnormal behavior.

puberty Sexual maturation; the time at which the individual is able to perform sexually and to reproduce.

quantitative trait loci (QTLs) Genes that collectively contribute to a trait for high intelligence.

rational-emotive therapy A cognitive behavior modification technique in which a person is taught to identify irrational, self-defeating beliefs and then to overcome them.

reaction formation Defense mechanism in which a person masks an unconsciously distressing or unacceptable trait by assuming an opposite attitude or behavior pattern.

reality principle In Freudian theory, the idea that the drives of the ego try to find socially acceptable ways to gratify the id.

reciprocal determinism The concept proposed by Albert Bandura that the behavior, the individual, and the situation interact and influence each other.

reciprocal inhibition Concept of Joseph Wolpe that states that it is possible to break the bond between anxiety provoking stimuli and responses manifesting anxiety by facing those stimuli in a state antagonistic to anxiety.

reflex An automatic movement that occurs in direct response to a stimulus.

regression Defense mechanism in which a person retreats to an earlier, more immature form of behavior.

reinforcement Any event that increases the probability that the behavior that precedes it will be repeated; also called a reinforcer; similar to a reward.

reinforcement therapy A behavior therapy in which reinforcement is used to modify behavior. Techniques in reinforcement therapy include shaping, extinction, and token economy.

REM Sleep There are two main categories of sleep, Non-Rapid Eye Movement Sleep (NREM; which contains stages 1–4; basically everything except REM), and Rapid Eye Movement Sleep (REM). REM sleep is a sleep period during which your brain is very active, and your eyes move in a sharp, back-and-forth motion as opposed to a slower, more rolling fashion that occurs in other stages of sleep. People often believe mistakenly that humans only dream during REM sleep, although humans also dream during slow wave sleep (stages 3 and 4). However it is true that the majority of our dreaming occurs during REM sleep.

repression Defense mechanism in which painful memories and unacceptable thoughts and motives are conveniently forgotten so that they will not have to be dealt with.

residual schizophrenia Type of schizophrenia in which the individual currently does not have symptoms but has had a schizophrenic episode in the past.

resistance Psychoanalytic term used when a patient avoids a painful area of conflict.

resolution phase The last phase in the human sexual response cycle; the time after orgasm when the body gradually returns to the unaroused state.

Restricted Environmental Stimulation Technique (REST) Research technique in which environmental stimuli available to an individual are reduced drastically; formerly called sensory deprivation.

retrograde amnesia Forgetting information recently learned because of a disruptive stimulus such as an electric shock.

reversible figure In perception, a situation in which the figure and ground seem to reverse themselves; an illusion in which objects alternate as the main figure.

Rorschach Inkblot Test A projective personality test in which subjects are asked to discuss what they see in cards containing blots of ink.

safety needs Second level of motives in Abraham Maslow's hierarchy; includes security, stability, dependency, protection, freedom from fear and anxiety, and the need for structure and order.

Schachter-Singer theory of emotion Theory of emotion that states that we interpret our arousal according to our environment and label our emotions accordingly.

scheme A unit of knowledge that the person possesses; used in Jean Piaget's cognitive development theory.

schizophrenia Severe psychotic disorder that is characterized by disruptions in thinking, perception, and emotion.

scientific method An attitude and procedure that scientists use to conduct research. The steps include stating the problem, forming the hypothesis, collecting the information, evaluating the information, and drawing conclusions.

secondary appraisal In appraisal of stress, this is the evaluation that an individual's abilities and resources are sufficient to meet the demands of a stressful event.

secondary reinforcement Reinforcement that is effective only after it has been associated with a primary reinforcer; also called conditioned reinforcement.

secondary traits In Gordon Allport's personality theory, the less important situation-specific traits that help round out personality; they include attitudes, skills, and behavior patterns.

secure attachment Type of infant-parent attachment in which the infant actively seeks contact with the parent.

self-actualization A humanistic term describing the state in which all of an individual's capacities are developed fully. Fifth and highest level of motives in Abraham Maslow's hierarchy, this level, the realization of one's potential, is rarely reached.

self-efficacy An individual's sense of self-worth and success in adjusting to the world.

self-esteem A measurement of how people view themselves. People who view themselves favorably have good self-esteem whereas people who view themselves negatively have poor self-esteem. Self-esteem affects a person's behavior dramatically.

self-evaluation maintenance model (SEM) Tesser's theory of how we maintain a positive self-image despite the success of others close to us.

self-handicapping strategy A strategy that people use to prepare for failure; people behave in ways that produce obstacles to success so that when they do fail they can place the blame on the obstacle.

self-serving bias An attribution bias in which an individual attributes success to his or her own behavior and failure to external environmental causes.

semantic memory Type of long-term memory that can use cognitive activities, such as everyday knowledge.

sensation The passive process in which stimuli are received by sense receptors and transformed into neural impulses that can be carried through the nervous system; first stage in becoming aware of environment.

sensitivity training group (T-group) Therapy group that has the goal of making participants more aware of themselves and their ideas.

sensorimotor period Period in cognitive development; the first two years, during which the infant learns to coordinate sensory experiences with motor activities.

sensory adaptation Tendency of the sense organs to adjust to continuous stimulation by reducing their functioning; a stimulus that once caused sensation and no longer does.

sensory deprivation Situation in which normal environmental sensory stimuli available to an individual are reduced drastically; also called REST (Restricted Environmental Stimulation Technique).

serial learning A verbal learning procedure in which the stimuli are always presented in the same order, and the subject has to learn them in the order in which they are presented.

sex roles The set of behaviors and attitudes that are determined to be appropriate for one sex or the other in a society.

shaping In operant conditioning, the gradual process of reinforcing behaviors that get closer to some final desired behavior. Shaping is also called successive approximation.

short-term memory Part of the memory system in which information is only stored for roughly 30 seconds. Information can be maintained longer with the use of such techniques as rehearsal. To retain the information for extended periods of time, it must be consolidated into long-term memory where it can then be retrieved. The capacity of short-term memory is also limited. Most people can only store roughly 7 chunks of information plus or minus 2. This is why phone numbers only have seven digits.

signal detection theory Research approach in which the subject's behavior in detecting a threshold is treated as a form of decision making.

similarity Gestalt principle in which similar stimuli are perceived as a unit.

simple phobia Excessive irrational fear that does not fall into other specific categories, such as fear of dogs, insects, snakes, or closed-in places.

simultaneous conditioning A procedure in classical conditioning in which the CS and US are presented at exactly the same time.

Sixteen Personality Factor Questionnaire (16PF) Raymond Cattell's personality test to measure source traits.

Skinner box B. F. Skinner's animal cage with a lever that triggers reinforcement for a subject.

sleep terror disorder (pavor nocturnus) Nonrapid eye-movement (NREM) sleep disorder in which the person (usually a child) wakes up screaming and terrified, but cannot recall why.

sleepwalking (somnambulism) NREM sleep disorder in which the person walks in his or her sleep.

social cognition The process of understanding other people and ourselves by forming and utilizing information about the social world.

social cognitive theory Albert Bandura's approach to personality that proposes that individuals use observation, imitation, and cognition to develop personality.

social comparison Theory proposed by Leon Festinger that we tend to compare our behavior to others to ensure that we are conforming.

social exchange theory Theory of interpersonal relationships that states that people evaluate the costs and rewards of their relationships and act accordingly.

social facilitation Phenomenon in which the presence of others increases dominant behavior patterns in an individual; Richard Zajonc's theory states that the presence of others enhances the emission of the dominant response of the individual.

social influence Influence designed to change the attitudes or behavior of other people; includes conformity, compliance, and obedience.

social learning theory An approach to social psychology that emphasizes observation and modeling; it states that reinforcement is involved in motivation rather than in learning, and proposes that aggression is a form of learned behavior.

social phobia Excessive irrational fear and embarrassment when interacting with other people. Social phobias may include fear of assertive behavior, fear of making mistakes, or fear of public speaking.

social psychology The study of how an individual's behavior, thoughts, and feelings are influenced by other people.

sociobiology Study of the genetic basis of social behavior.

sociocultural Emphasizes the importance of culture, gender, and ethnicity in how we think, feel, and act.

somatic nervous system The part of the peripheral nervous system that carries messages from the sense organs and relays information that directs the voluntary movements of the skeletal muscles.

somatization disorder Somatoform disorder in which a person has medical complaints without physical cause.

somatoform disorders Psychological disorders characterized by physical symptoms for which there are no obvious physical causes.

specific attachment phase Stage at about six months of age, in which the baby becomes attached to a specific person.

split-brain research Popular name for Roger Sperry's research on the syndrome of hemisphere deconnection; research on individuals with the corpus callosum severed. Normal functioning breaks down in split-brain subjects when different information is presented to each hemisphere.

SQ5R A technique to improve learning and memory. Components include survey, question, read, record, recite, review, and reflect.

stage of exhaustion Third stage in Hans Selye's general adaptation syndrome. As the body continues to resist stress, it depletes its energy resources and the person becomes exhausted.

stage of resistance Second stage in Hans Selye's general adaptation syndrome. When stress is prolonged, the body builds some resistance to the effects of stress.

standardization The process of obtaining a representative sample of scores in the population so that a particular score can be interpreted correctly.

Stanford-Binet Intelligence Scale An intelligence test first revised by Lewis Terman at Stanford University in 1916; still a popular test used today.

state-dependent learning Situation in which what is learned in one state can only be remembered when the person is in that state of mind.

statistically significant In inferential statistics, a finding that the independent variable did influence greatly the outcome of the experimental and control group.

stereotype An exaggerated and rigid mental image of a particular class of persons or objects.

stimulus A unit of the environment that causes a response in an individual; a physical or chemical agent acting on an appropriate sense receptor.

stimulus discrimination Responding to relevant stimuli.

stimulus generalization Responding to stimuli similar to the stimulus that had caused the response.

stimulus motives Motivating factors that are internal and unlearned, but do not appear to have a physiological basis; stimulus motives cause an individual to seek out sensory stimulation through interaction with the environment.

stimulus trace The perceptual persistence of a stimulus after it is no longer present.

strange-situation procedure A measure of attachment developed by Mary Ainsworth that consists of eight phases during which the infant is increasingly stressed.

Glossary

stress Anything that produces demands on us to adjust and threatens our well-being.

Strong Interest Inventory An objective personality test that compares people's personalities to groups that achieve success in certain occupations.

structuralism First school of thought in psychology; it studied conscious experience to discover the structure of the mind.

subject bias Source of potential error in an experiment from the action or expectancy of a subject; a subject might influence the experimental results in ways that mask the true outcome.

subjective organization Long-term memory procedures in which the individual provides a personal method of organizing information to be memorized.

sublimation Defense mechanism; a person redirects his or her socially undesirable urges into socially acceptable behavior.

successive approximation Shaping; in operant conditioning, the gradual process of reinforcing behaviors that get closer to some final desired behavior.

superego Sigmund Freud's representation of conscience.

surface traits In Raymond Cattell's personality theory, the observable characteristics of a person's behavior and personality.

symbolization In Sigmund Freud's dream theory, the process of converting the latent content of a dream into manifest symbols.

systematic desensitization Application of counterconditioning, in which the individual overcomes anxiety by learning to relax in the presence of stimuli that had once made him or her unbearably nervous.

task-oriented coping Adjustment responses in which the person evaluates a stressful situation objectively and then formulates a plan with which to solve the problem.

test of significance An inferential statistical technique used to determine whether the difference in scores between the experimental and control groups is really due to the effects of the independent variable or to random chance. If the probability of an outcome is extremely low, we say that outcome is significant.

Thanatos Sigmund Freud's term for a destructive instinct such as aggression; also called death instinct.

Thematic Apperception Test (TAT) Projective personality test in which subjects are shown pictures of people in everyday settings; subjects must make up a story about the people portrayed.

theory of social impact Latané's theory of social behavior; it states that each member of a group shares the responsibility equally.

Theory X Douglas McGregor's theory that states that the worker dislikes work and must be forced to do it.

Theory Y Douglas McGregor's theory that states that work is natural and can be a source of satisfaction, and, when it is, the worker can be highly committed and motivated.

therapy In psychology, the treatment of behavior problems; two major types of therapy include psychotherapy and biological therapy.

time and motion studies In engineering psychology, studies that analyze the time it takes to perform an action and the movements that go into the action.

tip-of-the-tongue phenomenon A phenomenon in which the closer a person comes to recalling something, the more accurately he or she can remember details, such as the number of syllables or letters.

token economy A behavior therapy in which desired behaviors are reinforced immediately with tokens that can be exchanged at a later time for desired rewards, such as food or recreational privileges.

trace conditioning A procedure in classical conditioning in which the CS is a discrete event that is presented and terminated before the US is presented.

trait A distinctive and stable attribute in people.

trait anxiety Anxiety that is long-lasting; a relatively stable personality characteristic.

transference Psychoanalytic term used when a patient projects his feelings onto the therapist.

transsexualism A condition in which a person feels trapped in the body of the wrong sex.

trial and error learning Trying various behaviors in a situation until the solution is found.

triangular theory of love Robert Sternberg's theory that states that love consists of intimacy, passion, and decision/commitment.

triarchic theory of intelligence Robert Sternberg's theory of intelligence that states that it consists of three parts: componential, experiential, and contextual subtheories.

Type-A behavior A personality pattern of behavior that can lead to stress and heart disease.

unconditional positive regard Part of Carl Rogers's personality theory; occurs when we accept someone regardless of what he or she does or says.

unconditioned response (UR) An automatic reaction elicited by a stimulus.

unconditioned stimulus (US) Any stimulus that elicits an automatic or reflexive reaction in an individual; it does not have to be learned in the present situation.

unconscious mind In Sigmund Freud's psychoanalytic theory of personality, the part of personality that is unavailable to us; Freud suggests that instincts and unpleasant memories are stored in the unconscious mind.

undifferentiated schizophrenia Type of schizophrenia that does not fit into any particular category, or fits into more than one category.

variable interval (VI) schedule Schedule of reinforcement in which the subject is reinforced for the first response given after a certain time interval, with the interval being different for each trial.

variable ratio (VR) schedule Schedule of reinforcement in which the subject is given reinforcement after a varying number of responses; the number of responses required for reinforcement is different for every trial.

vestibular sense Sense that helps us keep our balance.

vulnerability-stress model Theory of schizophrenia that states that some people have a biological tendency to develop schizophrenia if they are stressed enough by their environment.

Weber's Law Ernst Weber's law that states that the difference threshold depends on the ratio of the intensity of one stimulus to another rather than on an absolute difference.

Wechsler Adult Intelligence Scale (WAIS) An intelligence test for adults, first published by David Wechsler in 1955; it contains verbal and performance subscales.

Wechsler Intelligence Scale for Children (WISC-III) Similar to the Wechsler Adult Intelligence Scale, except that it is designed for children ages 6 through 16, and helps diagnose certain childhood disorders such as dyslexia and other learning disabilities.

Wechsler Preschool and Primary Scale of Intelligence (WPPSI-R) Designed for children between the ages of 4 and 7; helps diagnose childhood disorders, such as dyslexia and other learning disabilities.

withdrawal Unpleasant physical reactions that a drug dependent user experiences when he or she stops taking the drug.

within-subject experiment An experimental design in which each subject is given all treatments, including the control condition; subjects serve in both experimental and control groups.

working memory The memory store, with a capacity of about 7 items and enduring for up to 30 seconds, that handles current information.

Yerkes-Dodson Law Popular idea that performance is best when arousal is at a medium level.

Sources for the Glossary: The majority of terms in this glossary are from Psychology: A ConnecText, *4th Edition, Terry F. Pettijohn. ©1999 Dushkin/ McGraw-Hill, Guilford, CT 06437. The remaining terms were developed by the* Annual Editions *staff, 2001.*

Index

A

abortion debate, 73
advance directives, 100–101
advertising and children, teens, 151–158
aggression, 28; research on, 168–172
Alzheimer's disease, 43–44, 70
American Psychiatric Association, 204
American Psychological Association, 141
amygdala, 201
Anderson, Susan, 15
anthropology, molecular, 36–37
antidepressants, 202–203
archaeology, 33, 34; sites, 34
Aronson, Elliot, 173
assisted suicide, 102
attachment bond, 76
attitudes, longevity and, 96–97
autism, 39–41; aggression in, 40; immune deficiency in, 39–40; viral infection in, 40
autism-related genes: chromosome 6, 40; chromosome 7, 41; chromosome 13, 41; chromosome 15, 39

B

Baby Boom generation, 93–95, 181; and aging, 93; as parents 83–84
Barbie doll, 153
behavior: childhood, 10, 27; homosexual, 31; human, 49
Bering Land Bridge, 34
biological clock, 52–55
biotechnology, 33
blood types, 34
brain: embryo, 71; hemispheres, 69; human, 42, 49; imaging, 45; networks, 9; surgery, 44
brain disorders, 42, 44; hereditary, 43
Breedlove, Marc, 28
bullying, 86–89; anti-bullying legislation, 87; anti-bullying training, 87; National Education Association statistics on bullying, 87
Buss, David, 145

C

Carducci, Bernardo, 125
centenarians, 97
children, raising, 10; social/moral development, 81
chimeraplasty, 43
choices, good and bad, 197–199
chromosomes, 28; Y chromosome markers, 35

circadian rhythm, 52
classroom hostility, empathy, 173–177; jigsaw classroom, 174
coaching, sports, 59
cognitive processes, 15; cognitive psychology, 15
cohanim, 33, 35
Coleridge, Samuel Taylor, 49
Columbine High School, 86–87
conflict resolution programs, 88–89
consumerism, in childhood, 151–158; in teens, 154
coping mechanism, avoidance as, 6
coronary artery disease, 70, 184
cortisol, 53, 63, 169, 200. *See* stress
couples' communication, 136–150; in conflict, 178–179
crowding, research on, 168–172
cultural biology, 21–23
cultural differences, 15; analytical logic, 16; dialectical approach, 16
Czikszentmihalyi, Mihaly, 57, 59

D

Dante, 47
De Quincey, Thomas, 49
de Waal, Franz B. M., 168
denial, as a distortion of reality, 196
depression, 203–205; clinical, 203; seasonal, 52; depression and anxiety, relationship between, 205
desires, research on basic, 206–208
devaluing, as a distortion of reality, 196
development, fetal, 72–73
discipline, 10; consequences of, 10–11; punishment as, 10–11; strategies of, 10
DNA (deoxyribonucleic acid), 21–23, 32–34, 37, 43
domestic violence, 160–161
dopamine, 50
drug trials, 64–65; "double-blind" studies, 64–65
ducts: Muellerian, 28; Wolffian, 28

E

early childhood education, 78
"edutainment", 79
Ehrlich, Paul, 20–26
Ekman, Paul, 120, 122
elevator effect, 171
Emerson, Ralph Waldo, 12–14
emotional intelligence, 111–114; assessing, 112–113; curricula, 113–114
empathic teaching, 114

empathy, nurturing, 116–119; in young children, 116–118
end-of-life: care 98–104; costs, 103; movement, 100; resources for information about, 103–04
endorphins, 50, 76
evolution, biological, 20–22
expectancy theory, 63; mind over matter, 62
extraverts, 14

F

facial expression, 120–121
Faludi, Susan, 159
Father Knows Best, 151, 162
feminism, 162, 166
Firestone, Robert, 143
flow, mental, 57, 59; "in the zone," 56
focusing, mental, 56
Freud, Sigmund, 9, 49
friendship: characteristics of, 108–109; networks of, 108; social interactions and, 107–108; in older adults, 109
Frost, Robert, 59
fruit flies, 52, 55
fundamental attributional error, 16

G

gender: awareness, 29; biology, 27; relationship, 29; differences in communication, 179
generalized anxiety disorder (GAD), 200–201
gene-environment interactions, 24
genetic defects, 29; single-gene disorders, 41; susceptibility genes, 41
genetics, 33–37; behavioral, 31–32; evolutionary 21–23; and determinism, 21; and identity, 24; and genetic engineering, 44; and genetic markers, 34; and population, 34
genome: screens, 41; human, 43; and genotype, 44; and gene therapy, 43
gestation, 71; and amniotic fluid, 72; and pre-natal environment, 74; and pre-natal response to stress, 74
Gottman, John, 136

H

habits, breaking bad, 197–199
Hamer, Dean, 31–32
happiness: feel-good, 206; value-based, 206
health-care proxy, 100–101

Index

hedonism, 47
heritability, 24
HIV (human immunodeficiency virus), 70
Homo sapiens, 33
hormones, 28, 30. *See also* stress
human behaviors, 21
human natures, 25–26
hunter-gatherers, 33
Huntington's disease, 44
hypothalamus, 52

I

idealizing, as a distortion of reality, 196
impotence, 70
infant development, 75–77
infidelity, in relationships, 142–143
intimacy, in relationships, 141–144; fear of, 143
introverts, 14

J

James, William, 49, 59
jealousy in relationships, 145–148
jet lag, 54
Jung, Carl, 3

K

Kennedy, John F. 163

L

language, 22
limbic system, 50
long-term care insurance option, 103
lying: clues to, 122–124; and polygraphs, 122; Verdicator and, 124

M

Malcolm X, 206
male menopause, 70
masculinity, and manhood in America, 159–167
Maslow, Abraham, 4
media: kids and, 81; marketing to children, 81, 151–158
Medicaid, 102–103
Medicare, 102–103
medicine: custom, 37; molecular, 34
Medigap, 102–103
melatonin, 52
memory: avoidance, 9; forgetting, 9; inhibition, 9; losses, 9; storage, 43; working, 43
men's health, 69–70
mental conditioning, 56–59; mental toughness, 57; visualizing, 56, 191
migrations, 33
mind-body relationship, 45

Million Man March, 160, 166
monoclonal antibody technique, 44
motivational training, 57
mutagens, 53

N

nature vs. nurture, 22, 24
Neanderthals, 37
nervous system, human, 22
neural regeneration, 44
neuron, 49
neuropeptides, 50
neurotransmitters, 39, 49
Nisbett, Richard, 15–17
norepinephrine, 200–201. *See* stress
Nuland, Sherwin, 49

O

obesity, 70
Oedipus complex, 195
older workers, 182–183
Ozzie and Harriet, 151

P

pain: management, 98; medication, 99; as "fifth vital sign," 99
parenting: 10–11; 81–85; lost art of, 81–82; and discipline and authority, 84; parents-advocates (buddy adults) and, 83; and peer parenting, 83; teaching morality and, 85; and parent as career coach, 84
Parkinson's disease, 44
pathology, psychological, 2–3
Paxil, 128, 202. *See also* antidepressants
Penfield, Wilder, 49
performance: ideal performance state (IPS), 57; peak performance, 59
personal secrets, revealing of, 131–135
personality: adult profile, 12; biology of, 31–32; stability of, 12–13; traits, 14
personality inventories: MMPI (Minnesota Multiphasic Personality Inventory), 12; NEO Personality Inventory, 12
pharmacotherapy, 203
phenotype, 40, 44
Pines, Ayala Malach, 141, 147
placebo effect, 45; placebo response, 60; nocebo response, 61
play, 78–80; research on, 78; play date, 79; play deprivation, 78, 80
pleasure, 47–51; biology of, 47; civic pleasure, 47
pleasure theory, 206
posttraumatic stress disorder (PTSD), 88
pre-frontal cortex, 42

pregnant women who work, 74
premature infants, 72–73
prevention, of psychological problems, 4
projecting, as a distortion of reality, 196
Promise Keepers, 160, 166
prostate, enlargement of, 70
Prozac, 202–203. *See also* antidepressants
psychology: developmental, 6; fetal, 71–74; humanistic, 4–6; molecular, 31; personality, 6; social, 6, 15–17
psychotherapy, 194, 203; group therapy, 185

R

Radcliffe Public Policy Institute, 182
Reiss, Steven, 206–208
relationships: dominance in, 6; interpersonal, 7
relaxation response, 63
religion, 45
repression, Freudian, 9
reproductive genetics, 28
research, fetal, 71–74
reward deficiency syndrome, 50
robots, 44, 45; sentient robots, 46
Rockdale County, Atlanta, 83
Rogers, Carl, 4
Rosen, Emmanuel, 194–196

S

school recess, 79–80
seizures, 44
self-esteem, 6–8; definition of, 191–192; low self-esteem, 7; programs, 8
self-help, myths of, 189–193
self-hypnosis, 57
Seligman, Martin E. P., 3
sensuousness, 48
serotonin, 40, 50. *See also* SSRIs
Sesame Street, 157
sex: youth, 83; group, 83; fellatio, 85
sexual identity, 28–29
sexual passion, 147
shame transaction, 77
shyness, 125–130; Internet bonding and, 129
sleep disorders, 52, 55
smoking, 70
SNRIs (serotonin norepinephrine reuptake inhibitors), 204
sociometer theory, 6
Spears, Britney, 82
Spielberg, Stephen, 207
spontaneous healing, 60
sports psychology, 57–58; U.S. Olympic sports, 58
SSRIs (selective serotonin reuptake inhibitors), 202–203

stem cells, 44

stress: emotional isolation in, 185; hormones, 53, 63, 169, 200; management, 58, 184–186, 189; positive or negative, 58

suprachiasmatic nucleus (SCN), 52–54

T

tai-chi, and yoga, 190

Tannen, Deborah, 178–179

teens: and Internet, 90; as millennial generation, 90–91; *Newsweek* poll on teens, 91; social behavior, 92; social groups, 91–92; stress and hostility, 91

temperament, 12

testosterone, 28–30, 69, 70

thalidomide, 40

Thomas, Lewis, 185–186

Toffler, Alvin, 181

tranquilizers, 201

twins: identical, 31, 39; Siamese (Chang and Eng), 24

two-career couples, 181–182

Type A, Type B personalities, 184–185

U

unisex, 28

V

venlafaxine XR, 204–205

violence, and guns in school, 86–89

W

well-being, 2, 13

work, and private life, 180–181

World War II, 3–4, 159, 162

Y

Yankelovich, Daniel, 181

youth: and alienation, anger, and revenge, 86–89

Z

Zeigarnick effect, 132

Zimbardo, Philip, 125

Zoloft, 202–203. *See also* antidepressants

Test Your Knowledge Form

We encourage you to photocopy and use this page as a tool to assess how the articles in *Annual Editions* expand on the information in your textbook. By reflecting on the articles you will gain enhanced text information. You can also access this useful form on a product's book support Web site at *http://www.dushkin.com/online/*.

NAME:

DATE:

TITLE AND NUMBER OF ARTICLE:

BRIEFLY STATE THE MAIN IDEA OF THIS ARTICLE:

LIST THREE IMPORTANT FACTS THAT THE AUTHOR USES TO SUPPORT THE MAIN IDEA:

WHAT INFORMATION OR IDEAS DISCUSSED IN THIS ARTICLE ARE ALSO DISCUSSED IN YOUR TEXTBOOK OR OTHER READINGS THAT YOU HAVE DONE? LIST THE TEXTBOOK CHAPTERS AND PAGE NUMBERS:

LIST ANY EXAMPLES OF BIAS OR FAULTY REASONING THAT YOU FOUND IN THE ARTICLE:

LIST ANY NEW TERMS/CONCEPTS THAT WERE DISCUSSED IN THE ARTICLE, AND WRITE A SHORT DEFINITION:

We Want Your Advice

ANNUAL EDITIONS revisions depend on two major opinion sources: one is our Advisory Board, listed in the front of this volume, which works with us in scanning the thousands of articles published in the public press each year; the other is you—the person actually using the book. Please help us and the users of the next edition by completing the prepaid article rating form on this page and returning it to us. Thank you for your help!

ANNUAL EDITIONS: Personal Growth and Behavior 02/03

ARTICLE RATING FORM

Here is an opportunity for you to have direct input into the next revision of this volume.
We would like you to rate each of the articles listed below, using the following scale:

1. **Excellent: should definitely be retained**
2. **Above average: should probably be retained**
3. **Below average: should probably be deleted**
4. **Poor: should definitely be deleted**

Your ratings will play a vital part in the next revision.
Please mail this prepaid form to us as soon as possible.
Thanks for your help!

RATING	ARTICLE	RATING	ARTICLE
	1. Positive Psychology: An Introduction		37. The Teening of Childhood
	2. Making Sense of Self-Esteem		38. The Betrayal of the American Man
	3. Repression Tries for Experimental Comeback		39. Coping With Crowding
	4. Private Lives: Discipline and Knowing Where to Draw the Line		40. Nobody Left to Hate
			41. Speak No Evil
	5. The Stability of Personality: Observations and Evaluations		42. Work, Work, Work, Work!
			43. Don't Face Stress Alone
	6. How Culture Molds Habits of Thought		44. Self-Help: Shattering the Myths
	7. The Tangled Skeins of Nature and Nurture in Human Evolution		45. Think Like a Shrink
			46. Bad Choices: Why We Make Them, How to Stop
	8. The Gender Blur		47. Chronic Anxiety: How to Stop Living on the Edge
	9. The Personality Genes		48. Up From Depression
	10. Where We Come From		49. Secrets of Happiness
	11. Autism Is Likely to Be Linked to Several Genes		
	12. The Future of the Brain		
	13. The Biology of Joy		
	14. The Tick-Tock of the Biological Clock		
	15. Into the Zone		
	16. Mind Over Medicine		
	17. The Seven Stages of Man		
	18. Fetal Psychology		
	19. Four Things You Need to Know About Raising Baby		
	20. What Ever Happened to Play?		
	21. Parenting: The Lost Art		
	22. Disarming the Rage		
	23. A World of Their Own		
	24. The Road Ahead: A Boomer's Guide to Happiness		
	25. Live to 100? No Thanks		
	26. Start the Conversation		
	27. Friendships and Adaptation Across the Life Span		
	28. Emotional Intelligence		
	29. Nurturing Empathy		
	30. What's in a Face?		
	31. How to Spot a Liar		
	32. Shyness: The New Solution		
	33. Revealing Personal Secrets		
	34. Welcome to the Love Lab		
	35. Finding Real Love		
	36. Prescription for Passion		

(Continued on next page)

NO POSTAGE
NECESSARY
IF MAILED
IN THE
UNITED STATES

BUSINESS REPLY MAIL
FIRST-CLASS MAIL PERMIT NO. 84 GUILFORD CT
POSTAGE WILL BE PAID BY ADDRESSEE

McGraw-Hill/Dushkin
530 Old Whitfield Street
Guilford, Ct 06437-9989

IIIııııIIııIııIııIIdIıııIIdıIıIdıIdıIııIIdıIddıl

ABOUT YOU

Name   Date
_____   _____

Are you a teacher? ❒   A student? ❒
Your school's name
_____

Department
_____

Address   City   State   Zip
_____

School telephone #
_____

YOUR COMMENTS ARE IMPORTANT TO US!

Please fill in the following information:
For which course did you use this book?
_____

Did you use a text with this ANNUAL EDITION?   ❒ yes ❒ no
What was the title of the text?
_____

What are your general reactions to the *Annual Editions* concept?
_____

Have you read any pertinent articles recently that you think should be included in the next edition? Explain.
_____

Are there any articles that you feel should be replaced in the next edition? Why?
_____

Are there any World Wide Web sites that you feel should be included in the next edition? Please annotate.
_____

May we contact you for editorial input?   ❒ yes ❒ no
May we quote your comments?   ❒ yes ❒ no